To serve is to love

To serve is to love

*The Canadian story of the
Sisters Servants of Mary Immaculate*

Sister Claudia Helen Popowich, SSMI

with a foreword by Vladimir J. Kaye

Sisters Servants of Mary Immaculate, Toronto

*To Mary Immaculate
our mother and model
whose life was a continuous hymn
of love and service*

*to our deceased sisters
who gave themselves
to the invincible love of Christ
for His people
under her protection and inspiration*

*to our living sisters
that they may be stirred to deep devotedness
by this story
of our birth and growth*

*to those future generations of Sisters Servants
who, although yet uncalled,
will fill another volume
with their holy lives and good deeds*

this book is dedicated.

Foreword

Sister Claudia is well qualified to undertake this arduous and formidable task of writing the history of the Congregation of Sisters Servants of Mary Immaculate of Canada or, perhaps more correctly, of the Canadian-American Province of Christ the King. It is not solely the story of a congregation but also a detailed history of the establishing of schools for the children of Ukrainian pioneer settlers in the west, of the founding of rural hospitals, orphanages, evening classes for adults, and homes for the aged, and of the filling of the gaps which otherwise would have remained unfilled by provincial authorities unable to cope with them.

Born in Sudbury, Ontario, Sister Claudia received her elementary education in her native city and secondary education at the St Catharines Collegiate Institute. After entering the Congregation of Sisters Servants of Mary Immaculate in Toronto, she continued her studies at the University of Saskatchewan, Saskatoon, obtaining her BA degree magna cum laude in 1959 with majors in English and history. In 1966 the University of Ottawa conferred upon her an MA degree for a thesis in English literature. A very capable educationalist, she has taught in all high schools and academies conducted by the Sisters Servants in Canada and in the United States: Sacred Heart Academy at Yorkton, Saskatchewan; Immaculate Heart of Mary Academy in Winnipeg (where she served as superior and principal); Mount Mary Immaculate Academy at Ancaster, Ontario (serving as principal for two years); and St Mary's Villa Academy at Sloatsburg, New York. On October 2, 1967, she became the first woman to work at the Sacred Congregation for the Oriental Churches in Rome, where for two years she acted as an administrative secretary for the oriental missions.

In the summer of 1966, at the request of Sister Frances Byblow, provincial superior, she started to collect material for the history of the Sisters Servants in Canada and the United States, which she completed in 1971 after her return from Rome. Although written in a narrative style, it is based entirely on documentary material and all facts are fully substantiated by relevant quotations and references. She describes with meticulous accuracy and detail the growth of the Canadian province of the institute from the very first day of arrival of the four sisters in Alberta in the autumn of 1902 to the present day.

Sister Claudia has added new and important facts concerning the activities of the sisters in the field of education and in the social and religious services performed in the Ukrainian rural and urban communities of the Canadian west, which contributed to the gradual integration of this large ethnic group into the general Canadian picture. Coming from a different environment and culture the Ukrainians were confronted with problems of adaptation to new conditions; but they eventually achieved economic establishment and subsequent acculturation. They all experienced the fear of insecurity and encountered serious problems connected with the change of mode of life.

In this particular field the sisters rendered their great service. They helped the immigrant settlers and their children to overcome the problems of adjustment by serving as a link between them and the new world. One of the main such links was education, and Sister Claudia describes vividly the tremendous obstacles and almost unbelievable sacrifices the sisters faced in overcoming the difficulties and establishing schools in remote rural districts. 'In their personal daily living ... the sisters denied themselves butter and meat and eggs, and heat and electricity' in order to save money and to maintain the newly established (1905) St Nicholas School in Winnipeg. 'St Nicholas School depended solely upon the sisters' own precarious ability to finance it.'

Not only in Winnipeg but in other places in the west 'their educational work ... so hesitatingly launched in the close quarters of an unpretentious convent at Edmonton, in the nave of a rustic log chapel at Mundare, and in the dismal basement of a mission church at Winnipeg, was expanding of its own momentum.' They overcame the seemingly insurmountable difficulties and before two decades passed the number of schools increased tenfold, culminating in 1953 with the opening of Mount Mary Immaculate Academy at Ancaster.

Later the Sisters Servants took another bold step – they opened the doors of their academies and welcomed youngsters of other ethnic and religious groups with startling impartiality. Sister Claudia explains why the doors of the schools were opened to non-Ukrainian and even non-Catholic students: 'The sisters believed that their Ukrainian students, by retaining a pride in their national origin, could effectively interpret Canadian culture to Ukrainians, and Ukrainian culture to Canadians, particularly to their fellow students of other ethnic groups. Experience had taught them that the lasting friendships formed by Ukrainian girls with students of other nationalities and cultures, such as those from Central and South American nations, almost automatically seemed to eliminate prejudice – which usually springs from an unconscious animosity toward the unknown. Their correspondence with the members of the staff after their return to their own country indicated that these daughters of diplomats, businessmen, and professionals not only affectionately remembered their teachers and schoolmates but also retained a warm regard for Ukrainians in general.'

Sister Claudia deserves warm recognition for producing such a complete and profusely documented history of the Canadian Sisters Servants of Mary Immaculate, which vividly depicts the sisters' self-sacrifice and their valuable contributions in the educational and humanitarian fields for the Ukrainian community in particular and for Canada in general.

V. J. Kaye

Ottawa, Ontario
July 1971

Author's preface

As history, this Canadian story of the Sisters Servants of Mary Immaculate is unique perhaps only in the details of its beginnings. If more time has been devoted to analysing these than to celebrating their successful issue, it is because they yield the most precious revelations of the characteristic spirit and approach of the Sisters Servants confronting, like every Canadian pioneer and foreign missionary, the challenge of the new and unknown.

Their story, however, cannot be separated from that of the Ukrainian Catholic Church – the people of God – in Canada and the United States. For as a religious congregation the Sisters Servants are not a grouping of like-minded women united for philanthropic purposes. They are a community for living together in the service of Christ in His Church, a service which reaches out in different ways to the needs of the human family in general and of the Ukrainian family in particular. Among their numbers are young adults and nonagenarians, short and tall, brilliant and mediocre, musical and tone deaf, enthusiastic and melancholic. They are the family of man writ small – a living commentary on the description of St Paul of the work of the Spirit: 'Now there are varieties of gifts, but the same Spirit' (1 Cor 12:4–12).

And just as for everyone and everything 'there is a season ... and a time for every purpose under heaven' (Eccles 3:1–9), so, too, for the Sisters Servants, there was a time for their birth at Zhuzhyl, an unknown Ukrainian village; for their initial growth in Europe; for their joy and sorrow when, as a young missionary group in the Canadian west, they experienced the growing pains of a rather skeptical beginning; for their suffering, especially during the Second World War, as they watched the Ukrainian Catholic Church in Ukraine – and within it a part of their own institute – being subjected to waves of terror that left it with little more than its anguish and a broken body; and, finally, for their love which has continued to topple obstacles that might have prevented them from fulfilling their mandate of service.

It is not so much the experiencing of these paradoxical aspects of life that is most lasting, however, but rather the meaning and hope which the experience holds for each of those who grow and are enriched by it.

Hence, in the chapters of this book, I have not been concerned only with reporting events in which Sisters Servants prominently figured, but much more with searching for the meaning in terms of their dedication and commitment. For here there is sufficient universality, sufficient applicability, sufficient common chord to have relevance for more than the present generation, and for more than yesterday. And since this is also a story of the Church, it embraces in its scope the sisters' co-missionaries – their bishops, and the religious and secular clergy – those tireless, thorough, vigorous, and determined men, whose courage and confidence seem to have been as boundless as the country; and their people – not celebrated heroes, but heroes all the same – good people trying to live out their lives decently in terms of their own commitments and obligations and opportunities in the face of tremendous odds.

Regretfully, however, on this canvas of almost seventy years of achievement it has been possible to pause only here and there to paint in a name, since this study has dealt only with highlights – points that stand out in a somewhat cursory review. It therefore remains for another writer at another time, perhaps, to develop it further, or to find in the end of this book the beginning for another. At this point, therefore, I simply say, 'To be continued.'

*   *   *

It must be confessed that I entered upon the writing of this history without being aware that the institute's most valuable documentary source, the original chronicle – containing copies of official correspondence, community assignments, personal appointments, accounts of pioneer experiences, and the apostolic strivings of over a quarter-century – was non-existent. It had been taken to Europe in 1936 by Sister Veronica Gargil (then the superior general), and lost during the Second World War. Consequently, primary source material for the early period had to be sought beyond the archives of the congregation. Both research and writing, therefore, became a long, drawn-out affair, since a part of the story had to be pieced together from bits of information culled from official and private correspondence, and the diaries of persons such as Archbishop A. Langevin, OMI, Bishop E. Legal, OMI, Bishop N. Budka, Rev. P. Filas, OSBM, and Rev. A. Lacombe, OMI. The study was further prolonged by my unexpected summons to Rome in October 1967 to undertake an assignment at the Sacred Congregation for the Oriental Churches. Only after I returned to Canada in November 1969 did the work proceed in earnest.

Some of the documentation for the later period, beginning in 1934 with the establishment of the Canadian-American Province of Christ the King, is contained in the provincial archives of the Sisters Servants at Toronto. Except for local mission chronicles and files the provincial chronicle, entry register, mission reports, visitation summaries, obituaries, as well as correspondence files, souvenir booklets and programmes, photographs, and scrapbooks were consulted here; other archives from which source materials were drawn are identified in the notes. It should be observed that in the text the full name of a sister (religious, baptismal, surname) is given only in an initial reference. The accepted English spelling of all surnames has been retained even when it does not conform to the system of transliteration being followed. The more recent term 'Ukrainian rite' rather than 'Ruthenian' has been used, except in quoted documents and printed works. Abbreviations of religious orders and congregations which appear refer to the following communities: FSC – Brothers of the Christian Schools; CSSR – Congregation of the Most Holy Redeemer (Redemptorist Fathers); OFM – Order of Friars Minor (Franciscan Fathers); OMI – Oblates of Mary Immaculate; OSBM – Order of St Basil the Great (Basilian Fathers). Source materials originally in languages other than English have been translated. The *Jerusalem Bible* text has been used for scriptural quotations and the *Documents of Vatican II*, trans. ed. J. Joseph Gallagher, gen. ed. Walter M. Abbott SJ (New York, 1966), for quotations from the decrees of Vatican Council II. Moreover, since complete references are given in the notes a bibliography has not been compiled.

*   *   *

It gives me great joy to feel that by virtue of this history, whatever may be its failings, I have been united with innumerable guides, advisers, and friends who have given generously of their time, energy, and advice in its preparation. I am thankful to them all, but I wish to thank especially ...

... my community, for the time and opportunity to make this study, particularly Sister Jerome Chimy, superior general; Sister Justine Kowal, provincial superior; Sister Frances Byblow, former provincial superior, who encouraged me to undertake this work and made numerous helpful suggestions in the manuscript; former provincial superiors Sister Elizabeth Kassian, Sister Bernadette Warick, Sister Boniface Sloboda, and Sister Vincent Yaremovich (American province), who patiently suffered all manner of interrogation and offered valuable insights; Sister Ruth Yakimyshyn, superior, for many personal kindnesses; Sister Monica Mantyka, for assisting with the index and statistical lists; Sister Andrea Kruk, for typing the final portion of the manuscript; Sister Ruth Aney, for preparing the jacket, maps, and photographs; all those Sisters Servants who answered countless appeals for information, who were so tirelessly hospitable and thoughtful during my numerous incursions of their files, and those who stopped by, or wrote, to say 'I'm praying for you';

... Archbishop Mario Brini, secretary of the Sacred Congregation for the Oriental Churches, Rome, who, during my two years with the congregation, graciously permitted me to prolong my annual vacations for the purpose of research; the Ukrainian Catholic bishops in Canada and the United States for their interest and advice, particularly Archbishop-Metropolitan Maxime Hermaniuk, CSSR, who made available the early files of the Winnipeg Archeparchy, which yielded a rich harvest of source materials;

... the late Dr G. W. Simpson, former head of the Department of History, University of Saskatchewan, Saskatoon, and member of the Board of Governors, who inspired and nourished my interest in history in his brilliant classes, and under whose guidance I began this study;

... Dr V. J. Kaye, notable author and historian, for his unstinting assistance after Dr Simpson's death in 1969, especially in sharing the fruits of his own extensive research, and in offering to replace his close friend, Dr Simpson, in writing the Foreword;

... Rev. L. A. Cormican, OMI, professor of English at Carleton University, Ottawa, for his critical reading of the manuscript and perceptive observations, which contributed much to its present form;

... the authors of published works and dissertations, Senator Paul Yuzyk, J. G. MacGregor, Rev. J. Denischuk, CSSR, Dr M. R. Lupul, and Dr B. N. Bilash, for generously permitting me to quote from their writings;

... Rev. A. Welykyj, OSBM, superior general, author of the first complete history of the Sisters Servants, for help on particular points concerning the institute; Rev. J. Jean, OSBM, for providing me with a priceless store of documentary materials collected over a period of sixty years; Rev. R. Danylak, chancellor of the Toronto eparchy, for many helpful suggestions and for contributing a scholarly article on the Ukrainian Catholic Church to the appendix of this book; Dr G. Luckyj, Department of Slavic Languages and Literatures, University of Toronto, for checking the transliteration in the Notes; Mr G. Hallowell, assistant editor at University of Toronto Press, for the final editing of the manuscript – a gallant performance under considerable pressure;

... Rev. N. Delaquis, chancellor of the Archdiocese of St Boniface, and Msgr M. G. Doyle, chancellor of the Archdiocese of Edmonton, for assistance in locating relevant documents contained in their respective archdiocesan archives; and Rev. M. Daciuk, OSBM, former provincial superior, for permission to consult his Order's archives at Mundare, Alberta;

... the officials who, in 1966–7, went beyond the call of duty in helping me to gather scattered source material: the late Rev. E. Tardif, OMI, former archivist of the Western Canada Historical Institute, Edmonton; Mr H. A. Taylor, provincial archivist, Edmonton; Mr A. R. Turner, provincial archivist, Regina, and the members of his staff, particularly Mr E. Morgan; Mr D. Bocking, assistant provincial archivist, Saskatchewan Archives Office at the University of Saskatchewan; Mr C. H. Logie, former director of school administration, Department of Education, Regina; Rev. C. Kinderwater, executive director of Alberta Catholic School Trustees, Edmonton; Mr W. G. Gillis, regional director, Welfare Department, Yorkton; Mr C. E. Wadge, editor of the *Yorkton Enterprise*;

... the following friends and helpers: Rev. A. Luhovy, Rev. O. Kupranec, OSBM, Rev. C. Tremblay, CSSR, Rev. B. Humeniuk, Rev. M. Berko, Brother Methodius Koziak, FSC, Brother Clement Tobin, FSC, Mrs Keitha Frances, Mr Pat Gleason, Mr C. G. Langrill, Dr N. C. Strilchuk, the late Dr W. G. Lazaruk, Mr H. M. Jackson, Mrs Anne Lopechuk, Mr J. I. Tesla, Sister Marie Thérèse Larochelle, CSJ;

... Mrs Stella Neweduk, who typed thousands of words and who, together with her husband, Dr Michael, and the boys, cheerfully suffered interruptions and inconvenience on my behalf;

... my mother, and the members of my family, particularly those in Toronto – Bill and Natalie, Michael and Carmella, and their wonderful children – who, hardest of all, had to live through the writing, and whose prayerful encouragement and love saw me through;

... Our Lady, under whose direction, so to speak, this book was written. I am left with the impression that because of her intercession the finished manuscript reached the publication stage not because of my abilities but rather in spite of my limitations.

At the moment of the book's completion my feelings can most appropriately be expressed in the words of that gentle seventeenth century author, I. Walton: 'If I have prevented any abler person, I beg pardon of him, and my reader.'

Sister Claudia Helen Popowich

Toronto, Ontario
July 1971

Contents

Illustrations

Compassion at Dauphin and gaiety at Winnipeg – they have a common source
At Edmonton, Alberta, age and youth discover the best of each other

No matter what the age, the goal is understanding – Edmonton, and Hamilton, Ontario

Two in Toronto, Ontario, share a mutual love
Our Academy girls, Yorkton, Saskatchewan

To be a nurse is to give of oneself – Kitchener and Ottawa, Ontario

Once in a lifetime – Winnipeg

In Toronto ladies learn to prepare altar bread
When making plans, five heads are better than one – Toronto

The Marian Pilgrimage at Ancaster, Ontario

Teaching summer catechism, Courtland, Ontario

To serve is to love

CHAPTER 1

A time to be born...

On a crisp November night in the year 1902 four religious sisters, members of the practically unknown Ukrainian Congregation of Sisters Servants of Mary Immaculate, detrained in Edmonton, Alberta, to commence a life of prayer and service in the Canadian Northwest.

They were the first missionaries to be sent abroad by their fledgling congregation, which had been born just ten years before in the obscure village of Zhuzhyl in Ukraine.[1] Surprisingly enough, however, before another ten years had flown by, these first sisters were followed by others who set forth on a mission to Brazil, and then by still others, over the years, who initiated apostolates in Italy, Czechoslovakia, the United States of America, Yugoslavia, Poland, France, England, Germany, and Argentina. Today, at 118 mission centres in twelve nations on three continents, 1,020 Sisters Servants serve in churches, schools, hospitals, nurseries, homes for the aged, academies, seminaries, and episcopal residences. They spend themselves in prayer and in intellectual, charitable, and physical pursuits for the realization of man's temporal needs and his spiritual aspirations.[2] Thereby they participate, as did their pioneer sisters, in the history of cities, states, nations, and the Church – itself born in a stable.

Until the founding of this congregation the only religious institute for women existing in Ukraine was the semi-cloistered Basilian Order which, historians believe, had established a monastery in Kiev as early as 1037.[3] Inevitably, however, the monastic community was adversely affected by the turbulent history of this nation which, for years, was forced to bear the brunt of Lithuanian, Polish, Austrian, and Russian suzerainty, and which, throughout these political upheavals, found its religious life eroded by a potent anti-Catholic prejudice, which was bolstered by a non-Catholic doctrine. The result was that 'toward the end of the nineteenth century not one monastery existed in Russian-controlled territory where previously there had been eighty-two, while in that of Austria only two managed a feeble existence.'[4] Against this background it is easy to understand why there was no active religious institute for women of the Ukrainian rite in the country, comparable to those numerous Latin-rite communities of sisters which combined an active apostolate with a life of contemplation.[5]

Increasingly, however, the need of the Ukrainian nation for this kind of religious community had become apparent to a group of zealous Basilian priests. Most of these men had recently completed their clerical studies in the monasteries of their order which, since 1882, had been undergoing an internal and external reform under the Jesuits.[6] Although they burned with a real desire to effect a much-needed spiritual renewal throughout the land, these priests realized that the means whereby they could make any significant impact were limited to conducting missions, preaching, educating young men, and publishing religious books and periodicals. They recognized, therefore, that if their spiritual endeavours were to effect any permanent results, they would have to be followed up by continuous, persistent, and devoted service, especially among children, girls, and women. It was the Jesuit, Rev. Gaspar Schepkowski, master of novices and major superior of the reformed Basilians, who best expressed the exigency of the situation when he stated: 'Believe me, Reverend Fathers, until your efforts as pastors and missionaries are supplemented by the apostolic works of an active congregation of women, your results will be far from fruitful, because the primary and most vital requisite for the religious and moral revival of a nation depends upon the formation of its women and children. And for this essential task it is imperative to have sisters.'[7]

His view was shared by Rev. Jeremias J. Lomnitsky, OSBM, who had experienced at first hand the distress that came from being unable to advise, in any constructive way, most young Ukrainian girls who desired to become religious.[8] Since the Basilian nuns accepted candidates only from the intelligentsia, others could become sisters only if they changed their rite and entered a Latin-rite institute.[9] Obviously another religious congregation was needed to enable Ukrainian girls who desired to make a religious commitment, but who could not meet the academic or financial requirements of the Basilians, or who wished to participate in a more active apostolate, to do so. Then, too, such an institute was needed to enrich the education and training of children, especially in poor villages, with the spirit of the Gospel; it was needed to guide and inspire Ukrainian women to foster in their personal lives and within their families the virtue of true Christian living; it was needed to ensure that not only the wealthy élite of the cities but also the middle class of the towns and the peasants of the villages would benefit from its prayers and good works.

Aware that there was no dearth of religious vocations in Ukraine, Father Lomnitsky from time to time had considered the possibility of founding such a congregation. But he had not yet approached his superiors for the required permission because he knew well that such a venture could not even get off the ground unless it were assured financial stability, at least during the crucial formation period. He understood that any attempt on the part of the Basilians to raise money for such a purpose at any of the parishes in which they preached or conducted missions would probably be doomed, since there were individuals even among the clergy who often stung them with their antagonism. One reason for this lamentable state of affairs was their order's reform by the Polish Jesuits; many persons and groups erroneously concluded that the Basilians must be so thoroughly impregnated with the Latin rite that they would doubtlessly carry out a systematic programme of Latinization among the Ukrainian people.[10] Such an attitude could have a devastating effect upon a fund-raising campaign and also cast a negative reflection upon a new religious community. Hence Father Lomnitsky could only hope that if and when a moment for the implementation of his plan did arrive he would be able to find a patron willing to support it.

An occasion unexpectedly presented itself. Prior to his intended departure to a new post in the town of Rava, Rev. Canon Cyril Siletsky invited Father Lomnitsky and three other Basilians to give a mission in his parish of Zhuzhyl in May 1891.[11]

Zhuzhyl, a fair-sized village in the province of Galicia, was well known for its national consciousness and cultural contributions. Its people were unsophisticated, diligent folk whose joy was in the simple things of life: the rich black soil which they worked in the sweat of their brow and which was their only sustenance; the Byzantine-styled church which had been built through their personal sacrifices and dedicated labour, and which externalized the faith that supported them through all the vicissitudes of life.[12] But they were also a determined people who at this particular moment were ready to move mountains to prevent their parish priest from leaving them. Profiting from Father Lomnitsky's presence they prepared a delegation which eagerly presented him with a petition to influence Father Siletsky to remain in their village. For all their good intentions, however, their request would likely have been ineffective, regardless of any amount of urging by the Basilian, if it had not been for the fact that six of their daughters had already begged the missionary to assist them to enter a Ukrainian religious congregation.[13]

For Father Lomnitsky these two unexpected developments were inseparably linked. He was convinced that if he could persuade the pastor – whom he greatly esteemed and admired – to remain in Zhuzhyl, he would not only satisfy the parishioners but might also succeed in winning Father Siletsky's support for the erection of a new community of sisters. Then, not only prospective candidates from this village but from the entire nation as well would be enabled to become members of an institute which would carry out, in the name of the Church, an apostolic and charitable activity belonging to the very nature of the religious life. Without delay, therefore, he acquainted the older priest with his project and, without difficulty, recruited his help. 'This was one of the happiest moments of my life,' Father Lomnitsky later confessed, 'because this virtuous and wise man was now involved in the noble and holy endeavour.'[14] Joining in his jubilation were the prospective postulants who, having learned that Father Siletsky had agreed to act as the intermediary in the material affairs of the institute, and that Father Lomnitsky had accepted the responsibility of its spiritual formation, recognized that a new congregation would soon be in the making.[15]

And it was. In the ensuing months matters such as drafting the constitutions, obtaining permission from ecclesiastical as well as civil authorities for its erection, choosing and training one candidate to assume leadership within the institute, and preparing the remaining postulants for their reception into religious life were undertaken.

Before long Father Lomnitsky submitted the first constitutions to the metropolitan ordinary for approval.[16] In their temporary directives they contained three significant stipulations: that the diocesan visitor and superior of the congregation, until such time as the institute would be ready to govern itself, would be a Basilian monk; that the conferences and retreats for the sisters would be given by religious priests; that the entire leadership on behalf of the Ukrainian hierarchy be granted to the metropolitan ordinary in Lviv. In general they were patterned upon the constitutions of the Latin-rite Congregation of Sisters Servants, which had distinguished itself by its zeal for and adaptability to the varied circumstances and needs of the apostolate among the Polish people. This was the kind of institute which, comprised of its own daughters, could give the Ukrainian nation a new lease on its spiritual life. When, therefore, on May 6, 1892, the constitutions received official approbation from Metropolitan S. Sembratovich, the first major step in this direction had been taken.

Having procured ecclesiastical sanction, Father Lomnitsky spared no effort to gain governmental authorization for the enterprise.[17] And in this he encountered his first major obstacle. The Austrian officials insisted upon a financial guarantee of 40,000 florins (approximately $19,280) for the new foundation, and it was only through the intercession of Count John Sheptytsky, the father of Metropolitan Andrew Sheptytsky, OSBM, that the governor of Galicia, Count Casimir Badeni, temporarily approved the proposed institute.[18] Thus another hurdle was successfully cleared.

The challenging task of selecting a young woman to be the first leader of the community now confronted Father Lomnitsky. In this weighty responsibility he had as a model Christ Himself who, at a particular time in His life, likewise had had to make a momentous choice. And strangely enough, as the exemplar of 'the servant of the servants of God,' Christ had chosen Peter – an unpolished, tactless, and often brash old fisherman who could make no claim to noble ancestry, significant wealth, social prominence, superior education, or to any of the other trappings which worldlings usually consider indispensable to success. From a merely human point of view it might appear that the priest's choice of Michaeline Hordashewsky for the first superior and co-foundress of the new congregation was a serious error. The members of her family, for instance, were not included in the wealthy, prominent, educated, and socially desirable circle of the urban élite. They were good, hard-working, middle class citizens of the western Ukrainian city of Lviv, who could modestly admit only to an average economic, social, and educational background. They neither envied nor sought to emulate those who tried to capture the admiration or esteem of men simply on the basis of material advantages or worldly achievement. When they were enabled to earn a decent living, one which would permit them to raise their children in an environment that would be healthy in its physical, moral, social, and educational aspects, they were content. Nor were they religious or political fanatics; yet the love which united them into a close family unit simultaneously embraced God, the Church, and the nation. Such was Michaeline's humble lineage and the Christian spirit in which she had been nurtured.

Then, too, she was altogether inexperienced in the organization and administration of any sizeable association, much less that of a religious institute. When she had first revealed to her spiritual director, Father Lomnitsky, a desire to consecrate her life to God, she had visualized herself only as a member of the long-established Basilian Order (since it was the only one of her rite in existence) and not the co-foundress of a new one. A few years before, in anticipation of her entry into religious life, she had, with her director's permission, made a vow of perpetual virginity. During this period she had lived with the hope that the priest, who was both her confessor and friend, would assist her to gain admittance to the order.[19]

God's plan, however, differed from hers. With unquenchable optimism Father Lomnitsky found himself sketching for this particular penitent a picture of the community which, as yet, existed only as an inspiration in the mind of God and men. He outlined for her the urgent spiritual needs of her people: those of women and children; the growing concern of the

Ukrainian hierarchy and clergy about their own inability to meet these needs, and their ever-increasing belief that a zealous institute of sisters might help to offset what was becoming a substantial spiritual deficit.[20] He pointed out, too, how her desire for personal sanctification could be realized within the framework of a congregation which would assume a responsibility for the spiritual renewal of her people. Obviously the Basilian was confident that this young woman, only twenty-one years of age, could accomplish much to further the work of Christ on earth. Perhaps his conviction was reinforced by an appreciation of the virtuous life she led, and his discernment that her lively disposition and sympathetic personality were augmented by integrity, determination, energy, and common sense.[21] Above all, because he knew that she truly loved God, he was certain that her ever-increasing awareness of this love would enlighten, guide, sustain, and console her in the future, and thus enable her to accomplish the difficult assignment he was asking her to accept.

His proposal seems to have come as a surprise, since Michaeline did not give him an answer immediately. There is no record of how long the Basilian had to await her decision, but her eventual positive response to God's call echoed that of her exemplar, Mary: 'I am here at your service' (cf. Lk 1:38). Although at this moment she could not foresee the interior and exterior trials which she would be called upon to undergo as a Sister Servant, her deep faith and hope in God's Providence gave her the courage to place her hand in that of her Master. Nor did she ever withdraw it.

Naturally, her expressed willingness to cooperate in the founding of the new congregation set in motion a significant chain of events. First, it was necessary that she enter a thriving religious order in which she would be given an opportunity to observe, at first hand, how a group of individuals, pledging themselves to give witness to Christ in the world, fostered the unity and apostolate of the Church by developing and sharing their personal gifts and graces in a common life. This kind of milieu would permit an intimate acquaintance with the nature, vows, membership, and manner of life within a religious institute as well as with its management, administration, and responsibilities. Such knowledge and experience would be an invaluable asset for her in providing a sound foundation for her own community.

By June 1891 arrangements which would enable Michaeline to fulfil the requirements of her postulancy with the Felician Congregation were completed.[22] Father Lomnitsky and these sisters, who were of Polish extraction and members of the Latin rite, both evidenced, through this Christian gesture of mutual cooperation, a true spirit of ecumenism. One has only to recall that centuries of historical events often involving political and religious conflict between Poles and Ukrainians had constructed what seemed to be an impenetrable wall of ill-will and distrust.[23] The charity and understanding of this priest and these sisters, however, transcended a barrier of suspicion and misunderstanding; not by any means did they wipe out every vestige of old antipathies, but in a small way at least they counteracted its injurious effects upon men of both nationalities by their Christian collaboration to foster the new institute which would exert itself to spread the gospel message of goodwill among men.

Whether the proposed community of sisters would ever take root and flourish depended to a great extent upon the future life and actions of this unassuming Ukrainian girl. On June 17, 1891, the day on which she was to begin her religious training, Michaeline experienced the poignancy of leaving the warmth of her family circle, of parting with lifelong friends, and of renouncing a young girl's rather carefree existence in order to follow the call of the Master. Surely His words, 'You have not chosen me, but I have chosen you' (Jn 15:16), must have meaningfully resounded within the deepest recesses of her soul as she travelled from Lviv to Zhovkva, the city in which the Felician novitiate was located. Here she lived and learned and prayed until August 22, 1892, when she returned to her family home to await her reception day.

The stage for this memorable event was the Church of St Onufrius in Lviv. Here a large congregation of clergy and laity witnessed the touching ceremony at which Michaeline Hordashewsky received the habit of a Sister Servant on August 24, 1892, and thus became the congregation's first novice.[24]

Whether any other religious habit served as a model for the one she accepted that day, whether she herself designed it or followed the suggestions or instructions of others, is not known.[25] What was significant was the fact that she now wore a distinctive garb which, to her contemporaries, signified religious consecration. As was the accepted form for religious habits, its general style coincided with the common dress worn by women of that period: ankle length, full pleated skirt, long wide sleeves. The dark blue of the dress, scapular, and cincture set off the white coif which in turn provided a striking contrast with the black veil covering her head. For her, as for hundreds of sisters who would follow in her footsteps, these colours were symbolic: she associated the blue with Mary, the white with purity, the black with penance.[26] Each of these — Mary, purity, and penance — would become a meaningful part of her religious life. Besides accepting a religious garb she also chose as her patron the Ukrainian martyr, St Josaphat, who gave his life for unity within Christ's Church; henceforth, then, she would be known simply as Sister Josaphata.

Since only a few days remained before the feast of the Assumption of the Blessed Virgin, the day chosen as the birthday of the congregation, Sister Josaphata found it necessary to depart immediately for Zhuzhyl, where the new community would begin its inconspicuous life.

Upon her arrival she met the eight young women who were to be her fellow religious, and whose path to the convent had hardly been strewn with roses. 'Indeed, there were many trials we had to overcome,' acknowledges one of them, 'the greatest of which was the opposition of our parents. Nevertheless, the good God helped us to bear the deep suffering occasioned not only by their refusal to listen to us but also by the obstacles they placed in our way.'[27] But no man can block the realization of God's designs, even when He chooses to carry them out by the most insignificant of His human creatures. It is hardly surprising, therefore, that even though initially the fathers and mothers involved failed to discern God's action in this event, they eventually did find the courage to listen, to remove all obstacles, and to impart their parental benediction to those of their children whom He had chosen.

For their reception into religious life the postulants had received a spiritual preparation from Father Lomnitsky and Father Siletsky, both of whom were profoundly conscious of the necessity for the religious formation of this initial group that would, they believed, prove to be an extraordinary instrument for the spread of Christian ideals in their troubled land. Consequently, among Father Lomnitsky's most cherished priestly works during this period was his direction of these girls. In his frequent visits to Zhuzhyl he made a special effort to know them, to guide them, to discover whether they genuinely desired to make a religious commitment, and to determine whether they possessed the physical, mental, moral, and spiritual attributes indispensable for the religious state. For his part, Father Siletsky greatly assisted the Basilian by providing instruction in scripture and Church doctrine. In addition, recalls one of the aspirants, 'on Sundays or holy days, after the celebration of the Divine Liturgy, we met with Father Siletsky for explication of our recently compiled constitutions, or for a period of spiritual reading.'[28]

Since the spring of 1892 both priests had also quietly and calmly moved ahead with plans to provide a dwelling for the new community. In this they were assisted by the offerings of building materials and volunteer labour of the local people. By August most of the important work of additions to and the restoration of a building purchased in Zhuzhyl for the first convent were completed. A house with a spacious garden had been procured from a widow, a Madame Huminova, for 1,500 gold florins (approximately $723). Half of this sum was to be paid in currency while the balance was to be redeemed through the sisters' care and maintenance of the widow for the remainder of her life.[29]

In spite of the rainy morning of Saturday, August 27, there was a festive spirit abroad as the villagers, summoned by the church bells, prepared to participate in divine worship.[30] The congregation, whose numbers had been increased by the presence of friends and relatives from surrounding villages, would not permit their spirits to be dampened by the weather as they joined their pastor, Father Siletsky, their missionary friend, Father Lomnitsky, and many other priest visitors in prayerful thanksgiving to God for His blessing upon a vital project. This, indeed, was a day which the Lord had made. The Eucharistic celebration was followed by a stirring sermon preached by Father Lomnitsky, who chose as his theme Christ's call: 'Follow me' (Jn 1:43; Mt 9:9). Then, a rather unusual scene took place in that village church. One of the postulants recorded it for posterity thus: 'Upon the completion of his stirring sermon Father Lomnitsky added: "God has invited some of your daughters to consecrate themselves to His service. Are you willing to offer them to God, especially you, their dear parents and relatives?" Whereupon, deeply moved, the people responded: "We wholeheartedly offer them to the Lord." ' Meanwhile the postulants themselves could scarcely remain unmoved by this unique drama. 'Indeed,' commented one of them, 'words are incapable of expressing our feelings, for only one who has experienced such a moment can understand what I would have written here.'[31]

Returning to their homes and their families, with whom they fully shared the mingled joy and pain of that day, the girls remained keenly conscious of the fact that within a few hours they would begin a new chapter in the story of their personal life and in the annals of the Ukrainian Catholic Church.

Late that afternoon the church bells once again invited the villagers to prayer, but now the sun had pierced the clouds and seemed to externalize the joy which prevailed so positively that day that it seemed almost tangible. After the vesper service eight postulants and one novice were conducted in procession to their new home, which was then solemnly dedicated.[32]

The official designation of the new institute as the 'Congregation of Sisters Servants of Mary Immaculate' proclaimed to the nation that the young women who would choose its manner of Christian living would give witness to Christ through their personal consecration to Him and their dedicated service to His people. Because it was a servant Church which Christ had established by coming 'not to be ministered unto but to minister' (Mk 10:45), these Sisters Servants would strive, throughout their lives, to become closely identified with this servant Church both in fact and in the eyes of men. They would devote their lives to prayer and to the kind of service, especially among children, that Christ Himself set up as a condition for admission to the kingdom of heaven: to feed the hungry, clothe the naked, care for the sick, and shelter the homeless. In addition, they would strive to relieve the infirmities of man's spirit: the impoverished mind, the unformed intellect, the heart thirsting for love and beauty. This service would, moreover, be permeated with the spirit of Mary Immaculate, their model, who, in her entire bearing, whether at the Annunciation, in Bethlehem, in Egypt, in Nazareth, Cana, or on Calvary, had shown herself to be the Lord's handmaid – courageous and ready to serve. Mary's desire to give of herself to others, a desire which grew out of her love for God, fashioned the substance of her prayer, 'I am here at your service' (cf. Lk 1:38). Henceforth, a similar response would echo within the soul of each Sister Servant as, growing in an awareness of God's personal love for her, she would endeavour to bring her neighbour to an experience of this love too. And through this service she would be loving both God and man.

It was twilight when the memorable programme formally inaugurating the new congregation ended. The final speech had been said, the final benediction given, and finally the sisters were at home together. For the first time those nine young women, who formed the nucleus of a new religious congregation in the universal Church, joyfully welcomed each other as members of one religious sisterhood.[33] Their postulancy and noviceship were before them. The interval would be one during which each would strive to grow in wisdom and in grace. When it was completed the Church, which had fostered their development through its ordained ministers, would rightfully expect these women to be the Christian leaven within a society whose soul yearned to be raised beyond the drudgery of a daily duty that can so easily become the sum total of a man's life. Man needs to perceive that life in the true sense of the word is anything but absurd and human life far from folly.

But the preparation for this demanding responsibility was in no way spectacular; their day was interwoven with prayer, study, and work. Each week one or another of the Basilian Fathers, usually Father Lomnitsky, travelled from the monastery at Kristinopil to preach conferences, hear confessions, and instruct them on various aspects of their new way of life. This teaching was supplemented during the week by Father Siletsky, especially in the field of scripture study and catechetics.[34]

Within a few weeks two more postulants were accepted into the institute so that on the feast of St Michael, November 21, 1892, there were ten who received their religious garb and were admitted into the canonical novitiate year.[35] On this same day Sister Josaphata pronounced temporary vows of poverty, chastity, and obedience, and thus formally completed her novitiate training. She was now better prepared to supervise the programme set up for the young novices and to plan the manner in which the community would begin its service to the nation.

In so far as their apostolate was concerned, the particular purpose of the congregation as outlined in the first constitutions included teaching, nursing, and the care of churches. Both teaching and nursing require study and a definite period of practical training, but because their numbers were still so few, whereas the mission field was as broad as the country and already awaited them, the sisters realized that they could not all expect to benefit from any formal professional training immediately upon completion of their novitiate. Yet it was essential that they acquire a basic theoretical and practical knowledge in both these fields.

In the area of teaching it was of primary importance to decide first where the greatest need for sisters existed. It took little deliberation to conclude unanimously that in most villages and even towns the youngest members of Christ's Mystical Body, children between the ages of two and six years, were the most neglected. The sisters knew that such pre-schoolers as well as some of their older brothers and sisters were often left to shift for themselves throughout the better part of the day after senior members of the household, including both parents, left for work in the fields or wherever they could earn a livelihood. It was dire economic need and not a lack of concern which created a situation in which not only was there seldom anyone to minister to these children's physical needs but also their spiritual and mental development were left almost entirely to chance. This, of course, was long before the passage of compulsory education laws, so that only a small proportion of the population had received more than an elementary education. This lamentable state of affairs, partly the result of centuries of domination and exploitation by other nations, helps to explain why many Ukrainians outside of the cities were engaged in occupations requiring little or no formal training; and ordinarily a child's lot was much the same as that of his parents. The sisters, conscious of how much there was to be done in education, decided to devote themselves to these youngsters from the beginning of their apostolate by establishing nurseries. In this way they could lay a firm foundation for a child's future growth: they could develop a healthy body; they could enkindle the first spark of intellectual curiosity; they could satisfy the natural craving of a human heart for its Creator by introducing a child to God through his family and the world about him. In these nurseries they could give a child an understanding of himself, his world, and his destiny. Later, when their numbers had increased and more sisters could be trained in pedagogical skills, the congregation would be ready to move into more advanced areas of education to participate in the development of the mind and heart of the nation's youth.[36]

Having reached this decision the sisters immediately implemented a plan whereby each member would have an opportunity to receive some basic nursery training, at least during the latter part of her noviceship. Consequently, on May 15, 1893, a separate wooden building constructed on the same property as the convent was opened as the first nursery of the community.[37] Here the children of Zhuzhyl ate, played, rested, learned, and prayed under the watchful eyes of the teachers-in-training. These in turn were guided and instructed by Sister Arsenia Anne Hordashewsky, a half-sister of Sister Josaphata, who had entered the institute shortly after its foundation. Prior to this she had completed a course in Lviv in nursery administration under the direction of the experienced Felician Sisters.[38] Her teaching in Zhuzhyl had far-reaching consequences, for within forty-six years, until the Second World War struck a crippling blow to the further development of the European community, there were seventy-four such schools scattered throughout the country.[39]

In regard to nursing the sisters recognized that it was not feasible to open a hospital of their own in the near future. They desired, however, to alleviate physical pain, to minister to the many needs of those who were ill, and to console the sick in the midst of their suffering and pain. And while it is true that this can best be accomplished in a hospital, the sisters concluded that they could reach a greater number of the poor if they visited them in their homes. These were the people who could never afford hospital care; therefore, so far as the sisters were concerned these were the people who needed them most. Besides, the institute was just as indigent, so that any type of hospital building was out of the question. As a result, they organized a simple public health service which called for each convent to have at least one sister on its staff who would be capable of visiting and helping to care for the sick of the area in which the mission was situated. It is remarkable that from the earliest beginnings every sister

– even if she were involved in teaching – attempted to acquire some knowledge of home nursing care. Eventually almost every religious could assist a doctor, where the patient was fortunate enough to have one; and where no physician was available she knew how to ease the pain of less serious illnesses. It was not until 1894 that the first step to provide formal training for nurses was taken with the enrolment of Sister Anastasia Anne Melnyk and Sister Alexandra Anne Muzyka in an accredited nursing school.[40] In the early years the majority of sisters were self-taught; they studied medical texts and handbooks; some even utilized herbals and thus acquainted themselves with the medicinal properties of plants. Undoubtedly their methods and medications would be frowned upon today by those in the medical profession, but in the nineteenth century, and particularly in rural areas, their work was Schweitzer-like in its effects. This is verified by a homely excerpt included in an account of a cholera epidemic which broke out in the village of Samolusky shortly after a convent was erected there in 1894: 'The sisters nursed the sick twenty-four hours a day. Often they spent the night passing from one house to another with the elderly pastor, Father Uhnovich, providing medical assistance and spiritual comfort to those who had no one else to help them.' This passage ends with the quiet statement: 'We helped to save many lives.'[41]

The third particular purpose of the institute involved the care of churches, in many of which dusty altars, unswept floors, soiled and often torn linens or liturgical vestments awaited a woman's hand to make all things clean and new. And even in the less neglected churches a nun's touch in the sanctuary would assure both pastor and people that someone who cared was looking after the house of the Lord. To this end the sisters learned to make varieties of floral arrangements and became proficient in sewing altar linens and liturgical vestments.[42]

But more important than the effort they expended upon such inanimate objects as a church, or altar, or flowers, or vestments was their close contact with the living Church – the people of God. Each evening after the day's work was done many villagers, particularly girls and women, joined the sisters in singing 'Moleben.'[43] Before the chapel service began the sisters 'taught the girls to sing various parts of the Divine Liturgy, or hymns, or they read to them from some basic spiritual authors.'[44] Certainly the Second Vatican Council of our day would have found nothing wanting in their communication or dialogue with the laity.

Besides preparing themselves for an active apostolate a portion of the sisters' time each day was spent in earning their daily bread. Although it is true that they had been assisted in the purchase of their convent by the offerings of many good people, they did not expect to be continually supported by such funds. Accordingly, they provided for the necessities of life through their own manual labour. Nor was there anything glamorous about the tasks they performed. Sister Athanasia Theodosia Melnyk, one of the first postulants, recalled their early efforts to earn a living: 'To support ourselves we did the weeding, potato digging, reaping, and hay-making in the gardens and fields of our parents and in that of Father Siletsky.'[45]

Perhaps because they did work hard they were better able to appreciate the toil of the common people, and were open to ways of assisting them. For instance, aware that many of the village girls whom they guided and instructed during their evening meetings would one day be engaged as servants in the homes of the wealthier district landowners, they undertook the duty of teaching them as much about home economics and general housekeeping as possible. In this way they hoped to equip these girls to fill their positions with a greater sense of personal dignity and confidence. It seems, however, that the sisters' 'lowly labour' and interest in 'common chores' led some people, even clergymen, to misconstrue the very essence of their religious vocation and the purpose of their apostolate. An interesting passage in an article written by Rev. D. Tkachuk, superior general of the Basilian Order, and printed in 1933, revealingly discusses this absurd viewpoint and effectively says the last word on the subject: 'It is sad to have to admit that in the beginning many people, even some priests, had an erroneous concept of the congregation. These seemed to think that the Sisters Servants were simply efficiently trained servants and that within a few years we would have many excellent maids. This is a completely perverted notion. In the Latin rite there are many congregations whose purpose it is to train women for this kind of an occupation, but simply because these religious sisters teach girls to be efficient in their work does not mean that they themselves automatically become maids. Our Sisters Servants, therefore, have never been nor are they now candidates for positions as domestic servants.'[46]

The congregation's vital existence in the Church must be dated from April 6, 1894, the day on which five novices pronounced their vows. Together with Sister Josaphata they now formed a zealous band of six professed sisters eager to plan an active role in the missionary life of the Church.

And they did. Within a decade, because of the increasing numbers of postulants, the sisters founded seventeen missions, established a new novitiate in the larger center of Kristinopil, conducted sixteen nurseries in which they cared for and trained approximately eight hundred children, ministered to homeless children in their orphanage, visited and nursed about fifty patients daily in nine missions, assisted the sick in their convalescent home, and managed the household and food services department of the Lviv Seminary. In this way the original hopes of those who had devoted so much time and effort to establish the institute were being fulfilled.[47]

And in 1902 the Church ceased to regard the congregation as an infant among existing religious orders, even though it was only ten years old. Father Lomnitsky relinquished his office of major superior on July 12, and on September 26 the authority of this position together with the awful responsibility of guiding the rapidly maturing institute to new ventures passed to Sister Josaphata.[48]

A few months later, with the arrival of four Sisters Servants in Edmonton, Alberta, one of the first branches of this sturdy stem would be grafted to the vine of the Church in Canada where, nurtured by faith and strengthened by trust, it was to grow ever more fruitful and add its own remarkable story to the annals of the congregation.

CHAPTER 2

A time to seek...

In Europe the Congregation of Sisters Servants was evolving in a very special way. Canada, across the seas, thousands of miles away, was beginning to experience a gradual inflow of European immigrants, including some from that very area where the Sisters Servants originated.

It began in a small way on September 7, 1891, when the first two 'Ruthenian workers,' Ivan Pylypiw and Wasyl Eleniak, from the Carpathian village of Nebiliw, disembarked at Montreal.[1] The tiny trickle begun then, swelled into a flood in the late nineties. Taking note of this phenomenon in 1896 *The Times* of London stated: 'The wholesale emigration of peasants from Galicia, which during the past few years has constantly occupied the attention of the Press and governing circles in Austria, shows no signs of abatement. Lately the provincial authorities have again received explicit instructions from Vienna to check by every available means the ever-increasing exodus. Notwithstanding the publicity given to accounts of the hardships and privations awaiting the emigrant in foreign countries the movement is gaining ground, and is now noticeable in districts where it was formerly almost unknown.'[2]

While Europeans of all sorts participated in the immigration flow which continued until forcefully stopped by the First World War, the first group of Ukrainian immigrants settled in the vast empty acres of western Canada in the 1890s. They seemed a strange and unfamiliar people. Few Anglo-Saxons knew who they were; fewer bothered to find out. Government officials reported them as 'Austrians,' 'Galicians,' 'Bukovinians,' 'Ruthenians' – everything but 'Ukrainians.' The nomenclature used in these reports seems to have been based predominantly upon the geographical areas from which these people had emigrated, probably because the authorities could find no other way by which to identify them.

To a great extent such confusion can be attributed to the fact that 'a stateless nation which becomes a minority within an alien body politic is invariably exposed to political, social, and economic pressure aimed at the obliteration of its identity.'[3] Having suffered many masters, Ukrainians had often been subjected to such pressures; they had tasted the humiliation of being discriminated against in the rights to hold public office, to receive commissions in the armed forces, to establish schools in which Ukrainian would be the language of instruction, and to be admitted to educational institutions. Eventually their national name fell into obscurity in both the Russian and Austrian empires where they were officially forbidden to use it.[4]

Upon their entry into this new country they again were not destined to hear themselves referred to as Ukrainians. As late as 1915 the Saskatchewan newspaper, the *Yorkton Enterprise*, was deploring what it considered to be a loose use of terms: 'Both Ruthenians and Poles living in Canada object strongly to the name "Galician" because it has been used indiscriminately by unthinking Canadians in contemptuous reference to the Slav immigrants.'[5] But it was to be a long time before a correct form would replace those which were adopted almost as terms of reproach by immigrants who had preceded the Slavs to this land. In 1920 these new Canadian citizens were still insisting 'usually with accompanying patient explanation' that they were Ukrainians. Actually it was not until 1940 that they could consider their struggle as having achieved some measure of success, for by that time on both official and unofficial fronts there remained 'only rare isolated pockets of resistance still fighting for the lost cause of names fading into obsolescence.'[6]

Perhaps the Ukrainian immigrants, because of their long history of foreign domination, needed, more than other Slav newcomers, to experience the warmth of a welcome or at least an attitude of acceptance upon their arrival to Canada. Instead (and this is evident especially from contemporary newspaper editorials), they were quite generally derided as uncouth, often because their appearance in the Immigration Halls in odd native dress was far from meticulous after a journey of thousands of miles over land and sea in third-class accommodation; they were ridiculed and labelled ignorant often because they were strangers to the cadences of English speech; they were socially scorned and dubbed uncultured often because they were unacquainted with the institutions and customs of the country. It made little difference to those Anglo-Saxon Canadians who raised a discriminating vociferous protest against them that, although 'the majority of the Ukrainian immigrants were poor farmers in their native land, there were also a number of families among the early settlers who were of a class of small landholders descended from the ancient Ukrainian nobility that still cherished the old traditions of status, learning, and leadership.'[7]

In 1895 Dr Josef Oleskow, professor of agriculture at the University of Lviv, in a letter to the Department of the Interior in Ottawa, had suggested that since a great number of Ukrainian agriculturalists desired to leave their native country because of overpopulation, subdivision of land holdings, heavy taxation, and unfavourable political conditions, Canada, with ample good free land for settlement, would be wise to accept these thousands of poor but diligent and thrifty farmers.[8] But it seems that references such as this, which promised Canada a group of enterprising and experienced agriculturalists at a time when the country desperately needed them, counted for nought. Politicians, preachers, journalists, and even ordinary citizens raised their voices in a pompous plea to their fellow countrymen to preserve against dilution and contamination everything that they considered typically Canadian: its blood, its government, its institutions; its culture, customs, and ideas; its integrity, grit, and intelligence; its energy; ambition; and anything else that might come to mind.

This generally prevailing attitude is exemplified in an excerpt from an article entitled 'Undesirable Immigrants' in Winnipeg's *Daily Nor'Wester*, dated September 23, 1896: 'Parties of Galician immigrants continue to arrive in Winnipeg. If our foreign immigration agents cannot send us a better class of immigrants than these it is almost time to consider whether we might not dispense with immigration agents altogether. The southern Slavs are probably the least promising of all the material that could be selected for nation building ... There is a class of immigration which retards rather than promotes progress. The uncleanly and illiterate are an evil rather than a good ... It is bad enough if these people come to us of their own accord; but it is monstrous that we should be paying agents to induce them to come.'

Similar fears were articulated in the House of Commons. Frank Oliver, the honourable member for Edmonton, stated in 1902 that 'the western prairies are the seat and cradle of the future population of this dominion. They are the seat of power and control. As that population is, so will this dominion be. If you fill those prairies with people with different ideas, different aspirations and different views from your own, you are simply placing yourself under a yoke. You are swerving your country from that destiny which your fathers intended, and which you fondly hoped you were achieving.' This was clearly a censure of Sir Clifford Sifton's prosecution of a vigorous immigration propaganda campaign in eastern European states. The minister of the interior was herewith being warned that Canada would suffer a setback unless every effort were made to replace European immigration with that from the British Isles, for, as Mr Oliver continued, 'if we, as Canadians, wish to get the fullest benefit from the settlement of the Northwest Territories, it is necessary that that settlement should be, as much as possible, of people not only much like ourselves, but altogether like ourselves, not only in ideas of civilization but also in political traditions; in other words that we should draw upon the British islands as much as possible for the western country.'[9]

Even as early as 1899, however, officials involved in immigration were convinced that British settlers would be unable to cope with the difficulties of pioneering life in the Northwest. In his yearly report to the Canadian high commissioner in London W. T. R. Preston, inspector of agencies in Europe, included this significant statement: 'But one has only to be thrown into contact with these people here to be assured that they are not likely to leave their positions of ease and comfort upon English farms, and assume cheerfully the alleged responsibilities attached to pioneer life in a new country ... the project to induce them to emigrate to Manitoba and the North-west might, in my humble opinion, be abandoned.'[10]

At the turn of the century it would have been impossible for the critics to conceive that within seventy-five years, when Canada would be celebrating its centenary, the response of the 'Galicians' to the back-breaking task of building a nation would be inscribed in the records of law and government, 'of agriculture and industry, in education and the arts,' and that the signature of their loyalty would also be written 'on the fields of battle of two world wars in defence of Canada.'[11]

Neither could the settlers themselves have envisioned their astounding achievements. In the 1890s and early 1900s, as they looked out over the unbroken land of their homesteads, covered with stone and brush, decaying tree trunks, withered grasses, dank muskeg, and treacherous swamps, set in the middle of a trackless wilderness, they had need of every ounce of courage, determination, and faith to break that first furrow, and with it to begin to shape their careers and to make their distinctive contribution to Canadian life. Despite the loneliness, fear, the poverty, and the labour, they were determined to succeed, for these 'first phase immigrants differed radically from those who followed them during the second and third phases of Ukrainian immigration. They came to Canada on their own volition with the intention of settling permanently on the land, establishing homes in the new country, bringing up children as future Canadian citizens. Psychologically they did not suffer from lack of vertical mobility, as did many members of the subsequent two phases.'[12] On the contrary, seeing in this country a promising tomorrow for themselves and for their children as free individuals, they gladly spent their energies in the exhausting task of bringing their farms under cultivation, acre by acre. At first they found themselves strangers in their new homeland, particularly since they could not communicate in its official languages; for this reason they chose homesteads in close proximity to each other in order that they would not be entirely bereft of fellowship, and not, as some believed, because they shunned association with other peoples. As a result Ukrainian colonies mushroomed in the Northwest, attesting to the deeply ingrained impulses of these people for an organized community life.

In these early days every settler through sheer necessity was an artisan. He had to make everything he needed. His simple home was ingeniously constructed from materials he found on the homestead: logs were utilized for walls and rafters; a blend of clay, water, and straw served as outdoor and indoor plaster; swamp grasses sewn together provided thatch for the roof. Indeed, the Ukrainian pioneer's home, tools, utensils, and furniture were plain and rough, but his resourcefulness in fashioning even these out of the crudest of raw materials, his adaptability to life under wretched conditions, and his manifestation of a community consciousness in the midst of a wilderness, demonstrated the solid stuff out of which this immigrant was made. Reports from colonization agents in the Northwest to Ottawa were soon punctuated with statements such as that written by C. W. Speers in 1903: 'They are very progressive; and, although they commenced life a few years ago poor, they are now very comfortable, and soon will be well fixed. This is seemingly characteristic of the Galician settlers, who are among our very most progressive.'[18]

For the majority of the Ukrainian pioneers, however, a number of houses situated within a particular geographical area did not constitute a settlement. They longed to see within the district a school, no matter how small or ill-equipped it might be. They yearned for a church such as they had known in their native land, where, together with their priest, their families could experience the joy of common worship, and where, in association with one another, the pioneers could derive the refreshing comfort of human companionship even on these vast prairies. Almost immediately such matters began to claim their attention.

Readily discerning their own disadvantages in not knowing the English language, most of them resolved that their children would not be similarly handicapped. Then, too, since they themselves had been deprived of the right to a full education in Europe, they desired that their children should benefit from the opportunity of an education guaranteed to all Canadians. The only drawback was the fact that a mere handful of schools existed in their settlements; their repeated requests, however, eventually found western agents including appeals for schools in reports to their seniors. In 1899, for instance, C. W. Speers wrote concerning the colony of Ukrainians settled northeast of Saltcoats (in today's province of Saskatchewan): 'There is no public school of any kind in this colony, although there are about 125 children of school age. Therefore, the necessity of the establishment of English-speaking schools must be apparent, as this seems to be the universal wish of the Galician Colonies that have been established.'[14] Speers' statement indicates that the struggle of these settlers to provide an education for their children had begun even before the nineteenth century ended. Eventually one school after another was constructed, often at the cost of much sacrifice and personal expense; then followed the almost impossible task of obtaining teachers to staff them. Wherever they could, these settlers strove to acquire instructors of their own race, who would be able not only to educate their offspring but also to assume leadership within the community and act as a liaison between it and the rest of the world.[15]

Inevitably issues involving their rights in education, particularly in regard to having their children taught by teachers who spoke Ukrainian in addition to English, led them into the political arena. And despite the belief of certain Canadians that 'people emerging from serfdom, accustomed to despotism, untrained in the principles of representative government, without patriotism ... are utterly unfit to be trusted with the ballot,'[16] the subsequent participation of these men and women in the political life of the nation was so successful that in this field 'they surpassed all other Slavic groups.'[17] And the announcement on December 22, 1969, by the Right Honourable Pierre Elliott Trudeau, prime minister of Canada, of the appointment of Dr Stephen Worobets, the son of a Ukrainian pioneer, as lieutenant governor of the province of Saskatchewan, attested to the fact that Ukrainians had indeed borne out the prophetic statement of J. T. M. Anderson, Saskatchewan inspector of schools, that the descendants of these immigrants would make a valuable contribution to future Canadian life and citizenship.[18]

Man, however, does not live by bread and learning alone. The majority of these pioneers suffered a great deal because they were without religious consolation. It was easier to procure a teacher than a priest. With their own hands and their own materials they could and did erect their domed churches; but there was no one to conduct services in them. The bitterness felt as a result of this spiritual impoverishment permeates the following passage in a letter written by a settler from Yorkton, Assiniboia, in 1901, to the American newspaper, *Svoboda (Liberty)*:[19] 'All national groups have their own pastors; all of them are able to hear the word of God preached in their own language except us, Ukrainians, who must live our lives as though we were less than human beings.'[20]

In an endeavour to satisfy a growing spiritual hunger the people improvised services. Another letter in *Svoboda*, dated February 21, 1901, from a settler in Stuartburn, Manitoba, briefly describes this practice: 'At present we are in the process of completing our church where, on Sundays and holy days, we meet for public worship. Even though we are without a priest we endeavour to bring a bit of happiness into our lives by joining the cantors in the singing of Matins and Vespers.'[21] But such meetings were not enough. The increasing frustration at having no priest to celebrate the Divine Liturgy or to administer the sacraments prompted the pioneers to send simple but sincere appeals to clergymen through the newspapers. One such entreaty reads: 'Together with other settlers we appeal to and beseech our spiritual fathers both in Galicia and in America to send us one from among themselves at least now, in our fourth year here. For their efforts on our behalf God will reward them with health and a long life and we in turn will try to repay them with whatever we shall have.'[22]

A number of questions arise spontaneously at this point: Why should the Catholics from Galicia have been so neglected from a spiritual standpoint when there were already Catholic missionaries in the Northwest? Could not these settlers have attended **Mass when** celebrated by these priests? Could not these missionaries have ministered to their needs by baptizing their children, marrying them, or burying their dead – at least until they had their own clergymen? If indeed these Christians accepted the universal teachings of the Catholic Church and professed a unity with Rome, the answers seem obvious. Certainly they seemed to be perfectly clear to the Latin-rite bishops of the Catholic dioceses of the Northwest: Archbishop A. Langevin, OMI, of St Boniface; Bishop V. Grandin, OMI, Bishop E. Legal, OMI, of St Albert; and Bishop A. Pascal, OMI, of Prince Albert. These prelates were at a complete loss to understand why the Ukrainian people, who claimed to be Catholics, 'showed themselves ill-disposed toward the Latin priests.'[23]

The perplexity of these churchmen is not at all surprising. History, particularly that of modern times, has illustrated time and again that the occidental mind has often been baffled by the eastern mentality; here was simply another instance of West failing to comprehend East. It would be important for these bishops to acquaint themselves with the religious rite of this people if they hoped to understand, accept, and assist them.

They had, first, to know that in 1596 by the Treaty of Brest-Litovsk this Eastern-rite Church (sometimes referred to as 'Greek Catholic' or 'Uniate') renewed communion with Rome while retaining its own distinct hierarchy;[24] and, second, that although it differs from the Latin rite in its entire heritage of spirituality and liturgy, of discipline and theology, this tradition belongs to the full catholic and apostolic character of the Catholic Church.[25] Some of the more obvious variations in this rite include the use of the Old Slavonic language in the liturgy,[26] distinct chant, ceremonies, and liturgical vestments, and the option of candidates to the secular priesthood to marry before ordination.[27]

The Canadian bishops would also have to understand that Ukrainians had passionately attached themselves to these distinctive elements, which expressed their own national genius, largely, perhaps, because these aspects noticeably differentiated their rite from that of their Polish rulers who through the years had made successive attempts to destroy their national consciousness by forcing the Polish language and Latin rite upon them.[28] The inevitable reaction had set in: Ukrainians had fiercely resisted these impositions. Their resentment of these elements within the Polonization attempts[29] increased with each generation until the Polish language and Latin rite became synonymous with 'oppressor.' Any Ukrainian who became a Catholic of the Latin rite was labelled *Latynnyk*, which name, so far as Ukrainians were concerned, might just as well have been 'national enemy.' It made little difference to many of them that intrinsically such as individual's religious affiliation remained the same; that is, he was still a member of the Catholic Church. The majority of his people considered him a turn-coat, and hence a traitor who they felt should be, and was, held in utter contempt – particularly since 'Latinized' Ukrainians generally adopted the Polish language and customs together with the rite.

It was precisely this kind of antagonism that confounded the Canadian bishops. They stood by as helpless witnesses to schism as some of these settlers, lacking their own clergymen, and having brought with them as almost second nature this hostility toward the Latin rite, turned from Catholic priests to Russian Orthodox, Baptist, Presbyterian, and other ministers.[30] The following excerpt from an article submitted by a Canadian pioneer to *Svoboda* reveals the kind of suspicion and prejudice that was sometimes encountered: 'The French Catholics have already extended their paws and are quite convinced that we will soon be within their grasp. As you can see, fellow Ukrainians, these are the people who are preparing to destroy us. Slowly we are being led into the Latin rite; systematically we will be forced to adopt the Polish tongue until finally we will be *Latynnyky* – rosary mumblers, and scapular wearers.'[31] Such an attitude, which had been moulded by history, permeated the relations of some Ukrainians with Catholics of the Latin rite in their new homeland, even though the actual circumstances that had given it birth and the subsequent conditions that had nourished it did not exist here. But since it takes a long time for attitudes and animosities that have been centuries in the making to die, their end would indeed be slow a-coming. At times the helping hand of a Latin-rite priest, whose concern for souls prompted him to extend it, would be seen as a 'paw' waiting to 'grasp' a Ukrainian soul, and the expression 'They want to Latinize us and our children,' was to be heard in Canada for many years. Such an outlook generally proved to be more destructive than constructive: it bred distrust where there could have been understanding; it separated where there could have been Christian unity; and the Mystical Body of Christ suffered as a consequence.

In these early years, what emerged with any kind of clarity was the fact that these people would remain Catholic only within the framework of their own rite and that unless something were done to strengthen their faith the Ukrainian Catholic Church in Canada would be dead before it had scarcely begun to live. For a time, Archbishop Langevin had believed that Latin-rite priests could handle the situation, but Rev. A. Lacombe, OMI, Bishop Grandin's vicar general, and one of the giants in the exciting history of the west, strongly discouraged this view in a letter to his archbishop: 'No, no, never will we be able to retain these good people within the Catholic Church by endeavouring to do so through the Latin rite.'[32]

If, then, language and rite were the chief stumbling blocks, the bishops and priests concluded that a possible solution might be to have members from interested religious congregations learn the language and even accept a change of rite if this would enable them to minister to the spiritual needs of the Ukrainian immigrants. In 1901 Archbishop Langevin sent petitions to the Oblates, Redemptorists, and the Assumptionists asking these orders to prepare a few of their subjects for this mission work by sending them to Galicia 'to learn the language and study the ways of the people.'[33] He was prompted to adopt this course of action after efforts to persuade responsible officials in Rome, Vienna, and Lviv to assist in the cause had generally met with failure.

In 1898 Bishop Pascal had visited Vienna where he had outlined the problems and the need for Ukrainian clergy in the Canadian Northwest to Austrian officials and bishops.[34] It was here that he had learned more about the only monastic order for priests of the Ukrainian rite existing in Galicia, namely, that of the Basilians, and had become convinced that this order should be persuaded to undertake the Canadian mission. Monks could provide a continuity that was absolutely necessary, especially for the Ukrainian settlements which, between the years 1897 and 1900, were visited sporadically by a few Ukrainian priests, none of whom were tempted to remain in Canada for any length of time.[35] Perhaps the initial poverty of the settlers, the countless numbers of parishes that needed to be visited, the hardships involved in reaching them, and the extreme climatic conditions were the discouraging factors which persuaded these clergymen to seek a more congenial life and ministry in the United States. Whatever their reasons they came, they saw, and promptly left. The Basilians, on the other hand, could assure a measure of stability since if one of their members departed or was recalled his place could be filled by another. Then, too, monks were celibates. This was a crucial factor because, at this time, according to the policy of the Sacred Congregation for the Propagation of the Faith in Rome, married priests were ineligible for the ministry in this country. The dilemma lay in the fact that a majority of the Ukrainian clergy was married. Rev. A. Jan, OMI, visiting western Ukraine in the summer of 1902, was dismayed to discover that 'scarcely thirty are not married.'[36] Since none of these married clergymen could volunteer for Canadian service even if they had so desired, the advisability of advocating a Basilian foundation for this country became increasingly apparent.

Having done what he could in Austria Bishop Pascal had proceeded to Rome where on December 19, 1898, he had presented to the cardinal prefect of the Congregation for the Propagation of the Faith the first memorial of the Canadian Catholic hierarchy dealing with the spiritual needs of the Ukrainian immigrants in Canada. It contained an eloquent plea to the congregation to lend its aid in obtaining Basilian priests for Manitoba. If by January 7, 1899, Archbishop Langevin, in a letter to Bishop Grandin, could enthusiastically exclaim 'we are going to receive Basilians!'[37] then it seems that at least one bishop was convinced that positive results would crown Bishop Pascal's efforts in Europe. The archbishop's exuberance proved to be premature, however. Only one Basilian priest, Rev. D. Poliwka, OSBM, who was not a Ukrainian but a Slovak, arrived in Winnipeg on October 21, 1899, remained for a few months, then emigrated to the United States just before the year ended. Thus, at the dawn of a new century, those who had expended so much time, effort, and expense in seeking the means to resolve the Ukrainian problem found that in this self-imposed task they were not much further ahead than when they had begun.

With what was either desperation, or determination, or both, the bishops decided to try again. This time, to represent them in European capitals, and to speak on their behalf with pope and emperor, with cardinals and counts, they chose the 'Big Chief of the Prairies,' Father Lacombe, a man who felt as much at home in Countess Melanie Zichy's drawing room as he did in Chief Crowfoot's tepee or in a CPR caboose.[38] On February 15, 1900, with little besides his worn crucifix and his paternal heart filled, as he himself said, with love for the unfortunate Galicians, this silver-haired emissary embarked upon his significant mission.

His travels took him to France, then to Italy, Germany, Austria, Belgium, and back to France. At every opportunity he pleaded for the Ukrainians in Canada. And when in May he arrived in Rome he besieged those prelates who could assist his cause, particularly Cardinal Ledochowski, prefect of the Congregation for Propaganda. The Austrian ambassador in Rome discovered that accidentally he too was now thoroughly acquainted with the difficulties facing the Austrian emigrants. Even Pope Leo XIII found himself listening to the complex situation when on June 28, at an audience arranged by his friend Bishop Merry del Val, Father Lacombe spent most of those memorable moments speaking, as he notes in his journal, about the Ukrainian problem.[39] Two days later he bade farewell to Rome. Only time would reveal whether or not his appeal had been heard.

By September 5 he was in Vienna seeking the cooperation of the Austrian premier and the minister of foreign affairs. Time and again he patiently reiterated the reasons for his mission in soliciting aid for his Ukrainian brethren in the form of funds to erect churches and chapels, and for priests to minister in them. He tried to make these officials understand that this was the only way to retain these people in their ancient faith.[40]

Having no intention of returning to Canada before he had exhausted every possible source of assistance, Father Lacombe journeyed to Ukraine to confer with Bishop Andrew Sheptytsky and the superiors of the Basilian Order. Perhaps as a gesture of its interest in his assignment, as well as a mark of deference to the adventuresome ambassador himself, the Austrian government thoughtfully defrayed his travelling expenses from Vienna to Stanislaviv, together with those of his two companions who were, surprisingly enough, two nuns: the provincial superior of the Franciscan

Sisters and a companion-sister. The former, 'a brilliant and zealous woman and a member of one of the leading families of Austria, had promised Father Lacombe to secure in Galicia several nuns for orphanages in Canada. She was also to act as his interpreter and, to some degree by her family influence, as his advocate.'[41] Her extraordinary undertaking in Galicia regarding sisters for Canada initially focused attention upon the need for Ukrainian women religious in the Northwest.

Upon his arrival in Stanislaviv where his itinerary permitted him to spend only a few days, Father Lacombe's thoughts were dominated chiefly by the need for priests, not sisters. His host was His Excellency, Andrew Count Sheptytsky, the young prelate who had been elevated to the episcopacy only a year before and whose unusual career fascinated the elderly priest. The son of a count, Bishop Andrew was one of the few remaining members of the ancient Ukrainian nobility; he was highly educated and fluent in seven languages. Renouncing all personal ambition he had resigned his commission as a cavalry officer and on May 28, 1888, had entered the Basilian Order during its period of reform. Five months after Father Lacombe's visit, on January 17, 1901, he would be enthroned as archbishop of Lviv and metropolitan for all Ukrainian Catholics of Galicia. As archbishop he would become a privy councillor of Emperor Francis Joseph, a member of the Austrian House of Lords, and assistant to the papal throne. Despite the diversity of their backgrounds, the meeting which took place on September 16, 1900, between the simple Canadian priest and this youthful patrician primate was a milestone for both men: with it began a friendship which lasted a lifetime. In the two days they spent together Father Lacombe recognized and was deeply impressed with the profundity and authentic humility of this great prelate, with the qualities of mind and heart which, as he later informed Archbishop Langevin, had won for this churchman 'the respect and love not only of his own faithful, but of those belonging to the Latin and Armenian rites as well.'[42] Considering the prevailing political, religious, and social tensions, this was no mean feat. And for the first time during his European pilgrimage Father Lacombe found himself holding discussions with a man whose love and concern for the Ukrainian immigrants completely eclipsed his own.

His brief association with Bishop Sheptytsky convinced Father Lacombe that if this physical, spiritual, intellectual, and moral giant could himself witness the situation in the Northwest he would move mountains to aid his people. To the immigrants such a visit would bring immeasurable joy. And so, on the spur of the moment, without having had an opportunity to consult his bishops, the old missionary suggested a Canadian tour. But even he was surprised at the prelate's immediate and positive response to his proposal. Nothing, the bishop confessed, would give him greater pleasure than to serve these settlers as just another missionary, but since circumstances made this impossible he would be delighted to visit the Dominion in order to meet his people, to speak with them, and to study their problems. Both men recognized that this would be possible only if the invitation were formally extended by the Canadian bishops and endorsed by Vatican and Austrian officials. Nevertheless, it was with the hope that they would soon see each other again that the two friends parted.

Father Lacombe completed his special European assignment with a one-day visit to Lviv, where he met with the superiors of the Basilian Order, and to Vienna, where he was granted a private audience with the emperor, Francis Joseph. He was greeted at the royal palace with much pomp and ceremony, but the coolness with which the Austrian monarch received his impassioned plea for assistance effectively dampened Father Lacombe's spirits. Hence it was a somewhat dejected ambassador who, having completed his mission, returned home.

Upon his arrival in Canada Father Lacombe discovered that the invitation which he had so spontaneously extended to Bishop Sheptytsky had released a veritable flurry of correspondence between Canada and Europe. Repeated petitions from Canada's bishops, its apostolic delegate, and Bishop Sheptytsky himself, for authorization to proceed with plans for the trip, were directed to Vienna and Rome. They seem to have fallen upon deaf ears. In a letter dated September 11, 1901, the now 'Metropolitan' Sheptytsky admitted as much to Father Lacombe: 'Having learned that Cardinal Ledochowski has opposed rather than supported my project I am temporarily postponing it until next year. In November I shall be in Rome where the matter will be discussed, and if it pleases God I will come during the following year ... I am convinced that we shall see each other again.'[43] This disappointing development prompted Archbishop Langevin to revert to his idea of preparing Latin-rite priests for the neglected Ukrainian missions. The metropolitan, on the other hand, was determined to utilize what he believed would be only a short interval before his own Canadian tour; therefore, with papal approval, he delegated his secretary, Rev. Basil Zholdak, as his official visitor to the Ukrainian Canadians. This young priest who, to date, had been the only one to answer the primate's call for volunteers to Canada, was commissioned to submit a detailed report to the metropolitan upon the completion of a personal study of conditions overseas.

The wisdom of this decision was proved shortly after Father Zholdak's arrival in the Northwest when glowing accounts concerning him and his work began to reach the archbishop in Lviv. Satisfaction with the young clergyman was expressed by Archbishop Langevin who stated that 'the work of this zealous and pious missionary has been that of an apostle of Jesus Christ, and the good accomplished in the midst of the Ukrainians by his ardent preaching, by administration of the sacraments, especially those of penance and the Eucharist, and by an irreproachable life, has been immense. Already the diocese of St Boniface, and the vicariate of Saskatchewan have been evangelized.'[44] Never before had any of the few Ukrainian priests who had temporarily served in Canada been so well-disposed toward the Latin-rite hierarchy. Father Zholdak's attitude amazed the bishops and his general conduct won for him their respect, trust, and assistance, thus facilitating his work and travels among Ukrainians.

But an old story repeated itself. His cooperation did not escape the censure of some of the more suspicious-minded among his own countrymen; they accused this man, who had crossed an ocean and parts of two continents to assist them, of Latinization, with all its traitorous implications.[45] Nevertheless, despite such condemnation by the clamorous few, the silent majority rejoiced in his presence, confident that his love for them and a sincere interest in their welfare would serve as the basis of his recommendations to the metropolitan.

By the summer of 1902 Father Zholdak was ready to journey to Ukraine, present his report, then return to continue his work among Ukrainian Canadians. In his visits to the numerous settlements of the Northwest he had discovered that only one Catholic priest, the zealous Belgian Redemptorist, Rev. A. Delaere, was gaining the confidence of Ukrainians and managing to keep within the Church those of the Manitoba and Saskatchewan colonies which he visited.[46] Then, too, having witnessed the confusion which widely prevailed among his people and which arose from the tireless proselytizing efforts of schismatics (as those who adopted the Greek Orthodox religion were called) and protestants, Father Zholdak concluded that this situation could be altered only if Metropolitan Sheptytsky would send missionaries to Canada immediately. Therefore, on July 4, 1902, accompanied by Rev. A. Jan, OMI, he embarked on the steamer *Lake Ontario* bound for Liverpool.

His young companion, Father Jan, was being sent to Ukraine by Bishop Legal[47] with orders to remain there to learn the language in the event that no Ukrainian religious would consent to come to Canada.[48] For this purpose the bishop could not have selected a better man, since this French Oblate, in the course of his ministry at St Joachim's parish in Edmonton, had become acquainted with many Ukrainian immigrants who had settled in the town. And although he had been concerned with their spiritual well-being he had become even more anxious about the numerous young Ukrainian girls, many of whom had emigrated without their families and were now engaged as servants in Edmonton. There were approximately three hundred of them here and although they were generally pious and reserved the priest realized that in their circumstances they could unwittingly become victims of material and spiritual exploitation. Desiring to help them he recruited the teaching assistance of sisters from the religious Congregation of the Faithful Companions of Jesus, and in February 1901 organized a night school where three evenings a week these girls attended classes in English, religion, and handicrafts.[49] The gatherings, which averaged about twenty girls each evening, provided the priest with an excellent opportunity to meet each girl personally, to encourage, advise, and guide her, especially through the first rough months in a bewildering new environment. This unique project was strongly endorsed by Bishop Legal, who often visited the school, attended the students' dramatic performances, and even participated in their infrequent but gay picnics.[50] It is unlikely, however, that either Father Jan or the bishop foresaw the effects of the 'Ruthenian Young Ladies' Club' on the evolution of the Ukrainian Catholic Church in Canada: from its membership would come the first Canadian Sisters Servants of Mary Immaculate.[51] Nor could Father Zholdak or Father Jan have guessed that as a result of their present quest for missionaries not only priests but also Sisters Servants would be Canada-bound within a few months.

The first weeks in Lviv after their arrival on July 24, 1902, were arduous and disappointing ones for the two envoys. Almost immediately they had been informed that the Basilians would have accepted the Canadian mission if they had not already depleted available personnel by sending priests to Brazil.[52] On July 30 a discouraged Father Jan wrote to his superior general: 'The more I see and hear, the more convinced I am that we cannot hope to procure priests from here ... We shall have to count only on ourselves, hence the scholastics must learn Ukrainian ... I have begun to study this difficult language, but since there is neither a grammar nor a French-Ukrainian dictionary, I am endeavouring to learn at least enough to enable me to administer the sacrament of penance and to teach catechetics. This is far from being a pleasant task, but since it is for souls I do not complain.'[53] Certainly at this bleak moment it seemed that any shred of hope still being harboured by the Canadian hierarchy for the successful outcome of this mission might just as well be abandoned.

Yet within one week Father Jan was able to leave the city certain that both priests and sisters would soon arrive in the Canadian west.[54] Exactly what caused this complete reversal of events is not known, but on August 19 a much-relieved Father Zholdak conveyed to his friend, Father Lacombe, the good news that 'three Basilian Fathers, one lay brother, two secular priests, and *three Basilian Sisters* [author's italics] are going to leave Galicia for Canada at the beginning of October.'[55] Within a month Father Zholdak faithfully followed up this generalized information by sending Father Lacombe a list of the missionaries, which included the names of Rev. J. Lomnitsky and four Sisters Servants, not 'three Basilians' as previously denoted by Father Zholdak.[56]

Their departure from Lviv was scheduled for October 7, 1902, but even before the missionaries had completed packing a number of personnel changes were made, with Rev. P. Filas, OSBM, replacing Father Lomnitsky, and Father Zholdak becoming the only volunteer from among the diocesan clergy. The four Sisters Servants included Sister Ambrose Marcella Lenkewich, Sister Taida Helen Wrublewsky, Sister Isidore Pauline Shypowsky, and Sister Emilia Klapowchuk.[57]

And so, after countless disheartening and futile attempts by the French hierarchy to obtain missionaries, Metropolitan Andrew Sheptytsky was sending a few of his nation's priests and sisters to be a beacon of spiritual hope to Ukrainians amid the hardships, burdens, and loneliness of Canadian pioneer life.[58] Truly, they would have to be the salt of the earth.

CHAPTER 3

A time to plant...

The train bearing the nine missionaries moved out of the Lviv railway station on October 6, 1902, and as familiar scenes and landmarks of city and countryside slipped by Sisters Ambrose, Taida, Isidore, and Emilia became poignantly conscious that they had indeed begun their arduous journey from the old world to the new.[1]

These four women mirrored the youthfulness of their congregation: the oldest among them, their superior, was twenty-six-year-old Sister Ambrose, while the youngest, Sister Emilia, had just recently observed her twentieth birthday.[2] Since none of them had been members of the institute long enough to have been admitted to final profession, each was still bound only by temporary vows of poverty, chastity, and obedience. There existed an interesting diversity in their national origin: Sister Isidore and Sister Emilia were Ukrainian, Sister Ambrose was Polish, and Sister Taida was German. Of the four, only two had received any professional training, although each had gained experience in the congregation's apostolate by direct participation in its works over a number of years. Having recently graduated from a nursing school in Lviv Sister Ambrose was the group's official nurse, and Sister Taida its linguist. The latter's background differed most from that of her companions. Sister Taida had received an education in languages and music from governesses and tutors because her father had not permitted her to attend German public schools. At the time of her entrance into the institute she possessed a basic knowledge of English, spoke Ukrainian and Polish fluently, and was qualified to teach German, French, and music. She had volunteered for the Canadian mission but her health was so poor that many had questioned the wisdom of selecting her for an assignment which most believed would prove physically trying even for a healthy woman. In choosing her Father Lomnitsky may have considered that together with her zeal and spirit of dedication her knowledge of English and French would be invaluable, while her certification to teach music could provide a source of income for the initial support of the young community.[3]

The personal differences which existed among these sisters simply emphasize that here were four individuals who were bound by a powerful tie: they had been drawn together not by some chance mutual attraction but by the spiritual magnetism of a love which, transcending natural differences, had moved them to volunteer for this service.

Perhaps because they were all young the sisters enjoyed every moment of the trip to Hamburg where they were to board a steamer for the Atlantic crossing. Here, the Sisters of St Charles Borromeo opened both their doors and hearts to them; in fact, it was in their impressive chapel that Sister Isidore renewed her religious vows.[4] For two days the four companions were avid tourists in this famous port from which thousands of European emigrants had preceded them to North America. Then, on Saturday afternoon, October 10, they joined the Basilians and Father Zholdak on the *Moltke.*

Their lengthy ocean voyage was interwoven **with** the pleasant and the unpleasant: there were the bright, delightful days with clear skies and a gently rolling ship in a sparkling sea; and there were the overcast, forbidding intervals of rising winds and a heaving ocean. Finally, on October 20, when their ocean liner carefully picked its way into New York harbour, the immigrants caught their first glimpse of the new world – the impressive skyline of America's foremost metropolis.[5]

Awaiting them on the dock were a number of Ukrainian American priests with whom the Basilians and Father Zholdak would spend the day; among them was Rev. N. Dmytriw, who had ministered to Ukrainian settlers in Canada from 1897 to 1898.[6] Also on hand were a few Sisters of Mercy who, at Father Lacombe's request, received the sisters into their convent, but so graciously and warmly, recalls Sister Ambrose, that they made the Sisters Servants feel immediately at home on a new continent.[7]

The arrival of the missionaries in New York sparked a hurried editorial in the October 23, 1902, issue of *Svoboda* entitled 'Last Minute News,' which began: 'Four Galician priests under the leadership of Father Filas have arrived in New York whence they will proceed to Canada. Included in the group are a number of Ukrainian Sisters Servants who will care for the children of the Canadian Ukrainian immigrants.' This general introduction was followed by a more personal note: 'We send Father Filas, whom we know to be an ardent Ukrainian patriot, a sincere welcome.' This statement was rather strangely augmented by those which followed: 'May God assist you to carry out His works for the good of the Church and your nation. Overcome French, Polish, Russian adversaries. Never forget that you are sons of the Church and of an unfortunate Ukraine. Do not disappoint the hopes which your Fatherland places in you.'

This passage certainly made an unusual demand upon a group of

Catholic missionaries. They were being rightly asked to carry out the work of God, which meant, of course, that all of their actions should be motivated by love. But they were also exhorted to 'overcome' certain groups of people, among them the French and Poles. The editor of this newspaper was in effect transplanting antagonisms which had existed in Ukraine toward the Latin rite to Canada, where he now saw the enemy in two Catholic groups belonging to this rite: the French and Polish peoples. It is unlikely, however, that the Basilians and Sisters Servants, who had already travelled far to bring Christ to their people, could have been persuaded to inject a note of discord and strife into their Christian message of the brotherhood of man.

Prior to the missionaries' departure from Lviv, Father Zholdak had begged Father Lacombe to procure reduced railway fares for them since, as he explained, 'Galicia is poor; consequently, we priests and sisters who are setting out from this poverty-stricken country are also indigent. From New York we must purchase railway tickets for ten persons to Ottawa. This would cost approximately $100, which is certainly an immense sum; therefore, with all my heart I ask you to obtain CPR fare reductions for us.'[8] The Oblate missionary went one step further: he obtained cheaper tickets from New York to their final destination – Edmonton.

On October 23 the party reached Montreal where it was greeted by Father Lacombe, and shortly thereafter by Archbishop Langevin. Both clergymen were overjoyed that their efforts to procure Ukrainian missionaries had achieved the arrival of these men and women. Here the sisters experienced their first taste of Canadiana as they acquainted themselves with the historic sites and imposing churches. Then they travelled to Ottawa where Archbishop D. Falconio, apostolic delegate, imparted the Church's blessing upon their future work.[9]

It had been difficult to decide where, in the west, the group should begin missionary activity. Each of the three western bishops had hoped that a mission would be established in his diocese, but recognizing that at this time schism threatened Ukrainians in Alberta more than elsewhere Archbishop Langevin notified Metropolitan Sheptytsky on October 25, 1902, that 'the Basilian Fathers and these courageous sisters will proceed to Edmonton';[10] thus only Father Zholdak would remain in Winnipeg. It seems that permission for the entire group to begin apostolic work among the Ukrainians in Bishop Legal's diocese of St Albert was given somewhat reluctantly, since Archbishop Langevin specified that within a month Father Filas was to return to establish another foundation in the archdiocese of St Boniface.[11]

The most punishing part of the entire passage from Ukraine seems to have been the last lap – those final thousands of miles from Ottawa to Edmonton. Because the train rolled across vast expanses where there were few towns, and because whenever it did stop the missionaries could afford to spend very little for food, they suffered hunger to a painful degree.[12] 'We admired the courage and the joyful spirit of our sisters,' recalled Father Filas, 'for they endured the demanding journey without the slightest complaint.'[13] But even though they were tired and hungry the missionaries could not help but be fascinated by the prairies. For here the atmosphere and surroundings were truly western, and they were caught up, despite themselves, by the sheer magnificence of the land's sweep as mile after mile it rolled away from the shiny railway tracks, then rose and fell and rose again until it vanished into the sky.

Finally, on Saturday, November 1, their train pulled into the station at Strathcona, 'the railway town of the Edmonton district situated on the south side of the Saskatchewan overlooking the river from the high bank of the valley.'[14] It was almost midnight.

Since the date of their arrival had been uncertain there was no one on hand to meet them; they therefore hired a coach which soon deposited them at the Victoria Hotel where they planned to get a night's lodging. But a group of priests and sisters surrounded by baggage can scarcely go unnoticed in any town at any time of the day or night. It was merely a matter of minutes, therefore, before a Mr Picard, learning that they were the Ukrainian missionaries whom the Oblates of St Joachim's parish were expecting, notified the superior, Rev. H. Leduc, OMI, of their arrival. Moments later they were being welcomed in a brightly lit parish rectory by an enthusiastic group of Oblates.[15]

The exhausted Sisters Servants were offered a welcome temporary residence in the General Hospital conducted by the Sisters of Charity (Grey Nuns) of Edmonton. When Father Zholdak had first learned in August that sisters would be sent to Canada he had been understandably perplexed, since no preparations had been made to receive women religious. His anxiety permeates the letter he had immediately sent to Bishop Legal: 'Humbly and sincerely I beg Your Excellency to make arrangements for our sisters to live in a convent until they have a home of their own among the Ukrainians. During this period they would be able to render assistance to Ukrainian patients in the hospitals as well as teach catechism to the Ukrainian working girls. It is absolutely necessary that they temporarily reside in a convent, for there is no other place prepared for them.'[16]

Bishop Legal seems to have acted at once. On October 2 he had informed Father Lacombe of a more permanent solution to Father Zholdak's problem: 'At Edmonton, we are remodelling the old church where the sisters will have a large apartment and where, if necessary, they will be able to gather our young Galician domestic workers of the city for religious instruction. The apostolic delegate has written to me, as he has to you, to announce the arrival of the missionaries. His Excellency need not fear that we will have any difficulty in receiving the sisters. On the contrary, we are prepared to receive them; we are awaiting them.'[17] The 'large apartment' mentioned in this letter is further described by the bishop in his diary as 'two fair-sized rooms prepared for the sisters above the church sacristy in which some work remains to be done but which the sisters will be able to occupy in a few days.'[18] Since it was a week before they moved into these living quarters, the hospitality extended to the Sisters Servants by the Grey Nuns was gratefully accepted, deeply appreciated, and never forgotten.[19]

The first snowfall of the year was softly blanketing Edmonton when later that Sunday morning, after a few hours of rest, the sisters made their way to the hospital chapel for a Mass. Unexpectedly, however, the Grey Nun escorting them opened the door to a room that was jammed with Ukrainian working girls, most of whom were students of Father Jan's night school. Evidently news of the missionaries' arrival had sped through the town, and these girls had wasted no time in organizing an informal meeting with their very own religious. The exuberance which prevailed at that gathering is best related by Sister Ambrose: 'In the first burst of enthusiasm it was difficut to distinguish our spontaneous expression of gladness from the girls' joyous chorus of greetings. And suddenly each of these young women whom we had never seen before, became very dear to us.'[20]

This encounter proved to be merely a harbinger of more to come. That afternoon the Ukrainian youth of the town injected a special fervour into their welcome of the priests and sisters by presenting a programme of recitations and songs of their own composition. The emotion of the moment was described by the *Edmonton Bulletin* on November 3: 'There was a large assembly at the convent F.C.J. [Faithful Companions of Jesus] to greet them. The good people tried to give expression to their welcome and their recognition of the noble sacrifices made on their behalf, but words failed them. In spite of the elation and satisfaction natural to the occasion, they were too deeply moved; tears of joy came to their rescue. It was truly an affecting scene; the tears were contagious to those who witnessed them.' The article continued: 'It is to be hoped that under the fostering influence and inspiring instructions of these good missioners the Ruthenians of this diocese will have a grand future.'[21]

This hope was echoed in his journal by Bishop Legal who, that day, recorded the following sentiments: 'We have learned that the Basilian Fathers and the Sisters Servants of Mary have already arrived. Thanks be to God! Let us hope that now we shall be able to keep our Galician population in the unity of faith. It is really providential and I do not regret Father Jan's trip, which was crowned with such success. While the sisters whom he brought from Europe to take charge of our housekeeping are very helpful,[22] the arrival of these monks and sisters of the Greek-Ruthenian rite is a much more important event.'[23] In the light of these comments, it is scarcely possible to doubt the love of this ecclesiastic for Ukrainians and the sincerity of his desire to help them to remain Catholics within their own rite and 'in the unity of faith.'

A trip to St Albert was scheduled for the following day. Here the missionaries would meet the prelate under whose jurisdiction, in the absence of a Ukrainian bishop, they would work among their own people. Bishop Legal was looking forward to the visit, for he had already been informed that the party was making 'the best possible impression.' Then, with what seems to have been tongue-in-cheek regarding feminine curiosity, the bishop made the following note in his journal: 'I am anxious to see them, as is everybody else in St Albert, particularly the sisters at the convent. They asked me, for instance, how the new sisters are dressed; venturing a guess I answered, "in blue." And I was surprisingly accurate, for their habit really is a dark blue.'[24] The prelate seems to have been especially struck by the youthfulness of the sisters, for he commented: 'All are very young; even the superior does not seem to be more than thirty years of age.' He must also have taken special notice of Sister Taida's ability with languages, since he ended his journal entry with the observation that 'one of them speaks English well and is also fluent in German.'[25]

After a brief reception, held the following day by the convent sisters for all of the missionaries, it was necessary to return to Edmonton in response to an announcement which had appeared in the *Edmonton Bulletin*: 'On Wednesday evening there will be a reception for them [the missionaries] at the c.m.b.a.[26] night school. We hope the ladies with their usual kindness will allow the girls to attend.'[27] The ladies apparently did permit the girls, their Ukrainian maids, to participate in the affair during which Bishop Legal and the Oblates noted with satisfaction that the Ukrainians of Edmonton had turned out en masse to greet their priests and sisters.[28] These events were climaxed on November 9 when seven religious orders joined a predominantly Ukrainian congregation to participate in the Divine Liturgy celebrated in the Ukrainian rite.[29] And so, having counted their blessings, renewed their noblest aspirations, and prayed for the grace to rise above defeat, failure, and discouragement, the Sisters Servants began, in Canada, to fulfil the mandate which the Church had given them.

Within a week Sister Ambrose and her small community moved their few personal belongings into their temporary convent. The two-room apartment prepared for them was in an attic which extended over the sacristy of St Joachim's Church. One entered their living quarters through a door leading from the sacristy to a steep flight of stairs that, in turn, led into their kitchen-refectory-reception room. And, although the slanted ceiling was low, the walls and floor constructed of rough unpainted beams and wide boards, the rooms sparsely furnished, it was home – at least for a while.

Nor did they suffer privation while residing there. Each day an Oblate lay brother provided them with a sufficient supply of water, fuel, and food, the cost of which, they learned later, had been borne by the bishop. It is not surprising, therefore, that the community annalist felt impelled to record for posterity the enduring debt of the congregation to these good people: 'Let it never be forgotten that Bishop E. Legal, OMI, and the Oblates of Mary Immaculate were our initial Canadian benefactors. Without any fanfare and without desiring anything in return, they performed countless deeds of kindness on our behalf. May God reward them here and in eternity; may they be remembered in our prayers as long as our congregation shall exist.'[30]

After they were settled in their attic home, little time was lost groping for something to do. A part of their day was spent in earning a living through needlework by filling orders for the women of St Joachim's parish; it is likely that the Oblates encouraged the ladies to assist the sisters in this way. In addition, they cared for cleanliness and order in the church; visited Ukrainians in the hospital or nursed them in their own homes; met with immigrant families to listen, advise, and console. Their evenings were generally devoted to catechetical work among the Ukrainian working girls whom they instructed either in the little attic convent or at the night school. On Sundays and holy days they taught music, emphasizing in particular liturgical singing, in an effort to foster the girls' more active participation in the Divine Liturgy.

They also discovered that they, too, had much to learn. Bishop Legal was both surprised and impressed, as he confessed to Father Lacombe, to find that 'the Ruthenian sisters who arrived just two weeks ago are already vigorously engaged in learning English from their teachers, the Faithful Companions of Jesus, and are also teaching young Galician working girls catechism and prayers in their language.'[31] Thus, within a matter of two weeks, the sisters had assumed the roles of wage-earners, nurses, social workers, students, and teachers. By so doing they had set in motion all the major elements of their social apostolate. And this service was their real expression of a higher process – a process of continuing self-consecration to God – for which they had come together as a religious community.[32]

Shortly after their arrival in Edmonton the three Basilian Fathers had divided the many Ukrainian colonies among themselves so that they could visit each one from time to time. It soon became apparent, however, that a more permanent arrangement was required. In December Bishop Legal and Father Filas agreed that the best way for the missionaries to reach their people would be to establish a mission in a district heavily populated by Ukrainians, and also to begin a foundation in Edmonton, in conjunction with which the bishop believed it would be possible to establish two schools in opposite parts of the town to accommodate all Ukrainian children. It was decided that these schools would be conducted by the Sisters Servants as soon as they could prepare themselves, together with any postulants, to undertake this teaching assignment.[33]

The proposed foundations in Edmonton and in a suitable rural area made it necessary to obtain land for each of them in town and country. On December 22 Bishop Legal informed Father Lacombe that his diocesan council had decided to buy a whole block in the eastern section of the town of Edmonton for the future foundation of a Greek-Ruthenian parish. 'We must purchase it immediately,' he wrote, 'because the price of land is increasing enormously; at present we will be able to buy this block at a comparatively low cost, for its price has been fixed until a particular date. It contains thirty-eight small lots on which have been constructed one frame house, one log dwelling, and a stable; the land and the buildings can be obtained for $2,300.' The negotiations involved in the purchase of this property were actually completed on December 17, 1902. Within a month, on January 23, 1903, Father Filas assured the establishment of a rural mission by buying two homesteads on the north shore of Beaver Lake, situated approximately sixty miles northeast of Edmonton. The great numbers of Ukrainians who were settling in this region (which was renamed 'Mundare' two years later), seemed to indicate that a mission here could become an important religious centre for Ukrainian Catholics of the entire district.'[34]

Bishop Legal's plan that the Sisters Servants conduct two schools in Edmonton could be realized only if they remained in the town to continue their studies in English and, later, to acquire the requisite pedagogical training. If it were imperative that they also begin to serve at Beaver Lake, the sisters could be divided into two groups, one of which could remain in Edmonton and the other at the rural mission. Such an arrangement would permit at least two of their members to take advantage of the educational opportunities available in Edmonton.

Providence, however, ordained otherwise. Just after midnight on December 6, 1902, exactly two months after she had left Lviv, Sister Taida Wrublewsky, the young German religious who had consecrated her life and many talents for the benefit of the Ukrainian people, became so critically ill that she was rushed to the General Hospital.[35] Although she rallied somewhat, her physical condition deteriorated steadily through the winter, and on Saturday, May 23, 1903, in the first Canadian spring which God had permitted her to experience, it became obvious that Sister Taida would soon sacrifice in death her zeal and great desire to devote herself to the mission for Ukrainians in this country. Bishop Legal, who was called to her bedside, made the following entry in his journal: 'At about eleven o'clock I was informed that Sister Taida was becoming weaker. I had already seen her earlier that morning but now she was indeed sinking rapidly. I left for the hospital at once. Here we began the prayers for the dying. I recited them in Latin, and Father Dydyk repeated them in Old Slavonic, their liturgical language. Father Leduc led us in the recitation of the rosary, but before we had completed the second decade our little sister was no longer of this world but in the place of rest. She had been a kind and pious nun, very simple, and filled with the good will which characterizes her companions. At last, after her period of suffering, she was experiencing joy and peace.'[36]

It was a heart-rending moment for the three remaining Sisters Servants. Within six months after their arrival in Canada they had lost one who had been a sister, friend, and fellow missionary. 'This is a great trial for our Galician sisters,'[37] wrote Father Leduc to Father Lacombe; and indeed it was. With the death of their companion the sisters knew grief and a deep sense of loss; they knew, too, a momentary apprehension at the thought of their future in this sparsely settled Northwest, which had already claimed one of their own. At the same time their deep faith enkindled a supernatural joy, for, as they often said later, Sister Taida had been called by God to launch their community in heaven while they were launching it on earth.

The funeral took place on Empire Day, Monday, May 25, 1903, which, because it was a national holiday, permitted many people, particularly Ukrainians, to participate in the burial service. In the presence of Bishop Legal, many Oblate missionaries, and women religious from the various congregations of Edmonton, Father Dydyk officiated at the ceremony which was described by the bishop as being 'very long but very pious and solemn.' The pallbearers, the three Sisters Servants together with a few of their religious friends and teachers, the Faithful Companions of Jesus, carried the simple black coffin upon their shoulders from the hearse to the cemetery plot that had been paid for by the parishioners of St Joachim's because the sisters could not pay for it themselves. On their behalf Father Dydyk, speaking in Latin to the non-Ukrainians present, 'thanked all those who had come to give the sisters this last expression of sympathy.'[38] The many acts of kindness they had received from clergy and laity alike profoundly touched the sisters and helped them to face the challenge of a future which they could only guess would prove to be formidable.

Sister Taida's death compelled Father Filas, as the superior of the entire missionary band, to make a decision concerning the three remaining Sisters Servants. Since they could not now be separated into two groups, he had to choose between leaving all of them in Edmonton (as Bishop Legal hoped that he would do) and transferring them to the rural mission at Beaver Lake. There seems to have been little hesitation on his part in adopting the latter course, perhaps because the construction of a log cabin, which could serve as a convent, had been begun on the Basilian homestead early in May. But whatever his primary motive, and regardless of whether the sisters agreed that his plan was the best for the future of their Canadian community, the fact remains that on July 3, 1903, Sisters Ambrose, Isidore, and Emilia, accompanied by Father Filas, left Edmonton in a wagon driven by Mr A. Lesiuk, who had already become the sisters' close friend and generous benefactor. In fact, it was he who had purchased $90 worth of lumber and logs, which had been hauled to the Basilian farm from Chipman by a group of Ukrainian farmers from that area, and which were being used to construct their cabin.[39] For two days the wagon, heavily loaded with its five passengers and their belongings, creaked across sixty miles of rugged trails and through dank swamps. And when, thankfully, they reached the Beaver Lake settlement, the sisters were informed that their house, being built on the homestead three miles away, was far from complete. But no sooner had they accepted the hospitality of the Lesiuk family to remain in their home until they could occupy their own convent, than Father Filas, for some unknown reason, decided that even though their house was still unfinished the sisters should move out to the homestead directly. On July 11 Mr Lesiuk drove them and their few earthly goods to the Basilian farm.

No one would have blamed the sisters if they had gasped in dismay at the sight which greeted them. There, set amid scrubby bushes, old fallen tree trunks, and a profusion of dried grasses and tangled weeds, was their new home – a simple two-storey structure that literally stood exposed to the elements: it had no doors, no windows, and no roof. Because the cracks between the logs had not yet been filled in with clay the sisters could see from one side of the house clear through to the other. On the second floor there was only one long room, obviously meant to be the dormitory. A few old beds and a crude table were the sum total of their household furniture. With no stove, no cupboards, and no shelves of any kind it was useless to unpack even their few cooking utensils. Still more disturbing, however, was their discovery that they had no well – hence no water. And on top of all this they learned that they would be alone on this farm, which appeared to them to be in the middle of a wilderness, until accommodation for the Basilians would be provided on the homestead.[40]

The arduous life of the sisters in these harsh surroundings began with Mass and Communion on the following day, July 12. It was, according to the Julian Calendar observed by the Eastern Church, the feast of Saints Peter and Paul; hence Father Filas chose them as the patrons of the mission. But not every day would so begin. Whenever the Basilian priest stationed at Beaver Lake was travelling to one or another of the numerous colonies committed to his ministry, often a month at a time, the sisters' personal and communal prayer would be their only source of spiritual nourishment. Never before had they been called upon to endure such great religious privation and almost total human isolation. They would need to be prudent and wise beyond their years, bold yet cautious, courageous, holy in their own spiritual life, and impervious to the most dangerous enemy of every missionary – discouragement.

Perhaps the greatest consolation to the sisters was the enthusiasm of the populace. Father Filas happily informed Bishop Legal of this in his letter of July 15, 1903: 'Our people have received the sisters with even a greater affection than they received us.'[41] This was fortunate, for until they could clear the brush from a piece of land on which to plant their own vegetables the sisters had to depend almost entirely upon the kindness of the farmers of the district for the barest necessities of life; it was impossible for them to provide for enough food at a time when they had no garden, no poultry, or even a cow. And these good settlers who did not possess much in the way of goods or money themselves, shared with the young missionaries the little they could: butter, eggs, flour, and vegetables. Eventually a Mr Muzychka even donated a cow, which became their most prized possession.

Before long, however, the sisters found that dependence upon public support has its pitfalls. The first generous response of the farmers seems to have cooled, probably because, not knowing how little the sisters did have, they failed to realize just how dependent they were upon the help of friends. As a result, 'during a period of two weeks there was no bread or sugar in the house. In a word, they had nothing. They lived for two weeks on milk alone.'[42] Hunger, cold, and strenuous physical labour naturally began to take their toll of the sisters' health, so that illness was added to their list of hardships.[43]

All through the summer 'farmers continued to work on the convent whenever they could spare the time. The Basilian lay brother travelled to Edmonton for the lumber to roof the house, but because it usually took a week to make the return journey over the rugged terrain, the work was delayed again and again.'[44] And that unfinished roof created quite a dilemma for the sisters, for 'every time it rained they had to move their beds from place to place, even beneath the boarded portion, if they hoped to escape those areas where the water trickled in between the cracks.'[45]

At the same time the sisters found themselves grappling with other pioneer problems, most of which, after much travail and error, they somehow managed to resolve. When, for instance, Sister Ambrose found herself faced with the task of plastering the log cabin, she had not the faintest notion of how to make the clay, used throughout the west by Ukrainian pioneers. But simply following her maxim that 'when there is nobody else to do your job, you learn what you need to know on the spot because you must,' she combined what she thought looked like a reasonable amount of clay, water, and straw, kneaded it with her feet, began to plaster the house without much ado, and hoped all the while that her mixture would hold. Being a nurse, she was unused to these kinds of assignments; and often after she was in bed at night she would run her burning hands over the wall beside her cot in an effort to cool them off, in order to be able to fall asleep.[46]

It soon became apparent to the sisters that they would be involved in much heavy physical labour if they hoped to survive on the homestead. Except for the Basilian lay brother, there was no one but the three of them to do the farm work. With each passing day, as the number of chores increased, it became more difficult to achieve a sensible balance in their prayer life, their apostolic tasks, and their farm duties. There was precious little time for the study of English, or of anything else for that matter. And while it is true that whenever Father Filas was at the mission the sisters could count on benefiting from spiritual conferences or other lectures, such periods were rare because of the numerous colonies of which the Basilian was the pastor.

Against such a background of work it scarcely seems credible that the sisters could have expected to take on additional duties. But because they had not lost sight of their chief reason for coming to Canada – service to man in his spiritual and human needs – they tried to coordinate their time and ability to fulfil an active apostolate in catechetics and health care.

On the Sundays and holy days when Father Filas was at the mission, horse-drawn vehicles of all kinds would bring in settlers from miles around for participation in the Divine Liturgy, which was held outdoors until the little chapel, being built alongside the convent, was completed. Before the services began or after they were over, when the priest ordinarily heard confessions or baptized or married, the sisters gathered the childen together, separated them into age groups, and in the shade of a tree or the convent talked with them about God, about their relationship to Him and to their fellow men. They interwove catechetical instruction with the teaching of hymns, the liturgy, and even included game songs, which children enjoy so much. And whenever Father Filas was away, many families came on Sundays, as usual, to participate in a simple service led by the sisters; most often it was comprised of singing hymns and parts of the Divine Liturgy, a homily, and spiritual reading.

Then, too, because in western Canada at this time a doctor was a rarity, the sisters made sick calls at a moment's notice every day of the week. In this way their nursing skill, especially that of Sister Ambrose, was put to practical use at once. If the sick could not be brought to the convent for treatment, the sisters travelled by wagon or cart to farmhouses scattered throughout the district. And any given visit entailed more than a soothed brow or a soothing cup of tea. If they were in a home where the mother of the family was ill, their work was done not after they had assisted the patient but only after they had scrubbed and fed the children, cleaned the house, and had prepared a meal for the husband who would come home tired and hungry and often discouraged after a hard day's work on his uncleared land. And before they returned to catch up on their own farm chores, the sisters instructed a member of the family about how to care for the patient until they came again. Their service was immediate and effective, but it was also *Christian*, as it was meant to be.[47]

If, indeed, there is any truth in the saying that only a happy nun will attract others to the religious life, then unquestionably, amid their obstacles and uncertainties, the three sisters must have been cheerful givers, for before long 'many girls asked to be admitted into the congregation.'[48] It had seemed highly improbable that any young woman, even a farmer's daughter of this pioneer period, who also had to work hard, would have desired to enter their ranks after witnessing the labour of these religious in the midst of destitution. Father Filas, when informed by the sisters of their prospective postulants, expressed a negative opinion about accepting them. 'Would you,' he asked them, 'expect these girls to endure the trials and tribulations which are now so much a part of your lives?'[49] There was no escaping the truth that their life was hard, but when the sisters refused to admit the young women on these grounds they simply declared: 'If you can bear such suffering for the love of Christ and our people, so can we.'[50]

And so, on August 14, eight months after their arrival in Canada, the first Canadian postulant, Mary Letawsky, arrived at Beaver Lake from Edmonton. She had attended Father Jan's night school, had been active within the Ukrainian community which had belonged to St Joachim's parish until the arrival of the Basilian Fathers, and, because there were no sisters of her own rite in Canada, had planned to enter the Congregation of Sisters of Charity (Grey Nuns) of Edmonton. But she had been forestalled in this by Father Jan who had learned about the imminent arrival of the Ukrainian sisters. Through her subsequent association with them at the Ruthenian Young Ladies' Club meetings and at the night school, she felt drawn to them by what she described as their 'wholehearted commitment to the Church and its people.'[51]

But her hopes of becoming a Sister Servant were almost dashed on the day that her father drove her to the convent at the Beaver Lake mission. Having pulled up his wagon at the farmhouse, he made no attempt to dismount; instead he simply stared in shocked disbelief at the material privation which stood starkly exposed: the building without doors or windows, with just half a roof, and with walls only partially plastered; the few chickens perched on a ladder, which was propped against the house, that seemed to be all the poultry the sisters owned. 'You must be out of your mind, my child, to want to remain here,' he exclaimed. 'Is this your idea of a convent?' Undoubtedly her father's reaction was anything but encouraging, but Mary Letawsky had absolutely no intention of turning tail and abandoning her vocation. Fortunately she elicited immediate support from two of the sisters who came out to meet them. 'They greeted us warmly,' she recalled, 'and then they said: "A moment ago we had very little; but the Mother of God has just given us something precious – you – and through you, the deep joy we now experience." And that,' added the postulant happily, 'completely disarmed my father.'[52]

As the first member to be accepted into the Canadian novitiate, Mary Letawsky symbolized the seed of that future generation of Sisters Servants who, born and raised in Canada, would carry on the spiritual and social mission which the first three sisters had just initiated. Then too, she was a great comfort and help to them in these first months. With Sister Ambrose, for example, she finished plastering the convent. The result, she remembered, 'was rather depressing because the clay darkened the entire house. When we eventually did obtain a stove,' she added, 'its pipe had to be extended through the window opening because we did not have the money with which to buy the materials required to build a chimney. But since we could not afford window panes either, smoke swirled back inside whenever there was the slightest breeze, and blackened the interior still more.'[53]

Life at Beaver Lake in the first few weeks and months had its more memorable moments. One such event was Bishop Legal's first visit to the sisters after their departure from Edmonton. His journal entry for August 30, 1903, briefly describes it: 'We eventually arrived, surprising the three sisters who had not been expecting us. The house destined for their convent is quite large and seems to be well built; the clay plastering, which has been carefully done, will certainly keep it warm in winter. It should be finished in about a month. Opposite the house is a lovely hill from which one can see about fifty farms. It is there that the Fathers intend to build their church and monastery.'[54]

As their distinguished guest looked over the farm, no little consternation was going on behind the scenes, particularly in the kitchen. 'At that moment we hadn't a crumb of bread nor a piece of meat in the house,' related the postulant, Mary Letawsky; 'therefore, Brother Jeremiah was speedily dispatched to kill one of our few chickens, while I hastily set about to bake a batch of biscuits. But when a sudden gust of wind sent clouds of smoke back into the house, we finished cooking that meal with watery eyes and amid gasps for air.'[55] That night, a pleased bishop recorded in his diary: 'These good sisters tried their best and succeeded in serving us a very good dinner.'[56] His flustered hostesses were doubtlessly relieved to observe that their visitor had seemed blissfully unaware of the smoky circumstances under which his meat and biscuits had been prepared.

That autumn September 21 – the day on which the Eastern Church commemorates the Blessed Virgin's birthday – had a dual significance for the Sisters Servants: it marked the first mission ever to be given by the Basilians at Beaver Lake, and also the entrance into the congregation of two more postulants, Pelagia Tymochko and Josepha Krysko. Thus, before winter set in, things began to look brighter. Their religious family was beginning to grow.

Soon it was Christmas Eve. And before they broke bread at the traditional Holy Supper, their mission superior and spiritual director, Father Filas, paused to remind them of their blessings: 'Sisters, no king in his palace can know more happiness than we experience this evening, for we are here on a mission for Christ who, my children, did not have even as much as we, be that ever so little. Let us, then, rejoice in the Lord.'[57]

The sisters had great need of such encouragement, particularly during the first two years when, according to the annalist, 'in addition to their regular farm chores, they were obliged to plaster the farm buildings as these were erected; prepare meals for the labourers who assisted the Basilians in their construction projects; clear the land of trees and brush in order to bring additional areas of the farm under cultivation; and do the gardening, haying, and stooking as well.'[58] Sister Ambrose became increasingly alarmed about the situation, especially because it deprived postulants and novices of the time required to prepare themselves for their religious life and its apostolate. But, for the time being at least, it was a problem that could not easily be resolved, since the very existence of the novitiate depended not only upon the spiritual assistance but also upon the economic help provided by the Basilian Fathers, the latter in return for the sisters' work on the farm.

But what worried the community most at the end of the second year was the fact that, by remaining only at Mundare (the former Beaver Lake settlement), they were ignoring the majority of the fifty thousand Ukrainians who, according to Archbishop Langevin, had settled in the dioceses of St Boniface, St Albert, and the apostolic vicariate of Saskatchewan by the end of 1903.[59] Still, it hardly seems possible that the sisters could even have considered opening another mission at a time when they had a membership of exactly ten sisters – all but three of whom were still either postulants or novices – and total assets that amounted exactly to zero.[60]

Against that background their plan to begin a new foundation in Edmonton in the spring of 1905 appeared to be sheer folly. But before they had made their decision they *had* looked at reality. Their Church was poor. Their people were poor. They were poor. Of this fact they were well aware. But what did this matter in a missionary country? What did anything matter so long as they could fulfil the mandate which the Church had given to them as its missionaries.[61]

For two years they had borne the burden and heat of the day in one small area of the Canadian Northwest. But at the same time they had implanted there the seed of their religious congregation. And they believed that, just as seeds deposited by the autumn winds germinate in the spring, so, too, with the grace of God, the tiny grain they had diligently sown for the good of their Church and its people in Canada would take firm root and grow. This, however, remained to be seen.

CHAPTER 4

A time to grow...

As envisaged by the sisters, their apostolate in any future foundation would resemble that carried on at Mundare; that is, it would consist of an active participation in parish life through tasks as simple but as varied as moderating the Association of the Apostleship of Prayer and scrubbing the church floor. When, therefore, on April 27, 1905, twenty-two-year-old Sister Emilia Klapowchuk, accompanied by a novice, Sister Josaphata Tymochko, and a postulant, Caroline Bleschak, unpacked their few personal belongings in their new Edmonton convent, a weatherbeaten frame house situated on the south side of the newly constructed St Josaphat's Church, the sisters had little premonition that almost immediately they would be thrust into a field for which they had not had an opportunity to prepare themselves adequately: that of education. This first humble teaching endeavour, together with those that were undertaken almost simultaneously at Mundare and Winnipeg, would bring immediate, far-reaching changes in the institute's governmental structure.

It must be remembered that in these early years of the twentieth century the Catholic hierarchy of the Northwest, particularly Archbishop Langevin and Bishop Legal, seems to have been of the same mind and spirit as those American bishops who at the first Plenary Council of Baltimore in 1852 had taken the adamant stand that every Catholic child be educated in a Catholic school. The predominantly Protestant atmosphere of the American public schools, in some of which a suspicious and often hostile attitude toward Catholicism was manifested, was considered by the bishops to be unsuitable for Catholic children in that it constituted a proximate danger to their Catholic faith. It was out of this concern that the unique American parochial school system emerged.[1] For similar reasons the French-Canadian prelates regarded Catholic education as one of the Church's most vital apostolates in the west. They exhorted the laity to enter the teaching profession, but even though 'the shortage of teachers in these provinces [of the Northwest] in the early part of the present century necessitated a short training period.'[2] few had sufficient educational background to be admitted to the Normal schools. It was the exception rather than the rule for a student to proceed beyond the eighth grade.

Women, especially, were a rarity in any of the professions, for the role of women at the beginning of the century differed radically from that of the era which began after the Second World War. Working women, either single or married, did not as yet constitute a class, nor did career women constitute a category. Therefore, in an effort to procure as quickly as possible the personnel needed to fill numerous vacant teaching positions, the bishops called upon religious institutes of women to accept an educational mandate from the Church. The response, although generous, was nevertheless far from sufficient to meet the great demand; hence most major superiors found themselves in the agonizing predicament of having to assign teaching posts to sisters who, although capable of doing fine work in a classroom, were unfortunately professionally unqualified. These sisters in turn were compelled by circumstances to shoulder the heavy burden of teaching without sufficient academic and pedagogical preparation, while at the same time striving to acquire the requisite diplomas. This was the beginning of the never-ending cycle of teaching – summer school – teaching which prevailed for years in almost every religious institute; it was an exhausting year-round schedule that taxed the spiritual, mental, and physical strength and well-being of many teaching sisters – despite their good will. But because they regarded Catholic education as the Church's most pressing current need, and consequently their own most meaningful apostolate, Canadian religious congregations patiently accepted this hardship from the earliest beginnings. Eventually they even learned to live with it, for it was the only way in which they were able to provide year after year an increasing number of qualified instructresses for the Catholic school system in the Northwest.

Although most active institutes of sisters participated in this educational endeavour, it was upon the bilingual congregations that the greater demands were made, primarily because of the intimate link existing between language and religion in the French-speaking parts of Canada. For besides sharing the fears of the American hierarchy regarding the public schools, the French-Canadian bishops and laity were also convinced that 'the future of the Catholic religion in Canada was closely tied to the survival of the French language. Any attack on the latter was an attack on the Church, and the deepest political and religious loyalties were closely affected by the school question in the Territories.'[3]

This view was carried over from the French language to those tongues spoken by the thousands of immigrants from the eastern European countries whose settlements had already begun to dot the west at the turn of the century. In his report to the Congregation of Oblates, dated July 20, 1901, Archbishop Langevin had noted that if the children of these new settlers were to remain in the faith of their fathers it was imperative 'to found schools as quickly as possible and to place Catholic teachers in them.' Confident that 'a religious women's community would do immense good in these new colonies,'[4] especially in satisfying the need for Catholic teachers of many ethnic origins, the archbishop planned to establish 'a community of women to teach in the schools of the Ruthenians and others.'[5] In June 1902 he had enthusiastically informed Metropolitan Sheptytsky of this project: 'At this moment I am working in view of founding an institute for the formation of certified school mistresses who will teach in the schools of the new colonies. I shall accept Polish, Ruthenian, and German girls.'[6]

However, with the arrival of the Sisters Servants in Canada four months later, the necessity of establishing a new congregation to serve the Ukrainians no longer existed. It was replaced instead by the need to provide these religious women with an adequate opportunity to learn English so that they could in the near future attend Canadian schools, and thus prepare themselves for the teaching apostolate awaiting them. It was for this very purpose that Bishop Legal had provided the means whereby they had begun their study of English almost immediately after they had settled in Edmonton in 1902. But Father Filas' subsequent decision to transfer all of them to Beaver Lake shortly after the death of Sister Taida in the spring of 1903 had been a major setback in this regard.[7] It became obvious to Archbishop Langevin and Bishop Legal that if their desire to see Ukrainian children taught by their own religious teachers were to be realized they would have to convince Father Filas that educational training was an indispensable requirement for the sisters. Thus, even after he was recalled to Ukraine in January 1905 to assume the post of provincial superior of the Basilian Order, and was replaced as head of the mission in Canada by Rev. S. Dydyk, OSBM, both bishops continued their correspondence with Father Filas concerning this question, feeling, perhaps, that in his new prestigious position he could do much to advance the cause which they believed would greatly enhance the development of the Ukrainian Catholic Church in Canada. Their initial pleas, however, seem to have been ignored, for in a letter to Bishop Legal dated April 23, 1905, Father Filas flatly stated: 'I am opposed to having our sisters from Ukraine *and their new associates* [author's italics] attend schools to further their education, because I think that this can serve no useful purpose.' Instead, he advocated a programme whereby the Sisters Servants and the Latin-rite bishops would sponsor the education of girls who expressed a desire to enter the institute upon the completion of their studies.[8] Certainly, in the light of

Father Filas' negative attitude toward the schooling of the existing group of sisters, a teaching apostolate for them seemed as remote as the moon. For with no opportunity to study English in the predominantly Ukrainian settlement at Mundare, it hardly seemed likely that any Sister Servant would soon see the inside of a classroom either as a student or a teacher.

Such was the situation in the spring of 1905 when Sister Emilia and her companions, having surveyed the ramshackle condition of doors, windows, floors, and ceiling of their Edmonton house, plunged boldly into a veritable sea of activity: in between their periods of community and private prayer they dealt with whatever household repairs they themselves could manage; they performed the housekeeping chores in their own home and in that of the Basilian monastery, which was situated on the north side of the church; they planted and tended their garden (practically their only source of food) which covered every spare inch of the mission property; they cared for the sacristy and the church; they instructed children, youths, and adults in catechetics and liturgical singing; they organized and moderated children's and youth sodalities as well as a number of pious adult societies; they visited the sick in hospitals and nursed the ill in their own homes; they collected and distributed clothing among the poor of the parish. This period, composed of days brimful with a multiplicity of physically demanding duties, is summed up by the annalist in only one brief statement: 'Our present assignments, numerous and exhausting, make our beginnings here rather trying.'[9]

Although he was happy to witness the sisters' active engagement in the parish apostolate, Bishop Legal had not relinquished his hope that they would participate in the Catholic education of Ukrainian children. In an effort to launch such an apostolate, he persuaded Sister Emilia to open a nursery in the tiny convent. Knowing that this young superior already possessed 'a good command of the English language,'[10] and that her previous experience with nurseries in Ukraine would enable her to administer one capably in Canada, the bishop was convinced that she and her companions would be successful in instructing pre-school children. He hoped, moreover, that this introduction to the Canadian system of education would form the basis for a future effective teaching involvement, at least on the elementary school level within the diocese.

The nursery school opened by the sisters within a few months after their arrival in Edmonton had a most unpretentious beginning. There was an initial enrolment of just three children, who studied in the shabby frame convent which soon came to be known as 'the sisters' school'; the same room which was used as the community chapel, dining room, and recreation area was also the classroom; the table which became the altar during the celebration of the Divine Liturgy and a dining table during mealtimes served as the children's common desk after the school bell rang. Without doubt the instruction was straightforward and simple, and accommodations and facilities far from adequate.

Still it was better by far than the kind of instruction being received by hundreds of Ukrainian children in the Northwest. Except for a few outstanding exceptions, schools attended almost solely by Ukrainians received the poorest assortment of teachers, 'often seedy old veterans of the schoolmaster's trade who filled in for a few months now and then, or young university students from the East who came out for a brief period during their summer recesses. In most cases the qualification of the last for teaching was a permit hastily granted by the Department of Education which could not find sufficient teachers unless it did so. Few of them remained to teach school for more than one year, and in many cases they quit during their brief summer term, with the result that many a Ukrainian school might have two or more teachers a year, as well as periods when it had no teacher at all.'[11] Whenever a teacher was available, however, the children usually faced a language problem because few of them knew English, and they generally confronted a teacher 'who knew no Ukrainian and had to fumble his way along to establish some communication with his charges, so that most of the time of the harried teachers and the unfortunate students was spent in instilling the rudiments of English. It would have been ideal if the school boards could have hired Ukrainian teachers, but, except for one or two individuals living in Winnipeg, none of these were available.'[12]

Besides these disadvantages, parents were concerned about the fact that their children were being taught by people who did not have the slightest conception of the Ukrainian background and culture, nor the Ukrainian Catholic faith. Perhaps this is why, incredible as it may seem, the nursery school insisted upon flourishing, so much so that it was not long before the sisters were compelled to think of expansion in order to relieve unhealthy congestion. With no bank account or building fund upon which to draw, they were forced to borrow from the only resource available, namely, Sister Josaphata Tymochko's dowry, which, incidentally, consisted of $500 and three cows! In a manner that was to become characteristic of the Canadian institute, the sisters met their problem head-on and solved it without much fuss: with their borrowed cash they went shopping and bought a school.[13]

Today's sophisticated and 'superior' world may smile at this first building transaction that involved simply an unimposing hut, which at best could be converted into only one average-size classroom. Nevertheless, for the sisters it was a precious acquisition, and the day on which it was towed to the mission property and set up a short distance from the convent was one for rejoicing. After all, what difference did it make that much of its outside layer of paint had peeled away, or that most of its windows were cracked or broken? It was their first school, and as such it held the promise of a more ample educational programme for a greater number of children in an improved classroom situation. For the young community this was enough.

But effective teaching means efficient teachers. As early as April 17, 1905, Father Filas had informed Archbishop Langevin that his proposal for the schooling of prospective candidates to the Congregation of Sisters Servants had already been implemented: 'I have heard from Alberta that the sisters there have found young girls and have started to send them to school to learn the English language and to become school teachers.'[14] On the other hand, the sisters were well aware that the arrangement to educate prospective candidates – a plan for which they assumed most of the costs at a time when they were living from hand to mouth – would not provide qualified teaching personnel for many years. For, as noted by the annalist, 'the applicants have very little education because their parents live on widely scattered farms from which it is difficult to send their children to school regularly.'[15] In most cases, the girls involved would have to complete their elementary education before proceeding to high school and later to a provincial teachers' college. Moreover, the project was risky in that those sponsored might not enter the congregation at all. Therefore, despite Father Filas' contrary view in this matter, and in an effort to assure that they would be able to function ever more knowingly, actively, and fruitfully, the sisters dared to initiate their own programme to provide some of their members with a chance to upgrade their personal academic status. Unfortunately lack of funds and the great number of parish tasks in which they were engaged did not permit more than one or two sisters to be set aside for studies at any one time; but a beginning had to be made.

And it was. By 1910 the effects of this wise decision were felt in Edmonton when Sister Josaphata Tymochko, the second postulant in the Canadian novitiate, received her teaching permit. She immediately reorganized the existing nursery school into a graded elementary school for Ukrainian children, and by this bold action formed the nucleus for the later St Josaphat's Separate School in Edmonton, which became the first officially recognized elementary school conducted by the Sisters Servants in Canada.[16]

Almost simultaneously, still another school was in the making at Mundare. Early in 1905, having noted that quite a number of Ukrainian children of the district were not enrolled anywhere, either because of the language barrier or because schools in the rural areas were still widely scattered, Sister Ambrose, relying on a few of her novices, offered these youngsters a simple course of academic instruction and Christian guidance. The pupils were taught in the nave of the mission chapel, which was separated from the sanctuary by a portable screen. Certainly theirs was a unique classroom, in which, by the end of this first year, sixty bright and alert children were daily developing the gifts of mind and spirit with which God had endowed them.[17] For a long time Bishop Legal had been waiting for just such positive action as that which he now witnessed at Edmonton and Mundare. At last the Sisters Servants in his diocese had taken their first weak but resolute steps in the direction of a meaningful teaching apostolate.

Meanwhile, in the archdiocese of St Boniface, Manitoba, Archbishop Langevin was continuing his efforts to procure Sisters Servants for a school in Winnipeg. On July 2, 1904, he had expressed his deep concern for the Catholic education of Ukrainian children in a memorandum to the Austrian emperor, Francis Joseph: 'Already English, German, and Polish Catholics have their special schools, which they maintain at their own expense. The Ukrainians, who are poorer, would have difficulty in making this new expenditure, but they must have a separate school. A Basilian Father opened a school in Winnipeg this last spring, in a little house which the Sisters Servants of Mary, of Galicia, who are already established in the diocese of St Albert, are going to occupy this autumn, if they are not already settled there. I repeat, there are more than four thousand Ruthenian children without a school.'[18]

The autumn of 1904 came and went, however, and still no sisters arrived in Winnipeg. But this is not surprising, for how could they? After the opening of the mission in Edmonton there remained only two other professed Ukrainian sisters in the diocese of St Albert, namely, Sister Ambrose Lenkewich and Sister Isidore Shypowsky; and with a novitiate to conduct at Mundare, together with the additional responsibilities of household, farm, and school, it was impossible to withdraw either of them to establish another centre anywhere until some of the novices completed their training.

Obviously, the only alternative was to tap sources in Ukraine for additional personnel. Without further hesitation Archbishop Langevin directed a steady stream of insistent entreaties for more sisters to Father Filas, hoping, perhaps, that through his intercession these appeals would be considered favourably by Sister Basil Myshok, the major superior of the Sisters Servants. In all likelihood the ultimate response to his persistent requests evoked a sense of dismay as well as relief, for although Father Filas' letter of April 17, 1905, stated that sisters were being sent to Canada, it also specifically indicated that their apostolate would simply include 'caring for the church in Winnipeg and performing household duties at the mission.'[19] For all intents and purposes it seemed that the archbishop's efforts had yielded very little indeed.

It was almost summer when, on June 16, 1905, tired almost to death after their journey across an ocean and nearly two continents, Sister Athanasia Theodosia Melnyk and Sister Alexia Anne Chykalo detrained in Winnipeg.[20] But their physical exhaustion was no match for their exuberant youth and zeal, and so they could view with eager anticipation the scene of their eventual apostolic pursuits.

Winnipeg, situated on the site originally founded by La Verendrye in 1738 when he erected Fort Rouge at the confluence of the Red and Assiniboine rivers, had been incorporated as a city in 1873. Lying as it did almost midway between the Atlantic and Pacific oceans, and sixty miles north of the boundary line between Canada and the United States, it had become an important distributing centre after the completion of the Canadian Pacific Railway in 1885, and had subsequently attracted thousands of the early Ukrainian immigrants.

Fully cognizant of the fact that their mission among their people in this expanding city would demand all the self-sacrifice that they would be able to muster, the sisters nevertheless joyfully counted their blessings and faced the future with truly sanguine hope. For, after all, Divine Providence had guided them safely to this new country. Then, too, when they could sufficiently repair and scrub down the decrepit mission house on Flora Avenue which had been allotted to them, they would have a reasonably habitable convent;[21] nor were they exactly penniless, since they had meticulously avoided spending much of the grand sum of $100 provided for their travelling expenses by their superior. And just as soon as they could manage to obtain a sewing machine to make a religious habit for a postulant who had been awaiting their arrival impatiently for almost two months, they would have one other sister in their midst. She was Agatha Petrushkewich, just a slip of a girl who had entered the French Institute of Sisters of Charity of St Boniface (Grey Nuns) three years previously, and who, when hearing that religious women of her own rite were expected to begin an apostolate in the city, had immediately applied for, and had received, permission from Archbishop Langevin to enter the Congregation of Sisters Servants. Hence, two days afterwards, in a moving and impressive ceremony held in the mission church on the feast of Pentecost, Agatha was received into the community as Sister Nicholas. The sisters regarded this as another event in the gradual working out of God's superior and inscrutable designs for them. 'We are grateful,' wrote Sister Athanasia, 'that at the inception of our mission in Canada, we have the joy of welcoming among us our first new member, who will, by sharing in our apostolic labours, help us to bear the sufferings and crosses which will be an integral part of our lives here through our daily witness to Christ.'[22]

Later that same week the little community of three fulfilled the pressing but pleasurable duty of visiting Archbishop Langevin, and experienced for the first time the warmth of his paternal gentleness. His open-hearted welcome, his assurance of prayers for the fruitful outcome of what he termed 'their lofty but difficult assignment for Christ and His Church,'[23] his sincere promise ever to be a father to them, 'a promise which he kept as long as he lived,'[24] together with his episcopal blessing, set their hearts aglow with happiness. They were acutely aware that in this exemplary prelate they had an authentic friend. And they would have great need of friends.

June and July slipped by amid the thousand-and-one details involved in organizing a household and a multitude of apostolic works. The community even instituted a sewing centre for liturgical vestments because, as the annalist notes, 'every priest and parish had need of these.'[25] And although their schedule grew tighter with each passing day, the sisters, quick to perceive that they must adjust their plans to conform with new realities, worked out a programme whereby Sister Alexia and Sister Nicholas would be enrolled in one of Winnipeg's English-speaking schools, while Sister Athanasia would shoulder the bulk of the group's responsibilities in home and in parish. Such action was vehemently called for if these religious were to be intelligent Canadian citizens, if they wished to discharge their duties better, and if they desired to function in a more intimate and fruitful manner. The venture, holding as it did the promise of a daily grind of arduous mental and manual labour, would demand patience and perseverance and perspiration; of all of these the sisters were willing to give.

Regrettably, almost as soon as their proposal was conceived it had to be shelved. Early in August Rev. Mathew Hura, osbm, the superior of the mission, informed the sisters that two of them would be required to assist with the teaching in the bilingual school which he had established for Ukrainian children the previous year. Despite any regret which they might momentarily have experienced, the sisters calmly renounced their own wishes and readily embraced this additional duty, hoping that their work with children in Europe together with their great desire to discharge their new assignment efficiently, would give them more than a fleeting chance of success. Ever conscious of their missionary role, however, their principal motivation to teach stemmed from their profound awareness of the need to help intensify the daily growth of Ukrainian children to Christian living, or, as they so simply expressed it, 'to keep our children in the faith.'[26]

All in all, the arrangement could hardly have been considered a splendidly sensible one, and therefore, even though they might not have foreseen its long-range effects, the sisters recognized that they were being thrust into an awkward situation. For while it is true that Father Hura's sudden decision to have Sister Athanasia conduct morning classes in Ukrainian and Sister Nicholas to teach in English during each afternoon did bring the Sisters Servants into the field of education within the province of Manitoba, it also had a detrimental effect: by thwarting the project of the pioneer sisters in Winnipeg to pursue regular Canadian courses of studies, this good priest unwittingly prolonged the time before the sisters could qualify for provincial teaching certificates. Thus was laid the basis for the subsequent false assumptions and even accusations to the effect that Sisters Servants teaching in Winnipeg years later were still unqualified. Having their professional status viewed with a jaundiced eye could not help but have a demoralizing effect upon many competent and fully certified sisters who were afterwards assigned to teach here, and upon their pupils and the parents of these children as well.

The unexpected reversal of their plans lent fresh impetus to the sisters' search for other avenues which might lead to some form of academic assistance. Part-time studies seemed a tentative solution to their problem of bridging a language and learning gap; and so, resorting to their flair for derring-do, they set up a private night school in their convent by hiring a Miss Nellie Petryk to instruct them for two hours each evening, and arranged for additional Saturday courses at St Mary's Academy, conducted by the Congregation of the Holy Names of Jesus and Mary. Thus during the ensuing five years Sister Athanasia and Sister Nicholas, in a methodical and unflamboyant fashion, consistently attended to their studies, and at the same time constantly worried about earning enough money to pay for their lessons. Because their original purse of $100 had long since been squeezed dry, and whereas lodging and food were their only remuneration for work in parish and school, any mite they did receive came in a trickle-down way primarily from extra sewing orders and from the occasional small monetary gifts thoughtfully sent by Archbishop Langevin.

Nor, for the time being, could this rather precarious financial situation be altered. The prescribed monthly fee of fifty cents for each child attending the mission school could be scraped together only by a few immigrant families; hence Father Hura, with whom the money was deposited, had the unenviable task of endeavouring to generate enough funds to operate the school by pooling the precious few dollars paid by parents and the meagre income of the mission. The utilization of their small earnings for this purpose meant that the missionaries' daily living was stripped of everything except the barest necessities. But the combination of a keen sense of duty, catholicity, and community solidarity prompted both pastor and sisters to make every concerted effort to keep the school open; and with this as their first priority, it is little wonder that to achieve their specific end no personal or communal sacrifice was deemed too great.

During the year 1905 the enrolment of a handful of children in the plain school building located at the busy corner of Winnipeg's McGregor and Selkirk avenues jumped to 160, but the teachers' anxiety for their pupils' safety also increased, especially for those in the primary grades who were compelled to cross the dangerous intersection, with its heavy street-car traffic, a number of times each day. This constant hazard spurred Father Hura and the sisters to transfer classes to the basement of the recently constructed St Nicholas Church in the spring of 1906.

Even though they thought that they had looked at the actualities and considered all the possibilities they were soon to rue their decision, for although the church was new its basement was just a basement – dingy, dank, and unheatable. To make matters worse, so much water seeped in through the poorly fitted windows that when it rained both sisters and children were faced with the gruelling task of bailing it out by bucketfulls. It was a most stunning setback. In their concern for their young charges the priest and sisters had merely managed to make a bad situation worse.

These disheartening results were enough to take the steam out of any missionary; nevertheless, the sisters continued to teach, the enrolment continued to multiply, and Father Hura continued to scrimp and save to keep things going. One semester succeeded another and although the material situation remained basically unchanged, a continuing harmonious relationship was quickly established between the teaching sisters and the children. 'It is strange,' noted the annalist in 1906, 'that in spite of the inconveniences our children must endure, they have developed so deep a devotion and loyalty that, whenever a family must move to a farm outside the city, the pupils weep at having to leave us and their school.'[27]

But abruptly in 1907 the organization of the Winnipeg mission was radically transformed. Hitherto, in order to sustain their apostolate in both parish and school, Father Hura and the sisters had expended their physical resources in a common effort and had contributed their material assets to a common fund. But shortly after his appointment to the dual post of provincial superior of the Ukrainian Basilians and of canonical visitor for the Sisters Servants in Canada, Rev. S. Dydyk saw fit to sunder this combined endeavour by relieving the priests of his order of the management of St Nicholas School and assigning to the Sisters Servants sole responsibility for its administration and maintenance. Understandably startled and shaken by Father Dydyk's rather electrifying adjustment, the sisters looked upon his proposal as 'a most frightening enterprise.'[28] They hadn't the slightest notion how they could secure the funds needed to maintain the school; furthermore, they were oppressively conscious of their financial limitations, especially since, in the absence of a separate school system in Manitoba, they could expect not even a shred of governmental assistance. Hence the sisters can hardly be blamed for feeling as if an albatross had suddenly been hung about the very neck of their institute. But the stakes were high – nothing less than the spiritual, academic, moral, and social well-being of hundreds of Ukrainian Catholic children. Naturally, there was nothing to be done except to swallow their panic, accept this latest formidable burden, and trust in the Lord – a course which the sisters had long since discovered to be a positively unfailing preventative against discouragement whenever, as at this moment, they had little to go on except faith.

An immediate honest and careful appraisal of their position revealed that as long as St Nicholas School depended solely upon the sisters' own precarious ability to finance it – regardless of whether it was comprised of a partitioned church basement or, as later, a more suitable school building – so long would it be chronically beset by debts and its very existence remain in jeopardy. And this in spite of the fact that, with dogged perseverance, the local religious community struggled to tap every available source in order to raise money. Thus month after month and year after year, out of an abiding heart-deep concern for the Christian education of Ukrainian youth, no sacrifice was avoided, no effort spared. In their personal daily living, as the annals reveal, the sisters denied themselves butter and meat and eggs, and heat and electricity; after school hours, on weekends and holidays, they knocked on countless doors and begged; they accepted every order placed with them for needlework, even though to fill each one they were compelled to work far into the night; they constantly prepared children's concerts, organized bazaars, and sponsored teas. Only in this manner did the nickels and dimes, and sometimes quarters, come in to support their cause. School closure, however, loomed menacingly above the horizon for over sixty years; therefore it is hardly surprising that every succeeding Winnipeg superior found herself forced to acquire the holy ambition of getting out of debt.[29]

But their educational work in the west, so hesitatingly launched in the close quarters of an unpretentious convent at Edmonton, in the nave of a rustic log chapel at Mundare, and in the dismal basement of a mission church at Winnipeg, was expanding of its own momentum. Within a scant five years a burgeoning Ukrainian population in and around Edmonton brought with it such increasing numbers of children to the sisters' doorstep that, by 1910, there was no escaping the fact that the one-room school purchased a few years before had become totally inadequate. With a magnificent grasp of the obvious, Sister Josaphata, who had succeeded Sister Emilia as superior of the Edmonton community, determined that a more functional building was indispensable; one that, in the light of a broader apostolate, would serve as a convent, an elementary residential and day school, and a hostel for working girls.

For besides fulfilling their regular teaching assignments the sisters had sought out young Ukrainian immigrants, girls who had come into the city either directly from Ukraine or from the surrounding colonies to seek employment. The hearts of these religious burned in anguish for each young woman who was experiencing the inexpressible loneliness of one who suddenly finds herself exposed to the grim business of earning a living in a strange environment, bereft of any family reinforcement, and unable to communicate in the official language of the country. Recognizing that they could not ignore this problem in the way they ignored their own hardships, and prompted by a compassionate desire to lessen the girls' difficulties of adaptation to a new land and culture, they organized night classes for them in their tiny schoolhouse. Brought together in shared worry and concern, the sisters and ladies from the neighbouring Sacred Heart Parish provided instruction in English and religion, and at each session supplemented learning with their outgoing friendliness and hospitality. This was a valid and enlightened social service long before 'social service' came into its own in Canada.

Without doubt, such enriching encounters made it increasingly distasteful for the students to return to their boarding houses, which were generally dismal places operated by mercenary individuals who had few scruples about defrauding an unsuspecting immigrant. To Sister Josaphata, a woman who embraced in her unstinting Christian affection those with whom she lived and for whom she worked, it seemed curiously insensitive not to consider the welfare and happiness of these girls. Her enthusiastic interest raised the bright hope that if multiple efforts were exerted in their behalf, a hostel might become a reality. But how to finance such an ambitious venture? She was familiar enough with the maxim that money is the root of all evil, but never before had she been so convinced that very little good can be accomplished – or evil avoided – without its aid. However, with both her religious community and most Ukrainian immigrants limping along on the skimpiest of incomes, it was obvious that she could not harbour even a vague expectation that they would be able to finance the multi-purpose edifice she was contemplating.

Aware that no neatly wrapped package of solutions to her genuinely prickly problem would present itself, Sister Josaphata simply resorted to her own initiative and, resolutely pinning her hopes upon the institute's staunchest supporters – the bishop, the Basilians, and the women from the neighbouring Latin-rite parish – issued a bold appeal for support. The result? Before long there was a building fund which boasted a bank balance of $400, the sum netted from the first fair ever to be held in Edmonton for the benefit of Ukrainians. The project had been organized by ladies whose surnames – Hughes, Neil, Caseman – indicate that the sisters had aroused a lively interest in the welfare of their people among many Anglo-Saxons. True, $400 wasn't much, but at least it was a starting point. The Basilian Fathers, for their part, provided a permanent site for the school by donating four lots out of the half-block of land originally purchased for the Ukrainian mission.[30] And finally, Bishop Legal, whose heart must often have undone the diocesan treasurer's balance sheets, magnanimously accepted the responsibility for both the plans of the proposed structure and the bulk of its costs.

The prelate's more than favourable consideration of the sisters' development programme was a breakthrough of startling proportions, for because of it the previous problematic situation changed character entirely. Within four months after construction had begun in August 1910, the bishop was able to outline for Father Filas the progress that had been made in building the school and in procuring the money to pay for it: 'A home for the Little Sisters of Mary Immaculate is almost completed adjacent to their old house in Edmonton. This convent, hostel, boarding and day school, will cost approximately $8,000, and is being financed by means of a loan of $6,000, which will be paid for in yearly payments of $600 from the fund obtained through the annual collections held in each diocese for Ukrainians. In addition, the Catholic Church Extension Society of Toronto has promised to provide $500 for four years in order to pay off the remaining $2,000 debt. I do not hesitate to predict that this convent school will accomplish much good.'[31] Thus, for the time being at least, the bishop's efforts on their behalf freed the sisters from anything like consternation regarding mortgage payments. Then, too, the assurance of Sister Josaphata's monthly teaching salary of $60 lessened somewhat the gnawing anxiety stemming from their personal obligation to maintain the convent school, and thus permitted them to participate in their apostolate of prayer and service more fully and with greater tranquillity of mind.[32]

In Winnipeg, on the other hand, each day grew a little more anxious in the face of ever-rising perplexities connected with the operating costs of St Nicholas School. Although the sisters lived as cheaply as possible, and thus managed to pay the price needed to fend off school closure, their inability to afford repairs resulted in the continuing physical deterioration of the dark, damp, and mouldy cellar school under the church. In 1909 a rather weak scheme – born not of emotion but of desperation – for carrying out a door-to-door canvas among their people in an effort to raise funds for a decent school failed dismally. 'We collected almost nothing,' confessed the convent chronicler, 'but that little, together with the sum of $100 offered by the archbishop, we deposited in the bank, postponing for the time being all plans for another building.'[33]

If it accomplished anything at all, their action did succeed in focusing attention upon the persistent poverty which characterized their lives, thus winning for them at least one other faithful benefactor, Rev. A. Cherrier, a member of Archbishop Langevin's archdiocesan council. He was a godsend to the sisters. For, having discovered that the 'Ukrainian sisters' were depriving themselves of food in a struggle to make ends meet, Father Cherrier's kindness spilled over beyond his own French parish as, assuming the role of Good Samaritan, he made certain that a basket of groceries somehow found its way to the convent each month. So it is hardly surprising that it was to him the sisters appealed on May 25, 1911, when, after a heavy rainfall, they beheld their pupils' desks floating about the church basement in a murky sea. One glance at the mess was sufficient for the good priest. Hastily dispatching a letter to his archbishop (who was just then preparing to travel to Rome), Father Cherrier begged the prelate to consider favourably his proposals for a new school in order that the existing intolerable state of affairs be resolved; and he seconded his proposition with a personal offering of $1,000.[34] Fourteen anxious day later things began to happen. On June 8, without the remotest hint, Father Dydyk surprised the sisters with the astounding news that the archbishop had ordered the immediate construction of a two-storey school at the corner of McKenzie and Flora avenues, in close proximity to the mission church. It was to be financed with money drawn from a fund established by the Canadian episcopate at the first general council held in Quebec in the autumn of 1909. At that meeting the Latin-rite bishops had voted to apply a portion of each year's diocesan collections over a period of ten years toward the support of Ukrainian Catholic works in western Canada.[35] The school, therefore, would be a gift to the Ukrainian people not from one person or group but from Latin-rite Catholics across the land.

The sisters were jubilant, for not even in their wildest imaginings had they envisioned such a turn of events. Once again, in their hour of need, Archbishop Langevin had reflected his concern for their Church and people not only in words but in specific concrete actions. And because they were convinced that from schools such as theirs the Ukrainian Catholic Church would receive an effective spiritual leadership, the sisters regarded his assistance in this instance as an acceptance of responsibility of the highest order. On the other hand, in his readiness to help it seems as if the archbishop had somehow dipped into the future and had seen how fruitful his deed would be through those priests and sisters and even a bishop – all former students of St Nicholas School – who would one day strengthen their Church by spending themselves in a ministry of love among Ukrainians throughout the nation.[36] And so, for the moment at least, the sisters were able to forget that the responsibility for the larger school still rested with them, and that they would have to continue to strain mightily to support it.

No one was to observe more closely this gradual broadening of the institute's apostolate than Metropolitan Andrew Sheptytsky, who arrived in Winnipeg on September 27, 1910, ten years after Father Lacombe had invited him to visit the settlements of Ukrainians in western Canada. After participating in the Eucharistic Congress held at Montreal on September 5–16, 1910, the prelate was finally able to realize his dream of seeing at first hand the life of his people in the land of their adoption. He desired to go 'everywhere the missionaries go, and to accompany them, so as to make observations, taking into account all of the problems and difficulties, striving to gain the most exact information with regard to the dispositions, prejudices, and opinions of Catholics; and even of their opponents, so as with full knowledge of the case to reckon for the future the probability of triumphs or failures.'[37]

And this, precisely, is what he did. From September to November the metropolitan crisscrossed the length and breadth of the prairies, visiting larger centres and dropping in on little out-of-the-way settlements; celebrating the Divine Liturgy with his people; preaching the Gospel; hearing their confessions; baptizing their children; and listening to touching accounts of endeavours to carve a future out of a wilderness. These people were his beloved children; hence their spiritual and material hardships were also his.

Among those he visited were the Sisters Servants, four of whom had carried his blessing with them to this country in 1902. Now, just eight years later, he was witnessing the initial fruits of their silent and strenuous efforts. As the only Ukrainian women's religious congregation in the nation the institute naturally came under the metropolitan's close scrutiny. What he found was a membership of just nineteen sisters divided among three missions within the provinces of Alberta and Manitoba, and subject to the ecclesiastical jurisdiction of two Latin-rite ordinaries, Bishop Legal of St Albert and Archbishop Langevin of St Boniface. Perhaps it was the element of geographical and occupational fragmentation, a factor which he knew could substantially weaken any fledgling community unless it were secured by a sound community structure, that prompted the metropolitan to consider the institute's survival in Canada to be a moot question indeed. Accordingly, in each of their convents he asked the same burning question: 'Sisters, do you think that your congregation will be able to survive in Canada?'[38] The metropolitan's concern, however, had not focused on a new situation; rather, it had surfaced one with which the congregation had managed to cope from the earliest years. As a result, the development of the institute's internal government and authority – without which stability would indeed prove elusive – had unobtrusively kept pace with its more obvious external growth. For this reason the metropolitan's query received a spontaneous response from the sisters at each mission: 'We firmly believe that with God's help our Canadian institute will thrive.'[39]

Undeniably, this kind of structural maturation had been anything but easy. As long as the community had functioned only at Mundare, no problem concerning leadership or government had arisen. Sister Ambrose Lenkewich had continued to conduct local affairs in consultation and cooperation with each Basilian superior of the mission and with the local ordinary, Bishop Legal; this in conformity with the constitutions approved for the congregation at the time of its founding in 1892, and in accordance with which the Canadian sisters had regulated their religious life and apostolate.[40] However, with the establishment of the convent at Winnipeg within the archdiocese of St Boniface, all matters, even that as routine as the transfer of a sister from one mission to another, had become more complicated because two separate ecclesiastical entities were involved. Almost overnight, then, this minor expansion had brought with it a need for a major superior who would oversee the affairs of individual houses within each diocese and deal with matters pertaining to the institute as a whole. To this end, and in the absence of any other appointment by the European motherhouse, Sister Ambrose had assumed the responsible post almost as a matter of course.

Such action is not surprising since time and again during the community's first five years in the west the sisters had been compelled to exercise their own initiative in the organization and conduct of their life and work. During this formative period there had existed an almost total blackout with regard to official communications and specific directives from Ukraine. This can be attributed to the fact that at this time the European community was itself undergoing a period of reorganization and further formation.[41] Whatever the reasons, this silence on the part of European superiors permitted the Canadian sisters to remain eminently in command of their own course. They saw their local situations from their own passionately committed point of view and dealt with each in their own independent manner. This kind of autonomy inevitably affected their communal life in that, although the constitutions remained unchanged in essence, some accidental differences in such areas as the apostolate and religious garb came to be added.[42] And these gradual modifications, issuing especially from the sisters' educational undertakings, eventually blended new tones into the complexion of the Canadian congregation, thus lending it an appearance somewhat dissimilar from that of the maternal community in Ukraine.

It was possible that so marked a degree of self-sufficiency could, in time, divorce the Canadian institute from the control of the motherhouse. That higher superiors in Europe were aware of just such an eventuality is evident from the fact that in 1909, one year before Metropolitan Sheptytsky's visit, the Canadian sisters finally received two key notifications from Europe: first, that Sister Vitalia Mykush had been elected major superior of the entire congregation; and, second, that Sister Ambrose Lenkewich had been appointed to be her Canadian assistant, with the authority to govern the mission overseas on the basis of specifically spelled-out powers; namely, to accept and dismiss aspirants, admit postulants to the novitiate and worthy candidates to temporary profession, appoint local superiors, transfer sisters, grant permissions and assign penances in the spirit of the vows and constitutions.[43] By making the Canadian assistant responsible to the major superior and her council, Sister Vitalia succeeded in temporarily reforging the link of unity in the congregation, which had been wearing rather thin.

At this time, Sister Ambrose was the only remaining member of the original four sisters who had founded the mission in Canada, since both Sister Isidore Shypowsky and Sister Emilia Klapowchuk had been recalled to Ukraine in September 1908.[44] Although tiny in physical stature, her contemporaries described her as great in those human attributes that really count. God had led her to a new land where she had raised a spiritual family in His name, a family comprised partly of a small but influential community of sisters whom she had trained in the novitiate and had later continued to guide with maturity and true insight, and of those countless men, women, and children whom she and her fellow religious had taught and nursed in their scattered prairie farmhouses. Steeped in humility, and with a good conscience and a genuine faith, she had borne adversity with a quietness of mind and heart that bespoke of heroism. For seven years she had played her part in the central role of superior with great dignity and unfailing poise. And if, by chance, she had been living with the hope of being relieved of the burden of governing, she must have tasted keen disappointment. For now all the lonely decisions were officially hers.[45]

Nor had Sister Vitalia acted too soon, since there was evidence that greater instability might ensue from the misunderstanding of the reasons for Sister Ambrose's appointment by the western bishops. For some inexplicable reason the hierarchy interpreted this move to mean that the motherhouse desired that 'the Canadian sisters form a distinct and independent religious community.'[46] And believing that the surest and most immediate way to achieve this goal would be for the professed sisters to elect their own major superior, the bishops scheduled an election for February 17, 1910. It was to be administered by Father Dydyk, whom the bishops now appointed as the Sisters Servants' diocesan visitor with the power to 'modify their rules in what concerns the new goal which these sisters must pursue; that is, teaching in the primary schools, even those which are controlled by the government.'[47] In this proposal the bishops' predominant concern for a Catholic education for Ukrainians in the west is clearly manifested, for its prime objective seems to have been nothing less than the establishment of a completely independent Canadian Congregation of Sisters Servants, with a totally new constitution based on a teaching mandate only. Its implementation most assuredly would have been against the community's best interests, and would have struck at the very heart of the institute, since the issue of unity was at the proposition's very core.

This potential hazard must have been clearly grasped by Father Dydyk. He knew the congregation well, and therefore would have fully appreciated two crucial points involved in the situation: the canonical validity of Sister Ambrose's appointment, and the necessity for the Canadian community to remain within the originally established Institute of Sisters Servants if it hoped to retain its identity – for the proposal contained the seeds of future division in an unwieldy hodgepodge of independent diocesan branches of Sisters Servants in various parts of the country. But whatever the reasons which motivated him, Father Dydyk seems to have been persuaded that, in this case, no action was the best action. In short, no election was held, nor do any of the existing annals make the slightest reference to the bishops' directives, a fact which suggests that few sisters, if any, had ever known of them. For the time being, therefore, a rather ticklish situation seemed to have been brought under control. Not by any means was it a dead issue, however; and it might well be heightened again should fervent advocates of separatism appear.

In sum, by the time Metropolitan Sheptytsky visited them in 1910, the sisters, having weathered many a storm that had threatened their stability, had emerged with a firmer grasp of their destiny. Such intangible growth, however, is hardly ever visible to a casual visitor. And so, even though in their new school which he joyfully dedicated in Edmonton on October 30, 1910, the metropolitan saw striking evidence that the Sisters Servants were becoming productive and contributing members of their Church and nation, he nevertheless seems to have persisted in his fear that the magnitude of the missionary task among Ukrainians in Canada might prove to be too much for the struggling community. He called upon God to sustain its life and works: in the prayerful atmosphere of the novitiate chapel at Mundare, he formally consecrated the Congregation of Sisters Servants in Canada to the Sacred Heart of Christ. This spiritual giant acknowledged simply that by this act he had implored the Sacred Heart to bless the institute with many good vocations so that it would never be confronted with a crippling shortage of dedicated hearts and willing hands. For he was convinced that the Sisters Servants would have to labour and sacrifice much to keep their fellow countrymen in the faith.[48]

This conviction stemmed from what the metropolitan had seen of Ukrainians in the course of his travels across the prairies. For one thing, despite their physical and material hardships, he had not found a people wallowing in a slough of despond; on the contrary, he had seen a people with a deep sense of purpose and a truly valiant spirit. He was convinced, therefore, that this pioneer drive, this striving for more and better, would see them through their trying times. But from the spiritual point of view it seemed to him that his people in Canada were 'like a transplanted tree, and consequently, sick and enfeebled.'[49] With only a few missionary priests and sisters to guide them, the metropolitan feared that spiritual disunity, much of which he believed resulted from the proselytizing efforts expended by numerous religious sects, would sever the vital union of branch and vine – Ukrainians in Canada from the Holy See. Consequently he believed that only a strong unifying force could keep them in the faith. And he concluded that this essential unifying element for them would be a bishop of their own language and rite. 'Even if all the missionaries of the Ruthenian rite in Canada were people out of the ordinary,' he wrote upon his return to Lviv, 'it would be extremely difficult for their work to find a centre of action and a moral unity by itself and without a Ukrainian bishop, if only because of the different dioceses and individual differences.'

He, perhaps better than anyone else, understood how magnanimous the Latin-rite bishops had been in their paternal concern and kindness toward his people. But, as he explained to the Canadian episcopate: 'It is one of the successes of the schismatics and others – the most painful of our cause – that they have managed to characterize as enemies of the Ukrainian nation the chief representatives of Catholicism and the Catholic hierarchy. It is painful to have to admit it, but the fact is there. Founded on the old prejudice of these people against the clergy and the episcopate of a rite which is not theirs, and of a nation which seemed hostile to them (and often was so), the schismatics have managed to make this idea one of the principal points of Ukrainian public opinion and patriotism in Canada. And it has become almost a mentality, a fixed idea, one might say.' The metropolitan, furthermore, was certain that there was now no way of replacing 'by anything else the authority of a Ukrainian bishop'; and he explained his position thus: 'The Christian of the West, inclined by nature and by tradition to individualism, is personally attached to the Apostolic See. The attachment to his bishop is a part of his faith in the Holy See. The Oriental, no less attached to the constitution of the Church, is so in another way: it is his priest and his bishop whom he considers in the first place, and it is in their attachment to the Apostolic See that he is also attached to it. Clearly this was the catholicity of the Christians of the ninth century: it was by their bishop that they were attached to the Church, not by the person of the Pope. In the West these ideas have been modified in the course of centuries by the whole tendency of Western civilization. In the East the mentality has remained what it was centuries ago.' On behalf of his people, therefore, Metropolitan Sheptytsky entreated the Canadian episcopate: 'May God, in whose hands are the hearts of kings, and no less of bishops also, inspire Your Lordships to find the best means of saving these souls for whom Christ died, and who are in such imminent danger of being separated from the Church and of being lost for all generations.'[50]

His plea was heard. In fact, the sense of urgency which characterized it seems to have contributed in no small measure to the speed with which the Holy See, ever solicitous for her children of all rites, responded to this magnificent appeal. On July 15, 1912, Pope Pius x elevated to the dignity of the episcopacy Rev. Nicetas Budka, prefect of the Ukrainian Theological Seminary in Lviv, delegating to him jurisdiction of the newly created Ukrainian Catholic ordinariate of Canada, with its see in Winnipeg. Typical of the sentiments expressed in most Catholic publications in Ukraine at the news of this nomination is an article printed in the periodical *Dushpastyr* (*Pastor of Souls*): 'Our Catholic brethren in far-off Canada, having been forced to leave all that was dear to them in their homeland in order to seek a better life for themselves and for their children, rejoice at the news of this appointment. Yet they have reason for still greater jubilation, for their new bishop is truly a man of God; one who consecrated his life to help the needy and who now desires only that all our Ukrainian people in Canada be faithful children of God and of the Holy Catholic Church.'[51]

Undoubtedly, it was a challenging mandate which the new bishop received, since his was a diocese – numbering well over seventy-five thousand Ukrainian Catholics – that stretched from the Atlantic to the Pacific, and from the United States border to the Arctic, in a country he had never seen. None the less, he had some understanding of the problems faced by his fellow countrymen in North America since, prior to his appointment, he had served as the diocesan director of emigration. Unfalteringly, therefore, Bishop Budka welcomed the unexpected summons to serve the Church in Canada, and soon after his consecration, which took place in St George's Cathedral, Lviv, on October 13, 1912, he departed for Winnipeg, arriving there on December 19.[52]

The joy of the Ukrainian community was real, for to his people the bishop was the long-awaited shepherd of a flock which desperately needed him. His presence among them evoked a general surge of optimism. To quote the annals: 'Priests, laity, and our congregation have placed great faith in our bishop, believing that as a father he will be attuned to the needs

and interests of our people, and will thereby bolster the spiritual consciousness of us all.'[53]

At this historic juncture of a newly created ecclesiastical structure for
their Church in Canada, ten years had elapsed since the Sisters Servants
had begun their mission in this country. On the face of things, the decade
seemed to have produced few demonstrable results; for while it was true
that in the two years since Metropolitan Sheptytsky had visited them their
membership had more than doubled, and they had opened one other
school in Sifton, Manitoba, their growth had not been marked either by
tremendous brick-and-mortar expansion or by any exceptional acts. But
graced as these pioneer sisters were with great faith, imagination, and zeal,
their spiritual life and apostolic works were becoming more and more an
expression of true and lasting benefits; consequently, their influence was
being felt in home and school and parish. Ironically, however, each small
step taken in response to the Church's mandate to bring the compelling
message of the scriptures to their people through a life of prayer and service, seemed to them to underscore the distance still to be travelled toward
achieving this goal. For even though it was already evident that their institute was one of surprising vitality, its accomplishments up to now would
mean little if they were not prologue to more important visions of the
spiritual and human needs of their people in all parts of Canada. Hence,
motivated by a renewed sense of mission, and under the guidance of a
dedicated bishop, the Sisters Servants entered in spirited fashion the unfolding of still another phase of apostolic endeavour.

CHAPTER 5

A time to build...

The manner in which the Sisters Servants could respond to the all-pervasive pressure being felt among them for some positive action to prevent a ripple of disunity from swelling into a tidal wave of schism, was set out in clear relief by the indefatigable Redemptorist missionary, Rev. A. Delaere. This priest of Belgian origin, who had unceasingly and conscientiously toiled among Ukrainians since 1899, and who had adopted their rite in 1906 to serve them more directly, was anything but complacent as he witnessed at first hand the spiritual handicaps of the Ukrainian community on the prairies.[1]

With startling clarity he exposed these facts of life in his *Memorandum* published in 1909, and explicitly recommended to the Church the means by which it could effectively assault the myriad problems besetting the Ukrainian community: 'To inculcate or preserve Catholic life among this multitude of people who are being harassed by the novel ideas they find in Canada,' he wrote, 'it is not sufficient to baptise their children, to hear their confessions once a year, or sometimes only once in two or three years, to remain only a few hours in their midst and then desert them again for several months and leave them under the care of their guardian angels, or in the hands of schismatics or heretics. I repeat again, we need a thorough organization: we need schools and other institutions thoroughly Catholic. We also need nuns to give a Catholic education to children and to undertake among these Ruthenians other works that are just as urgently required among them as among other Catholics in this country.'[2]

To the secularistic mind, Father Delaere's emphatic call for greater Catholic educational opportunity for Ukrainian children may seem relatively unimportant, or perhaps even somewhat ridiculous; but to the pioneer Sisters Servants, who believed that Christian education was especially designed to make a child conscious of the sacred as well as the profane, and hence good as well as clever, it was an inescapable challenge. This being the case, they felt that they could do nothing less than channel their personal and communal talents, energies, and resources into a broader educational involvement. This is why, during Bishop N. Budka's fifteen-year tenure in Canada, from 1912 to 1927, the congregation was characterized by its exploitation of any opportunity that presented itself for the instruction and care of children. At the same time, more by accident than by design, in their main thrust to give meaning to the timeless virtues of faith, hope, and charity through a teaching mission, the sisters unconsciously continued to weave subtle changes into the warp and woof of their community life.

Almost immediately after the establishment of the ecclesiastical see in Winnipeg in 1912, the sisters were confronted with some harsh realities. For one thing, they could expand their teaching scope only if there were more schools for Ukrainian children. But these would no longer be provided directly by the Latin-rite bishops as had been the schools in Edmonton and Winnipeg, since all financial assistance provided by the episcopal fund for Ukrainian Catholic works in the west was now distributed by Bishop Budka who, from the outset of his term in office, found it well-nigh impossible to meet even the most crying requirements of his vast territory, regardless of how thinly he spread every available cent. What is more, Ukrainians were still generally an impoverished segment of the Canadian population, whose resources could scarcely go beyond churches, even if other buildings might benefit the people. At the same time, it seemed highly improbable that a women's congregation numbering only thirty-two members could assume the responsibility of providing the Ukrainian community with those projects which Father Delaere had considered as indispensable.[3] Hence, in 1912, it was one thing for the sisters to recognize the need for an institution, but quite another to supply it.

When, therefore, early in 1913 Rev. N. Kryzanowsky, OSBM, superior of the mission at Mundare, concluded that a convent–boarding school–orphanage would have to be constructed in order to alleviate the congested classes still being conducted in the chapel nave, and to house the growing numbers of orphans being brought to the mission, the economic implications of the proposal weighed heavily upon the sisters. Not that there was any doubt in their minds about the prevailing need for such a building. For years they had endured the hopeless overcrowding of the chapel classroom, and for years they had borne the miserable cold of the interminable Alberta winters, especially when the old box stove was unable to generate enough heat for the log structure, buffeted by blustering north winds in sub-freezing temperatures. But having had to assume the complete maintenance of St Nicholas School in Winnipeg in 1907,[4] an operation that was constantly consuming their meagre earnings, they could be pardoned for exhibiting a singular lack of enthusiasm at the proposition of having to adopt still another liability.

They were certain, it is true, that if the enterprise were undertaken they could count upon the unstinting assistance of Father Kryzanowsky, a man who displayed those qualities most highly regarded in any missionary: diligence, caution, an open mind, an absence of distracting personal flair, and above all orderliness and efficiency. Despite this assurance, however, they were neither so naïve as to believe that anyone but they would be called upon to accept full responsibility for financing the school nor so foolish as to think that they could extract the required sum from their already threadbare community bag by any means but their own unflagging effort and hard work.

It was at moments such as this that one of their remarkable traits – a characteristic that emerges from the pages of their chronicles time and again – enabled them to whittle down a problem to the point where a formidable obstacle no longer seemed insurmountable: this was their ability to pry a measure of optimism from a generally dismal situation. And nowhere does this quality show up so definitely as when they had to adopt the proposal for a new school at Mundare. For in full knowledge of the economic pit into which their institute might be plunged, and without bewailing the fact that they were being driven by circumstances to follow courses which might prove disastrous, the members elected to pursue at once a means for financing the structure. And they chose the only way left open, fruitless as it appeared: begging.

Curiously though, this move was to be a blessing in disguise for both the Sisters Servants and the Ukrainian community. The simple fact is that from the moment they gamely embarked on their assignment until they returned home utterly spent, the sisters participated in a mission that transformed a simple fund-raising pursuit into a rewarding apostolic venture.

The basis for this result was their success in identifying closely with the people whom they had served from the commencement of their work in Canada. Through the years, a real interest in them had given birth to a genuine appreciation of their countrymen's hardships, of their noble aspirations for themselves and for their children; and it was this insight that had enabled the sisters to view even their failings with compassion and humanity, and consequently to serve them in this spirit. This, of course, afforded a love for, and an acceptance of, the Sisters Servants by Ukrainians in the west, a fact which now made it possible for the congregation to turn to them for aid.

The sisters readily perceived that their plan for a *kvesta* (gathering of alms) would serve a dual purpose; first, it would meet construction costs, and, second, it would provide them with a rare chance of meeting with hundreds of Ukrainian families, especially with those dwelling in remote farmhouses in the far-flung settlements of northern Alberta. For some time it had been evident to the sisters that what their people needed from missionaries in order to reinvigorate their Christian life during these hard pioneer days was not a complicated theology but rather the testimony of lives dedicated to God; lives filled not with a succession of extraordinary things but just with a direct, loving attention to their needs. This kind of witness and charity the sisters could give in lavish abundance.

Their quest during the winter, spring, and summer months of 1913 took them from heavily populated centres, which they ordinarily reached by train, to remote villages and hamlets, where they moved from farm to farm in the horse-drawn vehicle of some generous Ukrainian farmer. More often than not they rode along perched atop sacks of sugar or flour or bales of hay, and while this might have been an interesting vantage point for any two sisters if the weather were splendid and they were not travelling far, it held much to be desired when they covered mile after mile in the face of icy winter winds, in chilly spring rains, or beneath a searing summer sun.

In any given district, word of their presence as well as the reason for it usually preceded the sisters via the local grapevine, and thus eliminated the need for time-consuming explanations in each household. Invariably, the religious found themselves listening, comforting, encouraging, and often counselling. In fact, men, women, and children responded to their genuine piety and zeal so spontaneously that the sisters' evening, in whichever home they were scheduled to be lodged overnight, resembled a religious revival on a family level: formal catechetical instruction was interlaced with the stories of a saint or two, a few hymns, and common prayer. On the Sabbath or on other festive days, in the absence of a priest, it seemed that a revival of district proportions was being held when country folk from miles around gathered in a local farmhouse – if there were no parish church in the area – to worship with the sisters. And nothing gave the two religious involved more pleasure; for them, time was not money but a gift of God, which was not to be wasted. So they gladly gave it to these good people, and thus unconsciously were making a spiritual recompense for the material assistance they were receiving. For while, predictably enough, they did encounter deeply rooted prejudice, and occasionally even became convenient targets for attacks by those who despised the Church, more frequently the sisters were the recipients of contributions – beginning at one penny and averaging fifteen cents – which were made in a spirit of unaffected charity. Poorer farmers, unable to offer any monetary help, donated some vegetables, or a chicken or a few eggs to help feed children who were needier than their own.[5]

In July 1913, while many sisters were still soliciting far from the centres of population in lonely country areas, the construction of the proposed school commenced. Bishop Budka seems to have questioned the wisdom of erecting the building at the mission, which had found itself lying three miles south and east of the town of Mundare after the Canadian Northern Railway had come through in 1905. 'The school is being erected on the farm,' explained Sister Ambrose, 'because, on the basis of the advice we have received from the Reverend Fathers [Basilians] and our own observations, we have concluded that, from the economic point of view, it will be easier to support an orphanage and school in the country.'[6]

The bishop, himself an educator, and a man who possessed the rare virtues of candour and informality, soon arrived at Mundare, not to participate in any impressive ground-breaking ceremony but instead to devote his entire 'vacation' to digging the school's foundation. On August 8 he blessed the cornerstone, satisfied that construction was proceeding at a normal pace.

Unfortunately, the work soon foundered on a simple shortcoming – insufficient funds. Sister Ambrose, under growing pressure from mounting costs, found herself grappling with piles of unpaid bills. It was something of a jolt, she acknowledged to the bishop, to discover 'that funds previously collected have run out, and that not only is there no end in sight to our expenses, but present debts are proliferating so fast that our financial precariousness rather frightens me.'[7] Hard pressed and understandably distressed, Sister Ambrose, for one, had no intention of scuttling that saving *kvesta*; thus, once again, she requested permission to continue soliciting funds.

Admittedly, Bishop Budka's interest together with Father Kryzanowsky's aid proved to be great morale boosters as well as economic mainstays for the sisters. The eventual completion of St Joseph's School, however, they attributed primarily to the grass-roots support of the Ukrainians of northern Alberta; without it the sisters might have reaped a disastrous harvest of debts. Instead, by the middle of 1914 the mission possessed a school which contained living quarters and three fine classrooms, and had an enrolment of 126 children, eight-six of whom – mostly orphans – were in residence.[8]

Perhaps because it was a home for many homeless children, Bishop Budka had a special fondness for St Joseph's. This partiality revealed itself chiefly through his ceaseless endeavours to assist the sisters in improving the lot of their young charges. As might be expected, therefore, prevalent among his papers are cheery letters from Sister Ambrose thanking him for such commonplace but indispensable articles as 'a box full of children's coats';[9] and other notes from the children themselves, expressing their delight at having received his marvellous package filled with 'all kinds of toys.'[10] It warmed the Sisters Servants to know that their bishop, a modest and prayerful man, who greatly inspired them by his enlightening views and his priestly encouragement, had their interest so much at heart that 'although personally poor, his boundless charity, particularly toward children, often blinded him to his own needs.'[11] In the fullest sense, during this early period, Bishop Budka contributed much to the happiness of the sisters and children of St Joseph's, a school which, until 1926, was one of the few boarding academies available to Ukrainian children in this rural area of Alberta.[12]

In the autumn of that year, 1914, the sisters together with their fellow Ukrainians, especially those who had emigrated from the Austrian-controlled province of Galicia, experienced a sense of apprehension and concern when, for the first time in its history, Canada found itself fully involved in a war abroad, with Austria as one of the enemy. Despite the tensions that had been building up in Europe, Canadians had not given deep and serious consideration to the possibility of war. Europe had seemed a long way off, and the country had been preoccupied with its internal affairs. But almost immediately after its entrance into the fray, immigration from Austria ceased, and the first phase of Ukrainian settlement in Canada was abruptly ended. For nearly a decade only a few people would be permitted to enter the country; hence, for the time being at least, wives, children, and other relatives of Ukrainian immigrants could not be reunited with them here. When, on top of this, lines of communication with much of eastern Europe were also cut, those in the new world were indeed separated from those in the old.

Ukrainians who had been in Canada for some years were at this time gradually adapting to life in their communities. None the less, many still faced the grave problems of adjustment. They were discovering that they were alien in fact as well as in law, for they had brought to Canada a cultural heritage – language, ideals and traditions, concept of government, standard of living – that another society had worked out. In short, they had come with different mores and with a different life experience; consequently, the problem they faced in their new society was essentially one of cultural adjustment.[13]

And their children, many of whom had already been born in Canada, found themselves living on the fringes of two cultures. They were in the trying situation where it was possible for the cultural heritage of their parents to be largely lost for them at a time when they had not fully acquired Canadian culture, nor had been accepted on equal terms by Canadians. If, therefore, they were not to be oppressed by feelings of inferiority which, to some degree, could be extensions of the parents' own feelings as immigrants in a country so drastically different from their native land; and if the designation of 'foreigner' were to be eliminated to permit them to gain acceptance in every sector of Canadian life; they required training by people who understood the handicaps under which they were growing up.[14]

Both Bishop Budka and the Sisters Servants believed that it was imperative to give this second generation a knowledge of, and pride in, their inheritance, an understanding of the problems and achievements of their parents, and a recognition of the value of their cultural contributions, so as to bridge the gap between the two generations, prevent a reaction against their standards, interests, and attitudes, and thus give them a feeling of belonging in the Ukrainian community within the framework of Canadian society. Furthermore, they were convinced that these ends could best be achieved through education, preferably in schools such as those already established by the sisters in the provinces of Manitoba and Alberta. These facts strengthened Bishop Budka's resolve to broaden the sisters' educational influence by introducing them to a teaching mission within yet another province – Saskatchewan.

One of the most heavily populated Ukrainian areas in that province was the Yorkton district. Situated in east central Saskatchewan, about 278 miles west of Winnipeg, on the main line of the Great Northern Railway, Yorkton was strategically located at the hub of a rich agricultural area. As early as 1881 'York City' (as it was then called) became the nucleus of a thriving settlement made up of farmers mostly from York and adjoining counties in Ontario, and from England, Scotland, and Ireland. Its unique geographical advantages on what is known as the 'parkland' of the province were enticingly set forth for potential settlers by the Yorkton Board of Trade's brochure of 1910: 'It is not bare prairie,' it noted, 'but resembles more, as it is seen today, some of the best portions of the East coast of Scotland without the sea coast and ranges of mountains in the distance. Newcomers often remark that they expected to see nothing but plains and find instead streams, valleys, and beautiful groves as if nature had laid it out as a park, and great stretches of open land awaiting the plow.'[15] And it was precisely to put their hand to the plough on these 'great stretches of open land' that thousands of Ukrainians settled here. Before long the district was dotted with predominantly Ukrainian colonies such as Saltcoats, Canora, Preeceville, Kamsack, Norquay, Ituna, West Bend, and Calder.[16]

In response to a request by the French Oblate missionaries, who had long worked in the area, a group of Belgian Redemptorist religious established a mission centre in Yorkton on January 13, 1904. Because their membership included priests of both Latin and Eastern rites, they were able to serve various nationalities: Ukrainians, Poles, Hungarians, Germans, English, and French. In 1910, when they discovered that over 50 per cent of their 10,142 parishioners were Ukrainian, they established a religious centre in Yorkton for them. On September 19, 1913, the construction of a monastery was begun in the northwest section of the town; and shortly thereafter, on Christmas Eve of the same year, Fathers A. Delaere, N. M. Decamps, H. Boels, and C. Techuer, all of whom had adopted the Ukrainian rite, moved to the mission, which they dedicated to Our Lady of Perpetual Help – so beloved by the Ukrainian nation. By the following autumn, on August 23, 1914, Bishop Budka blessed St Mary's, the new mission church.[17]

Deeply concerned about the education of Ukrainian children, the superior, Father Delaere, began to harbour the remarkably bold idea that a school should be a part of the mission immediately; thus in 1914, when Bishop Budka visited Yorkton, he discussed with the prelate the need to procure a piece of land, situated on the northwest side of the church, which was particularly suited as a site for an educational institution. Since appropriate instruction for, and the guidance of, young Ukrainians had been uppermost in the minds of both men for some time, it is scarcely surprising that they readily agreed on two key points: that the moment was opportune to establish a school in the town to serve Ukrainians of the entire district, and that the Congregation of Sisters Servants of Mary Immaculate was the logical religious institute to found it.[18]

Acting upon Father Delaere's advice, Bishop Budka purchased two acres of the property selected by the Redemptorist and, shortly thereafter, was pleased to add to it two adjacent lots which were donated by a prominent citizen, Mr William Dunlop, who thus became the first non-Ukrainian benefactor of the Sisters Servants in Yorkton.[19] Confident that an elementary school of their own 'would raise the spirits and enhance the confidence of Ukrainian Catholics not only in Saskatchewan but also throughout Canada,'[20] the bishop asked Sister Ambrose to undertake the responsibility of building, maintaining, and staffing such an institution in

Yorkton.[21] This request, coming so soon after the onerous endeavour of the institute to construct St Joseph's School in Mundare, was to be a real test of the maturity and magnanimity of the young congregation.

It is unlikely that the sisters had any illusions that the proposal would be anything but easy to implement; but Sister Ambrose's immediate acceptance of the proposal seems to indicate that no inertia was sapping their vitality. In any event, the lack of delay enabled the *Yorkton Enterprise* to inform its readers on July 29, 1915, that 'Father Delaere, Superior of the Ruthenian Catholic Mission at Yorkton, announced this week that this Order [Congregation of Sisters Servants of Mary Immaculate] purposes erecting a school and orphanage for girls at Yorkton, similar to St. Mary's Academy in Winnipeg and the Sacred Heart Academy at Regina. Providing tax exemptions and sewer and water extensions to the property on Ontario Street are granted by the Council,' the article continued, 'work will be commenced this year ... Four teachers will be employed and the academy will be made a worthy acquisition to the educational institutions of the town.'[22]

To raise $25,000, the estimated cost of the building, the sisters knew that another *kvesta* was in the offing. And it commenced almost four months later, on November 18, 1915, when Sister Nicholas Petrushkewich from Winnipeg and Sister Macrina Pelagia Faryna from Mundare arrived in Yorkton. The gloomy basement of the parish church became their temporary convent. Luckily, because they immediately embarked on their quest for funds, they lived in it for just a few days at a time – whenever they returned to the town for a short rest from their travels throughout the district. In January Sister Nicholas, writing to Bishop Budka, briefly described their slow progress: 'The drive to solicit funds is going well; most people are receiving us very kindly. Yesterday we returned to Yorkton after travelling from colony to colony for five weeks. During the last two we collected very little because, owing to the extreme cold and heavy snows, the horses could move only with great effort; hence it was impossible to visit more than six homes a day. Even then, the poor animals were totally exhausted. To date, we have journeyed as far as Viscount,[23] and even though in many settlements we have received almost nothing, we are determined to pursue this vital assignment.'[24]

In May 1916 the sisters moved out of the church basement into a small rented house located at the intersection of today's Ontario Avenue and Darlington Street. It was a more pleasant dwelling, and from here the two religious carried on an apostolate of catechetics and home nursing care, continued to solicit funds, and organized a bazaar, to be held during the annual pilgrimage to the shrine of Our Lady of Perpetual Help at St Mary's Church on July 2 – one day before the scheduled blessing of the school's cornerstone.[25]

When the sisters eventually totalled the results of all their fund-raising work, they found that they had succeeded in raising the woefully inadequate sum of $2,000. By every estimate it was clear that if they relied exclusively upon almsgiving it would take years to erect a school. Consequently, in an effort to bypass a $23,000 roadblock, Bishop Budka recommended that the Sisters Servants request a $15,000 loan from the Sulpician Order of Montreal, a religious community well known for its support of Catholic institutions.[26]

No sooner had the bishop indicated this way out of their financial dilemma than he journeyed to Montreal to endorse the request personally and to prepare the necessary documents on behalf of the sisters. 'The matter regarding the loan has, thank God, proceeded better than anyone had envisaged,' he informed his vicar general, Rev. A. Redkevich, on May 18. And indeed his efforts must have met with instant success for within a week Sister Ambrose was instructed by the ordinary to have the building plans drawn up without delay. In addition, she was notified that Rev. N. M. Decamps, CSSR, the new mission superior in Yorkton, had been appointed by the bishop as procurator for the Sisters Servants, with authorization to make payments in their behalf during each phase of the school's construction.[27]

Events moved quickly, since these developments had lent fresh impetus to the matter at hand. In July 1916 the *Yorkton Press* carried the following announcement: 'Plans have been prepared and tenders are being called for a Sacred Heart Convent for the Rev. Ruthenian Catholic Sisters to be erected in the Cathedral grounds. The building is of ornate design and will be of brick veneer. It will be three storeys high with mansard roof. The building will be 45 ft. × 60 ft. and fully modern throughout. Mr. A. J. Papineau of St. Boniface, Man., is the architect in charge of the work.'[28]

The leadership of Bishop Budka and the Redemptorist Fathers in this matter, together with their optimism regarding the project's ultimate success, temporarily fired the sisters' hope and imbued them with a sense of certainty amid much of the uncertainty arising from their stunning communal failure to raise more than 5 per cent of the building's estimated cost. But it was not long before they recognized that even their loan was a somewhat piecemeal approach, for, at best, it only partially met their problem of financing the school. By September Father Decamps was urging the bishop to provide immediate assistance in the amount of $5,000, since the sisters' cash had already been spent. The situation placed considerable strain on the institute, and there seemed to be only one way to lessen it – by another *kvesta*.[29]

Despite these drawbacks, the sisters celebrated Christmas of 1916 in the new building which, even though not entirely finished, they had occupied on December 11. Then, just before the year ended, on December 30, Sister Athanasia Melnyk, the first teacher at Sacred Heart Institute, welcomed the first resident pupils who, surprisingly enough, were three boys: John Snidanko, Peter Snidanko, and Michael Kalinsky. And by the time classes commenced on January 11, 1917, the school had an enrolment of twenty-five pupils, seventeen of whom were in residence. By the end of June registration had jumped to forty-six children.

But by even the rosiest estimates the elimination of the economic pressure being experienced by the sisters in Yorkton seemed to be years away. Nevertheless, in reply to a telegram of good wishes received from Bishop Budka on the opening day, Sister Ambrose wired the following hopeful message: 'Thanks for congratulations. The times are hard indeed but we know the good hearts of our people who help us so much here around Yorkton.'[30]

The solemn dedication of Sacred Heart Institute took place during the annual pilgrimage on June 30, 1917; the entire event was graphically described by the *Yorkton Enterprise*: 'The third annual patron feast of the church of the Blessed Virgin of Perpetual Help was held on Saturday, Sunday and Monday last and was attended by 2,500 or 3,000 members of the parish. Special services were conducted daily, in addition to the regular services, by Bishop Budka. Over 1,000 confessions and communions were received and dispensed during the festival. People came from all parts of the parish which includes a radius of 50 miles, and even from Kamsack, Mitchellview, Shoal Lake, and Rossburn. Every train brought scores of worshippers, and on Saturday a special train arrived from Jasmin, which was filled to capacity.'[31] The *Enterprise* reporter duly added that 'a feature of the occasion was the benediction of the Sacred Heart Institute, a girls' school and orphanage adjoining the church. The building was completed last winter and at a special service on Saturday afternoon Bishop Budka officially opened the institution and blessed it. During the term which has just closed, upwards of fifty pupils were enrolled in the Institute, which has a staff of eight sisters and a Mother Superior ministering to their temporal and spiritual welfare.'[32]

In the following scholastic year, 1917–18, there were fifty-five pupils, twenty-two of whom were orphans. And among the stalwart pioneer sisters who cared for their 'temporal and spiritual welfare' during the first period of the institute's existence, and who also encompassed in their apostolic charity many sick and indigent residents of the town, were Sister Alexandra Mary Doiran, Sister Euletheria Anastasia Furtak, Sister Josaphata Tymochko, Sister Theresa Natalie Melnyk, Sister Eusebia Anne Matkowsky, Sister Taida Letawsky, and Sister Ignatia Anne Butryn.

This third school the sisters had built at the request of their ordinary. In this endeavour they had been assisted by bishop, priests, and laity, and there was no discounting the fact that its future existence hinged upon their continued support. But in the final analysis it was the sisters who, from this time forth, were saddled with the obligation of avoiding a financial crunch by seeking the means by which to operate and maintain the school as well as to repay what, for them, was a staggering debt.

First and foremost, however, the sisters' interest was centred upon the increasing numbers of children being entrusted to their care by parents from the provinces of western and eastern Canada. Consequently, within the scope of their teaching and training programme they sought to take in the whole aggregate of human life – physical and spiritual, intellectual and moral, individual, domestic, and social – not with a view of reducing it in any way but in order to elevate, regulate, and perfect it in the light of the example and teaching of Christ.[33]

This philosophy of education was echoed by Bishop Budka in his letter of January 10, 1917, to Father Decamps: 'It remains for all of us to draw now upon the interest to be accrued by this institution. And this interest is the Christian guidance of our children, a sound training in Canadian citizenship, a thorough academic programme supplemented by the study of our Ukrainian language and music. These are benefits that cannot be translated into dollars and cents.'[34] The quiet joy of the prelate in this new educational acquisition for his people is reflected in the prayer with which he concluded his letter: 'Bless O Lord, this good beginning made for the glory of your name, and for the welfare of our neglected youth, our Ukrainian nation and our new homeland, Canada.'[35]

With such lofty ideals animating them, it is easy to understand why the sisters struggled against challenging odds to keep their schools open and to establish new ones. These enterprises in turn fostered a keener awareness on the part of superiors of the importance of their institutes' educational role, and hence of the need for qualified teaching personnel. In 1917, for example, Sister Ambrose emphasized the fact that 'of the forty-seven members in the institute, a few have already received accreditation, while others are still studying. In addition, a number of aspirants are enrolled in teacher training courses in the provinces of Manitoba and Alberta.'[36] And in Edmonton during this same year Sister Elizabeth Sophie Kassian and Sister Theresa Melnyk participated in one of the earliest Ukrainian teachers' conventions to be organized in Canada. Unquestionably, the institute was involved in a rather modest educational programme, but it was nevertheless one that seemed to be moving steadily toward an ever broader participation – even during the war years, when the congregation was still wanting in human and material resources.

No sooner was the 1914–18 war over than Canadians were called upon to fight another foe – Spanish influenza – which struck the country with epidemic intensity. Originating in Spain, the highly infectious disease had spread quickly to the troops in France; in August it had reached Quebec, and then Montreal and Toronto. Within three months it swept across the Dominion, affecting one person in every six, and causing thirty thousand deaths – half as many fatalities as had been sustained in the four-year conflict.[37]

Throughout this paralyzing period of acute emergency when the impact of the epidemic was being felt in myriad ways, large and small, from Halifax to Vancouver, many individuals, charitable organizations, and religious institutions underscored their deep concern for the suffering by volunteering their assistance. And among them were the Sisters Servants. The initial impulse to help, and the subsequent performance of each of the five existing communities of Sisters Servants in Canada in terms of self-sacrifice and expendability in a moment of national crisis, are outlined in the local chronicles.

'In our city,' recounted the Winnipeg annalist, 'countless numbers of people have been stricken, and many die each day. In an effort to contain the epidemic, churches and schools have been closed; even then, however, our hospitals are overcrowded and the orphanages crammed with sick children. Doctors and clergymen face the colossal task of trying to minister to all those who call for their medical and spiritual help. Needless to say, the vision of the suffering and dying has sent a shudder of dismay through our ranks; hence, almost to a woman, we have found some way of serving those who are ill. But we are very few in comparison with the stricken majority. Some of our sisters have become totally involved in home nursing care, others assist the Grey Nuns at St Boniface Hospital, while, for three weeks, Sister Nicholas Petrushkewich and Sister Theodosia Katherine Senchuk have worked at St Joseph's Orphanage where most of the children and many of the Grey Nuns are seriously ill.'[38]

In and around Sifton, Manitoba, a rural municipality situated sixteen miles northwest of Dauphin on the CNR where the institute had founded a mission in 1910, the sisters fought the disease with nourishment and medication and solace. The task was far from easy, since the scattered farms limited the number of patients to whom they could minister daily. On November 12, for example, the chronicler noted that Sister Josepha Bilan and Sister Josaphata Tymochko had just returned home rather downhearted because they had visited only four families that day, when so many others still awaited them. But in view of all they usually did in each house, it is surprising that they managed to help even this many people. For instance, in one of the homes they had entered the sisters had discovered that the mother had just recently died, the father was dying, and all five of the children were desperately ill. After dispensing whatever medicine they could from their insignificant supply, the sisters had bathed the children, dressed them in fresh clothes they had brought, had scrubbed down the house, and cooked enough broth to last the family until their return.[39] Through this service, which they felt was far from adequate, they often succeeded in replacing fear and despair with confidence and hope.

Disturbing as the situation in Sifton was, it was scarcely less so in Yorkton where the capacity of the local Queen Victoria Hospital and the strength of the dedicated women who staffed it were taxed to the utmost. On November 6, 1918, at the request of the hospital authorities, Sister Taida Letawsky and Sister Stephanie Katherine Kinach joined the nursing staff in caring for an ever-increasing number of influenza patients.[40]

Other sisters from Sacred Heart Institute, who felt well enough to venture out of the convent, nursed the victims and consoled the dying in the town and in neighbouring settlements. During November and December they journeyed in an open wagon from one farmhouse to another, where they came to know at first hand the anguish of the neglected sick. For in these rural areas they found that not only was medical aid almost non-existent but that, worse still, even the hope of help – physical or spiritual – had been virtually extinguished. At times, almost frozen themselves, they stumbled into an unheated farmhouse in which an entire family lay stricken. In other instances they encountered starkly tragic scenes in homes where a parent or child, already dead, had not been buried because those who were still alive were physically helpless to perform this last service for one of their own.

Often the sisters brought back to Yorkton the orphans who had been abandoned even by close relatives. Missionary priests and members of the local police force were also bringing in so many children that before long youngsters were sleeping on improvised beds in the school corridors. But even Sacred Heart did not escape unscathed, for the disease eventually struck with such vehement fury that fifty children and most of the teachers became critically ill. When at last the ordeal was over the sisters thankfully counted just one fatality, a girl of fourteen.[41]

In Edmonton 'people are living in great fear for their own lives as well as for those of their dear ones,' recorded the chronicler. 'Our school, together with most others, is closed, as are churches, theatres, halls, etc. Our harried municipal authorities have ordered everyone to wear a handkerchief mask over nostrils and mouth when venturing outdoors, for the very air seems to be polluted. All of our teaching sisters have focused their attention upon relieving the physical and spiritual distress of the sick, whose unfortunate plight weighs heavily upon us all. A few of our members are cooking and caring for the students at the Taras Shevchenko Institute.'[42] But the sisters managed to cope with the work in the students' residence for two months only by continuously substituting religious who were relatively well for those who, sooner or later, were infected by the disease. At the convent things weren't much easier. 'Seven sisters and some of our orphans were recently ill,' wrote the annalist on October 26, 'and there was only one sister healthy enough to care for them all. Continuous day and night duty was, however, too much even for her, and hence Sister Lubov Katherine Chawrona was summoned from Mundare to assist her.'[43]

Farther north, in Mundare, a handful of sisters was nursing sixty-four children and their fellow religious at the outset of the epidemic. But as deaths from the disease began to take an ominous upward inclination in the district, the sisters converted St Joseph's School into a temporary hospital to meet the exigencies of the situation. Whatever beds they could find at the mission were set up in two classrooms, which became the wards for women and children. Into the third schoolroom they carried bales of hay, shaped each pile of fodder into mattress-like forms and covered them with sheets. It wasn't long before each of these unique hospital beds was gratefully occupied by a suffering man. A Mr Shandro demonstrated a Christian concern for his neighbours by visiting home after home, picking up those men, women and children who were completely bereft of medical aid and transporting them to the mission in what was probably one of the few automobiles in the area. The sisters bent to their business, nursing the sick, preparing the dying, consoling the bereaved, and scrubbing the rest. Before long, due to the increasing numbers of patients, they remained on duty almost around the clock. Father Kryzanowsky, too, was in constant attendance, not only to minister to the patients' spiritual needs but also to their physical wants as an orderly in the men's ward.

To begin with, the sisters waged their determined campaign against death with such homely medicines and means as lemons, broth, hot milk, dry cuppings, and their own ingenuity. 'Luckily for us,' recalled Sister Lubov Chawrona, 'Dr J. F. Belanger of Vegreville accidentally stopped by one day, and seeing our work, began to visit our patients daily, bringing with himself the medicines we had previously lacked.'[44]

After several months of this nightmare, the disease spent itself early in 1919. And it was perhaps Dr Belanger who best summarized the service that the sisters had rendered during the epidemic: 'You sisters have successfully completed a nursing examination,' he told Sister Ambrose. 'Here in Mundare you have saved the lives of more than three hundred people. But what I find most remarkable is that not one man, woman or child nursed by you in this improvised hospital has died.'[45]

From the start it had been an emotionally draining experience for the sisters. And if, in the aftermath, as they disinfected and put their convents and schools in order, they attempted to assess the effects of their rather precipitous plunge into nursing, they must have been aware of, and grateful for, rewards in human salvage that had been so extraordinarily rich. Invariably, they saw this as their witness to the Church's involvement in the world – an involvement that had stemmed from nothing more than their adamant refusal even to consider the notion that as members of a small, unknown institute they were incapable of offering much assistance to their fellow men, and hence to their country in a time of national need.

But almost as soon as this crisis was over they found themselves confronting another; one before which they felt absolutely helpless. In December 1918 the canker of religious and national strife, which had been recognized as a potential danger to Church unity by Metropolitan Sheptytsky in 1910, and which, through the years, had been steadily gnawing away at the very heart of the Ukrainian Catholic Church in Canada, caused a painful rupture within that Church. Schism became a sad reality when, at a convention held in Saskatoon, Saskatchewan, 'a group of dissatisfied leaders broke away from the Church, and established a new national church called the Ukrainian Greek Othodox Church in Canada. Despite his pastoral prudence and love for his people, Bishop Nicetas [Budka] was unable to stem the tide of the movement.'[46]

Although this was a blow that was deeply felt by bishop, priests, sisters, and laity, neither the faith nor the desire of loyal Ukrainian Catholics to enhance the healthful development of their Church was significantly shaken. For his part Bishop Budka was strengthened in his conviction that a fruitful religious future was possible only if the children of the immigrants were informed Ukrainians, intelligent Canadian citizens, and practising Christians.

In 1919, therefore, he persuaded the Catholic Extension Society of Canada to construct a school for Ukrainian boys in Yorkton, to complement Sacred Heart Institute which had been built to educate girls. In a magnanimous gesture the society, with Right Rev. T. O'Donnell as its president, granted $100,000 toward the erection of St Joseph's College. In a similar vein, the English-speaking Brothers of the Christian Schools, heeding the bishop's plea for a competent college staff, graciously accepted the direction of the new educational establishment, for at this time there existed no male Ukrainian religious order of teachers in the country. Thus, on May 6, 1919, Brother Ansbert M. Sheedy, Brother Stanislaus J. O'Reilly, and Brother James J. Valiquette arrived in Yorkton, ready to begin their apostolate as soon as the college was completed.

The educational aim of the new institution was clearly outlined by Bishop Budka in his address on the occasion of the laying of the cornerstone on September 7, 1919. The school, he stated, had been erected not only to pass on to children the wealth of the Ukrainian language and culture but also to educate the brain and the heart, with the view of making the pupils good Canadian citizens, good people, and leaders of high ideals in Christianity.'[47]

As in the case of all pioneer work, the brothers faced countless difficulties and obstacles, most of which arose from the suspicion entertained by some Ukrainian Catholics toward them. These people, 'blinded by prejudice and wrong information, considered St Joseph's nothing short of a Latinizing institution. The brothers tried to allay this growth of suspicion by visiting the parishes and by inviting the people to visit the college and observe the work done.'[48] Perhaps many people might have refrained from casting aspersions if they had but witnessed the devotion of these truly *Christian* brothers for their Ukrainian students. Theirs was a zeal that prompted even acts of heroic virtue, such as that of Brother Stanislaus, who offered his life to God 'as a holocaust for the success of our brothers' Ukrainian work in Canada.'[49]

Before long, even though they had been spared a mortgage, the brothers found themselves in financial straits as confining as those of their neighbours, the Sisters Servants at Sacred Heart Institute. In fact, 'on a number of occasions during the first eight years, the superiors of the

Brothers of the Christian Schools and the executive of the Church Extension intended to close the college, as it was going deeper and deeper into debt every year.'[50] From this common plight emerged a common sympathy, together with a real understanding and cooperation, between the staffs of St Joseph's and Sacred Heart. The Christian Brothers, with their richer and broader experience in educational affairs, often helped the sisters through sound advice, warm encouragement, and willingness to promote their work among girls. Entries such as the following punctuate the sisters' local chronicle: 'This year the number of resident pupils has increased considerably; this is due largely to the efforts of the Christian Brothers who, while touring the provinces of Saskatchewan and Manitoba in order to acquaint Ukrainians with St Joseph's College and to persuade boys to attend their school, have also encouraged girls to register at our institute.'[51]

During this period, when the Christian Brothers were organizing their work at St Joseph's College, the sisters at Sacred Heart were facing one of the more disturbing questions that had arisen in the aftermath of the recent influenza epidemic: where to care for the scores of orphans of preschool age who had literally been left on their doorstep. Needless to say their building contained scarcely any provisions or accommodations suitable for infants. Sister Ambrose concluded that this issue, which posed one of the most pressing problems of the day for the sisters, must be resolved immediately if the overcrowding in the Yorkton school were to be relieved, and if the youngest children there were to receive adequate care. But how? The institute was in no financial position to open an orphanage anywhere.

A way out of the impasse presented itself when Ukrainians in and around the village of Ituna – lying approximately fifty miles southwest of Yorkton – promised to provide a suitable building for a school if they could be assured that the Sisters Servants would direct it. Actually, this proposal was not a new one; it had been renewed almost yearly since 1916 when the sisters had first visited the district during their *kvesta* for Sacred Heart Institute. In fact, at that time, perhaps under good-willed pressure by the people there, Sister Ambrose had sought Bishop Budka's advice about whether to 'undertake the construction of a building in Yorkton or to remodel a hotel, which is on sale at Ituna, into a school. The chief disadvantage,' she observed, 'is that the place is without a church or resident priest.'[52] As it turned out, the school was built in Yorkton, as originally planned. Now, four years and a houseful of orphans later, with a Redemptorist monastery and a parish church already established in Ituna, and with its citizens still eager to provide for a school and orphanage, the sisters considered that the time was right to begin their sixth foundation.

A plan, drawn up by a group of interested parishioners, proposed that a committee be established to administer a fund, to be created by pooling interest-free loans of up to $500 provided by local farmers for the purpose of buying an appropriate building for the orphanage. The sisters were to repay the money whenever circumstances permitted them to do so. The proposal struck the sisters as being practical, realistic, and certain to eliminate undue economic strain at this latest mission.

Shortly thereafter, a newly established committee purchased a shabby village store that had sat forlornly at the edge of the village for a good many years and that now required a multitude of repairs in addition to a complete interior face-lifting. The group also made a down-payment on a piece of land consisting of two farms and forty acres, and costing $7,000. The renovation of the store was to be paid for by money drawn from the orphanage fund, while payments for the farm would be met by individuals who had pledged loans for this purpose. It almost seemed too smooth to be true.

Against that background, noted the annalist, 'Sister Ambrose, placing her faith and hope in God and the kindness of our people, sent the sisters to Ituna. They arrived there on July 18, 1920, almost as paupers, for all they possessed were the few articles donated by our other five communities which, because of their own indigence, were able to offer only some bedding and a few things for the chapel.'[53] As might have been expected, the sisters were relieved that *this time* things would be different; *this time* they would be free of a pressing mortgage and high interest rates.

But they weren't. No sooner were Sister Alexia Chykalo and Sister Theodosia Senchuk settled in their new home, which they named St Ann's Convent, than a nervous sense of here-we-go-again stole over them when they found themselves beseiged by demands for the repayment of loans by those friends who had so recently made them. This unexpected turn of events resulted from a classic case of mismanagement, perhaps because the good people of Ituna had tried to do too much too fast. Evidently, by not taking into consideration the skyrocketing construction costs in the immediate postwar period, the orphanage committee had underestimated the cost of extending and remodelling the old store. Building materials alone amounted to the sum of $8,000; hence money ran out before these costs, together with those for labour, had been met. The end result was such financial turmoil that a desperate committee gladly turned over to the sisters a stack of unpaid bills, a list of the persons who had made loans, and

Life was rugged but rewarding in the community's early days. Here, Sister Monica Mantyka and Sister Stephanie Diakovich are seated near a log cabin mission in the Peace River District, Alberta. Teaching school was a challenge when there was often no paper, no pencils – but, as Sister Monica says, 'We had the four walls, and a sealed-up window.' Below are sisters at a prairie mission.

When winter blasted Ituna, Saskatchewan, in the mid-1930s there was only one way to transport a homeful of children to the church a mile away. These sisters did it, with the help of a willing driver and a horse. The three sisters at the left are Sister Paula Dzygolyk, Sister Tekla Daciw, and Sister Josaphata Tymochko.

Below, the youngsters, together with a few members of the staff, at St Joseph's Children's Home in Mundare, Alberta. With the children are Sister Tarasia Hladio, Sister Hilary Lenyk, Sister Ann Smysniuk, Sister Severyn Hawryliuk, Sister Louise Matwiy, and Sister Celeste Diachinsky.

Sister Daria Sportiak has been a 'second mother' to children since the 1950s, when this picture was taken in Mundare, Alberta.
Sister Gertrude welcomes the war orphans who arrived at Ancaster, Ontario, in 1949 from refugee camps in western Europe.

Here is Sister Bernarda Chrunik, putting the girls in shape for a new season. This picture is taken at St Mary's School in Cleveland, Ohio. Sister Andrea Kruk shares a thought with children from her First Communion class at Saints Vladimir and Olga Church, Windsor, Ontario. And Sister Melanie Nakoneshny, at Immaculate Conception Cathedral, Philadelphia, Pennsylvania, prepares for the graduation Mass.

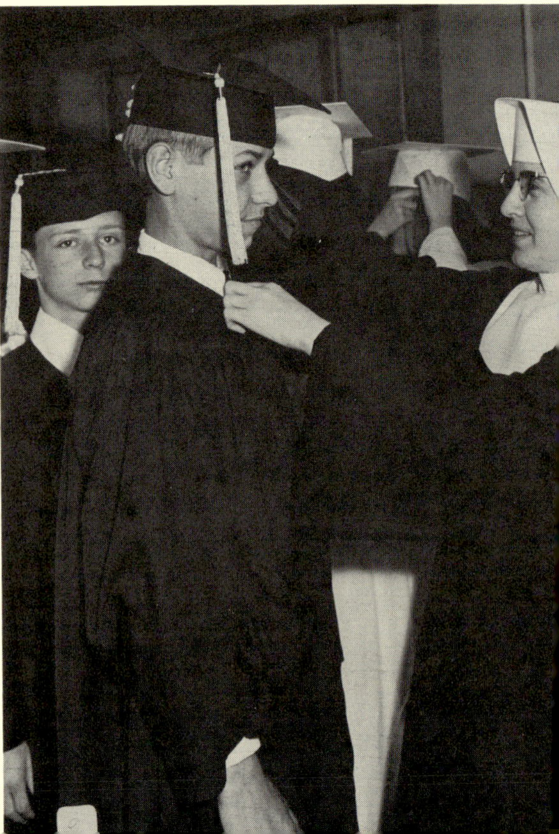

an empty orphanage fund. It was, undoubtedly, a major financial snag to untangle.

Perhaps all this might not have mattered quite so much if it had not been for the fact that almost everywhere the sisters turned they were plagued by creditors – and there was no hole to hide in. These events lent credibility to the unthinkable, that no sooner had the Ituna mission been established than it was teetering on the brink of dissolution. Nor could this grim possibility be wished away. 'There seemed to be no alternative,' explained the chronicler, 'except to resell the building and the farm to repay the debts, and permanently remove the sisters from Ituna.'[54] It was a bitter pill to swallow.

In an obvious effort to save the situation, their good friend, Father Delaere, now superior of the Redemptorists in Ituna, negotiated a loan for $10,000 at an interest rate of 9 per cent. This money enabled the sisters to satisfy most of their creditors, but 'the acquisition of this huge loan together with the interest was a tremendous burden for us,' confessed the annalist. 'What caused us additional grief,' she continued, 'was the subsequent suffering imposed upon Father Delaere by those who derided him for his act of charity by prophesying that his religious order would be faced with a great economic loss, since surely the sisters would be unable to meet their financial commitments.'[55]

Strangely enough, hardship and sacrifice once again drew out the best in the Sisters Servants. Amid all the humiliation and confusion that had arisen from the fiasco, they clung to a lively and indefatigable hope that somehow things would get better. And even though there was little enough to smile about in those days, the sisters in charge of St Ann's did smile. They knew they had a lot of blessings to count: their houseful of infants – and children are always something to smile about – and the roof over their heads – even if it were a heavily mortgaged one.

Such cheerful equanimity helped to make life bearable amid the direst poverty the sisters had ever known. At the same time, in order to survive, they had, of necessity, to be more rugged than the rugged conditions in which they lived. For instance, since their vegetable garden had not yet been planted nor their grain sown, they depended entirely upon charity for the food needed to sustain their orphans and themselves. And so, every week the sisters, women who would probably have never had to beg for food in their life, found it imperative to beg for every sack of flour, if they hoped to have some bread in the house. The mite that could be put away after they had made their most essential periodic purchases was designated 'for the debt.' And all of this was done because they believed that the orphanage was an important work and a merciful work – because hundreds of children who would otherwise be thrown on the state could find a home here.

As might be expected, foreclosure remained their bogeyman for years. But the fact that St Ann's had weathered the brunt of this storm of events was looked upon by the sisters as a miracle. 'We must never forget,' reminded the chronicler, 'that we are indebted for all this help to God and to our dearest Mother Mary who, ever since the moment of the founding of our congregation when she took it to her heart, has ever kept it under her loving patronage in times of greater and lesser stress. For this love, may she be praised forever!'[56]

In the face of all the crises, large and small, that pressed in from many quarters during these early years of rapid mission expansion, Sister Ambrose, as major superior, quietly pursued her own regular pace, dealing successively with each issue as it presented itself. A case in point is the period between 1920 and 1921 when, in the span of one astonishing year, she not only had to cope with the dismal Ituna affair but also had to marshal the resources of the institute to meet the greater educational demands being made upon the sisters in Edmonton and Sifton, by adding classroom wings to the two schools in these centres. She was fully aware of what a great burden the additional debt of $46,000 incurred from these undertakings would be for her fellow sisters.[57] It meant that the most frugal living conditions would exist in each of their institutions for a long time; in their personal quarters, food, and clothing the sisters would truly be the poorest of the poor.

Significantly enough, at this crucial moment in their history the respected figure of Metropolitan Andrew Sheptytsky unconsciously but dramatically and unforgettably regenerated and revivified the sisters' spirit of poverty. In the autumn of 1921 the prominent prelate made his second visit to Canada, this time, as he humbly explained, 'to beg on behalf of those Ukrainian children who have been orphaned by the cruel war and generally abandoned by society.'[58] The local chronicler thus described the sisters' first encounter with the metropolitan in Winnipeg: 'There he stood, a towering figure, noticeably weary, leaning upon his cane, yet with much zeal and more joy shining forth from his countenance. But what poverty he manifested! A Prince of the Church, a nobleman by birth, clothed in a religious garb that was worn thin and generously patched. Here before us stood a great and famous man who had chosen to beg for his conquered, humiliated, and indigent Ukrainian people.'[59] The modest manner and unostentatious appearance of the metropolitan forcefully reminded the sisters that it was a joy to be poor in the name of Christ for the good of the human family. His living example encouraged them to continue, in their own poverty, to give glad witness to the world that the Church is the Church of the poor, both in her spirit of detachment and in the harsh reality of her penury and suffering.

From the metropolitan, too, they learned about the poignant plight of their fellow Sisters Servants and their people in Ukraine, resulting from the political events that had occurred in the wake of the war. For both Poland and the Russian Bolsheviks had challenged the independent United Ukrainian Republic proclaimed in Kiev on January 22, 1919, after the collapse of the Austrian and Russian empires. And while the government which proclaimed this unity did not have at that time the physical force to protect it, this Act of Union represented the national objective of Ukrainian patriots, then and since. Before long the western part of Ukraine was occupied by Poland, and Ukraine proper was overrun by the Bolsheviks. It became necessary, therefore, for those who had engaged in resistance activities to flee from the country.

Among these refugees were former officers and men of the Ukrainian armed forces, many of whom succeeded in crossing the Carpathian Mountains and received asylum in Czechoslovakia. Civilian refugees emigrated to a number of European countries. When, however, restrictions governing the admission of immigrants to Canada were relaxed, many of these people took advantage of this development as early as 1922, thus initiating a second phase of Ukrainian immigration to this country. In the decade 1924–34 a total of 59,895 Ukrainians arrived in Canada to begin life all over again.[60]

This second phase group of settlers differed from the first in that there were no illiterate persons among them, and although the agriculturalists predominated the intellectuals were next in number. Because this group expected to return to their home-country 'whenever conditions change,' they displayed politico-refugee characteristics which prompted them to remain within the ethnic community, and to maintain close contacts with their European counterparts; they had no inclination to become too deeply rooted in the new world. This, in turn, greatly retarded their integration and their economic adjustment in the new country. Not until the Second World War would their integration be speeded up and differences which existed at the beginning between the members of the first and second phase groups be erased.[61]

For the most part these immigrants tended to be more urban than rural; consequently their numbers in the cities and towns of the west and in those of the industrial east notably increased.[62] As early as 1922, when the influx of newcomers was just getting underway, the Sisters Servants observed that with the increase in the Ukrainian population more of their children were attending public schools. This meant that these youngsters were not receiving instruction in catechetics or the Ukrainian language. In an effort to compensate for this deficiency, the sisters organized night school classes in their six missions; thereafter, on each school day, from 5:00 to 7:00 PM, they taught children in their own institutions or in parish halls, where these were available. In March 1922, for instance, after a full day's teaching at St Nicholas School in Winnipeg, Sister Lubov Chawrona and Sister Magdalene Euphrasia Hupalo travelled daily to the suburb of Elmwood to instruct ninety-four children.[63] In November of the same year, one group of sisters stationed in Edmonton was teaching in the suburb of Strathcona, another in Beverly, and still another was instructing 150 public school children in the local parish hall.[64]

Almost as a matter of course – perhaps because of their varied apostolates – the Sisters Servants had been developing such flexibility and adaptability that they seemed to adjust spontaneously to changing situations. Thus, as more Ukrainians settled in the cities and the sisters recognized that on a daily basis there were not enough of their own members to handle the growing number of night schools being opened in each new parish, they simply reorganized their schedules. By teaching in two parishes on alternate days, by organizing Saturday and Sunday classes for other groups, they were able in most centres to quadruple the pupil enrolment.

It is well to recall that the sisters were conducting these night schools in religion and the Ukrainian language in the 1920s long before Ukrainian was being offered as an accredited course in any Canadian high school or university. For this reason it was almost impossible for a sister to upgrade her knowledge of the language in any existing educational institution. Consequently, some of the Canadian-born sisters were prepared for this night-school apostolate by one or another of the European-born members who organized classes in their own convents; others had to rely solely upon their own private study of grammar, literature, and history. It became a year-round apostolate which, according to Rev. A. Truch, OSBM, was carried on 'in towns and in rural centres; in day and night schools; throughout the academic year and during vacations; in school buildings, in parish halls and in private homes; in bright classrooms and in dingy church basements; in various neighbourhoods and diverse circumstances. Without this instruction,' observed Father Truch 'many youngsters would never have spoken Ukrainian. And although not all of the sisters knew the language equally well, nor did they instruct in a similar manner, none the less, they succeeded in implanting in the hearts of thousands of children an appreciation of their heritage,'[65] and imparted a knowledge of the language which enabled them to feel at home in Ukrainian organizations and social circles as well as in their religious rite. Through their work in this field the sisters demonstrated not only that they were profoundly concerned about maintaining a vitality within their Church but also that they were in step with the changing situation within the Ukrainian Canadian community. In truth, their initiative in this area sparked an interest in Ukrainian night schools that still shows no signs of waning.

There were times during these early beginnings when the Sisters Servants, as one religious body, experienced the profound truth that life is a battle – for everyone; and that in it, at one time or another, everyone is badly beaten. One such moment was the summer night of July 24, 1924, when, at the Sifton mission, the sisters awakened to a nightmarish reality: their building was in flames. There was no place for either horror or fear as the fire, which had been sparked in the barn and which had already consumed the livestock, speedily whipped across to engulf the old wing of the school where their orphans were asleep. Within minutes, some sisters were hurriedly carrying drowsy youngsters out of the inferno while others were swiftly guiding older children out of their doomed home.

As the smoke cleared in the early morning light the sisters surveyed the smouldering ruins of their school in shocked disbelief and in the sad awareness that this was to be a suffering for the entire institute. The fruit of fourteen years of personal and communal sacrifice had disappeared in a few short hours. Nothing but a mass of rubble marked the places where the barn and dormitories had stood. Of the new wing – erected only three years before at a cost of $30,000, and not yet paid for – only the walls remained; heat, smoke, and water had combined to produce a perfectly uninhabitable interior. Gazing at the rubble after that anxious and prayerful night, some of the sisters voiced the rather strange thought that the Sifton mission seemed to have been foredoomed to failure, since it had been an on-again, off-again affair for fourteen years.

It had been in September of 1910 that Archbishop Langevin 'had directed Rev. A. Sabourin [who had adopted the Ukrainian rite in 1908] to build a spacious Ukrainian church, with a basement large and convenient enough to contain the classrooms of a proposed "Missionary

School." The priest was also ordered to construct a three-storey residence for the professors and students, and to remodel the old Ukrainian Greek Catholic chapel into a convent for the Sisters Servants.'[66] The chief purpose of the Missionary School, as outlined by the *Ukrainian Ruthenian*, was 'to prepare Ukrainian youth for a priestly and religious life in a manner suited to this country and our people here by means of an approved programme of studies and through the practice of Christian virtue.'[67] In addition, 'courses designed to meet the needs of those students who wish to meet the entrance requirements to a provincial Normal School'[68] were to be offered.

Without question, Father Sabourin had received a challenging assignment, for to construct the proposed church and school in the small village of Sifton was to be no mean feat. Without delay, he enlisted Archbishop Langevin's support in obtaining two Sisters Servants to help lay the groundwork for what the prelate hoped would be a flourishing apostolate 'from the point of view of fostering a spiritual growth in the Church and of developing the Congregation of the Little Servants of Mary Immaculate.'[69]

The hazards of overeagerness were evidenced before long in the immediate results following the sisters' ready acceptance of this mission. For upon their arrival in Sifton on December 1, 1910, Sister Alexia Chykalo and Sister Veronica Mary Melnyk discovered that their convent, the former village chapel which was being remodelled for them, was still far from habitable. For the time being they moved into a tiny uninsulated hut that seemed incapable of keeping in any heat. 'It was so cold,' recalled Sister Alexia, 'that we found it impossible to sleep. Even during the day we never felt warm. Day and night the icy winter winds mercilessly blew in through the cracks in the walls, and around the windows and doors.'[70] A month later, on January 3, 1911, having found the dismal living and working conditions in which they had to function wellnigh unbearable, the sisters unexpectedly backtracked and returned to Winnipeg.

The following autumn, on August 18, 1911, with their convent still undergoing renovations, Sister Alexia and Sister Veronica again returned to Sifton. Within a few weeks they were joined by Sister Josaphata Tymochko, who had been assigned to teach the younger boys and girls at the Missionary School. Now, with a group of three sisters, it was possible to enjoy a fuller and richer community life, even in the remote rural post.

Since the basement of the church, in which regular classes were supposed to be conducted, was also unfinished, the sisters set up a class-room in their own convent. Desiring to make the walls of the partitioned old school brighter for the children, they splurged on a bit of paint. But, as Sister Alexia explained, 'although we managed to cover the walls, there wasn't enough for the floor; hence this simply remained an un-painted eyesore until the spring, when we eventually saved enough money for the paint to finish the job.'[71] Finally, just before Christmas, on December 20, 1912, Sister Josaphata enthusiastically opened the convent school – with five pupils.

It was not until Rev. J. Jean, a French priest who had also adopted the Ukrainian rite, replaced Father Sabourin as director of the Mission-ary School on August 15, 1912, that the basement of the church was completed, the classrooms furnished, and the school officially opened on September 6.[72] In the ensuing months the sisters took up their duties in earnest. And although the apostolate pictured by the local chronicler seems rather commonplace, Sisters Servants at every mission could vouch that it was one which did not gain momentum through easy standards, half measures, and human temporizing; nor did its pleasures and rewards come in wordly trifles and ignoble ease, but only through patient sacrifice and hard work.

On March 1, 1914, for instance, the annalist rather breathlessly de-clared: 'This month, in addition to our teaching, cooking at the Mission-ary School, caring for the church and sacristy, tending the garden, per-forming our household chores and looking after the fifteen girls who are presently in residence at our convent, our community of five sisters is trying to make floral arrangements for seven churches.'[73] Beyond that, their convent served as the village counselling centre as well; explained the chronicler: 'An average of seven people a day seek our advice con-cerning their illnesses or personal problems.'[74] Furthermore, it seems that the sisters assumed responsibility for the well-being of outlying parishes and parishioners; on May 15, 1915, the annalist recorded that 'a few of our members travelled to Ethelbert [twenty-one miles away] to clean the church and decorate the altar of Our Lady for May devotions; two others, meanwhile, journeyed twenty-five miles to treat one of our patients, after which, in response to an urgent call, they proceeded eight miles farther to nurse a woman who was critically ill.'[75]

They did not, however, devote so much attention to the real social and physical ills they encountered that they neglected spiritual priorities. Perhaps more than other happenings, stories of conversions were faith-fully recorded. In fact, it almost seems as if members of the local community felt that even a brief, unvarnished delineation of the facts would suffice to enable future generations of sisters to appreciate and share the apostolic joy – so deep, real, and lasting that it can hardly be equalled by any other on earth – which they experienced at each such event. For a missionary forgets all the sacrifice that might have gone before, when, through her prayer and careful nurture, God grants a man the gift of faith, and she witnesses his new found love for the Lord manifested in a changed life and unexpected virtues. A simple case, typical of many others, was related by the annalist on December 10, 1915: 'Sister Taida Letawsky and Sister Augustina Salome Hawryliuk were called upon to nurse a sick farmer, an apostate, whom, time and again, they encouraged to make his peace with God, while he was still able to do so. One day, without warning, he declared that he wanted to make his confession. In no time at all the sisters had him bundled up and driven to the church where, with the grace of God, he joyfully returned to the fold. What is more, he is now an exemplary Catholic.'[76] An ingenuous account, to be sure, but one which reveals that Christ's parable of the lost sheep (Mt 18:12) was meaningful to these women.

The Sifton religious, long inured to poverty, felt its pinch more acutely in 1915 than previously, since now they found themselves solely responsible for a number of orphans who had been brought to them by priests, policemen, or concerned neighbours. Understandably, to provide for their ever-growing household soon became a day-to-day struggle. It is a scant surprise, therefore, that in the middle of December of that year 'the sisters were compelled to brave the cutting cold as they travelled from farm to farm in a desperate attempt to collect enough grain and vegetables to feed the children through the winter.'[77] To add to their trials, the convent, which had been 'renovated' in 1911, constantly demanded repairs. But with money less than scarce, any fixing that went beyond the sisters' modest carpentry skills was indefinitely postponed. And so it followed that they usually lived with situations as discomforting as that described by the annalist on December 10, 1915: 'We suffer much because the house is difficult to heat, and also because during the night so much water rises in our basement – where our kitchen and refectory are located – that every morning after the celebration of the Divine Liturgy we have to mop up about ten pailfuls. But when it rains, then we're really flooded!'[78]

Undoubtedly, theirs was an active apostolate. Too active, thought Sister Ambrose. For one thing, the heavy work schedule together with extreme cold and a continuous dampness so taxed the strength of almost every sister assigned to the mission (even though in these years almost all of them were young) that Sister Ambrose was compelled to make personnel changes more frequently than in any other convent. For another, she became much concerned about the sisters' spiritual well-being, especially after the Sifton community was asked to assume additional apostolic duties; for, as a deeply spiritual woman, she believed that an individual sister and her religious community are sustained only by unremitting prayer. A religious, she was convinced, must have time to pray or else she will become simply a tinkling cymbal. In a letter to Bishop Budka she defined her position: 'The sisters in Sifton are already finding it almost impossible to fulfil their spiritual obligations regarding community prayer, and often have to omit them. This state of affairs must not be permitted to continue. For my part, I do not desire to take upon my soul the responsibility of burdening them with still more work.'[79]

At this point, therefore, the future of the apostolate in Sifton remained uncertain; but a few weeks later it was decided that all personnel would be withdrawn and the convent closed until the situation could be remedied.[80] On September 21, 1916, after celebrating the Divine Liturgy, the bishop informed the faithful of the sisters' imminent departure. If, initially, the parishioners felt a shock, by no means did it render them speechless, for by evening so many delegations from the various parish organizations had approached the prelate with the promise to build a decent convent if only the sisters would remain that after consulting with members of the diocesan clergy including Rev. P. Kamenecky and Rev. M. Olenchuk, who were familiar with the sisters' work in the Sifton district, Bishop Budka permitted three sisters to carry on in a last-ditch attempt to salvage the mission.[81] At the conclusion of the 1916–17 school term, when the Missionary School was permanently closed, the sisters were directed to organize an elementary school in its place and to utilize the building formerly occupied by the professors and students.[82]

Within three years, however, even this proved inadequate to house an average of fifty children; therefore, in 1920, taking advantage of a bumper wheat crop, the sisters canvassed the farms for funds, and raised the sum of $6,000 for a classroom wing estimated to cost $30,000. Encouraged by the pastor, Rev. A. Kraykiwsky, who had been appointed to be the administrator of the entire project, the Sifton community tightened its belt in an effort to increase its savings, and optimistically embraced the burden of the construction, which began in June 1921.

Problems cropped up at every turn. To start with, the local farmers who had volunteered their labour incorrectly laid the concrete footing, with the result that the work had to be redone; this, of course, further multiplied the original cost. Next, the weather failed to cooperate; it rained so continuously that not only was construction hindered but the pumping of water from the flooded excavations constituted an extra drain on their savings. As weeks rolled by and other crises brought new costly postponements, the entire institute became perturbed. And there was good reason to be worried, for by the time the wing was ready the building accounts were in a sorry state, owing to erratically kept financial statements. Some sisters realized the magnitude of the problem and the precariousness of their position instantly, and others later, when bills that were supposed to have been paid were found to be still outstanding. All too painfully they became aware that their option to remain in Sifton was circumscribed by a host of debts from which it would not be easy to extricate themselves. It was Ituna all over again – only worse. This time, too, the morale of the sisters must also have been battered, for the chronicler ruefully remarked: 'Although the building was completed, it failed to gladden either our major superior or the rest of us.'[83]

For all the financial chicanery involved, however, the consensus of the sisters was that, while the good name of the institute had certainly been hurt by the whole bizarre mess, the wounds would heal, eventually. They were learning, and paying dearly for the lesson, that it was time to manage their own affairs. In that light, the chronicler's following morsel of advice to future generations of sisters is thoroughly understandable: 'Let our members know that they should prudently administer their own transactions, rather than depend upon others to do so for them, so that those to whom we may be indebted financially may not suffer a loss because of mismanagement.'[84]

No sooner had the institute begun to repay these liabilities three years later than fire virtually destroyed the school during that long July night in 1924. In the days and weeks that followed the most important factor in the mission's ultimate fate was the insurance; and when, at last, the sisters were informed that they would receive a sum of $2,000, a mere pittance in comparison to the total loss, the renovation of the existing wing could not even be considered. Hence, it came as no particular surprise to anyone when superiors concluded that 'there was no alternative except to abandon Sifton, and divide the existing debts among the other five houses, which would now have to share the common burden. By the end of the month, most of the Sifton staff had been transferred to other convents. And thus was interrupted in midstream the apostolate of the Sisters Servants in this part of Manitoba.'[85]

After this notable setback, those who expected to witness a congregation of sisters fearful of moving toward new horizons had to look elsewhere. For, sooner than anyone had anticipated, the Sisters Servants simply bounced back, and in 1925 headed down the road again – this time to Montreal, Quebec.

The number of Ukrainians in the cities of the industrial east had been rising steadily since the beginning of the second phase of their immigration to Canada in 1922.[86] As had been the case in the west, so too in the east, it became apparent quite early that the newcomers needed and desired teachers of their own language and rite. There was, however, one notable difference. In Quebec, French and English Catholic schools constituted the 'public' school system of the province. Consequently, the majority of staffs, both lay and religious, were comprised almost entirely of Latin-rite Catholics, few, if any, of whom had ever even heard that any rite other than their own existed in the Church. It was precisely this ignorance – so immediate and so hard to bear – that created much painful embarrassment for Ukrainian parents and their children. It was not uncommon, for instance, for a school official or a teacher, who regarded the strange rite with undisguised suspicion, to brand a Ukrainian child as a 'Greek Orthodox' in a public gathering or in a classroom, and perhaps to wonder aloud why he was enrolled in a Catholic school. Nor was it unusual for a Ukrainian pupil to be reprimanded and even punished for not attending services in the local Latin-rite parish; or, worse still, to be told that Holy Communion under the two species of bread and wine as distributed in his church was not Communion at all.[87] Not only was such an attitude demoralizing for Ukrainian children, but it held in it the seeds of the kind of bitterness that had characterized the relationship between Ukrainians and Poles in Europe, and this, just as the new Canadians were sinking their roots into Canadian soil.

These were some of the compelling reasons which prompted Archbishop G. Gautier to appeal to Bishop Budka for Sisters Servants. Primarily, theirs was to be a teaching assignment in two of the French schools that had the largest proportion of Ukrainian children. Another undertaking that would be just as important, however, was that of breaking down the existing barriers of prejudice and misunderstanding, for only then would their influence be enriching to all concerned.

Responding to the urgency and immediacy of the call to go east, Sister Ambrose sent Sister Josaphata Tymochko, Sister Taida Letawsky, Sister Lawrence Josephine Dzumaga, Sister Olympiada Anne Yawrotsky, and, later, Sister Sylvester Mary Werbicky to establish this latest foundation. Rev. M. Gregoriychuk and his parishioners were noticeably heartened and relieved at the sisters' arrival in Montreal on August 23, 1925. Gratefully accepting temporary residence in Mr N. Buchkowsky's truly Christian home, they subsequently went house hunting, found a fairly suitable home across the street from St Michael's Ukrainian Catholic Church, paid their first month's rent, moved in, named their convent in honour of St Therese, and began to prepare teaching materials for the school term scheduled to commence within a few weeks. No one doubted that the sisters meant to stay.

Beginning that September they taught religion and Ukrainian in the two schools of St John the Baptist and Jean Mance, spending a half day in each classroom. Before long, pursuing their educational apostolate still further with characteristic passion, they introduced Saturday and Sunday classes for pupils attending other city schools. This was a move that won for them the instant appreciation of parents.

The simple fact is that, as a result of their early success, two additional teachers, Sister Eusebia Matkowsky and Sister Julianna Rosalie Pankowsky, were hired to teach English to Ukrainian pupils in both of the French schools, commencing in the 1926–7 scholastic year. Astonishingly, within the short span of ten months the sisters had established themselves as proficient teachers in school and parish, and, perhaps more important still, they had so effectively thawed out the icy reserve that had initially greeted them that, more and more, the teachers of both Catholic rites were experiencing the rewarding effects growing out of their mutual respect, sincere cooperation, and real charity.[88]

In 1926, as the sisters approached their first significant milestone – a quarter-century of religious life and missionary activity in Canada – they resolved that the time was ripe to deal with a pressing matter that had been a source of anxious concern for years: their novitiate.

The Mundare convent had always been considered by members as the heart of the institute, not so much because it was the motherhouse,[89] but rather because, since 1903, when the first postulant, Sister Taida Letawsky, had begun her training at the old homestead, every Sister Servant had received her religious formation in this same house. Any sentimental attachment to this home by the sisters, because their religious vocation had been nurtured within its walls, was tempered by their personal experience; they were intimately acquainted with the advantages as well as the worst shortcomings of the novitiate 'on the farm.' No one, however, was better prepared than Sister Ambrose to evaluate the effectiveness of the training being offered there to the girls who were entering the congregation in small but constant numbers each year.[90] For no one had observed more closely or for a longer period, the conditions under which the young sisters were being formed, than she who had been the institute's first directress of novices and its only major superior to date.

And most of what Sister Ambrose saw, she did not like. For one thing, she did not like seeing postulants and novices bearing almost full responsibility for the practical management of the farm, and having to do a man's work in the fields and farmyard from dawn to dusk; she did not like witnessing, at the end of the day, their total exhaustion, which inevitably robbed them of both the time and the zest for prayer; she did not like the ever-increasing difficulty of enforcing rule 52 of the 1907 constitutions, which clearly stipulated that the final six months of the eighteen-month training period must be devoted to apostolic preparation. In a word, Sister Ambrose did not like the lack of religious and apostolic formation resulting from an impossible manual work load; a burden which was hindering individual sisters from realizing their fullest potential as religious. And although periodically, from 1909 to 1926, she had protested against this dismal state of affairs, she knew that any significant headway in altering the situation would be possible only when the institute itself was financially able to maintain and operate its novitiate.[91]

There had appeared a ray of hope that this worrisome problem might be resolved when, in 1910, Archbishop Langevin had asked the sisters to open a second novitiate in Winnipeg. This request seems to have stemmed from the prelate's continuing desire to train as many Sisters Servants for the teaching profession as possible. In January of this same year, for instance, the archbishop had reported to his clergy that of the fifteen Sisters Servants then in the institute some were already studying in Edmonton and would be applying for certification in that province. But, he added, 'already several girls, who have been studying in the convents of St Boniface, St Norbert, St Anne, St John the Baptist, and St Charles, are preparing to write their examinations for their diplomas, and there is reason to hope that these are precious subjects for the community.'[92] In the light of this fact it is not surprising that the ordinary should desire that Manitoba postulants receive their religious training in his archdiocese. For not only would there be time for a sound spiritual preparation under the direction of the local Basilian Fathers, but with educational institutions readily accessible the sisters' post-novitiate academic and pedagogical training would be assured.

Realistically, the chances of fully implementing the archbishop's proposal were slim. At the outset three chief obstacles stood in the way. In the first place, the house on Stella Avenue was too small to accommodate any additional sisters; secondly, the poverty of the Winnipeg home, resulting from the sisters' maintenance and operation of the mission school, put the support of a novitiate out of reach; and, finally, the current insignificant number of members in the congregation did not allow for a second novitiate staff. But in an effort to carry out, at least partially, the wishes of the archbishop, the sisters opened a novitiate in Winnipeg on February 12, 1912, shortly after the completion of the new St Nicholas School. Only aspirants from the provinces of Manitoba were included in the intensive formation course directed by Rev. A. Fillipow, OSBM. However, so brief was the existence of this training centre that only a total of five girls participated in the programme – among them the institute's first non-Ukrainian member, Sister Alexandra Mary Doiron, who was of French-Irish origin. What may have caused the project to founder even before it was three years old was Bishop Budka's lack of support, for in view of its small number of novices, the prelate, unlike Archbishop Langevin, believed that the second novitiate was unwarranted. Thus, for all its bright hopes, the handwriting was already on the wall. As it turned out, Sister Alexandra and Sister Daria Paraskevia Ushkowsky, who pronounced their vows on December 12, 1914, were the last novices to be trained here, since the girls admitted to the institute after this date were sent to Mundare; as a consequence, the Winnipeg centre unofficially folded up. And, in the end, it is doubtful that more than a handful of sisters experienced the slightest regret at its closing, largely, perhaps, because it had neither alleviated the vexing difficulties at Mundare nor altered the general novitiate picture to any significant degree.[93]

Perhaps unavoidably, therefore, in September 1917 Sister Ambrose appealed officially, for the first time in the congregation's history, to the other four existing houses for assistance in maintaining the novitiate at Mundare and in educating student sisters. Each local superior was requested to forward annually the amount of $4 for every sister in her home who was actively engaged in the apostolate. This, at best, was a feeble attempt to achieve a degree of self-sufficiency, for with a total membership of fifty-three, including postulants and novices, even a perfect response would not have constituted an impressive sum. But the action did effectively indicate that the sisters' hope of 'being on our own' was very much alive.[94]

After years of waiting, their dream for self-subsistence in Mundare began to come true in 1924, when four members of the Mundare staff – Sister Basil Catherine Starko, Sister Ignatia Butryn, Sister Suzanne

Starko, and Sister Taida Letawsky – took the initiative in this undertaking. They believed that for too long they had kept their eyes shut and focused on nothing in the face of a situation that had to be squarely met. That is why there never were four women as determined to exploit an opportunity than were they when they learned that a well-known widow, Mrs Mary Hewko, desired to sell her land, which was situated close to the parish church in Mundare. Its location can scarcely have been better, especially in view of the fact that for fourteen years, summer and winter, rain or shine, the sisters had walked eight miles to and from the church (usually barefoot to save their shoes) on Sundays, holy days, for May and June devotions, and any other special liturgical services. Immediate consultation on this unexpected development by the group of four sisters, who were convinced that the institute was no longer an infant and could therefore provide for itself, resulted in the conception of one of the institute's most imaginative efforts to date: the purchase of the land, the construction of a novitiate-school-orphanage, and a plan to support it by means of their own earnings.

Since they were particularly anxious to avoid affronting their long-time friends and benefactors, the Basilian Fathers, they decided to maintain a secrecy in the affair until the business deal regarding the property was closed. But what they thought was a successful conspiracy of silence wasn't so silent after all. For, from Winnipeg, Sister Ambrose, in an obvious expression of concern about the consequences of the sisters' financial initiatives, requested Father Kryzanowsky's help. 'I have learned,' she wrote on December 12, 1924, 'that the sisters wish to purchase Mrs Hewko's farm with Mr Dzygolyk's assistance. In order that this business be handled correctly, I will appreciate it if you, Reverend Father Superior, will be so kind as to look into this matter and advise the sisters as to how they are to proceed.'[95]

These unique women, however, coped with the dimensions of the project – beginning with the inevitable need to obtain the sum of $7,500 to pay for the land – in a manner that dramatized their doggedly optimistic mood. By begging, borrowing from the sisters' dowries, and by accepting Mr J. Dzygolyk's risky offer to buy half of the farm as part of a dowry for his daughter, Sister Paula Paraskevia, who was still a novice, they eventually purchased the property.[96]

Predictably enough, the sisters need not have feared the reaction of the Basilian Fathers to their desire to move from the farm. In response to a direct appeal by the bishop himself Father Kryzanowsky, who had been a sincere friend and wise adviser of the Sisters Servants ever since his arrival in Mundare in 1910, assured the prelate of his intention to assist in the project: 'As we have done to date, so shall we in the future encourage the faithful to contribute toward the maintenance of the orphanage and the payment of the debt.'[97]

The four sisters actively engaged in the proceedings initially emerged from the transaction as women whose expectations for success in their venture outdistanced their accomplishments; for not until the institute had conducted a year-long campaign for funds did Bishop Budka, on March 26, 1926, approve their construction plans. Within two months the sisters and orphans were ready to vacate the convent and school at the mission and settle in temporary quarters in the village. This step was taken in an attempt to save approximately $6,000 in building costs by dismantling the home and school that had served them since 1913 and using the materials in the new building. Mr A. Lesiuk's home, which comprised a part of the dowry of his daughter, Sister Gertrude Nadia, became a temporary novitiate and a storehouse for some of their furniture. An empty house which stood on the recently purchased farm came to life as soon as the children and most of the professed sisters moved in. Lack of bedroom space, however, made it necessary for most of the religious to sleep either in the unused chicken coop or granary. That, it turned out, proved to be a harrowing experience. For no matter how often the sisters swept worms from the rotting ceilings before lying down to sleep, the creatures insisted on dropping down upon them during the night.[98]

Later that summer, on July 13, the *Edmonton Journal* announced to Albertans that the Sisters Servants, hitherto living on the Basilian homestead, were coming to town. 'The Sisters of the Immaculate Conception have given a worthy hand [in the development of the Mundare mission],' the article explained, 'and have educated many children in the school which was begun on the homestead. A new convent of the Sisters of the Immaculate Conception is now under construction near the church. This is being erected of tile and brick, at the cost of $14,000.[99] It seems fitting,' concluded the reporter, 'that the corner stone of this structure should have been laid yesterday by Father Kryzanowsky who is head of the Basilian Fathers in Alberta.'[100] And it was equally fitting that Bishop Budka, the Ukrainian Catholic Church's pioneer hierarch, should have officially blessed the new St Joseph's Convent a few months later, on September 27. This was one of the final official functions attended by the ailing prelate before his *ad limina* visit to Rome toward the end of 1927.

As for the sisters, they were glad and relieved to be on their own at last. And because this newest project had considerably swelled the institute's total deficit, many of them presumed that their mission expansion would now slow to a crawl. Wishful thinking, perhaps; and not in keeping with the signs of the times. For to bear visible witness to the fulness of the Church's concern for Ukrainians in this country, many other apostolic activities would still have to flow from the congregation.

*   *   *

Against the background of Canadian life and culture, and simultaneously with their apostolic development, a gradual evolvement had been subtly modifying and transforming the original features of the institute. In 1917, for instance, Bishop Budka, keenly aware of this phenomenon, had observed: 'Although the sisters have been in Canada for fifteen years, almost all undertakings – and arduous ones at that – are still in an embryo stage. But at the same time as the congregation has endeavoured to meet new situations effectively, changes on the local level have been introduced in an unprecedented fashion. To make matters worse, lack of coordination – which is the effect of inadequate communication with superiors, who cannot afford the high costs of travel involved in regular visits to the widely separated missions – has resulted in a clutch of unauthorized practices that must either be eliminated or legitimately incorporated into the constitutions, so that uncertainty and misunderstanding may be removed and religious life firmly grounded upon sound principles. It is imperative that novel innovations cease at once, for it is undermining the peace and unity of the institute.'[101]

As an initial step toward 'stabilizing the constitutions by official acceptance of worthwhile practices which have emerged from the demands of life and missionary activity in Canada,'[102] the bishop directed Rev. N. M. Decamps, CSSR, in October 1916, to make a study of each local situation through an extraordinary canonical visitation[103] in the four houses of the congregation. 'Because we understand the concern of your major superior in this regard,' the prelate explained to the sisters, 'we feel that we can no longer wait until the end of the war to deal with this matter.'[104]

For his part, Father Decamps fulfilled the assignment so speedily that just over a month later, on December 1, 1916, he filed his visitation report and recommendations in which he dealt with six main areas: spiritual life, government, the novitiate, studies, transfers of sisters, and the religious garb.[105] The report touched off a whirl of paperwork in the chancery office and in the houses of the institute, for on the basis of its conclusions and suggestions Bishop Budka conceived a sweeping programme which, he believed, would strengthen the Canadian congregation.

To start with, he called for the election of a major superior and three councillors. Because Sister Ambrose had already held office for a longer period than the six years permitted by the constitutions, 'the ordinary, as the highest superior of the congregation,' stated Bishop Budka, 'takes this matter of the sisters in hand and, invoking the assistance of God and the Immaculate Virgin, hereby declares that a new major superior will neither be elected by a chapter nor appointed, but will be chosen by all professed religious, who will vote according to the procedures outlined in the constitutions and the advice we have received from competent sources. This election will be valid until a general chapter is convoked, which will occur when the necessity arises. In the meantime, however, the sisters will be bound by forthcoming decisions, implementations, changes and rules to be formulated on the basis of the visitation report. The major superior,' he emphasized, 'will be she whom the sisters will elect.'[106]

Altogether the Canadian Sisters Servants had been headed by no member but Sister Ambrose for fifteen years. From 1909 she had held that office by virtue of her appointment as assistant by Sister Vitalia, who had then governed the European community. And not until January 1912 had a council, comprised of two elected members – Sister Nicholas Petrushkewich and Sister Taida Letawsky – been stitched together to assist her. Two years later, within the unifying framework of the ordinariate for Ukrainian Catholics under Bishop Budka, the institute's governing body had been expanded still further: three members including Sister Josepha Bilan, Sister Euletheria Furtak, and Sister Athanasia Melnyk replaced the original two councillors at a moment when a healthy increase in vocations promised a broader apostolic activity. During the war years, however, when a communications blackout had effectively cut off the Canadian community from that in Europe, both the bishop and the sisters had become conscious of the need for a superior who possessed full powers as granted by the constitutions, rather than merely an assistant with the limited jurisdiction that had been accorded Sister Ambrose in 1909.

Excitement ran high as in February 1917 each of the forty eligible voters mailed her ballot to Winnipeg. There, in the chapel of St Nicholas School on the morning of February 10, Sister Melanie Sochatsky, Sister Veronica Melnyk, and Sister Nicholas Petrushkewich, the official tellers, tallied the votes in the presence of Bishop Budka. The outcome was a resounding vote of confidence for Sister Ambrose; she was to continue to lead the Canadian Sisters Servants. 'I was thoroughly convinced that I would be relieved of the office of major superior,' she confessed to the bishop, 'and I wholeheartedly desired this, for I am fearful when I think that I shall have to answer before God for the government of our entire Canadian community. I have long desired to return to the ranks so that, free from the pressures of this position, I could give more attention to spiritual things. But if it is the will of God that I should serve Him in this post, then may His will be done. I am depending upon God's assistance and upon that of Your Excellency. Thank you for your paternal blessing.'[107] To advise her, the sisters selected Sister Athanasia Melnyk, Sister Euletheria Furtak, and Sister Melanie Mary Sochatsky.

Although for a time some sort of change in institutional status had seemed a lively possibility, especially in view of the autonomous management of local affairs during the war years, it was generally expected that the principle of unity with the European community would be maintained. Significantly, however, these elections, which had been called by the ordinary, effected a pronounced chink in that relationship, for the Canadian congregation now became an independent diocesan entity united to the motherhouse in Ukraine only through common constitutions; but even these were being modified by the circumstances of their life and works in Canada.[108]

As a second measure in his programme of invigorating the institute, the bishop notified Sister Ambrose, on the day following the elections, that Rev. N. M. Decamps, CSSR had been appointed to replace Rev. S. Dydyk, OSBM, as canonical visitor of the congregation.[109] In short order Sister Ambrose, who personally welcomed the appointment, replied: 'In the name of our entire institute I express my appreciation to Your Excellency for appointing a canonical visitor who has always endeavoured to assist us.'[110]

Correspondingly, in response to the congratulations of the majority of the sisters, Father Decamps, in a circular to each local community, expressed his thanks, added a word of encouragement regarding the faithful observance of the constitutions, and reminded the sisters of the gratitude they owed to God for His marvellous graces and to the Blessed Virgin for her motherly intercession. He then significantly stated: 'After God and His Mother, the priests belonging to the Order of St Basil the Great are deserving of your appreciation. From the moment of your founding as an institute, these holy monks have fostered the growth of the young sapling, that is your congregation, within the vineyard of the Lord. They have nourished your souls with spiritual food, and have endeavoured to draw you to the Heart of Christ. And if, today, you are able to carry on an apostolate in Canada for the glory of God and His Church, this is due in large measure to their efforts on your behalf. For these and other countless benefactions from which you have derived much good, they are responsible. Therefore, be thankful to them, and prove by your holy lives that their strivings have not been in vain.'[111]

It seems, however, that the 'entire' congregation was not so pleased with the appointment of Father Decamps as Sister Ambrose had assumed when she thanked the bishop for the nomination. Either she had been unaware of, or had woefully underestimated, the effect of the appointment upon a small group of sisters stationed in Mundare, Edmonton, and Winnipeg who had not had as much missionary contact with the Redemptorists as had those working in Yorkton and Sifton. For them, the news seems to have been a bombshell. They were as shocked as they were apprehensive, since for the first time in their history a monk other than a member of the Basilian Order, with which their congregation had always been closely associated, would be scrutinizing their religious life and apostolate. In the first flush of this notification, therefore, they saw in the bishop's action a challenge to their time-honoured fidelity to the Basilian Order; consequently, the incident provoked a predictably strong defensive attitude on the part of some sisters. They forthwith proceeded to evince palpable disapproval by forwarding a formal petition to the bishop requesting the reappointment of a Basilian as the institute's visitor.[112]

Although it may have scored a dubious point for constancy, the wisdom of submitting the entreaty seems to have been exceedingly questionable, since such action was charged with the potential to spark more defiance than sweet reason. Most clearly, within the congregation itself, progressively strained relations among local houses might have arisen out of the spontaneous reaction of many members to take sides in the issue by assertion of their support for either the Basilians or Redemptorists. Such a division of loyalties could eventually have splintered the intrinsic bond of mutual trust that had hitherto united the Sisters Servants, and thereby have inflicted psychic wounds that would have been a long time in mending.[113]

On the other hand, the move was certain to pique Bishop Budka, who must have been surprised and perhaps somewhat nettled at the opposition that had greeted the appointment. That is probably why his responding action came to something less than what the petitioners expected. For, recognizing that Father Decamps could not adequately function as canonical visitor in the face of mounting tension, and hoping to clear the air of a climate that he must have perceived as divisive, he temporarily resolved the impasse by assuming the controversial office himself. Thus, in a letter to Metropolitan Sheptytsky, dated November 22, 1918, he declared: 'I myself must be the visitor of the sisters, of whom there are fifty in five convents.'[114] It was not until February 11, 1924, when he re-appointed a Basilian in the person of Father Kryzanowsky, that the healing process within the congregation might have been considered as off to a needful start.[115]

Despite this rather unsettling experience, the bishop proceeded to establish a more relevant rule for the sisters amid the contemporary atmosphere of uncertainty by modifying the existing constitutions and directives. These, he informed the members, 'are being based upon Church law as well as your just demands regarding your life and works, in order to correct prevalent flaws and strengthen weaknesses, so that the future flowering of your institute will be assured.'[116]

Surprisingly enough, not a shred of evidence exists to indicate that the bishop's constitutional implementations were ever received or enforced by the Sisters Servants. It seems likely that Bishop Budka never did succeed in completing the assignment which he had so willingly shouldered.[117] Almost surely, therefore, local innovation would have continued to be the rule indefinitely if it had not been for the fact that during Metropolitan Sheptytsky's second visit to Canada in the autumn of 1921 the sisters requested the convocation of a chapter of election and affairs.[118]

Thus, on September 19, 1921, eighteen elected delegates assembled at St Nicholas School in Winnipeg to select a new governing body and to stabilize their constitutions by thoroughly examining the current state of their communal affairs. In the presence of the metropolitan and the bishop, this first day of the first formal chapter ever to be held by the sisters in Canada was devoted to a study of, and a vote on, each of a group of recommendations submitted by individual members and houses. There were, however, three controversial resolutions upon which they focused their attention.

The first of these read: 'It is resolved that we sever all relations with the Sisters Servants in Galicia and form a distinct congregation in Canada under a different name and constitutions.' The second stated: 'It is recommended that a general chapter be convoked in Galicia for the purpose of electing a major superior to govern the three existing communities of Sisters Servants [that is, Galicia, Canada, and Brazil].' The third of these proposed that 'as an institute, we develop our life in line with our Canadian needs rather than with those pertaining to Galicia, but that, at the same time, we remain united as one congregation through common constitutions, except for directives relative to our Canadian situations.'[119]

If the resultant vote was any indication of the unity of thought among the delegates, then no fragmentation existed; for none but the last of these resolutions received their unanimous approval. Its acceptance plainly demonstrated that while the Canadian sisters had no wish to sever their sentimental and constitutional ties with the European institute from which their own community had sprung, they concurrently endorsed the notion that only an independence in the management of their affairs could foster both their religious life and missionary activity in Canada and the desire to remain a part of the original congregation of Sisters Servants.

But precisely because the institute's autonomy was still so untried, and hence so fragile, precisely because the path before it was still so indefinite, the delegates sought, by adaptation and modification of the constitutions and community prayer, to assure a spiritual and functional strength indispensable to any further beneficial development.[120]

The chapter of election, held on September 20, once again gave Sister Ambrose the mandate to guide the community as its major superior for another five-year term, together with her councillors, Sister Euletheria Furtak, Sister Nicholas Petrushkewich, and Sister Elizabeth Kassian. Moreover, for the first time Sister Ambrose was able to appoint a treasurer and a secretary. These posts were held by Sister Theresa Melnyk and Sister Athanasia Melnyk, respectively.[121]

It was, however, the second official chapter, held at Sacred Heart Institute in Yorkton on August 11–13, 1926, that spearheaded a dramatic change in leadership through its election of Sister Athanasia Melnyk as major superior. For the first time in twenty-four years, Sister Ambrose was permitted to step down from the institute's most responsible post to assume that of a councillor, in which capacity she continued to give of her positive piety, her zeal, and her experience to her new superior, to her fellow councillors – Sister Suzanne Starko and Sister Josephata Tymochko – to each member of the institute, to the hierarchy and clergy, and to her people.[122]

For her part, in a letter to the members, Sister Athanasia, who would now be required to face and attempt to resolve the concomitant problems of the institute, called for mutual understanding and support so that together, in the spirit of the Sacred Heart, they might fulfil the role for which their congregation had been called into being: to vivify the Church through their holiness of life and enhance the spiritual well-being of the Ukrainian people through a selfless apostolate.[123]

*   *   *

In November 1927 eighty-nine exuberant Sisters Servants celebrated the silver anniversary of their institute's existence in Canada. At the end of a hectic quarter-century, they expressed their gratitude to God for His bountiful goodness to them by joyfully participating in the Divine Liturgy of thanksgiving that was offered in each of their six convent chapels. It was a time, too, for pausing to catch their breath, to examine the meaning of what they had been through, and to contemplate the future.

People had come and gone. Their original staunchest friends and benefactors, Archbishops Langevin and Legal had both died in the interval.[124] Surprisingly enough, even Bishop Budka was no longer with them. When, on August 1, 1927, the Winnipeg chronicler had recorded that 'today His Excellency conversed with us about many beautiful things during a visit to our convent,'[125] neither she nor her fellow sisters had thought that this would be the prelate's final visit to St Nicholas School. But shortly thereafter he had departed for Rome on his *ad limina* visit and 'as his health was further failing, he was permitted to return to his native land where he was made auxiliary to Archbishop-Metropolitan A. Sheptytsky in Lviv.'[126] Nor could the sisters have foreseen that although this churchman, whose integrity and dedication had always elicited their admiration and affection, would be sentenced to endure unspeakable conditions of exile in Siberia during a war that was to engulf the world within a dozen years, he would never be broken, so that even in death at a remote outpost called Caraganda on October 1, 1949, he would remain, as they had known him in his pioneer life in Canada, a true son of the Church, a Confessor of the Faith.[127]

Events, too, had come and gone. And amid them their institute's individualism, its distinctive and distinguished marks of love and service, had been forged primarily by the courage of their poverty. They had known, as they had undertaken one venture after another for the benefit of their Church and people, that there was little chance that they would not become poor. Fortunately, they had realized early that to love it is necessary to give, and that to give it is necessary to be freed of selfishness. And so they had given – even their lives. For during these years 10 per cent of the total membership had died, at an average age of twenty-nine, mainly from tuberculosis caused by undernourishment, cold, and fatigue.[128]

Then too, since only twenty-five years had elapsed, the sisters could take no shelter in long-standing accomplishments. But already they were garnering a harvest of knowledge gained through experience – the first fruit of living and suffering, which always possesses the power to nourish the spirit and enrich the heart with the wisdom of love. And, if in the past, they had experienced intermittent doubts about their ability to contend with the demands made upon them by clergy and laity, they now reflected a growing sense of confidence, which emanated from their conviction that they were following the right course in Canada, even though they had little doubt that there would be detours, halts, and back-trackings as they pursued it. This healthy attitude had gradually etched itself into their consciousness primarily as a result of Bishop Budka's efforts. Time and again he had strived to impress upon them their worth in the Church, through exhortations such as the following: 'The most esteemed group in our Canadian mission, besides our priesthood, is the Congregation of Sisters Servants of Mary Immaculate. Not only does it exemplify the flowering of religious life but it also is educating our youth, one of the most precious integral parts of our nation. For this reason, each sister must be cognizant of her vital position in our Church, and this consciousness should encourage her to make every effort to assure that a rich personal spiritual life and a continuous striving for holiness may blossom before God, our ultimate goal, and also before the world which, seeing this good, may be edified and glorify the Lord.'[129]

And so, as they stood on the threshold of another period in their history, anchored in the Christian hope that makes life worth living – and death worth dying – they did not experience the discomfort of uncertain tomorrows. The end of one quarter-century was simply the beginning of the next.

CHAPTER 6

A time to heal...

In April 1929 Pope Pius XI appointed Rev. Basil V. Ladyka, OSBM, to succeed Bishop Nicetas Budka. In the interval of one and a half years following the prelate's departure for Lviv, it had become painfully clear that, despite the competent administration of the diocese by Rev. P. Oleskiw, Ukrainian Catholics were becoming increasingly disheartened at being without a spiritual leader. With such sentiment prevailing it is little wonder that on July 14, 1929, few Edmontonians of the Ukrainian rite were immune to the excitement and emotion generated by the consecration of their bishop-elect at St Joseph's Cathedral by Bishop Constantine Bohachevsky, apostolic exarch of Philadelphia.

Sharing in their mood the local annalist thus described the scene for future generations of Sisters Servants: 'It seemed as if all of nature in its summer best was rejoicing with us on that glorious Sunday morning when, here in Canada, one of our pioneer missionaries was to be elevated to the episcopate. Participating in the ceremony were over three thousand persons including the great and the small of various nationalities and rites; dignitaries of church and state together with common labourers and farmers pressed into every inch of the vast cathedral, while others followed the ritual from outside the church.'[1]

Such enthusiasm sprang from a real affection for Bishop Ladyka, who was no stranger to Ukrainians in Canada or the United States. Having been educated at the Grand Seminary in Montreal, and having subsequently travelled a great deal in the course of his missionary career, he was well acquainted with his people as well as with the circumstances under which they lived and earned their daily bread. Likewise, a cordial friendship, fostered by many years of collaborative apostolic activity, existed between him and the Sisters Servants; in truth, he had followed the institute's spiritual and missionary evolvement with great interest ever since his ordination to the priesthood in 1912. It was, therefore, with an outpouring of feeling betokening their happiness that, within a week, the sisters in Winnipeg joined the clergy and laity in welcoming the bishop to their city and, on July 21, in taking part in his enthronization. As the annalist recounts it: 'The day was hot and sticky, but in the eagerness to catch at least one glimpse of the newly consecrated bishop, few in the throng paid much attention either to personal discomfort or fatigue."[2]

Following close upon the receptions that were held in his honour on both civic and parish levels, the normal grind of daily duty soon unceremoniously plunged the young prelate into the diverse affairs of his immense ordinariate. To a great extent, his tact, discretion, sense of humour, and easy informality were to assist him to grow quickly in his new job and to resolve key issues in swift and quiet ways that often escaped public notice. A case in point was his startling appointment on July 23 – just two days after his official installation – of Rev. S. Dydyk, OSBM, as the canonical visitor of the Sisters Servants.

Two months later, on September 22, the bishop unobtrusively detrained at Mundare, where he blessed the cornerstone of Canada's first Ukrainian hospital which, predictably enough, was being constructed by those same sisters. Certainly, this latest undertaking strongly suggested to the prelate as well as to the members of the institute that the new major superior, Sister Athanasia, was learning early in her administration that the affairs of the congregation called for many quick decisions. From clergy and laity alike came a continuous clamour for new foundations, but apparently only the sisters were expected to perform practical miracles by uncovering ways and means for implementing their numerous and varied requests, among which had been the proposal for a hospital.

In truth, however, Sister Ambrose, herself a nurse, had harboured the concept of such a project as early as 1924,[3] probably as a result of the sisters' home nursing experience – which had continued uninterrupted since 1903 – their ordeal with hundreds of patients during the influenza epidemic of 1918, and their frequent *kvestas* throughout the district, all of which had served to convince her that Mundare was one of the most neglected rural centres as far as medical services were concerned. This, perhaps, was due to the fact that in the period prior to and immediately following the First World War the basic introduction of health care had been largely a matter for private institutions, philanthropy, and voluntary development. Hence most of the few hospitals existing in farming communities had been established primarily by religious and charitable organizations in an endeavour to help meet the desperate needs of the sick poor.[4] Until this time, however, no one individual or group had given much consideration to the possibility of building a medical centre in the predominantly Ukrainian settlement of Mundare; neither, for that matter, had the Sisters Servants been able to do so. Yet for all this, the idea of a hospital was not as farfetched as many might have thought. Crowded out by all the other missionary enterprises of the 1920s, shimmered a vision, however muddled and vague, that at some barely foreseeable future the institute would find itself in a position to extend, beyond that of simple home nursing, Christ's mission of healing **the sick**.

But for the moment there was nothing much that Sister Ambrose could do except plan ahead. In August 1925 she enrolled Sister Theophilia Mary Melnyk and Sister Marion Anastasia Shewchuk in a three-year nursing course at the Grey Nun's hospital in St Boniface, Manitoba. Following her example two years later, her successor, Sister Athanasia, registered Sister Gertrude Lesiuk and Sister Macrina Anne Schab at the Misericordia School of Nursing in Edmonton, and sent Sister Naucratia Stephanie Mizun to St Mary's Academy in Winnipeg for a commercial course that would prepare her for a possible position as secretary-treasurer of any future hospital. In this action could be found a flicker of hope **and a** promise of better health services for Mundare.

It was certain, however, that Sister Athanasia and her council would make the final decision to carry out the project only after carefully weighing its apostolic pluses as well as the institute's already significant economic minuses. Obviously, its missionary worth must have tipped the scales, for in short order, in the spring of 1928, the blueprint of a small, eighteen-bed hospital was prepared by Mr C. Gordon of Vegreville; a campaign committee to raise a sum of $20,000 was organized by Rev. J. Tymochko, osBM; and four Sisters Servants were dispatched to solicit financial support throughout Alberta. 'Preliminary problems which have held up the construction of the long-awaited hospital at Mundare have finally been resolved,' declared the committee in its official appeal for funds. 'Thus this group, which has been selected to coordinate fund-raising efforts for the enterprise in various localities, has already begun its work. To start with, we are agreed that building materials must be procured immediately so that as soon as the ground has sufficiently thawed construction can get under way.'[5]

At the eleventh hour, however, a bare month before work on the building was scheduled to start, Sister Theophilia Melnyk and Sister Marion Shewchuk, who had just completed their nurse training at St Boniface, defected from the institute without even waiting for a dispensation from their vows. And in the wake of this stunning setback, the sisters sadly learned that Sister Naucratia Mizun, who had been happily involved in her secretarial studies, had developed tuberculosis.

Amazingly enough, Sister Athanasia seems to have been quite unperturbed by these perplexing happenings. In fact, except for the initial impact of surprise and dismay, as well as a sense of sorrow at the flippant manner in which it seemed that Sister Theophilia and Sister Marion had regarded their religious vocation, the unexpected desertions did not cause more than the slightest ripple within the institute. Feeling that the remaining members had every reason to be optimistic rather than apologetic about the recent turn of events, the major superior stated: 'Perhaps it is better that the chaff should have separated itself from the wheat; and although it seems that those who have left used the institute to obtain an education, God has already more than compensated for any losses we may have sustained by blessing us with many graces. For His bountiful goodness may He be ever glorified!'[6]

One of the 'graces' to which Sister Athanasia was referring was the admission into the novitiate of Sister Theodora Katherine McNally, an experienced secretary who already possessed the training which Sister Naucratia – owing to her death two years later at the age of twenty-one – was destined never to attain. And even though any official opening of a hospital would have to be delayed until May of 1930, pending the graduation of the two student nurses at Edmonton, none of the original plans were jeopardized by the adverse developments.

Soon afterwards the sisters were heartened by the enthusiastic response of local farmers, twenty-seven of whom took the first step toward the realization of a hospital on July 6, 1928, by levelling the knoll upon which it was to be erected. Indeed, the project seems to have caught the imagination of town and country folk for miles around, beginning with members of the clergy, and including almost everyone from young N. C. Strilchuk, MD (a former student at the sisters' school in Edmonton, who was to be the hospital's first physician) to the oldest residents; totally engrossed in the venture, people offered whatever time, effort, and money they possibly could.

But because the sisters were hampered by unrealistic cost estimates that ranged from the original sum of $12,000 to the final amount of $37,000, even such wholehearted public support failed, that autumn, to camouflage the hard reality that work on the building would have to cease until additional funds could be raised. All was silent at the construction site throughout the winter of 1928. And not until the sisters had taken upon themselves a loan of $18,000 did workers once more appear. Although many farmers had pledged monetary donations few had made good their promise; in the meantime the project had been rapidly draining existing funds. 'The sisters will have to work hard for many years before this debt is paid,'[7] sadly acknowledged Sister Athanasia. Moreover, the hospital administration would have to become adept at operating on a shoestring. With things in such a pass Sister Gertrude, Sister Macrina, and Sister Theodora had every reason to throw up their hands in despair; instead, all through the summer of 1930 they strived 'to set up and organize the Mundare General Hospital according to the specifications of the Alberta government and the American Hospital Association.'[8] And so effective would their management be that, within ten years, on the basis of a 'low mortality rate, no obstetrical deaths, low surgical death rate, ideal bookkeeping, and well-operated facilities,'[9] the small western institution was received as a member of the American Hospital Association. Above and beyond that, however, from the day of its official opening on May 29, 1930, the sisters unreservedly implemented the philosophy of Catholic hospitals: to recognize man's unique composition of body and soul, and hence to embrace in the concept of total care the physical, emotional, and spiritual needs of every patient.[10] Such an ideal deepened their insight into nursing, enabling them to discover that which made it indispensable for society, that which ranked it among the most praiseworthy of specifically human services, and that which made it deserving of the recognition of both the ill whom they had in their care and of the families who had these patients in their hearts. Then, too, the second-year novices, who assisted in the hospital a few hours each day, had an opportunity to perceive the high precision and great delicacy of action and feeling involved in the profession; to recognize the spirit and virtue of charity which lent to the nursing sisters' work an intelligence, a fervour, and a special merit; and to appreciate that nothing was more revealing, more worthy, and more sacred in life's natural plan than human suffering. As the well-known catechetical compiler and writer, Rev. A. Luhovy, later affirmed, the sisters in this small country hospital daily performed a multitude of compassionate deeds that must have delighted the heart of Christ the healer.[11]

A similar buoyancy also characterized a number of other ventures launched during this period, even though these compelled Sister Athanasia to tread her way nimbly through a maze of related problems, particularly those involving personnel. For although there was a lot of energy in the institute as a consequence of the steady stream of vocations, very little of it remained untapped, owing to the multiplicity of apostolic tasks that each sister was called upon to perform.

Understandably, therefore, the unexpected communication from Bishop Ladyka, which reached Sister Athanasia barely one month before the commencement of the 1929–30 scholastic year, and which stated that 'the director of St Joseph's College at Yorkton requests two sisters to assume the management of the school's food services,'[12] not only caught the major superior by surprise but also occasioned no small degree of dismay, since most staff placements for the coming school year had already been completed. The move to procure sisters for the college was, however, interpreted as a step toward keeping it open to Ukrainian students during the depression, for few of the boys were able to pay much of their residential and educational fees. It was agreed that through wise food planning the religious could help to arrest the school's current downhill financial plunge. That, it turned out, was why the sisters' response was swift and decisive. Thus, when the students registered at the college in September they found Sister Augustina Hawryliuk and Sister Constance Eudoxia Malko directing the culinary department; within a month they also welcomed Sister Paula Dzygolyk who had come to help relieve the heavy work load.

Actually, assuming responsibility for the management of the food services department of an educational institution was not a novel undertaking for the Sisters Servants, since they were already performing a similar service at the Basilian Fathers' novitiate and scholasticate, which had been opened in Mundare in the autumn of 1923; in addition, they were soon to be engaged in housekeeping duties at Bishop Ladyka's residence in Winnipeg. Fortunately for the institutions concerned, society in general was still not as profession-conscious as it would be in the latter half of the century; consequently, neither were the sisters. For this reason religious women did not look upon institutional housekeeping or cooking chores as having little or no effect upon the life of society or the Church simply because these were 'unprofessional' or because they afforded little direct contact with the laity. On the contrary, because of their profound consciousness that they were women who had made a public consecration through their religious vows, the sisters involved in domestic duties looked beyond the pots and pans, the sink and stove, and saw their every act in the kitchen as one bearing an ecclesial character — especially through their vow of obedience. They saw their work as a living testimony of their love, a proof to the whole world of their desire to adore God at every moment of the day; hence they saw their actions as acts of worship, much akin to the liturgical public worship of the Church, even though not in the same sense. This outlook fostered a broad vision of their role in the Mystical Body, encouraged them to offer a constant, genuine service, and sustained them in the physically exacting duties that greeted them at the dawn of seven days of every week.

Almost surely this is why, at the close of that first year at the school, the Yorkton annalist could report that 'the Christian Brothers are very pleased with the sisters' management of their department, especially from the viewpoint of cleanliness, efficiency, and economy.'[13] In a similar vein, the historian of St Joseph's College, writing in 1955, and describing the contribution of the Sisters Servants, stated: 'Many of those Sisters, particularly Sister Paul, can rightfully share in the glory that belongs to the College. Their service will always be remembered by both students and staff. From the year 1929 to 1953, when the Sisters were removed by their superiors due to the shortage of Sisters in their own Congregation, they shared in the joys, sorrows and labors of the Brothers.'[14] More than anything else, therefore, it seems that the service of those sisters assigned to domestic work was one of interest and concern that not only helped the institution involved but also enabled these religious to grasp the fulness of their life and the apostolic dimensions of their being.

In the meantime, at Saskatoon, Sister Josepha Bilan and Sister Appolonia Anne Dzubinsky had opened a hostel for girls who came from rural areas to enrol in the local high schools, the teachers' college, or the university. The city, lying midway between Winnipeg and Edmonton, was not only the geographical and commercial centre of the northern part of the province, but was also its educational capital, being the seat of the provincial Teachers' College and the University of Saskatchewan. Hence the new residence on Avenue E was unquestionably a windfall for Ukrainian Catholic girls seeking a higher education, since up to now, owing to their difficulty in renting accommodation at prices they could afford, many students ended up light housekeeping in musty garrets where they shivered through January and sweltered through June.[15] Moreover, those enrolled in the city's high schools usually found themselves entirely on their own for the first time in their lives; homesickness and loneliness were their frequent and dangerous companions.

It appears that it was Bishop Budka who had first become concerned with their plight, having gained an insight into the situation through his periodic visits to Saskatoon. In the late autumn of 1927, just prior to his departure for Rome, he triggered a discussion on the subject during a meeting with Sister Athanasia, at which time he urged her to provide a home for these girls where their educational and social pursuits would be supplemented by a homelike and peaceful atmosphere and where their Christian values would be supported by personal prayer and by the example and guidance of the sisters. Such a project was indeed worthy of consideration, but, truth to tell, it gave Sister Athanasia cold comfort. She experienced an initial reluctance to commit the institute to the proposal, not because of a difference of opinion concerning the merits of a hostel, but rather because of an empty purse. As she wryly observed: 'Having requested that we establish a students' residence in Saskatoon, His Excellency forgot to ask, "Do you have the funds necessary to purchase a house?" '[16] Nevertheless, untimely as the plan may have seemed from the economic standpoint, and ill-inclined as Sister Athanasia may have been to rush precipitously into another costly venture, she embraced the idea as though it had been her own when she saw that, despite her personal misgivings, it was the express wish of the ordinary that she try to implement the plan.

Before long she was waist-deep in the discouraging task of trying to purchase a suitable building in a convenient location as cheaply as possible. Her spirits seem to have reached a doleful low ebb, for she wrote: 'We are now depending solely upon Divine Providence for help because human assistance is nowhere to be found.'[17] Her dispiriting search was abruptly interrupted by an unexpected summons to attend to an urgent matter in Montreal. And all the while she journeyed eastward the Saskatoon project lay both heavy and hopeful in her heart. She decided to share her troubles with Brother André, that great devotee of St Joseph.[18] 'This saintly man listened sympathetically as I explained my difficulties,' she related later, 'and then promised to join me in asking St Joseph to intercede in this matter. Fortunately, St Joseph heard our prayer, for shortly after my return to Saskatoon Mr W. O'Regan, a lawyer and trusted friend, who had recently arrived from Yorkton, helped us to purchase a large house for the sum of $8,800.'[19] And so, almost overnight, Sister Athanasia's lament about no 'human assistance' had been invalidated. And there were other friends: Mr J. Doherty of Winnipeg, who lent the sisters the $5,000 which permitted them to meet a portion of the building's cost; the Sisters of Our Lady of Sion, who shared their bread with Sister Josepha and Sister Appolonia until they were able to provide for themselves; the local pastor, Rev. M. Olenchuk, whose unstinting assistance was a boon during the first few burdensome months.[20]

In the end, the hostel proved to be a vital foundation. On the one hand, it afforded the religious an opportunity to work with young women from scattered parts of the province, as well as with the children and adults of the city and country parishes; on the other, it became a convenient house of studies for a substantial number of sisters who took advantage of the pedagogical training and university courses offered at Saskatoon. For her part, Sister Athanasia liked to remind the sisters that they had no one to blame for all these blessings but St Joseph.[21]

Astonishingly enough, the anxiety and hesitation that had marked Sister Athanasia's approach to the Saskatoon foundation seems to have evaporated in the autumn of 1928 when another convent was opened in Dauphin, Manitoba. That picturesque little town, lying in a rich agricultural valley 122 miles northwest of Portage la Prairie, had become the scene of intense religious activity in July of the same year. Rev. M. Pelech, whose manifold duties in half a dozen colonies in this part of the province prevented him from celebrating the Divine Liturgy or ministering to his people's needs in any one centre more than once a month, had begged Sister Athanasia to send two sisters here to supplement his work through a programme of religious and Ukrainian language instruction. It didn't occur to him that he would soon have a religious revival on his hands.

For what had instantly intrigued Sister Lubov Chawrona and Sister Epiphany Stephanie Svoboda about their assignment was its potential for a diversified apostolate. For instance, during the first religious service they had attended in the parish church, when it was obvious that only a handful of parishioners, mostly elderly, any longer participated in the Liturgy, they had sensed a generally apathetic attitude toward things religious. On the spot they had decided to expand their catechetical and language programme to include adults as well as children. For they believed that a greater literacy in the crucial areas of religion and rite would result in a deeper understanding of, and love for, Christ and His Church. Hence their aim, in all aspects of their teaching, was to bring their people to God.

Starting the first day the parish hall was in use from morning until evening. Religious instruction and language study, held in regular all-day classes, were followed immediately by extracurricular activities. Chief among these were the junior and senior choirs, organized by the sisters at once because their years of experience had revealed singing to be one of the easiest and most enjoyable ways for various age groups to become familiar with the Divine Liturgy. To assure that choral work would be continued after their departure in August, they trained a few of the musically gifted youngsters and adults to direct their respective groups. Most important of all, by planning Sunday services and by leading the people in prayer whenever Father Pelech was absent, they showed them how they could worship as a parish when they were without a priest. Wrote Sister Lubov: 'We met in the church each Sunday afternoon to pray the rosary, sing hymns, and "Moleben," and to study scripture; usually, too, one of us presented a homily on the Gospel of the day.'[22]

In the light of a renewed interest in things spiritual, it is natural that even as they left Dauphin at the end of six weeks the sisters had to promise to return. And they kept their word. Before school commenced in September Sister Lubov and Sister Vitalia Katherine Perepeliuk were back to establish a permanent mission. They occupied a six-room house rented for them by the parish, signed a contract with the church committee to teach night school classes for a monthly salary of $25.00,[23] then drew up their timetable. Included in their schedule, besides their teaching and parish responsibilities, was an apostolate to which the sisters gave top priority. Explained Sister Lubov: 'At the local hospital, which we visited almost every day, we assumed the role of interpreters between patients and medical staff, since few of the older Ukrainians knew more than a smattering of English. And perhaps we did bring a measure of comfort to the sick, especially to the dying, for many gave up their spirit clasping our hands and whispering a prayer.'[24] What is more, three evenings of each week were devoted to choir rehearsals, while on three others thirteen married women – the oldest of whom was sixty-five years of age, and all of whom were illiterate to the degree that they were unable to write their name in any language – were taught the A,B,Cs in the convent parlour.[25]

Not long afterward the sisters' strenuous efforts paid off even in a material way, for in March 1929, using a $500 parish gift as the down payment on a weatherworn house costing $1,500, they were able to move into a convent of their own – even though internally and externally it was in dire need of a facelifting. This was soon attended to by the indefatigable architect, Rev. P. Ruh, OMI, who chivalrously volunteered his services. As for the furnishings, reported the chronicler, 'essential articles were purchased only after we had earned some extra money from our needlework, floral arrangements, or the odd bazaar.'[26] And so, without much fuss, the sisters settled in Dauphin to prolong the apostolate that they had so unexpectedly established.

A parallel occurrence transpired in August 1931 at Regina, the capital city of Saskatchewan. As the annalist recounts it: 'During the course of a summer school in catechetics, the people pressed the teaching sisters to remain permanently in order to organize and direct a night school for their children, most of whom were attending public schools.'[27] This entreaty created a whole new set of problems for Sister Taida Letawsky and Sister Nicholas Petrushkewich, who, as much as they disliked to see a month's instruction potentially lost for lack of adequate follow-up, could not afford to stay on in Regina. For, to put it bluntly, they possessed little more than just enough money for their return fare to Ituna.

In a real sense, however, the sisters had little choice – they knew that the children needed them. 'Most of the pupils attending the course were being compelled to do so by their parents,' lamented the chronicler; 'they themselves, however, desired to dissociate themselves entirely from anything Ukrainian.'[28] Hence it was not the children's ignorance but their attitude that stung the sisters most painfully. Perhaps it was a sense of inferiority that was causing these children to rebel against the cultural background of their parents, or perhaps they were being impelled toward a hasty assimilation which generally robs second generation immigrants of the finer elements of old world culture and gives them but the veneer of Canadian life.[29] But whatever the cause, any move the sisters could make to counteract this negative way of thinking, feeling, and acting, even if only 'by motivating their pupils to learn and to hold in high regard the language, religious rite, literature, history, and culture of their forefathers,'[30] could be interpreted as a meaningful step toward narrowing the cultural gap that was threatening a sharp cleavage between one generation and another. From this viewpoint, the idea that the Sisters Servants should accept the challenge to attack the problem in earnest by settling in the 'queen' city was perfectly sensible, if not exceptionally heroic.

The notion of such a mission shifted rapidly from the realm of fantasy to the realm of distinct possibility when two days after her return to her convent at Ituna Sister Taida was authorized to open a house in Regina. 'Since the people were very reluctant to see them leave, it seems that the sisters had carried on a praiseworthy apostolate,' stated the annalist; 'and now, with the blessing of our superiors, Sister Taida and Sister Veronica [Melnyk] are leaving on September 14 to prolong their work among Ukrainian youth.'[31]

In short order, for $15 a month, Sister Taida rented a hut – a dismal excuse for a house – which had been abandoned ten years before; then, forming a two-woman scrub corps, the sisters effected a compulsory, swift clean-up. But the rent had chewed into their savings, leaving them with exactly $7; besides a house they had nothing. Recounted Sister Taida: 'Our poverty forbade us to buy a stitch of furniture, and therefore our house was as bare as Mother Hubbard's cupboard until a friend of ours delivered a stove and chair that he had salvaged from the clutter at the city dump. Nevertheless,' she added, 'we could have fared much worse.'[32] Despite their positive thinking, however, the sisters had no illusions about how hard daily living would be. At the same time, they were glad that they had set the stage for the missionary activity of their institute in still another centre of the Canadian west.

Before too long the sisters at every mission were fighting tooth and nail to keep their institutions from folding up. For if the general outlook in the west had been disturbing immediately following the economic débâcle of 1929, it became even more disheartening in the early 1930s. Throughout the country, and especially on the prairies, the impact of the depression was being felt – in the continuing falling prices for farm products, in the swelling ranks of the unemployed in towns and cities, and in the growing 'scarcity of money' reflected in a generally declining purchasing power amidst a psychological atmosphere of uncertainty and doubt that seemed to pervade the very fabric of Canadian society. In addition to the unprece- dented low price of wheat (fifty cents per bushel during December 1930), there occurred the climatic phenomenon of less than average rainfall and moisture-sucking winds that was turning the prairies into arid wastes. Canada, as a primary producer, was very hard hit. So, too, was the Con- gregation of Sisters Servants, saddled in the west with a crippling debt and with the grave responsibility of feeding, clothing, and educating scores of orphans in their children's home at Ituna as well as in each of their board- ing schools.

In the face of this bleak scene the sisters desperately resorted to any number of ways to provide for their charges. They earned a little from sewing liturgical vestments, making floral arrangements for churches, preparing hot meals for the crowds attending annual pilgrimages in Mun- dare, Yorkton, and Ituna (which most often meant cooking through the night preceding the feast day), selling religious articles, organizing annual bazaars, canvassing from door-to-door for used clothing, and altering these to fit their youngsters – ordinarily sewing late into the night after the scheduled work of the day was done. Only in this way, by sheer hard work, were they able to operate school and orphanage and even hospital from one day to the next. And during these lean years, in the chronicles of each of these institutions, the names of two benefactors appear time and again; namely, that of Rev. M. Pelech, a former student of St Nicholas School, and Mr J. Doherty of Winnipeg. One, a Catholic priest of the Eastern rite, and the other, a Catholic layman of the Latin rite, were both motivated to extend a helping hand to the sisters by nothing less than a truly Christlike charity. And the profound appreciation of the Sisters Servants for their occasional monetary offerings, or the 'twenty pairs of children's shoes,' or 'the box of the only toys our children have ever received,' is reflected in the prayer with which the local annalists ordinarily concluded their entries concerning these benefactions. The following excerpt, regarding a gift from Father Pelech, is typical of many others: 'May God, who sees how much we need this help for the children in our care, bless this good priest for his noble kindness to us.'[88]

And the sisters, who permitted themselves only the minimum in food and rest, continued to pay a high price for their service to others – the price of lives. For as before, in the seven years between 1927 and 1934, the institute buried on the average one sister a year, except that in this period, death – still resulting mainly from tuberculosis – claimed a younger group, averaging twenty-two years of age.[34]

Through the years the sisters' coordination of their spiritual, physical, and material resources together with their flexibility to adjust to changing situations and trends in Canada had given them a commanding edge over any other Ukrainian organization in the founding of vital institutions for their people. Along the way, too, a corresponding rapid increase in membership after the First World War had helped to staff each mission as it was opened. By the same token, however, the sudden influx of postulants had resulted in the institute's swiftly becoming top-heavy with sisters who were without a high school education, for superiors had taken Archbishop Langevin's advice to 'accept also those girls without an academic background or with little training because they can render great apostolic service as well as provide other members with the time for study.'[35] By 1925, therefore, the few teachers and nurses already educated by the congregation formed only a small minority of professionals. But even as early as this it was obvious that, if the teaching sisters, especially, were to function fruitfully, appropriate amendments to the constitutions would have to be adopted; having been written for a European community its only educational references applied to teachers in day nurseries.

Bishop Budka, for one, was convinced that unless implementations regarding the sisters' apostolate in Canadian schools were enforced immediately, the ranks of the Sisters Servants in this country could readily be riven by factional fissures arising primarily from a somewhat blurred understanding by many members of the professional responsibilities of each teaching sister. For already, 'on the one hand, the teachers believed that insufficient allowance was being made for the time required for study, correction of pupils' work, and lesson preparation, while on the other, the non-teaching members seemed to think that the teachers took too many liberties, did not assist sufficiently at community exercises, and did not bear their share of community burdens.'[36] That in fact is why, in the spring of 1925, the bishop had decided to 'formulate directives regarding the teaching sisters, which will be adopted at the nearest chapter of affairs,'[37] and had, therefore, requested each religious involved in education 'to state conscientiously, in writing, her personal observations regarding the existing difficulties, and to make suitable recommendations based on facts and her teaching experience, in order that instruction within the schools administered by the congregation as well as the general welfare of the sisters can be improved.'[38] Apparently the resolutions adopted at the chapter, held in Yorkton in 1926,[39] had not gone far enough, for a year later Rev. H. Workman, OFM, who had been requested by Archbishop H. O'Leary of Edmonton to discuss this matter with the local community, echoed Bishop Budka's thoughts by pinpointing the constitutions as the cause for any current disquiet among the sisters. 'The Rule,' he explained, 'was drawn up for Community Life in Eastern Europe, where other conditions prevailed and very different works were undertaken; therefore, if the Sisters here in Canada are to teach in the Public or Separate Schools, such provisions as would meet the requirements of the teaching sisters should be incorporated in the Rules. This would remove any suspicions on the part of the other Sisters that the teachers are not faithful to the Rules and Spirit of the Congregation.'[40] His was a timely appraisal, since it came at a moment when the members were accepting positions within the public school system of Alberta. Unfortunately, the entire matter seems to have been shelved, probably because of Bishop Budka's unforeseen departure from Canada.

Undeterred by their unsolved problems the teaching sisters moved to broaden their educational mission. In September 1927 Sister Ignatia Butryn and Sister Theresa Melnyk took charge of a new two-room public school at Brody, Alberta, about five miles northeast of Mundare, which had a registration of predominantly Ukrainian Catholic and Greek Orthodox pupils.[41] Moreover, by 1932, Sister Monica Mary Mantyka was the principal and teacher at Podola School, Sister Emmanuel Mary Dzubinsky was teaching at Koluz School near Chipman, Sister Joan Mary Magriy had joined Sister Ignatia at Brody, and Sister Benigna Mary Skaluba was teaching at Oleskow.

And since all of these public schools were situated within a radius of between five to ten miles of Mundare, each Friday afternoon, weather permitting, the sisters walked or, by paying a local farmer, were driven by whatever vehicle was available – wagon or buggy or automobile – to the novitiate house where, on Saturday and Sunday, they enjoyed the luxury of participating in the celebration of the Divine Liturgy, of praying in the presence of the Blessed Sacrament, and of refreshing their spirits in the company of a large group of religious.

During the week they lived in the one-, two-, or three-room teacherages provided by the local school boards; these were usually log or frame huts built beside the schoolhouse, in predominantly bush country. And as might be expected, in their daily round of occupations within and without the school, they came under the skeptical scrutiny of Catholic and Orthodox parents and trustees, for never before had sisters of any nationality or rite taught in these schools. So numerous were their 'extra' undertakings, however, that there was little time to worry about how others were evaluating their efforts. For instance, recalls Sister Monica Mantyka, 'at the conclusion of regular classes, we were involved in teaching religion and Ukrainian, in organizing and moderating the sodality and altar boys' club, in directing a choir, and in instructing older children and adults in preparation for their reception of baptism and other sacraments.'[42] And whenever, at the request of both Catholic and Orthodox families, they extended their teaching role to include the counselling and guidance of youth and adults of both religious affiliations, the sisters managed to relieve and warm the tense and frigid relationship stemming from the deeply rooted prejudice that often existed between the two groups in this pre-ecumenical era.

Finally, their salaries were instrumental in relieving some of the withering financial pressure being experienced by the sisters at the convent-novitiate-school at Mundare, as the economic recession dragged on. And although St Joseph's School had been academically upgraded in 1932 by the inclusion of grades six to nine, being a private institution it was as helpless to support itself as was the novitiate. Thus even when, in 1932, the wages of those sisters employed by public school boards were slashed from $150 to $60 a month, their small but steady income remained Mundare's material salvation.[43]

*   *   *

For the moment, no reasonable Sister Servant in the country would contend that all things in her institute were perfect, without flaw; for none was so naïve as to believe that where people lived and worked together, even if they were religious women, all conflict could be banished and idyllic harmony substituted. But imperfect though it was, and fallible humans that the sisters were, their congregation did provide them with an opportunity to live more profoundly and to labour more consciously, as they climbed toward maturity in Christ. The European sisters, for their part, believed that the spiritual awareness and the bond of fraternal charity which nurtured the life and the varied apostolic enterprises of their members in Europe, Canada, and Brazil could be further strengthened by the formation of a cohesive religious organism.

Somewhat unexpectedly, the first step in this direction was taken by the Sacred Congregation for the Oriental Churches in Rome on May 18,

1928, when it appointed Rev. Joseph Schrijvers, CSSR, as the apostolic visitor of the thirty-six-year-old institute, and authorized him to convoke a general chapter. In so doing, the Church inaugurated a course of action that eventually reversed the direction of diocesan jurisdictional fragmentation, paved the way for productive dialogue among the three groups of Sisters Servants, and ultimately shaped them into a vigorous, centralized sisterhood.

Father Schrijvers, who was to play a key role in helping the sisters to take their initial tentative steps towards that goal, was one of the first Belgian Redemptorists to change his religious rite, learn the Ukrainian language, and on August 21, 1913, begin missionary work among the Ukrainian people in western Ukraine. Highly esteemed by Metropolitan Sheptytsky and other members of the Ukrainian Catholic hierarchy for his zealous efforts on behalf of their countrymen, he was now being called upon to bring his authentic spirituality, energy, and imagination to bear in his guidance of the religious women confided to his direction by the Church.[44]

As might be expected, Father Schrijvers' assignment to summon the Sisters Servants to a general chapter was bound to provoke a thorough review by him of the position, within the institute, of the sisters in Canada and Brazil. Readily recognizing that the constitutions had continued to be a bond between them and Europe – thin at best but symbolically vital – he sought clarification of their status from the Holy See. On October 6, 1928, he was informed that these sisters were indeed members of the same institute with the right to be represented at the forthcoming chapter by their own delegation.[45]

Perhaps unavoidably, the Canadian community read Father Schrijvers's first letter dated October 29, 1928, with mixed feelings. In it, he notified them of his appointment, explained their canonical position within the institute, and extended an invitation to a general chapter to be held in Lviv on May 9, 1929 – adding, however, that he understood their difficulty in sending delegates, owing to the distance and cost of the journey.[46] Even those who, like Sister Ambrose and Sister Athanasia, had originally been members of the institute in Ukraine, and who had always entertained sentiments of affection for and a filial loyalty toward the European motherhouse, were somewhat taken aback by the possibility that, after more than a decade of unquestioned control over their internal and external affairs, they might now be required by a chapter to relinquish some of their autonomy. Those who had been born or raised in Canada, and who had entered the congregation after 1927 when it was already a self-reliant diocesan entity, found the idea of any loss of authority over their own affairs somewhat obnoxious. Thus a negative reaction to Father Schrijvers's communication was swift and predictable; the essence of the resolution advocating severance of all ties with Europe, which had been roundly defeated at the chapter held in Winnipeg in 1921,[47] was now incorporated into an unofficial but emphatic declaration that began to be heard rather frequently in almost every convent: 'We do not desire to be united with the European motherhouse.'[48]

In actual fact, however, the Canadian community had never formally cut its ties with the original congregation from which it had sprung, and hence still remained – as the Sacred Oriental Congregation had pointed out – a member of that institute. None the less, the strong emphasis on decentralized decision-making that prevailed, indicated that an examination and mutual discussion of the Canadian position was imperative if harmony were to be maintained; moreover, the logical religious body to review this matter was the general chapter, scheduled to convene the following spring. Unfortunately, the travel expenses involved and the required presence in Canada of Sister Athanasia, because of the multiple problems arising from the current hospital construction at Mundare, prevented any Canadian delegates from journeying to Lviv.[49] These reasons were accepted by Father Schrijvers as a sufficient excuse for non-representation at the meeting. In his reply, however, the visitor made it clear that in the area of authority he considered Sister Athanasia to be responsible to the European major superior, for he declared: 'I shall inform your major superior Sister Veronica [Mary Gargil], and the chapter, of your decision.'[50]

The same point was again stressed when, on May 15, 1929, four days after the conclusion of the chapter, Sister Veronica Gargil, whom the delegates had selected as major superior, informed the Canadian sisters of the election results, and then added: 'We are certain that you, dear sisters in Christ, will lend us your prayerful support and obedience, thereby easing the weighty burden of our office.'[51] Recognizing that the institute was travelling a narrow path between unity and separation, Sister Veronica did not intend to be diverted from her intention of bringing the sisters together. In her straightforward manner she established direct contact and thus indirectly reminded them that the communities in Europe, Canada, and Brazil constituted one and the same moral body of religious women who shared a common heritage and observed similar constitutions. It was clear that if this kind of relationship were to be permanently cemented the Canadian community for one would have to sacrifice a great degree of its self-sufficiency which for so long it had simply taken for granted.

Endowed with a great sense of discretion, Sister Veronica foresaw that splinters and hard feelings would persist so long as the constitutions lacked the approbation of the Holy See. Only definitive approval by the Church would halt further deletions or additions either by the sisters themselves or the local ordinaries, especially in mission territories. In Canada, for instance, some changes had been made during Bishop Budka's tenure of office, and still others had recently been introduced by Bishop Ladyka. On January 28, 1930, the prelate had sent to all Sisters Servants in his diocese a number of new directives, which he had said were based on the visitation report that had been recently filed by Father Dydyk. These rules, he had specified, were to be 'immediately put into practice without any discussion of them by the council of the institute.'[52] The prelate believed that his implementations, which substantially broadened the scope of the sisters' apostolate in education and health services, were 'necessary to meet requirements here in Canada.'[53]

Four months later he received the following communication from the Sacred Oriental Congregation: 'The Little Servants of Mary Immaculate, of the Ruthenian rite, who carry on their apostolate within your diocese and who, until now, have been an institute of diocesan right, have made a request to become a congregation of pontifical right; for this purpose they have submitted their constitutions for approval.'[54] The bishop was asked to submit any relevant observations concerning the Sisters Servants in his diocese. In his reply Bishop Ladyka summarized the sisters' missionary work, listed his own recent additions to their constitutions, and concluded with the following recommendation: 'According to my humble opinion, it shall be better if the Sisters in Canada will have no actual connection with the Sisters in Galicia: *de facto* the Ruthenian Sisters in Canada elect their own superior independently of the Sisters in Galicia. The Superior General in Galicia has nothing to do with the Sisters in Canada. The circumstances in Canada are different from those in Galicia, and the work must also be different. The Ruthenian Catholic Ordinariate of Canada shall be very grateful if the Holy See will deign to approve the Constitutions of the Ruthenian Sisters Servants of the Immaculate Conception of the Blessed Virgin Mary in Canada.'[55]

Bishop Ladyka's contention that the sisters in Canada were entirely independent of those in Europe emphasized the fact that before the revised constitutions, submitted to the Holy See by Sister Veronica, could be approved, the question of unity within the institute as a whole would have to be further clarified and accepted by the sisters and their local ordinaries in each country. Sister Athanasia and her council were therefore asked by Sister Veronica to affirm that the Canadian sisters desired 'to be united with the motherhouse in Europe; that is, with the chief governing body of the congregation.'[56] This was a rather startling request, confessed Sister Anthanasia, 'since, before this, none of us had ever been specifically asked whether we wanted to be unified, nor had we ever officially stated that we did not desire such unification. Moreover, we had never been officially informed that the major superior of the European sisters was also our highest superior; the respect and deference which have characterized our relations with Europe have stemmed from the fact that it was there that our congregation was born.'[57] It seems that even Sister Athanasia had failed to recognize that the clarification of their status by the Sacred Oriental Congregation, as communicated to them through Father Schrijvers, had been an official reminder that they were still Sisters Servants of Mary Immaculate and not something else. And this fact was confirmed within six months after Bishop Ladyka had sent his report to Rome, for in its reply the Sacred Oriental Congregation stated that 'It is not possible for the Little Servants of Mary Immaculate of Canada to be entirely independent of the same sisters in Galicia, and, at the same time, to constitute a part of that same institute. It is clear that if the sisters in Canada do not intend to remain united to those in Galicia, they not only cannot keep its name but must also change their religious garb.'[58]

But understanding the manifold problems involved, and interested in bridging vast geographical distances and a long-standing communication gap, the Holy See drafted a plan designed to avoid a cleavage and to heal internal differences by granting a degree of autonomy to each geographical region within a centralized structure through the formation of a 'province' for each area. As the chief pillar of the proposal, explained the Sacred Oriental Congregation, a province would enable the sisters in Canada to be governed by their own vicaress general, 'and thus to maintain a link with the motherhouse. This could also be done for the sisters in Brazil and Argentina on the one hand, and for those in Europe on the other; in this way the congregation would be divided into three provinces dependent upon the motherhouse in Galicia.'[59] Whether the sisters would see the proposal as one which would serve the real interests of their lives and works in Canada, and whether they would support it, remained uncertain; but each professed sister in Canada was given an opportunity to express her opinion through a referendum.

Inevitably, those members for whom the complexities of the issue were as frustrating as the uncertainties assumed a negative position; thus, before the vote was taken – and to the common chagrin of the sisters pressing for an affirmative stand in the matter – they presented the Holy See with a memorandum outlining the reasons for their opposition.[60] In general they feared that their constitutional amendments, which had been based on Canadian conditions, might not be considered important by the European community, and hence be either changed or, worse still, completely omitted from the revised rule; they feared that key positions in their Canadian council and local convents would be held by superiors born and raised in Europe, who might fail to understand the educational, social, and cultural background of their Canadian counterparts; they feared that in some of their external modifications or changes as, for example, those relating to their religious garb (the Canadian sisters wore a black rather than blue scapular, a ring, and a full-length cape after final profession), they would be required to conform to the standards and customs set in Europe.[61] And their troubled mood, that plainly arose from considerations beyond the purely religious, was becoming pervasive.

For his part, after having considered all aspects of the situation, Archbishop O'Leary informed the apostolic delegate that 'the Canadian branch should be kept independent, at least in regard to its own administration, and above all, financially.'[62]

In April 1931, in the depth of her own soul, each of the eighty-seven sisters eligible to vote began the lonely task of deciding how to cast her ballot. Before her were three propositions: (1) I am in favour of union with the congregation in Galicia, and of retaining the same constitutions, but with the addition of directives proper to Canada; (2) I am not in favour of union; (3) I am not in favour of union, but I desire that we retain the same constitutions.[63] The results, which were never released to the membership, indicate that the sisters, having weighed the risks, had found them acceptable, for 67 per cent of the total vote advocated union.[64]

Perhaps the most striking feature of the results was the revelation of the confusion that still surrounded the issue for 33 per cent of the sisters, who were still desirous of severing all European ties. And, in truth, the web of uncertainty that enveloped one-third of the community could not be unravelled by taking a vote, or by simply pretending that it did not exist. Father Schrijvers recognized this immediately upon his arrival in Canada in December 1931, for he encountered a troubled, uneasy sense of deepening concern. Therefore, in each convent he visited, he endeavoured to underscore the global implications of union for the institute as well as for Canada specifically. Then, too, he acquainted the sisters with those in Europe by vividly describing their life and apostolate; by pointing out that little besides local conditions differentiated them; and by emphasizing their common interests and their common concern for the glory of God, the good of His Church, and the welfare of His people. Wrote the Yorkton chronicler: 'Father's answers to our many questions were sincere and so clear that we recognized as never before what a great good union would be for us and for our entire institute. For one thing, we in Canada have acquired a parochial outlook, with each convent being more concerned with its missionary well-being rather than with that of the entire congregation. From unity we would derive a solidarity and strength that we have never quite managed to achieve alone. Many of us are therefore saddened by the thought that perhaps our votes, if they have been predominantly negative, may deprive us of an opportunity to reap the benefits about which Father Schrijvers spoke.'[65] In this way, having explored the issues, part of the opposing group was backing away from its original position, and thus the storm over the entire affair was giving way to sweetness and light. But because the results of the referendum had not been released to the members, they were left to wonder for over a year about what the ruling of the Holy See would be in the matter.

Curiously, though, news of the decision reached the sisters through an unofficial source, for during their annual retreat, which had commenced on August 19, 1932, their director, Rev. B. Kamenecky, OSBM, read to the assembled community the following article which had appeared in the newspaper *Nova Zoria* (*New Star*), published in Lviv on August 11, 1932: 'We have just learned from a reliable source that the Holy See has granted definitive approbation to the Congregation of Sisters Servants of Mary Immaculate, and has also sanctioned their constitutions for a trial period of seven years. This is the first institute of religious women within our Church to receive the explicit approval of the Holy See. The Congregation of Sisters Servants is comprised not only of its houses in western Ukraine, but also of those in Carpatho-Ukraine, Yugoslavia, Canada, and Brazil. After the decree of approbation is officially announced, a general chapter, at which all of these areas will be represented, shall be convoked for the purpose of electing a superior general and council. This chapter will also decide upon a location for the generalate. Thus, within forty years after its erection, the Congregation of Sisters Servants has grown to be a fruitful tree, for in that short time, not only has it introduced its charitable apostolate into each of our eparchies, but through its dedicated work among us, has called forth the love and esteem of our people as well. We offer the sisters our sincere congratulations.'[66]

'This announcement,' revealed the annalist, 'was received jubilantly by the majority of our members, especially by those who, from the institute's earliest beginnings, had witnessed the marvellous way in which Divine Providence had assisted it both in Europe and on this continent. The sisters had lived through more than one hardship and had borne the brunt of more than one derogatory remark from individuals who took it upon themselves to prophesy that our congregation would never receive the Church's approbation. But humans can never thwart God's will!'[67]

In a letter dated August 13, 1932, Father Schrijvers officially notified the sisters that on July 27, 1932, the Church had raised their congregation to the dignity of a papal institute;[68] he also confirmed that its constitutions had been approved for a trial period of seven years. In addition, continued their visitor, 'the Holy See has asked me to inform the religious that all houses of the institute (including those in Canada and Brazil) are united, and come under the jurisdiction of one general council. For this reason they cannot convene provincial chapters of election; such a chapter, if summoned, would be invalid. The sisters are to await further instructions from the Holy See, which I shall forward as soon as they are issued.'[69]

Immediately, in the chapels of their convents, schools, orphanage, and hospital, the sisters gathered to sing the *Te Deum*, endeavouring through this hymn of thanksgiving to express their gratitude to God for His goodness, manifested to them through the singular act of His Church.

Bishop Ladyka, upon being informed of the news, conveyed his thanks to the Sacred Oriental Congregation for the honour accorded the young institute, and expressed the hope that, since 'all the provinces and homes are united under one Directory, the sisters will work efficaciously for the glory of God and the salvation of souls.'[70]

Still another mark of the Church's esteem was the private audience with Pope Pius XI granted to Sister Veronica Gargil, now acknowledged as the highest superior of the Institute of Sisters Servants. In his paternal solicitude this kindly father of the whole Church expressed his satisfaction and joy that her institute had successfully passed its trial period and had been esteemed worthy to become an institute of papal right.[71] Truly, Father Schrijvers exclaimed, 'anyone who for one moment considers the present status of your congregation will see concrete proof of God's benevolence toward it.'[72]

The newly approved constitutions were to come into effect on September 21, 1933, from which day all members of the institute in all countries would be obliged to observe them. But since, inevitably, some misunderstanding arose within the Canadian community regarding the section dealing with the religious garb, Father Schrijvers informed the sisters that 'even though the Canadian Sisters Servants of Mary Immaculate are obliged to conform to the new constitutions as of September 21, 1933, they may, until the general chapter is held, wear the rosary, ring, and cape as has been the custom.'[73]

Desiring to bring to a speedy and satisfactory conclusion the centralization of the institute, the Holy See advised Father Schrijvers on January 5, 1934, to convoke a general chapter that would be held in Lviv on July 4 of the same year. In order to facilitate the election of delegates, the Sacred Oriental Congregation divided the institute into three provinces – Europe, Canada, and Brazil – each of which would participate in the assembly through its lawful representatives. This move signalled an end to the nearly exclusive powers that had been the preserve of each diocesan congregation and in its stead ushered in the principle of provincial subsidiarity, whereby the provinces, united to one another by common norms and purpose, would be responsible to a central governing body in which most authority would henceforth be vested.

On March 13, 1934, the sisters at Mundare played host to the sixteen delegates who had gathered to participate in a provincial chapter which had, as its prime function, the election of two members who would accompany the ex officio officials, Sister Athanasia Melnyk and Sister Ambrose Lenkewich, to Europe.[74] The crunch of the grim economic slump was felt in the absence at the assembly of the elected representatives from Montreal and Dauphin, who failed to attend because neither of their convents could afford the train fare to Alberta. For this same reason, too, only a total of four rather than eight Canadians would attend the chapter overseas. For all its former apprehension, however, the expectations that the province now pinned on its revived unity with Europe were stimulated in a host of quickened interests, and its zeal seemed to be enlivened by a surge of great expectations, as the participants voted to send Sister Josephata Tymochko and Sister Elizabeth Kassian to represent them at Lviv.

The Canadian delegation sailed from Montreal on June 8 aboard the liner *Ascania*. Both Sister Athanasia and Sister Ambrose, who had left Europe more than twenty-five years before, anticipated renewing acquaintances and revisiting the convents in which their religious life had been fostered. Together with Sister Josaphata and Sister Elizabeth, both of whom had emigrated with their parents while they were still very young, they nourished the hope that out of their participation in the chapter would emerge a deeper understanding of the European sisters – of the way they lived, the way they worked, the views they held, and why they held them.[75]

Almost one month later, on July 4, together with twelve delegates from the European province and two from Brazil, they assembled for the opening session of the historic meeting, presided over by Father Schrijvers. In the ensuing chapter of election, the capitulants selected Sister Veronica Gargil to be the institute's first superior general and six members of the European province to form the general collegial body.[76]

The deliberations of the chapter of affairs that followed abounded in an interesting and lively exchange of international ideas and viewpoints as the participants, in a desire to match their rhetoric with specifics, openly treated the issues peculiar to each geographical area, endeavouring to get at root problems and come up with fresh approaches. In sum, thought Father Schrijvers, it was a period during which God blessed the institute with many special graces. One incident in particular moved him deeply – so deeply, in fact, that he later described it in a letter to the Canadian community: 'The extraordinary manner in which God's grace works was manifested at the chapter, especially during the session at which the capitulants discussed the religious garb. At that time I briefly addressed the assembly regarding the obligation to conform to that section of the constitutions which clearly describes the distinctive habit of the institute. After I had finished speaking, your provincial superior, Sister Athanasia, and the three other Canadian delegates removed the rings and rosaries they were wearing and placed them before the superior general. This humble act touched the gathering so deeply that it is now indelibly inscribed not only in the history of the institute but more permanently in the hearts of all the sisters who were in that chapter room. Your sisters acted as true daughters of one congregation, which has as its patroness and heavenly mother the Blessed Virgin Mary.'[77] Undoubtedly this simple act of the Canadian representatives had spoken louder than a million words.

Fourteen ordinances – prescriptions which applied the constitutions to particular cases in a practical way – were approved by the first chapter. One of these, for example, stipulated that among themselves the sisters would use no titles; thus the superior general and provincial superiors would be addressed simply as 'sister' rather than 'Reverend Mother.' This was in keeping with the spirit of the constitutions which emphasized the equality of all members, even though, by virtue of their office, precedence would be accorded major superiors in all houses of the institute. As a capstone of sorts, the chapter also endorsed the resolution that the European province would be placed under the patronage of Our Lady of Sorrows; the Canadian under that of Christ the King; and the Brazilian under the protection of St Michael, the Archangel. The motto uniting them all would be: 'Glory to God, honour to Mary, to us peace.'

Finally, the chapter having been declared officially closed, the four Canadian sisters visited the village of Zhuzhyl, the birthplace of their institute. For all, and especially for Sister Athanasia who had been one of the original nine postulants, this was an unforgettable moment. Then, as a culmination of their historic adventure, they journeyed to Rome to re-affirm, in the heart of Christendom, their fidelity to Christ's Church. At Castel Gandolfo, the summer residence of the Roman pontiffs, they received the papal blessing which was, they declared, 'the highlight of the entire trip and an abundant recompense for the hardships involved in European travel.'[78]

Although on the surface it seemed that little had changed, in truth little remained the same; for the Canadian community had undergone an imperceptible, but none the less real, transformation in its progression from a congregation of diocesan right to a canonically erected province within a papal institute. Endeavouring to evoke a vigorous spirit that would set the Province of Christ the King upon a fresh and confident course, Sister Veronica appointed a new provincial council just one month after the conclusion of the general chapter. In her letter dated October 28, 1934, she announced that Sister Elizabeth Kassian had been selected as provincial superior, and that her four councillors included Sister Ambrose Lenkewich, Sister Fevronia Anne Prystupa, Sister Natalie Hedwig Klos, and Sister Lubov Chawrona.[79] 'Please accept this position,' wrote Sister Veronica to Sister Elizabeth, 'as the will of God and in the spirit of holy obedience; most surely our merciful Lord will bless and help you to fulfil faithfully the heavy responsibilities tied to this office.'[80]

And the diminutive, determined, and devoted Sister Elizabeth did just that, not guessing that she was destined to guide the Canadian Sisters Servants through fifteen years of bad times as well as good. A former pupil of St Nicholas School in Winnipeg, and one of the institute's first qualified teachers, she was both knowledgeable and perceptive, with a strong, precise, well-structured mind that did not suffer gladly fools, fanatics, or false reasoning. At the same time, as one of her former students, Brother Methodius William Koziak, FSC, asserted, 'she exemplified all that was noble and fine' in womanhood.[81]

In the best of times the position of major superior in a newly formed province would have been less than enticing. Now, at a time when it was imperative to heal old wounds and to cement the still fragile but vastly improved relations with Europe, as well as to sustain the members in the midst of an ever-worsening depression that threatened the very existence of their institutions, it was an unenviable, formidable challenge. Undoubtedly, the future was something of a minefield loaded with both opportunity and disaster; undoubtedly, the times called for effective leadership; undoubtedly, Sister Elizabeth was right for it.

CHAPTER 7

A time to blossom . . .

Sister Elizabeth, the first Canadian provincial superior of the pontifical institute, began immediately to define the role which her religious family would play in Canada for the next fifteen years. Perceiving the magnitude of the problems she would have to face, she launched a determined effort to fortify her Province of Christ the King by evoking a more forceful spirit of unity among its members and missions. In a single-minded endeavour, and with a clarity of goal, she set herself to the task.

Her first move was the centralization of the institute's Canadian head-quarters, a step intended to facilitate communication with the provincial council. Thus on December 1, 1934, the sisters were informed that hence-forth the provincialate would be in the city of Edmonton rather than in the out-of-the-way village of Mundare.

Next, she levied a monthly tax ranging from $10 to $20 upon five convents – Montreal, Winnipeg, Ituna, Yorkton, and Edmonton – for the maintenance of the novitiate and the education of professed religious.[1] Despite the widening ripples of hardship which continued to flow outward from a wheezing economy, and which would surely demand more per-sonal sacrifice if the superiors of these mortgaged missions were to meet this additional obligation, her action was both logical and timely. For one thing, the novitiate had unexpectedly been deprived of the teachers' salaries that had sustained it since 1928, when, six years later, as a result of hard times, public school trustees had dropped the sisters from the staffs of Brody, Podola, Koluz, and Oleskow schools, replacing them with unem-ployed lay teachers – usually members of their own families.[2] Therefore, in the short term at least, Sister Elizabeth's tax plan partially replaced this loss of revenue at a time when there was no other source upon which to draw.

Finally, she founded a bimonthly community periodical which the sisters voted to entitle *Zoria Marii (Star of Mary)*. Ostensibly, its pur-pose was to 'achieve a sense of oneness among the increasing number of Canadian convents,'[3] but Sister Elizabeth's ultimate aim was nothing less than to stimulate a greater constancy and a more than paper unity among the Sisters Servants throughout the world.

In the first issue, dated January-February 1935, she explained the immediate motivation behind the publication: 'We forward to you this initial copy of the *Star of Mary* which is being published for the greater glory of God, in honour of our heavenly Mother Mary, and for your benefit, dear sisters,' she wrote. 'As you well know some of our convents are separated by hundreds of miles, while others are located in remote rural areas where seldom anyone stops by to visit, to share news and views of community events, or simply to encourage our members stationed there. For each of us the *Star of Mary* will, I am certain, be a welcome guest which, through its pertinent religious and community content, will inform, cheer, and hearten. I am also convinced that this periodical will draw us closer together, and that out of this unity of mind and heart will emerge a deep understanding and a sincere mutual appreciation.'[4]

The enthusiasm with which the *Star* was received in Canada, Europe, and Brazil was unanimous. A commendatory job had indeed been done by the staff – comprised of two reporters from each convent – in their articles which catered to diverse reading tastes; for instance, the solemn 'Union with God' and 'A Prayer for Perseverance in the Religious State' were followed by the lighthearted 'Important Edmonton Events,' the newsy 'Hospital Highlights,' the humorous 'Sister Ignatia's Adventure with Fish,' and the touching 'Story of Little Nick.'

Impressed and pleased, Sister Veronica, their superior general, saw it as auguring well for the future of the entire institute. In a congratulatory letter to the editor, dated April 21, 1935, she admitted that the periodical could not have been inaugurated at a more opportune time 'since the houses within the entire congregation are becoming more numerous, and the sisters, united through charity into one large spiritual family, have a lively interest in, and a healthy curiousity about, the life and experiences of their fellow sisters.'[5] Thus at the outset of new undertakings, when the reorganized institute was just beginning to blossom into a more positive entity within the Church, the *Star of Mary*, simple and unpretentious in content and format, became an amicable link among the Sisters Servants on three continents.[6]

Modest as they were, these three innovations disclosed that the new provincial superior had begun her term of office on a positive note. And, in the first half of the year 1935, her province, tempered as well as prompted by a fresh realization of its potential, moved quickly toward a number of bold commitments of its members and resources. In fact, between 1935 and 1939 so many requests followed each new foundation that the openings and opportunities they promised injected a continuous stimulus into the stream of its mission movement.

One petition that appeared on Sister Elizabeth's desk early in February of 1935 was from Rev. M. Pelech. Currently stationed at Sifton, the Manitoba farming centre from which the Sisters Servants had departed shortly after their convent school had been destroyed by fire in 1924,[7] Father Pelech requested that four religious be assigned immediately to work with the Ukrainian youth of the entire district.[8] Action on the proposal was both swift and favourable. Indeed, doubts which might have arisen about whether after an absence of eleven years the sisters would accept the offer to reintroduce their apostolate at Sifton were dispelled when on April 17 Sister Euletheria Furtak, Sister Lawrence Dzumaga, Sister Barbara Theodora Prediliuk, and Sister Sozonta Tekla Iskiw left Winnipeg to open the new mission. On that very day, however, an incident occurred that threatened to deal the foundation a stunning blow: Bishop Ladyka notified Sister Elizabeth that the move to Sifton was being adamantly opposed by Archbishop A. Sinnott of Winnipeg.

It was this prelate who had assumed the sisters' debt in return for their property and building; it was also he who had subsequently restored the charred structure and had turned it over to the Polish branch of the Benedictine Congregation to be used as a private elementary school. Now, having learned that the Sisters Servants might return to the village, the archbishop made it clear to Bishop Ladyka that in his view the existing tension between Ukrainians and Poles in the Sifton district militated against having religious of the two nationalities and rites 'established side by side in such a small place.' A move in this direction, he contended, would only serve to stoke the existing fire of distrust. If, however, the people insisted that the Sisters Servants open a mission there, the archbishop declared himself ready to sell their former school for $20,000 in cash, and withdraw the Polish religious.[9]

Unfortunately, Sister Elizabeth received word of the archbishop's objection to the foundation on April 17, after the sisters assigned to Sifton had already left Winnipeg. Thus she suddenly found herself in a rather embarrassing predicament. In the first place, the institute did not have $20,000. In the second, to recall the sisters almost as soon as they arrived might simply add fuel to the racial enmity that ran deep.[10]

While she wrestled with her dilemma, the four sisters who detrained at Sifton that day discovered that almost every Ukrainian had turned out to meet them. Children excitedly squealed 'They're here!' while their parents, in turn, warmly called out 'Welcome back, sisters!'[11] After this unexpected reception, there followed a parade of sorts when the entire crowd gaily escorted the new arrivals up Main Street to the former rectory, now converted into a convent, where they were effusively greeted by the parish executive. Hopefully, the Sifton mission was on again.

Archbishop Sinnott's opposition, however, hung over the community until eventually, after many letters had passed between him and Sister Elizabeth, it was decided that the mission would be considered a temporary foundation until a transaction concerning the school building and land was finalized.[12]

In the meantime, for the four sisters on the spot, who recognized that they were by no means out of the woods and hence might be recalled at any time, the next few months slipped by quickly – perhaps because they were busy. There were people to see, particularly the sick; there were children, youths, and adults to instruct in Ukrainian or handicrafts or home economics. And since Sisters Servants never considered that it was enough for them, as missionaries, just to humanize, they broadened their catechetical courses and liturgical music programme to include all age groups as their chief means of dropping the seed of the Gospel into men's lives.

By the end of the year it was still too early to write off the possibility that at any moment the Sifton mission might be off again, since negotiations between the provincial superior and the archbishop were continuing. For their part, simply through quiet service and friendly daily contacts, Sister Euletheria and her small group unobtrusively did much to cool the flame of old prejudices that for years had smouldered close to the surface in the long loveless relationship between Ukrainians and Poles.

Better luck marked the institute's second venture in rural Manitoba, which grew out of a request by Bishop Ladyka that the sisters open a house at Komarno, about sixty miles north of Winnipeg. As early as January 1935 the prelate had requested permission from the apostolic delegate, Archbishop A. Cassulo, to transfer to the Sisters Servants the former Redemptorist mission which had served a predominantly Ukrainian district of some fifty square miles. He had estimated that the estate, sold to the Episcopal Corporation by the Redemptorists, and consisting of 160 acres of land, a small furnished house with a chapel room, and a number of dilapidated farm buildings, was worth about $1,400. 'Every year,' Bishop Ladyka had explained, 'I must pay taxes and insurance in addition to keeping the buildings from falling into disrepair; thus this property brings me no revenue whatsoever.' The ordinary's obvious low-keyed attempt to relieve the diocese of a financial headache did not, however, entirely lack a missionary motivation. It would be advantageous, the bishop pointed out, 'to transfer the property to the Sisters Servants who, according to their new constitutions approved recently by the Holy See, would work in the vast missionary field among the people who are poor both materially and morally.' Stressing the temporal and spiritual importance of the sisters' work, he further observed that instead of standing idle and draining the diocesan coffers the place 'could be used for the greater glory of God and the salvation of souls.'[13]

Impressive as all of this sounded, it remained true that merely to make the abandoned land and buildings functional the sisters would be required to pour into them long hours of hard manual labour and every penny they could save. They were, however, determined to refashion a thriving religious centre at Komarno.

It was on very short notice that the sisters assigned to effect this resurrection – Sister Augustina Hawryliuk, Sister Eusebia Matkowsky, and Sister Theodosia Pauline Iwasiuk – met in Winnipeg in May 1935, where, from sisters and friends alike, they managed to collect a motley array of household articles – everything from a pile of cracked dishes to a somewhat temperamental sewing machine. Then on May 21, teeming with ideas about how they would reap a spiritual harvest for the Lord at one swoop, they moved into their small convent. And scarcely had they put their house in order than things began to buzz in Komarno. Within a month youngsters were attending evening catechetical and language classes, aspirants to the Marian Sodality were helping to clean the church, St Anne was receiving a flood of petitions from women who had just become members of an association founded in her honour, children and adults alike headed for the convent in the evenings to learn liturgical and folk music or handicrafts, while many sick farmers were astonished to find the young sisters visiting and caring for them in their own homes.

Then it was summer, and from June to September they moved from village to hamlet for miles around, conducting catechetical and language courses. Often they were bone-weary; often they experienced a nagging frustration as a result of encounters with iron prejudices or religious indifference. Still, neither their joy nor optimism nor purpose diminished. 'It seems that when things were the roughest and toughest we had the funniest recreations,' recalls Sister Augustina. 'After all, we were doing the Lord's work. Besides, from our earliest beginnings we Sisters Servants had laughed at the physical and spiritual trials of a missioner's life. We had sacrificed and suffered to build houses in which to care for the needful young and old from among our people. And all because of an aching hope to drench our missions with the truth and beauty and wisdom of our faith.'[14]

Any ordeals the sisters had endured up to now were the mere shadow of a shade when compared with those they were destined to meet at Willingdon, Alberta – a small village lying approximately seventy miles northeast of Edmonton. For as soon as a mission was opened there on June 3, 1935, it became one of the most formidable crucibles in which the Sisters Servants were tested during the 1930s.

The Willingdon district had attracted many immigrants, mostly Bukovinians and Rumanians, from the moment the CPR had run its line through it from Edmonton to Lloydminster. By 1935 these people, most of whom professed the Greek Orthodox faith, comprised the bulk of the population; among them were only a handful of Catholics, either of the Eastern or Latin rites.

Two of the village's outstanding citizens, Mr I. Goresky, MLA, and his brother, Dr V. Goresky, both of whom were actively involved in civic affairs, recognized in 1934 that their community's most fundamental requirement was a hospital. In particular, Dr Goresky, a dedicated general practitioner, had witnessed time and again the grave complications to patients arising from their being transported to distant hospitals over the rough, ungraded country roads. Sparked by the Goresky brothers, public sentiment in favour of a hospital grew steadily until municipal authorities sought and received permission from the Department of Health to build one. This, it turned out, was all the two concerned men had been waiting for prior to petitioning the Sisters Servants to undertake the erection of a suitable building and to provide the personnel required to staff it. For its part, the municipality promised a building grant of $3,000 and a daily maintenance subsidy of $1.50 per patient.[15]

Obviously, so far as finances were concerned, the proposal was scarcely enticing. Less persuasive still was the fact that there was no resident Ukrainian Catholic priest in the area, and therefore Sister Elizabeth was concerned about the worrisome possibility that the sisters, together with the Catholic members of their staff and their patients, might not have an opportunity to participate regularly in the Divine Liturgy and to receive the sacraments. When, however, she was assured, first, by responsible governmental officials that her institute would be backed financially if it undertook the project, and, second, by the Basilian Fathers that a resident chaplain would be provided as soon as the hospital became operational, she and her council voted to establish a medical mission to serve Willingdon.[16] Despite the many ready promises, however, the birth pangs of the Sisters Servants' second hospital in Alberta were about to make themselves felt.

Owing to the fact that the institute was still young and had been growing too fast to have any reserve funds to appropriate for building purposes, the sisters were forced to negotiate a loan. Having received assurance that it would be forthcoming, they forged ahead with plans for a twenty-five-bed hospital. At the insistence of Dr Goresky, and with the permission of local authorities, they also agreed in May 1935 to establish a temporary hospital in the village. 'We calculated that we would have to use a house for this purpose for only about three months,' wrote one sister, 'since by that time at least a section of the hospital would be habitable.'[17]

A few weeks later, on a lazy June afternoon, a truck loaded with hospital beds, equipment, supplies, a few sticks of furniture, and four blue-robed sisters startled a handful of Willingdonians when it rumbled past the general store in a swirl of dust, halting finally before a small, weather-beaten house, which the sisters were renting for $20 a month. Like a flash, word swept through the community that 'those women who call themselves nuns' had come to town.[18]

These same women – Sister Gertrude Lesiuk, Sister Stanislaus Mary Koziak, Sister Theophane Helen Malowany, and Sister Onufria Helen Hnatiw – weren't too surprised to find that this creaky and draughty dwelling wouldn't be a temporary hospital until they had scrubbed down, disinfected, and spruced up the whole grubby place. But even before they could tackle this job, two of them were hastily summoned by Dr Goresky to treat their first patients – accommodated for the time being at the Willingdon Hotel.

The four missionaries found, too, that in between their nursing duties, unpacking, cleaning, and setting up a makeshift hospital they were beseiged by visitors. For although at first the people did not quite know what to make of them, they quickly warmed to the fact that these were the women who had taken upon themselves the responsibility of caring for their sick. Before long some came to chat and lend a hand; others to spill out their problems to these sisters whom they had only just met. And out of this simple but sincere association was emerging a living ecumenism; the sisters saw evidence of it in the confidence and friendship that manifested themselves even in the catechetical classes and choir rehearsals which Orthodox children, girls, and women were attending in ever-increasing numbers. The people, on the other hand, seeing the sisters bringing medicine to their sick, catechism and holy pictures to their children, sympathy and counsel to all, unofficially adopted them, so that by the time the construction of the hospital commenced in July 1935 they were already known throughout the district by young and old alike as 'our sisters.'[19]

Local farmers, thwarted by the painful squeeze on the domestic economy from contributing any monetary assistance toward the project, which everyone said would be the district's finest acquisition, rallied to the cause by volunteering their labour. Day after day, with almost a loving tenderness, the sisters and their people watched the structure rise, bit by bit. Then on September 15, the district emptied into the village to participate in the blessing of the cornerstone. The enthusiastic response that had resulted in the building's being roofed within three months seemed to predict that the official opening would take place in the spring. But this most talked-about event of the season was something that didn't happen.

By late fall there had developed an undercurrent of apprehension as the sisters had watched their initial bank balance dwindle to zero — and still no loan. Their jitters might have been more pronounced had they foreseen that, as a result of the provincial election in the summer of 1935, which had brought into power the Social Credit party, the money they desperately needed would never be forthcoming.[20] For at this time the attention of the public, especially that of business firms in all Canadian provinces, was focused on Alberta, whose electorate had just offered it as a subject for economic experiment. It was a measure of concern over the fiscal programme of this new government that prompted many finance companies to adopt a wait-and-see attitude, which soon resulted in a moratorium on loans that was to continue until the Social Credit party proved itself capable of engendering a sense of security and general confidence. An official of the Mutual Life Assurance Company explained it to Sister Elizabeth this way: 'Our company is not prepared to make further loans in the Province of Alberta at the present time in view of the present uncertainty of legislation in the Province.'[21]

The axe had fallen, and the Willingdon sisters found themselves among the first victims of this sudden shift in policy. In truth, however, it was fundamentally their premature confidence in acquiring the necessary loan that had nurtured the false sense of security which in turn had encouraged them to begin building before they had the necessary funds in hand. Already they were reaping a harvest of trouble for this error in judgment, made in a moment of zeal and compounded by lack of experience in larger construction projects.

Of course, the refusal by Mutual Life was a shattering blow and demonstrably a bitter foretaste of other setbacks to follow. Obviously, they were in deep, deep trouble. In fact, the immediate consequences were rather nightmarish. Everything came to a halt; construction was frozen and the sisters' reputation undermined. As countless creditors clamoured for payment, an unfounded distrust, fed by false rumours that the sisters no longer had any intention of completing the hospital, prejudiced some people, and thus sliced away at the moral support which they so sorely needed. On the face of it, a fiasco.

In spite of the fact that there were indeed causes for concern, the sisters remained unswerving in their faith and trust. 'We see our trials as a sign of God's love,'[22] wrote one of them. They comforted one another with the truth that the institute had travelled the road of suffering before. Perhaps. But this time the road loomed rougher than it ever had in the past. They did not have to bear their anguish alone, however, for it was shared by Sisters Servants across the country. Having been entreated by Sister Elizabeth to beg God's help in resolving the critical situation, they united in prayer to the one they knew never ceased interceding to God in their behalf – Mary Immaculate.

When it became obvious, soon afterward, that there was no immediate way through which to continue building, hope of moving the patients out of their uninsulated hut before winter – a prospect that had so tantalized them a few months before– turned out to be bleak. A measure of their sorrow and regret may be gleaned from this brief account by one of the nursing sisters: 'We shivered through that chilly autumn, trying to make the best of a bad situation, ever hopeful that by Christmas we would be nursing our houseful of patients in warm, roomy quarters. But September turned to October; even the harsh winter passed – in much the same way as do all things in this world. Then it was spring, and still the outlook for our future seemed as dim as ever. Before we knew it, the year had come full circle, and again after the warmth of summer we were experiencing the penetrating chill of autumn. Through it all, with its boarded-up windows and doors, our unfinished hospital – stark and lonely – stood against the endless sky, as if it belonged to no one.'[23]

They had indeed passed through an uncertain twelve months, and in the anxious present the matter still stood at stalemate. There was little likelihood of escaping from their weather-worn hut during the winter of 1936. Besides the trials that stemmed from cold and fatigue and financial worries, the sisters often experienced the pain of being able to participate in the Divine Liturgy only a few times a month in the summer, and even less frequently in the winter, when it was more difficult for a priest to reach the village. But this bruising suffering, too, they accepted as a reality of their mission work, and staunchly rejected the temptation to use it as a just reason for abandoning Willingdon.

A breakthrough in the intolerable standstill resulted from a decidedly simple plan of action promoted by the Basilians, Rev. M. Romanowich and Rev. A. Wynnyk, and endorsed by the provincial council.[24] The two missionaries professed confidence that even during these hard depression years there would be people willing to help complete the hospital by purchasing 5 per cent bonds in amounts ranging from $10 to $100, redeemable in five years. Before long, the requisite forms were printed and the project advertised in newspapers as well as from parish pulpits. And the real wonder for the sisters who travelled throughout the province selling the bonds was that people considered their purchase not a burden but an act of mercy. And so responsive were they that the sisters' anxieties evaporated in a spectacular outburst of Christian generosity that thrilled, astonished, and heartened them. 'There was no end to our rejoicing,' recalled one sister, 'when upon our return we discovered that, having raised enough funds to purchase windows and doors, and to finish the building's interior, we would be able to occupy our hospital by the end of October.'[25]

This was but wishful thinking. For at midnight of October 10, 1936, the building was gutted by fire. The awakened village rang with the startled cries of those who hastened to the scene of the blaze. Into the dawn, the sisters stood with their people watching the walls disintegrate in the heat of the flames; and as the fire raged unchecked one of them quietly remarked, 'We'll build it again.'[26] By morning, only two charred chimneys stood in the midst of the smoking ruins which, only yesterday, had almost been a haven for the sick.

Sister Elizabeth, having been hastily informed of the incredible turn of events, awakened the sisters at Edmonton to share the news. Humanly speaking, the episode was almost crushing in its cruelty, for, after almost a year of prayer, penance, and months of selling bonds, each sister had just begun to feel confident that the hospital would soon be a reality. Hence the unexpected, staggering loss could scarcely fail to inject a despondent note into the community mood. Never panic-prone, their provincial superior, who must have felt the blow more keenly than anyone, quietly said: 'It is obvious, dear sisters, that our hospital is destined to bring much praise and service to God and help to men since, from its very beginnings, the Lord has permitted it to be so severely tested.'[27] And with that she preceded them into the chapel where, in the presence of Christ in the Blessed Sacrament, they sang the *Te Deum*, St Ambrose's glorious hymn of thanksgiving.

Preliminary details of the fire soon filtered out to the other houses, and sisters everywhere waited anxiously for more precise information. But bad news often feeds as much on itself as on events; cynics, both within and without the institute, were quick to suggest that the hospital was a dead issue – finally. This time, even the most convinced optimists found it difficult to disagree.

Meanwhile, the Willingdon sisters, who had not been cowed by their material loss, were profoundly disturbed by a sudden strain in the amity that had existed between them and their people. 'A subtle accusation went abroad that we were guilty of arson,' revealed the annalist, 'that we ourselves had set fire to the building in order to collect the insurance.'[28] The fact of the matter was that the $20,000 hospital had been insured for only $12,000. And because the building had been unoccupied at the time of the blaze, the insurance agency was to haggle for two years before making payment, and this in the amount of just one-half of the indemnity. By all accounts, therefore, the episode was a misfortune for the institute that overshadowed every other problem; not only had it lost a building but it had acquired another debt, since the bonds that had recently been sold would be redeemable in the early 1940s.

It is clear, therefore, why shock waves were felt from one end of the Province of Christ the King to the other when it was learned that Sister Elizabeth was standing firm in her intention of not relinquishing the mission, even as suspicion and calumny against the sisters mounted. One factor in her decision may have been her belief that public opinion would increasingly turn in the sisters' favour when the ultimate success of the hospital venture became apparent. Convinced that there was no significant flaw in the enterprise, she looked upon it as a major responsibility to which the institute had committed itself, and hence one which she could not simply side-step. Her spirituality was rooted in the principle that a religious did her duty regardless of the cost or unpleasantness. There was no reason to believe that she was about to change that principle.

Concrete proof of her determination was soon forthcoming. Recognizing that the recent loss had badly eroded the institute's position to sell enough bonds or to borrow sufficient money from private individuals for rebuilding purposes, she appealed to the superiors of each of her houses to forward to the provincialate any portion of their scanty income that could be spared. For all its mildness the burden of her message was clear: the hospital would become a reality only if the sisters made a concerted effort to help themselves. And although the same old stumbling block – lack of funds – was to delay the task of starting anew, it would not reverse it. By scrimping and saving and funnelling any extra dollar into the Willingdon building fund, the institute began to inch toward its goal. In fact, so responsive was each local community that by August 1937 Sister Elizabeth was able to engage the services of the contractor, Mr L. Koss, to erect another building on the site of the hospital that had never been.

As a new structure began to rise quickly upon the ashes of the old, the sisters became cautiously optimistic. On September 19 the hospital was officially blessed by Father Romanowich, and on October 29, as workmen were putting the finishing touches to its exterior, the sisters joyfully made preparations to move their nine patients to a completed section of their new 'Hospital of Divine Providence.' However, they had to admit that the hut which they were at last leaving had served them well, for here, in spite of the crowding and the cold, they had nursed over three hundred patients in 1936 alone.

Yet one more personally wrenching experience was in store for them. A Mr Yahnitsky, who had gone beyond the unfailing kindness that is the mark of an exceptional Christian by leaving his own manifold autumn farm chores to assist in moving the sisters' belongings, was suddenly thrown from his loaded wagon by a team of startled horses; the sisters who rushed to his aid found him unconscious amid a mass of wrecked furniture. Ironically, it was he who became the hospital's first patient. With him and his family the sisters shared the sting of his painful injury; through his long convalescence they assisted him in a tangible way through their nursing skill and in a less tangible, but no less important way, through their prayers.

After this ordeal, the tide did turn in favour of the new institution. At the end of its first day, fourteen of its twenty-five beds were occupied; thereafter, because the Willingdon Hospital District is a fairly large one, the rate of occupancy was often higher than the building could accommodate. 'Our country hospital always hummed with activity,' related Sister Nestor Helen Kyba, one of the nurses. 'The maternity rate was high and often the building was too crowded for convenience, but we couldn't turn anyone away.'[29] Bukovinians and Rumanians liked to boast that 'in our hospital every person is considered a patient and not simply a case.'[30]

Dr Goresky and his successor, Dr Eugene Svarich, were later replaced by Dr William D. Cuts. A real spirit of cooperation grew up among the Willingdon doctors and their colleagues from Mundare, Vegreville, Lamont, and Two Hills, all of whom assisted each other in surgery and consultations. From this time, too, the nursing sisters began to accompany the doctor on country house calls. 'With roads still in poor condition with no grade or gravel, the transfer of a patient to the hospital in Dr Cuts' one-seat car was quite a feat,' recalled Sister Nestor.[31]

Throughout these early years, God's mercy never ceased to astonish and humble the Willingdon nursing staff. They believed that it was only with His help that they had finally snatched a happy ending from the jaws of defeat. This hospital, which could have been considered one of the institute's hardest tests up to 1937, therefore became – perhaps precisely because of the challenge it had posed – its greatest pride. No wonder one of the sisters felt compelled to write: 'For all His marvellous graces and goodness to us, may Divine Providence be praised now and forever.'[32]

One other pressing petition had been received early in February 1935, from Bishop Constantine Bohachevsky, OSBM, of Philadelphia. In his letter the prelate exhibited a single-minded determination to impress upon the Sisters Servants the fact that their entrance into the apostolate among Ukrainians in the United States of America could no longer be postponed. Explained the annalist: 'The bishop desires that our institute provide the housekeeping and food services staff for the seminary at Stamford, Connecticut. His Excellency seems to be convinced that this assignment will form the nucleus for a widespread apostolate in the numerous parishes of his vast diocese.'[33]

This invitation, however, was only one of many which the Canadian Sisters Servants had received from the United States during a period of twenty-five years. The first had come from Bishop Soter Ortynsky, OSBM, in 1910. This first Ukrainian bishop in the United States had been, since 1907, the ecclesiastical superior of the Catholics who had emigrated from various provinces of the former Austro-Hungarian Empire, other than those of Rumanian extraction. Already his people were dispersed throughout more than twenty states of the Union.[34] Believing that religious women could offer invaluable assistance to their countrymen in adjusting to an entirely different milieu, especially through their work with children and women, the bishop dispatched Rev. L. Sembratovich to Canada to confer with Sister Ambrose Lenkewich about the possibility of assigning a few sisters, who spoke English well, to assume responsibility for the direction of an orphanage, a centre for the sewing of liturgical vestments, and a Ukrainian evening school at Philadelphia. Inevitably, the proposal was torpedoed by circumstances themselves: with a total membership in the institute of only nineteen, including postulants and novices, the young community could ill afford to deplete itself by taking on missionary work in the neighbouring country.[35]

Bishop Ortynsky does not seem to have been a man who gave up easily. In August of the following year he directed three aspirants from the United States to the novitiate at Mundare. And although none of these – Mary Cherwonka (Sister Sophie), Anne Prystupa (Sister Fevronia), and Anne Zahryniuk (Sister Julia) – were Americans by birth, their arrival seemed to focus attention on the bishop's standing invitation for an apostolate among the almost half million Ukrainian Catholics under his jurisdiction.[36]

A year later, on December 24, 1912, another of the prelate's emissaries, Rev. K. Barysh, arrived in Canada from Galicia with two European postulants, Euphrasia Gnush (Sister Paraskevia) and Eugenia Malitsky (Sister Emilia), together with a professed religious, Sister Euletheria Furtak, all of whom had volunteered for the Canadian mission. 'It seems that Father Barysh has come here to appeal to Sister Ambrose to send sisters to the United States,' observed the chronicler of the Basilian Fathers, when the party arrived at Mundare.[37] And still there were no hopeful glimmerings. The institute's growing pains had not yet ceased; hence, once again, on the same reasonable ground of too few members, the invitation was firmly declined.

Even after Bishop Ortynsky's premature death in March 1916, when the Holy See did not name a new bishop but directed the apostolic delegate to appoint two temporary administrators, one for the faithful who came from the ecclesiastical province of Lviv (Galicia and Bukovina) and another for those whose origin was in some part of Hungary or Croatia, personal petitions from priests stationed across the United States regularly streamed into the obscure provincialate at the Mundare homestead. But the drive for sisters gained still greater momentum after 1924 when the Holy See set up two jurisdictions called 'apostolic exarchies' (in accordance with the renewed Oriental canonical terminology) – one of which was fixed at Pittsburgh under Bishop B. Takach for Byzantine-rite Catholics from the Subcarpathian region, Slovakia, and Yugoslavia; while for the Ukrainians who came from the north of the Carpathian Mountains, that is, Galicia and Bukovina, the apostolic exarchy was continued at Philadelphia. On May 20, 1924, the Holy See assigned Most Rev. Constantine Bohachevsky as apostolic exarch of this region; at the time of his appointment he was vicar general and canon of the Ukrainian Catholic diocese of Peremyshl in Galicia.[38] Strengthened by this mark of the Church's interest and affection, Ukrainians in the United States began a continual progress that was evidenced in the increasing numbers of parishes, priests, and schools that sprang up. The Sisters Servants, however, were still not ready to participate in this exciting development. But every refusal the clergy received from them seemed to trigger the same plaintive query: isn't there some way? The only offsetting crumb of comfort for both sides was the hope that the current upsurge in vocations to the institute might soon enable it to surmount the hurdle of insufficient personnel at which every effort so far had collapsed.

That the laity also harboured the hope of having Sisters Servants in their parishes is evidenced by an article in the Philadelphia publication, *Missionar* (*The Missionary*) of October 1932, in which after heralding the recently proclaimed papal status of the institute as a remarkable advance in its evolution, the editor stated: 'The Sisters Servants are already carrying on their apostolate not only in Galicia but also beyond the Carpathian Mountains in Yugoslavia, Canada, and Brazil. Since their founding they have through their life and works won the admiration, appreciation, and love of our people. Unfortunately, only our American eparchy is without Sisters Servants, whom we greatly need, especially for our children in the larger cities, who are deprived of Christian training and guidance. On this occasion we extend to them our sincere wishes for a fruitful growth within our Church and among our people, but at the same time, we express the hope that after the general chapter, which will be held in the near future, they will not permit this area of our Church to remain without their presence.'

Bishop Bohachevsky's latest petition was almost a follow-up to the appeal contained in this article. And for once it would not be easily denied since, in pursuit of his goal, the prelate had solicited and received the support of Father Schrijvers, then visiting in the United States. In view of the apostolic visitor's favourable intervention and enthusiastic endorsement of the bishop's appeal, Sister Elizabeth realized that the institute had no choice but to approve the request even at the risk of the outcry which the action might trigger at home. For there was little doubt in her mind that if the proposal were endorsed by her council a wave of indignation would sweep through Canadian Church circles, since many petitions from the clergy here had either been temporarily shelved or outrightly refused. Having made her decision, she forthwith assumed a hugely determined, hugely hopeful attitude toward the venture – conscious all the while that it would be she who would bear the brunt of any clerical displeasure – and informed Bishop Bohachevsky that the sisters would be on hand to begin their assignment at Stamford when the scholastic year 1935–6 began the following September.[39] Significantly, by paving the way for the first American mission, she reversed the Canada-only direction which had been followed thus far, and ultimately shaped another province within the institute.

When news of the impending mission broke, there was a brief flurry of speculation among the sisters about who would be selected. The appointments, posted shortly thereafter, put Sister Pancratia Pauline Solowiy in charge of a small community consisting of Sister Constance Malko, Sister Alphonsa Mary Chrunik, Sister Florence Antonia Wus, and Sister Catherine Natalie Huculak.[40]

Theirs was to be an unglamorous assignment – housecleaning and cooking and some catechetical work at the local parish. Too obscure, unimportant, and physically demanding for a group of young, eager, and buoyant religious, some might have concluded. And indeed, separated by long distances as well as by a national boundary from their other convents, they might time and again feel and taste the bitter gall of loneliness; after working hard from dawn to dusk and trying at the end of each day to soothe a tired back and calloused hands, they might time and again wonder whether humble tasks at St Basil's College counted for anything in the Church. All of this was true. But Sister Pancratia and her small band optimistically looked forward to the assignment which they were gladly undertaking in obedience. They realized that it was God who would do everything, not they; if He desired to bring forth some good from their mission, they knew they simply had to try not to get in His way; if He wanted their institute to involve itself in more direct evangelical pursuits within Bishop Bohachevsky's sprawling diocese, they knew He would bring this about in His own time. So far as they were concerned, theirs was a mission in the true sense of the word: there had been no running start, there were no footsteps to walk in, and no shoulders except their own to lean on.[41]

Early in August 1935, owing to an unexpected delay in the processing of their passports, only Sister Elizabeth and Sister Constance were able to leave Montreal for Stamford to make preliminary preparations in the two departments they would direct. Sister Pancratia and Sister Alphonsa joined them on August 29, just in time to help put the school in order before the students poured in. As it turned out, it was not until the feast of the Immaculate Conception in December, when Sister Florence and Sister Catherine arrived, that their community was finally united, and they honoured their patroness, Mary Immaculate, as a religious family.

Unquestionably, that day can be considered as having been of some moment for an additional reason, for to this first community of Sisters Servants in the United States was being granted the privilege of grafting a vital shoot of their institute to the Church in that nation, just as their missionary forebears had done in Canada thirty-three years before.

Two years later Sister Elizabeth and her council were finding it more and more difficut to resist the intense pressure to establish more missions in the United States; letters from the American bishop and his clergy, each containing essentially the same dog-eared request – that the sisters take charge of evening schools and parish organizations – were accumulating rapidly, largely perhaps because in 1935 they had shown a willingness to move beyond national boundaries, and hence one could not assume that willingness to be exhausted. When, therefore, in August 1937 three sisters arrived in Philadelphia to found St Mary's Home for the Aged, the question posed most frequently was not '*would* Sister Elizabeth make further commitments in the United States' but rather '*should* Sister Elizabeth make further commitments?' The danger was that in trying to respond simultaneously to both Canadian and American needs the institute might be trying to do too much too fast. Such a policy would mean assigning sisters to a mission almost immediately upon completion of their novitiate training, thereby depriving them of the time necessary to update themselves scholastically. The thorniest question, therefore, was 'would the congregation's future be mortgaged by postponing or prolonging the advanced academic and professional training of its members?' The answer was as complicated as it was important. Sister Elizabeth and her council leaned to the view that a protracted delay in building up an army of scholarly professional reserves might result in the congregation's ending up with some permanent scars in the future. At the same time they feared that continuous refusals of requests from the United States might call forth detrimental reactions from hierarchy, clergy, and laity, ranging from strained disappointment to outright bitterness. For Sister Elizabeth, especially, the cross-fire of pressures had created an unprecedented dilemma.[42]

In the end she was persuaded that any response the institute could make would be profoundly significant. Therefore, instead of calling a halt, or moving slowly in founding American missions, she actually speeded its pace. In fact, she reacted with such stunning alacrity that the swiftness with which houses were established in Bishop Bohachevsky's diocese between the years 1937 and 1939 virtually eclipsed that of any previous two-year period in the institute's history. A growing phalanx of small convents, usually with only two sisters, sprang up in Detroit; Minneapolis; St Louis; Syracuse, New York; and St Clair, Shamokin, Keiser, Wilkes-Barre, and Ambridge in Pennsylvania. And although it may have seemed that she was taking a risk by plunging into this commitment, Sister Elizabeth had already acquired a habit of making her risks pay off.

In each of the new centres the sisters lived in convents provided and maintained by the parish. The usual remuneration for each sister's work averaged from $20 to $30 a month; hence out of a maximum income of $60 the small community had to provide for its food, clothing, medical, and other personal needs. Inevitably, the going was sometimes rough indeed.

Personal concerns, however, seemed unable to divert their interest from their assignment; in each parish they set to work with the capability that springs only from constant, total absorption in a divine purpose. Almost overnight their apostolate paralleled that carried on in Canada: caring for the church; organizing and moderating Marian sodalities, altar boys' clubs, and married women's associations; conducting evening classes in religion and Ukrainian; visiting the sick in hospitals and homes; instructing converts; preparing youth and adults for baptism; and visiting fallen-away Catholics.[43]

Almost everywhere they faced a challenge similar to that encountered by Sister Ignatia Butryn and Sister Sozonta Iskiw when they arrived at Rev. V. Bilynsky's parish in Minneapolis on July 1, 1937. 'We found that the children, especially, had been spiritually neglected,' recounted Sister Ignatia; 'very few knew even the Lord's Prayer, fewer still understood Ukrainian, and practically none was able to speak the language. Under these circumstances it became necessary to use English as the language of religious instruction.'[44] Within a few days the sisters were listening to the music of the children's first stumbling prayers; they needed no other sound to make them happy.

The real rub, however, was the necessity to teach Ukrainian to a group of youngsters who had neither the slightest inclination nor intention of learning it. Most sisters had met with such initial resistance in Canada, but here it was worse. They were, consequently, faced with the challenge of enkindling a spark of interest in their charges for their religious rite, together with a consciousness of, and a legitimate pride in, the contribution which the assembled gifts and cultures of many nations, including Ukraine, were making to the ultimate enrichment of the United States.

They started from scratch. 'We decided to devote much time to lesson preparation in order to catch the imagination of the pupils in diverse ways, and thus arouse an enthusiasm for learning the language,' revealed Sister Ignatia. 'Most of them knew not a single word, and what was truly sad was their shame at being able to speak it for fear they might be branded as foreigners. We knew that those attending our classes were doing so only because of parental pressure, and hence we tried to make each hour both interesting and enjoyable, so that they would look forward to our next class. Fortunately, with the grace of God we succeeded.'[45]

If the wisdom of broadening the sisters' service in the United States had seemed exceedingly questionable in 1935, the paradoxical fact was that within a few years their work proved so impressive – even with just two sisters at a parish – that it won plaudits from bishop and clergy. It was, of course, still too early to measure the results of their activity with hard statistics, but already the centres to which they were assigned seemed to have come spiritually alive. Most priests were noticing that the sisters were making conscious Catholics in their parishes. Wrote Rev. B. Turylo, the pastor at Rochester, New York: 'The sisters have succeeded in teaching our children the Ukrainian language; they have shown our youngsters, through personal example, how to love God, their religious rite, and their heritage, and have thus drawn them toward all that is good. Through the sodalities which they have organized for our children and young women, they have pointed the way to a more fruitful Christian life. The frequent reception of the sacraments of penance and the Eucharist by the sodalists has set a worthy standard for the entire parish.'[46] The sisters' emphasis upon work among girls and young married women arose from their conviction that no family can be truly Christian without a truly Christian mother.

When on March 22, 1938, the first American-born aspirant, Katherine Oskorop (Sister Gabriel) from Olyphant, Pennsylvania, was admitted to the institute, the sisters saw in her and her immediate followers the foundation upon which the institute would be built in the United States. It was now obvious that Ukrainian Americans would be seeing more of the Sisters Servants.

Late in 1935, shortly after the establishment of the first American apostolate in Stamford, Sister Elizabeth received word that Sister Veronica would make a canonical visitation of the North American province in accordance with the 1932 constitutions, which prescribed such a review at least every three years. The visit, scheduled for the following spring, would undoubtedly offer the superior general more than a privileged peek at the roughest, as well as the smoothest, edges of missionary life. As head of the entire institute, who carried the hopes of the recently reorganized congregation for a resurgent future, she was responsible for the spiritual, intellectual, moral, and material well-being of every member. It became immediately obvious, however, that beyond its spiritual and administrative scope, the tour would scarcely avoid taking on an overtone of a sentimental journey, since no European major superior had yet met with the sisters on this side of the Atlantic.

With her customary thoroughness, Sister Elizabeth made preparations to host the guests, and so effective was her attention to detail that, together with her Christmas greetings to Sister Veronica, she enclosed steamship tickets for a liner scheduled to sail from the French port of Le Havre on April 18, 1936. And when, four months later, on April 27, the superior general and her secretary, Sister Valerie Dubyk, disembarked at Montreal, Sister Elizabeth was on hand to welcome them on behalf of each sister in Canada and the United States.

It was from this easternmost convent that the visitation commenced. For three months, from May 4 to August 3, Sister Veronica, a warm, gracious woman, whose strength of character was enriched by a sense of charity, travelled across the country keenly aware of the significance to the Church of this first official appraisal of the institute's Canadian offshoot which, in its youthful energetic zeal for the Lord's praise and service, had often proved impatient, impetuous, impulsive, and strongly independent, but which, perhaps because of its trials and errors, had evolved into a network of fifteen missions with a task force of 126 sisters.[47]

Sister Veronica recorded some of her first impressions in a letter to the sisters in Rome. Seemingly struck by the similar choreography of the official receptions throughout the province, she briefly described the procedure: 'According to the custom here, we are received in each convent in much the same manner. Upon our arrival, we are escorted by the sisters to the chapel where we sing the hymn, *To Your Patronage We Fly, O Virgin*, after which everyone unites in a prayer of thanksgiving for our safe journey. Next, the community gathers in the common room – always attractively decorated – where we are warmly greeted by the local superior. This ceremony culminates with our traditional *Mnohayia lita* [*For Many Years*]. As far as our homes here are concerned,' she continued, 'they seem quite adequate; each convent has its own chapel room but the Blessed Sacrament is reserved only in permanent houses – those owned by the institute.[48] Almost everywhere the sisters teach in schools; most of them also conduct Ukrainian language courses in the evenings for our children who, sad to say, are already very anglicized.'[49]

Through personal interviews with every sister, and her observation of the nature of their apostolic works, Sister Veronica soon recognized that a Canadian Sister Servant, besides being a woman of prayer, also had to be a combination of teacher, social worker, altruist, parish moderator, and shrewd business woman. The sisters, on the other hand, came to appreciate her patience, fairness, amiability, and charm; they were inspired by her genuine love for the Church, which manifested itself in a constant respect for its representatives. In sum, she captured their hearts. Confided the Mundare chronicler: 'From the moment we met her kind glance and warm smile, we loved her.'[50] It was not that she did so much to win the sisters' affection, admiration, and trust, but that she apparently did so little. She was simply herself. And it was this quality that endeared her to everyone.

In her conferences to each local community she exhorted the sisters to offer the clergy every assistance in their difficult parish work, and to the laity, particularly youth, something solid to stand on and something believable to work for. The world, she contended, had never gone wrong for lack of poets and prophets to proclaim ideals, but for lack of persons dedicated to putting ideals into practice.

In a final message to the entire province prior to her departure for Brazil, she wrote: 'With God's help and your prayers, my good sisters, I have completed my visitation in the houses of our Canadian province. I must confess that I am pleased with your spiritual life and apostolate, and am edified by the loving willingness with which you accept sacrifice and hardship in order to bring help to our people, especially the young. I shall pray that the Lord strengthen each of you and bestow upon every sister those graces necessary to fulfil ever more zealously every missionary work for His praise and the salvation and sanctification of souls ... I bid you all farewell with this prayer: May the blessing and peace of the Lord abide in your hearts and His love motivate your every deed.'[51]

Indeed, she would be missed. In truth, however, the spontaneous devotion which she had won was not only a resounding personal triumph but also a major benefaction for the entire institute, since, by making it easy in this initial encounter for Canadian religious to accept her leadership wholeheartedly, she was instrumental in fostering a greater confidence in the European government of the congregation. In that light, her Canadian visit could be considered a resounding success.

One of Sister Veronica's most astonishing moves regarding the Canadian community was the appointment (prior to her departure from Lviv) of a sister from Europe to direct the novitiate at Mundare. And, oddly enough, even though the somewhat unflattering implication of this step was that after a period of thirty-four years the Canadians were incapable of training their postulants and novices to the satisfaction of the general council, the news seems to have stirred no significant misgivings among the members.[52]

In making this startling change in the novitiate's directorship, the thinking within the general council seems to have been that, because in the past Canadian sisters had been more painfully conscious of what pulled them away from the European community rather than of that which held them together, it was necessary to create a climate in which regional differences would give way to an international allegiance. This, it was believed, could be achieved through a better understanding and appreciation of the mother province. In Sister Veronica's estimation there was no better place to begin than in the novitiate, and no person better qualified to bring about this fulness of unity than a sister born, educated, and trained in Ukraine; one who knew the Province of Our Lady of Sorrows at first hand. This then, was the real significance of the appointment, and not the fact that novices would become more fluent in Ukrainian or better equipped to serve their people through a superior knowledge and keener appreciation of their heritage – these were obvious fringe benefits.

Consequently, on June 19, 1936, when Sister Veronica was completing her visitation at the novitiate house, the new directress, Sister Josaphata Stephanie Kizlyk, arrived from Lviv to take up her duties at Mundare. From the very first it was clear that henceforth the novices would be guided by a woman characterized by a living faith, genuine piety, and an unlimited energy. But whether, with only a scant knowledge of English and a theoretical grasp of Canada, its culture, and its people, she could understand the Canadian girl entering the institute and prepare her adequately for a religious life and work in this country was an open question. Furthermore, the long-range effect of a strong European influence upon the next generation of Canadian-born sisters could only be guessed at.

Later that year in Winnipeg, on October 25 – a thousand trials and a million blessings after its opening in 1911 – St Nicholas School observed its twenty-fifth anniversary. As the history of the past quarter-century amply testified, a Ukrainian Catholic school existed in the province of Manitoba only because of the Sisters Servants. From 1907 they had provided its teaching staff and paid for the cost of operation and maintenance. In 1933, when high school grades nine and ten had been introduced by Sister Theresa Melnyk, the load had become heavier still.[53] They had managed to pull through thus far only by organizing bazaars, teas, concerts, and collections in which they were mercifully assisted by the 'St Nicholas School Committee,' whose executive was usually comprised of their pupils' concerned parents. The road to assistance from local parishes, besides that of St Nicholas, was proving longer than they had thought possible. For years all attempts to win such a modicum of support had met a dead end. It seemed that bishop, priests, and laity took for granted that the sisters' original commitment to teach was meant to be open-ended. When, therefore, in the course of the jubilee festivities Rev. A. Truch told a large gathering of clergy and faithful that it was 'not our work but the unremitting efforts of these pioneering women, the Sisters Servants of Mary Immaculate, in the cause of Christian education that has enabled us to meet in this school today,'[54] he could not have come closer to the truth.

Sacrifice had become a by-word at St Nick's. Chronicle entries over the twenty-five-year period attest to the sisters' day-to-day struggle to keep the school open – at great personal cost. For instance, since fuel constituted the biggest substantial drain on their scanty income, it became commonplace throughout the bitter winter months for the sisters to shiver their way through every weekend. Explained one of them: 'In order to reduce the fuel bill, we shut off the furnace after the children left on Friday afternoon until Monday morning, when they returned to their classrooms. And because our sleeping quarters were in the poorly insulated attic, we often awoke in the morning to find our hair hoary with frost and the water in our washbasins frozen solid.'[55] Healthwise, at the very least, the action may seem to have been highly imprudent, but only by penny-pinching were they able to exist. Moreover, it often became necessary to canvass for funds in the evenings and on weekends, as the chronicler disclosed in December 1929: 'The sisters have begun soliciting alms in the city so that we can pay our tax and fuel bills. Since it is clearly too late to hold a bazaar, and since we have no other means of raising this money, we are compelled to beg.'[56]

And the purpose of it all? A Christian education. For over twenty-five years they had been primarily concerned in their classrooms with enabling their pupils to distinguish between the two spheres of human order: the temporal and civil from the spiritual and religious, knowing full well that to the extent they succeeded, their students would become both good citizens and good Christians.

How well had they performed? Well enough, concluded Rev. A. Luhovy, who pointed out in his article, 'The Importance of Religious Institutes,' that the many priests, doctors, nurses, teachers, and businessmen numbered among the sisters' graduates had already proved their worth in various professions and occupations. Most important of all, in his estimation, was the fact that they were 'faithful sons and daughters of our Church.'[57]

In the final analysis, however lofty their goals and achievements, theirs was still the responsibility of staffing, administering, maintaining and operating the school, and with this task emerged a daily anxiety that often stretched their endurance to the breaking-point. It is understandable, therefore, why, amid the joy of a jubilee, some of the sisters who had dedicated the most productive years of their lives to St Nicholas School could scarcely help wondering whether they would ever be freed of what could be termed their 'perpetual crisis,' or whether it would rumble on unabated as long as the school existed.

Generally, however, the celebrations of the moment served to emphasize their debt to the past, especially to the kindly French prelate, Archbishop A. Langevin, who had built the school for Ukrainians in Winnipeg. It was fitting, therefore, that a few members of the staff, accompanied by a number of senior students, should visit his tomb at St Boniface. 'The roses we placed there,' confessed the annalist, 'were our anniversary remembrance of a beloved friend and benefactor.'[58]

On this note of quiet gratitude the sisters of St Nick's began the unenviable task of trying to keep the school running for another twenty-five years.

In all sectors of their apostolate, the Sisters Servants seemed to be forever probing, spending themselves, and pushing, refusing to accept the notion that they had already done all that was possible for an institute of their size and resources. Their missionary undertakings had always been characterized by the precious gift of initiative, a quality which had accelerated their mark beyond the humdrum advance that any group of committed women could maintain anywhere. In 1937 they again manifested their refusal to plod along at a leisurely pace when they involved themselves in still another apostolic work – the care of 'forgotten people,' the aged.

In the western provinces the number of retired Ukrainian pioneers was increasing steadily. Those who were fortunate to be cared for by their families, whether on the farm or in towns and villages, lived out their lives among their own – respected, venerable, and happy. Some, less fortunate, neglected or even totally foresaken by children and relatives, discovered that old age could be an agonizing experience. Doddering, infirm, and often mocked by the young, they had to fend for themselves when they could no longer do so. Still others, who had been transplanted from a familiar rural environment to the strange setting of an urban old people's home, either by concerned families who found themselves incapable of providing adequate care or by government agencies, often felt completely cut off from other men by the language barrier which generally existed. Many of those in private institutions operated by Latin-rite religious, felt deeply their deprivation of the Eastern-rite Divine Liturgy; hence even the Mass, which should have been for them a source of consolation, became instead a source of sorrow, for it was celebrated in a strange language and rite. It seemed to them that in their last years they had lost all that had been familiar and dear. Consequently, some sank into apathy and lethargy; others grew frustrated, bitter, and even terrified at the prospect of a solitary existence in the midst of many and, more likely than not, a lonely death.

In the Komarno district of Manitoba, priests and people of both rites began to appeal to the Sisters Servants, who had been in the village for two years, to take into their home some of the helpless aged of the area. Finally, in desperation, they brought to the convent doorstep blind old Mrs T. Olansky and her deaf, senile husband, Thomas, together with frail, bedridden Mrs A. Sapar. The sisters found that they could not turn these helpless oldsters away. Without much ado, therefore, they crowded their own beds and belongings into one part of the house, and in the other made space for fifteen patients. Shortly thereafter, having received authorization from the provincial Department of Health and Welfare to accept the aged into their home, and governed by the maxim that it is better to wear out than rust out, they added this demanding work to their farm and household chores, their parish activities, their night school teaching, and their home nursing visits. From this time the care of old people was one that delighted the soul of many a Sister Servant, some of whom, like Sister Alexandra Doiron, devoted the better part of their life to this compassionate service.[59]

Although St Basil's Home could scarcely be described as a 'country club' for select 'guests' (as some nursing homes for the aged are currently being advertised), the small, rather inconvenient house set in the middle of a thriving farming community provided the oldsters with a psychological uplift – that of spending their last years in cherished rural surroundings. Moreover, simple but homelike, it was a place where an institutional air could hardly be sniffed at all, and where an old man was a man and not a ruin. Whenever weather permitted, some puttered around with vegetables and flowers; the more sedentary eventually worked themselves up to be checker champs and needlework artists; those who were bedridden had someone with whom to reminisce or to ruminate on the caprices of the weather or the state of the crops. In other words, as noted by Archbishop-Metropolitan M. Hermaniuk, c ss r, in 1956, 'Here they found a real home with all they needed and desired: people of their own descent, a language in which they could communicate, liturgical services which could satisfy their spiritual desires, and above all the devoted care which only sisters can give.'[60]

The operating costs of the home were derived partly from the patients' monthly pensions of $20, of which $5 was to be deposited on their account for funeral expenses. For their part, the sisters underwrote all capital expenditures for necessary renovations, improvements, and equipment, and also provided their own nursing services. Any rare donation that came their way went right back into circulation to keep the home in operation or to provide some badly needed item that would provide the residents with a larger slice of comfort.[61]

In the autumn of 1937 their work with the elderly was extended into the United States as a direct result of Bishop Bohachevsky's donation of a twenty-four room, three-storey house in Philadelphia, which he stipulated was to be used as a clinic and home for senior citizens. When, on August 4, Sister Gertrude Lesiuk, Sister Theophane Malowany, and Sister Barbara Prediliuk moved into the old house at 719 Brown Street, they found their first task was to form the usual broom-and-bucket squad to scrub, paint, and renovate the building from attic to basement. The occasion for all the house cleaning and excitement was the blessing of the home by Bishop Bohachevsky on October 1, after which St Mary's Home for the Aged opened its doors to its first family of elderly residents.[62] 'May God bless your endeavours in this nation,' wrote the bishop to Sister Elizabeth in a letter thanking her for undertaking this apostolate and advocating further missionary commitments in his country.[63]

Shortly after she had assumed office in 1934 Sister Elizabeth had been alerted to the rapidly deteriorating state of the orphanage building at Ituna.[64] 'The structure is fast becoming an uninhabitable wreck,' lamented the provincial annalist. 'During the past harsh winter [of 1937] the sisters and children have suffered much from the relentless cold because of a dangerously defective heating system. The tattered condition of the build-ing, however, argues strongly against replacing the furnace, since its instal-lation would simply be a waste of money.'[65]

For their part, almost to a woman, the staff at St Ann's conceded that they feared for the children's health in a house that could not have been more poorly constructed. Thanks to the fact that the sisters in charge, headed by the indomitable Sister Paula Dzygolyk, were resolute women, not weaklings or misfits, do-gooders or romantics, the institution had re-mained afloat thus far. As one hard year had followed another during the early 1930s, they had faced an appalling shortage of almost everything needed to operate an orphanage, but their skilful management and imagi-native powers had done wonders to keep the children fed and decently clothed, and the building from falling apart. 'Only God knows how much prayer, patience, and perseverance were needed to walk that road,' re-called Sister Alexandra Doiron.[66]

What provided a clear signal that the old orphanage must go was a small fire that broke out at dawn on January 21, 1938. 'Luckily, not too much damage was sustained,' acknowledged the chronicler, 'but had it occurred during the night, we might have suffered a loss of life.'[67] This incident, which dramatized the fact that those at St Ann's were daily living on the brink of danger, persuaded Sister Elizabeth that a close hard look at the situation could no longer be evaded. Actually, the institute was trapped between painful alternatives: it could opt to terminate work with orphaned children by closing the mission, or to continue the apostolate by acquiring a large construction debt.

In the final analysis, little persuasion was needed to convince the council that closure was out of the question, especially in the light of the increasing number of family relationships which seemed to be weakening – a phenomenon that resulted in more children finding themselves homeless even while their parents lived. Besides, several of the youngsters currently in their charge had been so completely abandoned by all kinfolk that their total care and education, even beyond high school, had fallen entirely to the sisters. These responsibilities argued winningly in favour of remaining at Ituna. Even so, the sisters could not help wincing before the vision of a substantial mortgage.

Among those who first stepped forward to push the cause and arouse the sisters' hopes was Rev. S. Bachtalowsky, superior of the local Redemptorist community. It was he who arranged for a loan from his religious congregation;[68] in fact, so tirelessly did he involve himself in the project that the annalist felt compelled to state that 'in the history of the orphanage, as well as in that of our institute, his name shall be inscribed in letters of gold, since but for this good priest's encouragement and assistance we might not have had the courage to begin the enterprise until we had raised all the necessary funds.'[69]

A second loan from another old friend, Rev. M. Pelech, enabled Sister Elizabeth to approve plans for the proposed structure. By beginning at once they not only desired to provide a decent home for their young charges as soon as possible but also wished to complete the building in the year 1938 in order to commemorate a significant event – the 950th anniversary of Christianity in Ukraine. Undoubtedly the low-interest loans from their friends provided a tremendous boost to the building fund, but the sisters knew that they could not shrink the amount still needed without replaying an old script – conducting another *kvesta*.[70] In short order, therefore, while the brand new orphanage was already in the making, Sisters Servants from many convents fanned out in a multipronged effort to solicit public support in parishes across Canada and in the eastern American states.

It was no pleasant assignment, recalled Rev. S. Semchuk, who described the visit of two sisters to his parish: 'I can still see those sisters of ours as they arrived late in the autumn to beg on behalf of the orphans at Ituna. It was already a time of gusting snow and icy, penetrating winds. Wrapped in shawls, they proceeded from one farmhouse to another in a rickety car that barely sputtered along in a swirling wind and a biting, numbing frost. Everywhere, our good householders shared whatever they could, not permitting them to depart empty-handed; here they received a small monetary offering, there a chunk of meat, here some butter; and so it went the whole day through – all for the sake of children.'[71]

Meanwhile, at Ituna, it became imperative to vacate the old orphanage, since it was to be demolished and any suitable materials used in the new building. The question was where to house the children in the interval. At this point the villagers magnanimously rose to the occasion by erecting a two-storey log cabin on the sisters' farm with lumber obtained from the property. Besides its location close by the parish church, there was little to recommend the sturdy but damp house, since its facilities and accommodations ranged from the barely adequate to the totally inadequate. In spite of its drawbacks it was accepted gratefully as an unavoidable intermediate step between the old and the new. Consequently, when on April 19, 1938, children, sisters, furniture, and personal belongings were transported to the rustic dwelling, the staff worked with stubborn enthusiasm to make the cold, congested quarters as livable as possible. But they operated under a host of handicaps. In truth, however, the big troubles did not bother them as much as the little ones. The daily insignificant demands were the real terrors to meet; things like drawing enough water to provide for the washing of dishes, clothes, floors, thirty-three children, and whatever else needed a scrubbing – a chore that drained them physically even before they tackled the welter of other things that needed doing. Mornings found them up before the sun, and the evening was indeed far spent when they knelt for their last prayers of the day.

Construction of the new building, which had commenced on June 20, 1938, proceeded so smoothly that the official dedication was set for September 18. Although the mellow tints in the woods agreed that autumn was at hand, that day for the sisters was a springtime of the spirit, rich in hope. Together with the officiating clergyman, Rev. A. Delaere, the esteemed missionary who had bolstered their shaky mission at Ituna eighteen years before,[72] they participated in the ceremony that generated more fanfare and a larger turnout of clergy and laity from outlying areas than normally attended such occasions in a small rural village. Perhaps the reason for their interest was the fact that St Ann's 'Jubilee' Orphanage was a monument to both the sisters' faith and the generosity of priests and people across the land. Thus for everyone present it was a time of thanksgiving to the Lord for having permitted them together to achieve what individually they had only dared hope for.[73]

One unforeseen result of the campaign to raise funds for Ituna was the establishment in Toronto of the first mission in the province of Ontario. Since 1932, when the sisters had conducted a summer school in catechetics in that city, a goodly portion of the offerings for the support of the ophanage came from the industrial east, where the Ukrainian population was steadily increasing.[74] In 1931, for example, Ukrainians in Ontario numbered 24,426; by 1941 those living and working in the province reached a total of 48,158. This upsurge can be attributed to two trends: the tendency of immigrants to Canada during this period to be more urban than rural, and a secondary migration to the cities of those born in this country, with the consequent development of highly organized Ukrainian community enclaves.[75]

On March 15, 1937, in an all-out effort to touch hearts and open pocketbooks on behalf of the Ituna orphanage, Sister Michael Mary Rospad and Sister Euphrasia Justine Woloshyn left Winnipeg for Toronto. En route, at stop after stop – Fort Frances, Fort William, North Bay – they detrained to canvass for their cause, and consequently did not reach Toronto until April 29. Here they found that two priests, Rev. M. Olenchuk and his assistant, Rev. B. Humeniuk, served three parishes: St Josaphat's on Franklin Avenue in the west end of the city; St Mary's on Bathurst Street in central Toronto; and Sacred Heart (later Holy Eucharist) in the eastern sector. Through the courtesy of the pastor they were accommodated in one room of a parish house on Bathurst Street; the rest of the building was occupied by two other families.

Their fund-raising campaign got under way almost immediately. To their dismay, however, they found their efforts hobbled by disgruntled Torontonians who were not in the least reluctant to state that in their opinion it was a mistake to collect exclusively for an orphanage somewhere in Saskatchewan. As the chronicler explained: 'Our collection went poorly because most people wanted us to establish a mission here to serve the three parishes; they therefore emphatically declared that their donations must be used to purchase a convent in Toronto.'[76] Given this prevailing climate of opinion, together with the public pressure for a reordering of priorities in favour of a project closer to home, the sisters had little choice but to inform Sister Elizabeth of this development. Normally, the matter would have ended there, with the sisters being recalled to Winnipeg, had not their provincial superior viewed this call for sisters in a broader context – as a call from Ukrainians in one of the country's most heavily populated provinces.

Not wishing to remain idle before they heard from the provincialate, Sister Michael and Sister Euphrasia carried their orphanage cause to such centres as Montreal, Brantford, and Windsor, until on May 25 they were summoned to Toronto where Sister Elizabeth awaited them. She had come for an on-the-spot, hard-eyed look at the situation. Her appraisal, honest and searching, resulted in a pledge to provide the personnel for a mission if the parishes would provide a convent. The following Sunday, almost as if the convent were already a reality, two very elated priests informed their parishioners that the Sisters Servants were not leaving.

The decision could not have come at a more opportune moment, since just then rumour had it that the French Sacred Heart Parish was interested in selling its rectory at 438 King Street East. The building, adjacent to the church, held four distinct advantages for the sisters. First, since Ukrainians, who had begun to rent Sacred Heart Church for their liturgical services in May 1937, were already negotiating for its purchase, there was every likelihood that the sisters would be ideally located next door to a permanent parish of their own rite.[77] Second, the eighteen-room house was spacious enough to be used as a hostel for working girls and students. Third, public transportation from the area to the other two parishes was good. And, finally, by reason of its vulnerable location in relation to the houses in the eastern United States and western Canada, it would also be virtually a hospice for travelling religious. For all these reasons they decided to notify Rev. E. Lamarche, the pastor at Sacred Heart, that they would be willing to buy the property for $3,500. No one mentioned that for this purpose they didn't have even $3.50.

Having set their sights on a specific goal, the sisters pressed on to reach it. Notices of a forthcoming bazaar organized by them, and tickets for a raffle attached to it, soon flooded each of the three parishes, while they continued to canvass the city – this time, for a new house. On July 5 they were able to present Father Lamarche with an initial payment in the amount of $1,500, 'eight hundred of which we collected, and seven hundred of which had been lent to us by friends.'[78] That left them with exactly three months to raise the balance of $2,000. Like the good leader she was, Sister Elizabeth immediately dispatched reinforcements in the persons of Sister Matthew Sophie Nykoliuk and Sister Mechtilde Mary Byblow to take charge of the catechetical programme and thus free Sister Michael and Sister Euphrasia for fund raising.

The response was gratifying. On August 1 the sisters held open house. 'We first received our visitors in the church hall,' explained the chronicler; 'then we toured our convent, which was bare of all furnishings. Following this, everyone participated in a Moleben in honour of the Sacred Heart to thank Him for the grace of our having purchased the rectory.'[79]

Two days later they moved into their 'St Rita's Convent' to find it stripped even of its light fixtures. Now that they had a home, however, the fact that their chairs were orange crates and their beds the floor, seemed immaterial. Of immediate consequence, rather, were the benefits to be reaped: an active apostolate in three Toronto parishes, a foothold in Ontario from which to launch a summer catechetical programme for eastern Canada, and a hostel for girls working or studying in the city. In sum, a prize worth having.

With her term as provincial superior due to expire in the autumn of 1939, Sister Elizabeth, who had nudged and directed the institute's causes with reassuring cool since 1934, prepared to transfer her duties to whoever might succeed her. It came as a surprise to absolutely nobody, however, when on July 12 the general council manifested its confidence in her by notifying the members of the province that she had been selected to guide them through a second five-year period. The standard of leadership that she had supplied could, therefore, be read as a renewed mandate of sorts for her reappointment. To assist her, the generalate selected Sister Ignatia Butryn, Sister Natalie Klos, Sister Fevronia Prystupa, and Sister Monica Mantyka. 'It is hoped,' declared Sister Veronica, 'that the newly appointed council will guide the bark of the province safely and happily through any temporal tempests which might arise.'[80]

Her words were prophetic, since already Europe stood at the unfolding of a great war. God was about to submit the Sisters Servants in the Province of Our Lady of Sorrows to the spiritual, moral, and material ravages of a conflict the like of which the world had never known, and to a separation from their sisters in the west more complete than they had ever thought possible. In these circumstances it was perhaps inevitable that the Canadian-American province, second oldest in the institute, should surface as a leader and step into the governing void resulting from the isolation of the mother province.

CHAPTER 8

In time of war...

Ukrainian Canadians experienced anxiety and foreboding when in a startling manœuvre on August 23, 1939, Nazi Germany and Communist Russia became partners to a non-agression pact. The clearest signs of the designs of both nations were the German offensive that brought Poland under Nazi control within thirty days and a second treaty on September 28 which partitioned the defeated republic, with its area of 150,000 square miles and thirty-five million inhabitants, between the two signatories. As Ukrainians saw it, the action simply conceived another chapter in the long history of national injustice in eastern Europe. Specifically, where the communists were concerned, they were unable to submerge their suspicions that the Soviet leaders would place their own interests before those of other national groups – among them the Ukrainians – since more than half of the eastern portion of Poland, with a population of fourteen million and containing large agricultural stretches of Ukraine, was promptly seized by the Russians.

The new boundary ran through old Poland approximately in a line reaching from the southwestern tip of Lithuania to the northeastern edge of Hungary. The western half of the territory was annexed by the Germans and placed under a 'general government,' while most of the province of Galicia, including the populous Ukrainian dioceses of Lviv, Stanislaviv, and part of Peremyshl, fell into communist hands. In this territory, with the Red Army looking on, provincial assemblies were chosen which 'unanimously' voted for union with the USSR. On November 1–2, 1939, the Soviet Union, 'generously' agreeing to comply with the request, swiftly incorporated the former Polish territories into the Ukraine and White Russian constituent republics of the USSR.[1]

Sharing the growing concern of his faithful in Canada over these disturbing developments, Bishop Ladyka issued a pastoral letter on September 21 in which he aptly summed up their fears and conceded his own deep doubts concerning the future: 'Galicia, which for centuries has been one and indivisible, always true to spiritual values, has now been rent asunder by the communists. As a consequence, the achievements of centuries, particularly our churches, are in danger of being completely destroyed,' he sadly observed. 'I therefore call upon all of you to unite yourselves in prayer,' he added, 'imploring the Lord to bring this period of international travail to a swift end, to grant that the Ukrainian nation, under the leadership of its bishops – who will be strengthened by the example of their predecessors in a stalwart defense of the Catholic Faith – may experience better days, and that this conflict may soon be replaced by a lasting peace.'[2] The prelate undoubtedly hoped that the violent events occurring in eastern Europe would elicit a committed resolve from Ukrainians to work constructively together, regardless of organizational affiliation, 'to carry out all the responsibilities which this historical moment will demand of us as Canadian citizens.'[3]

For their part, Sisters Servants in North America found themselves intimately involved in the happenings 'over there.' At the heart of their anguish was the cruel uncertainty of the fate of their members who, at the close of 1938, had numbered 494 sisters, including forty-eight novices.[4] Paradoxically, therefore, the war, which was effectively beginning to cut off East from West, was also simultaneously cementing the bond of union between them and their European sisters as nothing else had ever done before.

Events moved quickly during the autumn of 1939. In October the Russian border was sealed, but not before Sister Veronica, her secretary, and three general councillors succeeded in making their way to the novitiate house at Kristinopil, located in German-occupied territory. 'In order to assure a freedom of movement for the governing body of the congregation,'[5] Sister Veronica acted swiftly to establish the generalate in this convent where, with the exception of aspirants from Czechoslovakia, all European candidates admitted to the institute were being trained. Here, although under the close scrutiny of authorities, religious were still permitted to live in their convents and fulfil some of their apostolic responsibilities.[6]

The world they had known, however, had already begun to crumble around them. Within a few months a great deal had changed; most notably, the members of the Province of Our Lady of Sorrows had become a divided family. Those who found themselves in territories occupied by the Soviets and those in areas under direct Nazi control or within the axis sphere might just as well have been living in two distinct worlds, so difficult was it to establish contact or even to determine the validity of bits of news concerning sisters and missions that did manage to filter through. Hence the picture of life on the 'other side' remained as murky as ever.

In November 1939 the first communication from Sister Veronica since the commencement of the war reached the provincialate at Edmonton via Rome. It was a profound relief for the sisters to learn that their superior general was alive, even though their fears for the welfare of the entire European community were scarcely diminished by the grim news contained in her letter. 'All of our houses except those at Kristinopil, Zhuzhyl, Belz, the schools in Peremyshl, Bosko, and Zhegestiv are under communist control.' she wrote. 'Only God knows how long things will remain this way. Almost every city in western Ukraine has been under attack. The tragedy of war has etched itself deeply upon all of us. Here at Kristinopil, bombings and shelling raids have battered the old section of our building as well as the new addition, which was almost roofed. Windows and doors have been blown out and the walls damaged.'[7] Characteristically, she seemed to be less disturbed by material losses than those concerning spiritual things. 'Many of our homes are now in communist hands,' she explained. 'At Berezhany, thirty-five orphans have been taken from us and placed in a Jewish orphanage. Our sisters have had to leave the schools because it has been impossible to conform to the godless demands of the Russians.'[8]

It was clear that in the face of overpowering atheistic opposition the sisters were endeavouring to cling to their Christian apostolate wherever and as long as possible. Before leaving Soviet-controlled Ukraine, Sister Veronica had encouraged them to remain in the midst of their people in order to strengthen them in their suffering by bearing witness to Christ in the daily struggle for one's own soul and the soul of a nation, and by ministering to their physical and material needs.[9] But the campaign to strangle the Church, a movement that by 1946 was to rise on a ferocious tide of arrest and expulsion of bishops, priests, religious, and laity to Siberian labour camps had already been unleashed by the communists. 'The Church is suffering more than any other institution in the land,' lamented Sister Veronica, as she proceeded to explain the brutal measures that threatened to strip the nation bare of its religious women: 'Many of our convents have been confiscated and our sisters dispersed. Some have returned to their families; others have resigned themselves to a hand-to-mouth existence, dwelling wherever they can find shelter. Pray for them, I beg you, my dear sisters, asking the Lord to grant them the strength to bear their sufferings for His praise, and the good of our Church, our institute, and our nation. Much prayer is needed to make reparation to God for great sacrilege. Only now do we fully appreciate what a tremendous grace it is to be able to profess one's faith publicly and to pray in freedom.' Then, almost as an afterthought, she added: 'There are seventy sisters here, among them forty-five novices and postulants. Indeed, we have many persons to support in these hard times, but we are confident that the Lord who feeds the birds will also remember us.'[10]

Sister Elizabeth translated her superior general's account of the European province's tribulations, yearnings, and poverty into immediate action. An urgent request went out from Edmonton to the entire community in Canada and the United States for special prayers to be offered each evening for God's protection of their sisters overseas. In addition, announced the annalist, 'the provincial council has appealed to all houses to make every sacrifice in order to send them some material assistance.'[11]

Predictably enough, as current events foreshadowed increasing disruptions in communication with, and travel in, Europe, few sisters entertained any hope that the second general chapter, scheduled to be held in 1940 for the purpose of electing a general council and evaluating the constitutions of 1932 after their seven-year trial period, would be convoked. Sister Veronica for one was certain that this was an impossibility. 'We had looked forward to seeing you at the chapter, at which time we had also wished to plan the observance of our forthcoming jubilee commemorating the fiftieth anniversary of our institute,' she wrote regretfully. 'Instead, Jesus is asking us to go through the fires of purgation in order to prove our worth. May His will be done; may we, with His grace, persevere in our Faith.'[12]

The matter of the chapter seems to have been one of concern for the Holy See as well, for on January 6, 1940, Father Schrijvers, writing to Sister Elizabeth from Rome, stated: 'The Sacred Congregation has informed me that the chapter has been postponed and that your superior general together with her council shall remain in office until further notice.'[13]

With regular channels of communication already closed, Sister Veronica acknowledged that proper recourse to the generalate by the province, regarding local internal affairs, would scarcely be possible, and hence she empowered Sister Elizabeth to deal with such matters within her geographical jurisdiction for the duration of the war.[14] Her vesting of broader authority in the provincial superior was a realistic move, and its timing superb, for although the institute in Ukraine seemed to be bleeding to death, that in Canada was vibrantly alive, bursting with good health and optimistic spirit.

This, in fact, was true of the entire Ukrainian Catholic Church in North America. At the end of 1929, for instance, when Bishop Ladyka had assumed office, only 46 priests were labouring in Canadian missions;

within a decade this number had doubled so that at the close of 1939 approximately 300,000 Ukrainians in 325 parishes and mission stations were being served by 90 priests; while in Bishop Bohachevsky's American jurisdiction there were 106 clergymen ministering to 290,688 people in 132 parishes.[15]

At this moment of consistent growth in North America on the one hand, and the effective throttling of the Church in Ukrainian lands on the other, the Holy See proclaimed to the world its pleasure and confidence in the Ukrainian Catholic Church in the United States and Canada by nominating a bishop for each country. The two appointments, that of Most Rev. Ambrose Senyshyn, OSBM, on July 6, 1942, as auxiliary to Bishop Bohachevsky, and that of Most Rev. Neil Savaryn, OSBM, on April 23, 1943, as auxiliary to Bishop Ladyka, were gratifying to their people. Thus hundreds joyfully participated in the ceremony that took place in St Nicholas Church in Chicago on October 23, 1942, when Bishop Senyshyn received the full plenitude of the priesthood from Bishop Bohachevsky, Bishop Ladyka, and Bishop Basil Takach; and a similar spirit of jubilation ruled the crowd that jammed St Michael's Cathedral at Toronto on July 1, 1943, to witness the consecration of Bishop N. Savaryn by Bishop B. Ladyka, Archbishop J. McGuigan (later Cardinal), and Bishop A. Senyshyn. Unquestionably, this action by Rome, which exemplified the solicitude of the Holy See for Ukrainians, further strengthened their Church on this continent.

Within the framework of this expansion, the pressures upon the Sisters Servants became more acute because of the almost unlimited requests for their services, especially in education. It seemed that even before petitions for sisters could even be considered by the council, many fresh demands were already piling up.

Sister Elizabeth, whose principal interest had always been in education, responded favourably to invitations for teachers whenever possible. In the latter part of the 1930s, for example, she had exhibited a notable willingness to place sisters in rural public schools. As a consequence, in 1936, Sister Benigna Skaluba had been assigned to a school at Candiac, Saskatchewan, and Sister Helena Kwasnicky to one at Zoria, Manitoba. In 1938 Sister Monica Mantyka had taken charge of eight grades in the poverty-stricken community of Heart River in Alberta's Peace River District.

Soon, however, Sister Elizabeth's educational policy came to reflect a different perception, for by September 1939 she had shifted toward a greater commitment of personnel to public and separate schools in towns and cities, largely perhaps because of the increasing numbers of Ukrainians settling in urban areas. In 1940, for instance, Sister Bernarda Anne Chrunik, who took up her duties in a school at Ukraina, North Dakota, became the first Catholic nun to be hired by the North Dakota State Board. Moreover, Sister Marion Pauline Zerebesky, who joined the staff of the Mundare District High School in September of 1945, and Sister Louise Pauline Matwiy, who began teaching in the local elementary public school at the same time, were the first religious to enter the Mundare public school system.

At the same time, the notable rise in the urban Ukrainian population resulted in an increased enrolment of Ukrainian children in separate schools. Unfortunately, ignorance on the part of many teachers about the Eastern rite to which these children belonged, soon created an emotionally charged cleavage between the teachers and their pupils' parents and pastors with the children unhappily caught in the middle, and wondering whether they really belonged to the Catholic Church. Aroused by the issue, and alive to its implications for home, school, and church, the Sisters Servants revealed a genuine desire to tackle the problem, convinced that they had a responsibility to these youngsters. When, therefore, in September 1939, their numbers in the Catholic schools at Edmonton were increased, and one of their members was engaged by the Separate School Board at Regina, a trend toward their greater teaching participation in publicly supported Catholic schools definitely emerged. Often, during this period, their apostolic interest in this direction was nudged by Latin-rite bishops, especially in regard to schools which had a goodly proportion of Ukrainian children. Among them, Bishop J. T. Kidd of London, Ontario, was most concerned, acknowledged the annalist: 'in fact, it is through his encouragement and assistance that we have accepted two teaching positions in a separate school at Windsor, for September 1940.'[16]

A secondary reason compelling the sisters to fill these openings was the assurance of a steady income, without which it was impossible to carry on their parish apostolate in most Canadian cities. 'If it were not for these teaching positions at Windsor,' declared the annalist boldly, 'our sisters there would be unable to conduct the evening school or work in the parish, for although its executive originally made a contract to provide them with a monthly salary of $50, it has reneged on its commitment. Strangely enough, wherever we have small houses in Canada, we are often confronted with this same difficulty; namely, that the parishes which promised the sisters a living wage do not fulfil their obligations. Usually the sisters receive a few dollars in the first or second month, but thereafter they are expected to fend for themselves. Simply to exist in such discouraging circumstances, therefore, they are obliged either to beg, sew liturgical vestments, or make artificial floral arrangements for sale to other parishes.'[17]

Having witnessed this type of situation time and again, Sister Elizabeth felt bound to refuse requests whenever she perceived that the sisters assigned to a mission might end up having to put more effort into earning a living than into their apostolate. A case in point was a parish in Vancouver. A petition, dated December 15, 1943, from Archbishop W. M. Duke, was forwarded directly to Bishop Ladyka, and read: 'Would it be possible to have two or three Ukrainian Sisters make a foundation here to look after Ukrainian children? I would be glad to help them to make a foundation, and I am sure they would save a great many souls. Please give me your advice in this very important matter.'[18] As it turned out, despite the archbishop's obvious interest in the spiritual welfare of Ukrainian children in that west coast city, the proposed mission never moved beyond the planning stage, primarily because the institute became disenchanted by the reluctance of those concerned to guarantee adequate provision for the sisters who would work there.[19]

Meanwhile, in the United States the current need was for sisters to staff parochial evening and day schools, which were being opened in almost every parish. The lively interest of Ukrainians in the parochial school stemmed from their dismay over the fact that the American public schools were emphasizing assimilation rather than integration. It was therefore hoped by hierarchy, clergy, and laity alike that the parish schools, which existed for the primary reasons that they offered religious instruction and taught the language of the group, would also, besides imparting to their children a knowledge and appreciation of American traditions, foster healthy attitudes toward their Ukrainian background and culture.[20]

The responsibilities of those religious assigned to the American schools in any parish differed little from the duties outlined in a letter to Bishop Bohachevsky by the pastor of Wilkes-Barre, Pennsylvania, in 1939: 'The tasks of the sisters shall include teaching in grades one to four, as well as in the evening school; providing a course in needlecraft for the older girls of the parish; preparing several children's concerts; conducting a youth church choir; and visiting parishioners and others at least once a month for the purpose of collecting offerings to pay for the maintenance of the school.'[21] They were, undoubtedly, in the main stream of parish life.

On the face of things, in both Canada and the United States, they were 'doing all right' as the idiom goes. Concern for their apostolate in all areas and the will to raise the scholastic level in their schools kept standards high. Whatever certification was required by provincial departments of education or health, was sought and obtained. At best, however, this business of constant up-dating was never easy, and it grew less so with the scramble for university credits and degrees, which soon became the only coin that would buy the recognition and certification that department officials demanded, and the only proof of competence which showed up on a transcript. The sisters found it imperative to supplement their Normal school training and experience by studies at universities during the evenings or on Saturdays, or during vacation time, even though it was strenuous and hectic, costly in time and tuition, and did not necessarily make better teachers or nurses. There was no alternative; the institute simply had to struggle to maintain the pace, while at the same time trying to safeguard the spiritual formation of the junior sisters and the health and spiritual growth of the seniors. The congregation experienced a tangible consolation for all its pains in the spring of 1940 when its first university graduates – Sister Cornelia Katherine Mantyka, Sister Marion Zerebesky, and Sister Mechtilde Byblow – received their degrees; now it could begin to deepen the scope of its services in private as well as in publicly supported institutions.

Whatever its merits, however, this educational policy turned up an area of contention; some members of the clergy were apparently piqued by what they viewed as simply the sisters' involvement in a great credit-chase. Others were inclined to call into question the whole breadth of the sisters' commitment, by failing to see the relevance to the Ukrainian Catholic Church of the sisters' teaching in both the public and Catholic separate school systems in Canada, interpreting these positions as a transfer of interest from Ukrainians and the Eastern rite to non-Ukrainians and the Latin rite. In their view the Sisters Servants were veering away from their principal mandate – that of fostering the faith among Ukrainians. These sentiments were underscored by the provincial superior of the Basilian Order, Rev. B. Baranyk, who, in a letter to Sister Elizabeth, dated June 15, 1945, stoutly complained: 'I take this opportunity to express the regret of some of our priests, arising from the sisters' reluctance to offer sufficient assistance in summer catechetics and to cooperate in the establishment of new institutions for the purpose of furthering their apostolate among our people.'[22]

Perhaps the ultimate irony of these charges lay in the fact that during this period in their institute's development the sisters had less reason than ever before to feel guilty of the charges. For between 1940 and 1945 they had founded no less than fourteen missions among Ukrainians in Canada and the United States; these included convents in the provinces of Alberta, Manitoba, Ontario, and Nova Scotia, and the states of New York, Pennsylvania, and the District of Columbia.[23] In the same interval the congregation affirmed that it had no intention of relinquishing the vital catechetical apostolate. For even in the summer of 1944, for example, when there were sisters enrolled in universities at Edmonton, Saskatoon, Kingston, Ontario, Washington, and Dickinson, North Dakota, as well as in the Ukrainian cultural courses being offered at Winnipeg and in the classes of language teaching methods and choral conducting organized by Sister Juvenalia Mary Kaniuk at Sloatsburg, New York, the institute none the less provided the personnel to staff ninety rural vacation schools in which 3,900 children received religious instruction. Taken on balance, all this added up to a pretty fair apostolic performance.

Ordinarily Sister Elizabeth treated complaints with equanimity. This instance was different, perhaps because she was quick to perceive the disquieting possibility that accusations of the kind made in the letter mentioned might irreparably damage the morale of the sisters, who could scarcely have been unaware of the undercurrent of criticism beginning to swirl around them. In reflection of that fact, and obviously bent on bridging any existing gap of misunderstanding, she resolved to explain both the complexities confronting the institute and the changing situations to which the sisters were realistically adapting within the framework of their religious vocation that, like any other, was not immune to the shortage of time, the emotions of the moment, and the human failings of its practitioners. Thus, in her reply of July 19 she spoke out loud and clear: 'It is painful for us to learn that some of the Reverend Fathers feel that we are failing to cooperate with the clergy in the opening of new institutions and in providing assistance in catechetical work. Regarding each of these charges our conscience is clear, for we are carrying on our apostolate as our resources permit. We cannot perform miracles. New houses are founded only as suitable personnel is available. More than this we cannot do ... Perhaps the Reverend Fathers do not realize that since our novitiate house has been reorganized our catechetical schedule has also been altered. In the past, when at least fifteen professed religious resided there, it was possible to serve a greater number of colonies in that district, and thus satisfy everyone. Today, however, the house is occupied only by the novitiate staff and novices, who obviously cannot be sent out for the summer to teach in numerous farming communities. Neither is it possible for the nursing sisters to leave their hospitals in order to assist in this kind of work, meritorious and important as it is. Furthermore, those members who teach in private, public, or separate schools must register in university courses if they are to continue to meet the academic and professional requirements of their respective departments of education. Nevertheless, while it is true that, as a consequence, fewer sisters than before are available for summer catechetics, every sister who is free teaches in as many colonies as possible. It is indeed difficult for us, therefore, to understand why some of our priests fail to take these factors into consideration.'[24]

Annoying as the criticism may have been, it does not seem to have produced any immediate adverse effects; neither cries of innocence nor a feeling of chagrin swept through the congregation. On the contrary, the complaints did have a redeeming attribute; they urged the Sisters Servants not only to develop their strengths, but also to recognize their short-comings.

Regardless of any remarks to the contrary, one of their strong points at this time was their work in catechetics, which was blossoming as never before. That first evening school for working girls at Edmonton, together with the home nursing visits of the original four missionaries in 1902, had offered their own forms of religious instruction, direct and indirect. Subsequently, every sodality, altar boys' club, women's association, and even every convent parlour, could write its own account of the teaching mission of the sisters – and no two accounts would be alike. So, likewise, every Saturday and Sunday class conducted in the cities and suburbs, as well as every vacation course held in rural areas, attested to the fact that they were bringing the gospel message to thousands of families from one end of the year to the other.

Among these religious undertakings, however, summer catechetics became the distinguishing mark of the Sisters Servants' apostolate in Canada and the United States. Largely, perhaps, because of the unslake-able need for religious instruction in rural districts, the movement had grown by leaps and bounds from 1904 when the first vacation school had been organized at Mundare. By the mid-1930s the sisters were literally blanketing the prairie countryside; Lamont, Myrnam, Borschiv, Plain Lake in Alberta; Norquay, Wishart, Goodeve, Hafford in Saskatchewan; Mountain Road, St Norbert, Fishing River, Oakburn in Manitoba – so reads the list of some of the 101 country towns and crossroads villages that felt their influence in the summer of 1935, for instance, when they instructed 5,076 children.[25]

Rev. Neil Savaryn (later Bishop), one of the early Basilian missionaries in Alberta, thus described their activity during vacation time: 'The sisters leave their convents each summer [from June to September] to conduct so-called "Ukrainian Summer Schools," which last anywhere from one to four weeks. The timetable includes catechetics, Ukrainian, and liturgical and folk music. The aim of the programme is to prepare the youngest children for the reception of their first Holy Communion, and to deepen the religious knowledge and cultural appreciation of the older group ... At the end of the course delighted parents, upon bidding the departing sisters farewell, can't seem to thank them enough for having taught their children such a great deal in so short a time. The youngsters, in turn, entreat them to return. For their part, the sisters, despite their fatigue, proceed to another colony where they begin all over again. Such vacation schools, which are admirably suited to conditions existing in this country, are conducted by the sisters every year.'[26]

In their own way, therefore, the Sisters Servants in North America had anticipated by more than sixty years the call for greater involvement in catechetics that came from Vatican Council II in 1965, when the council fathers declared: 'In fulfilling its educational role, the Church, eager to employ all suitable aids, is concerned especially about those which are her very own. Foremost among these is catechetical instruction, which enlightens and strengthens the faith, nourishes life according to the spirit of Christ, leads to intelligent and active participation in the liturgical mystery, and gives motivation for apostolic activity' (Declaration on Christian Education, 4).

Indeed, every summer mission they directed could produce its own small epic of conversions and reconversions, baptisms, marriages rectified, souls and bodies comforted, the while its children were schooled in eternal truth. Members of the clergy marvelled at the manner in which they often smiled their way into strange villages, braved the first opposition, endured burning sun or pelting rain to visit practically every family in the district, smoothed difficulties, calmed fears, explained away prejudices, weeded out old hatreds, and insinuated new hopes. Clergymen were astonished, too, at the inconveniences the sisters tolerated; 'they willingly teach in chapels, sacristies, parish halls, canteens, and on stages – all in an effort to impart religious knowledge and an appreciation of Ukrainian culture,' remarked Rev. M. Pelech.[27] And one of his fellow missionaries, Rev. S. Semchuk, concurred: 'I remember when our sisters arrived to teach at Olesha [Saskatchewan],' he wrote, 'where they were unable to find accommodation. Not at all miffed, they simply set up their living quarters behind the stage of the parish hall. And again, at Kowaliwka

[Saskatchewan], they lived in the sacristy. When I later asked them whether they had been afraid of dwelling in the isolated building, and what they had eaten, they quietly replied: "No, we weren't afraid; and as for food, we ate whatever the children brought – whatever was available." Not once did I hear a word of complaint, criticism, or protest; they seemed always to carry on calmly and generously.'[28]

Father Semchuk also illustrated the kind of assistance rendered by the sisters to priests in their scattered rural apostolate: 'Our Sokal [in Saskatchewan] seemed to have been forgotten even by God,' he admitted; 'it was as religiously fragmented as Babylon itself. In fact, when the sisters came to teach here for two weeks one summer there were only four families who were registered as parishioners. But God was about to perform a miracle in men's hearts through these missionaries. To their classes the sisters somehow managed to attract over forty children whose parents had left the Church either out of ignorance, prejudice, anger, or pride. Apparently, however, their hearts still hungered for the old truths, the old faith, for when the opportunity presented itself, all those who had apostacized, who hadn't seen the inside of a church for years, permitted the sisters to instruct their children. How gratifying it was to witness these youngsters approaching the sacraments of penance and the Eucharist, and to hear them sing the responses during the celebration of the Divine Liturgy. Quiet work and dedication performed these wonders and proved that the age of miracles is with us still.'[29]

In an endeavour to involve the laity in the institute's catechetical apostolate, Sister Mechtilde Byblow organized a teacher training course in religion for volunteers from among students attending Sacred Heart Academy in Yorkton. Assisted by the two Redemptorist missionaries, Rev. R. Chomiak and Rev. J. Korba, Sister Mechtilde launched the project in September 1940. By June most of the participants had been adequately prepared to provide sound religious instruction, and could henceforth be readily integrated into the regular vacation schedules. And they were. In due course, even though greater numbers of sisters found it necessary to attend summer schools, the religion programme was not adversely affected. In 1945, for example, the institute provided religious and lay teachers for 106 rural parishes, with a pupil enrolment of 4,004.[30] The benefits of the course were lasting, conceded Rev. A. Luhovy, 'for the children fondly remembered the experience and the knowledge that they had gained long after the sisters had departed, and this even though classes in their village were conducted for just two or three weeks, and only once every two or three years.'[31]

The last word on the Sisters Servants' contribution to the catechetical apostolate seemed to have been said by Father Semchuk when he acknowledged: 'Our people owe much to women such as Sister Taida [Letawsky] and Sister Isidore [Sophie Nozak] as well as many others who have carried the awesome burden of our spiritual progress in their seemingly weak hands. Thousands of children on the prairies will likely never forget their prayers, the truths of the faith, or their ethnic origin; all of this the sisters have given them. And they have done it without fanfare, without any recompense, and often even without receiving a word of thanks – all in the name of Christ for the eternal good of souls.'[32]

Within another area of their burgeoning apostolate, conditions proved ripe for a further flourishing of their missionary life in the United States through the opening of a motherhouse in that country in 1941. And the need was clear. A glance at the fourteen houses already established from New York State to North Dakota revealed that the fundamental flaw in the congregation's American structure was fragmentation; for with usually just two sisters serving at each mission, it was no exaggeration to claim that such isolation could easily corrode community unity.

As early as 1940 a candid assessment of the situation seemed unmistakably in the air at the chancery office in Philadelphia. Without doubt, Bishop Bohachevsky's sudden attentiveness to the problem facing the Sisters Servants in his diocese was born of charity and necessity. As he saw it, there were two good reasons for his proposal that the institute immediately procure a large house, preferably in the suburbs of some American city, to serve as the institute's focal point in the United States. One was that a home away from the voices of motors or railroads would permit the sisters a breather for a few weeks during the summer from the overheated centres in which they worked, and an occasion to acquaint themselves with new members as well as to enjoy the company of old friends from the other missions. The second was that the annual retreat, if made in a restful atmosphere, would be a refreshing spiritual and community experience, imperative, he believed, for religious assigned to American parishes, where the constant activity to which each sister was subjected throughout the year was an intoxication that could easily stifle spirituality. At every opportunity, therefore, the bishop sought to impress upon Sister Elizabeth the existing need for such a motherhouse.[33]

That there was no major obstacle to the congregation's carrying out the prelate's wishes at once was, in fact, an understatement. Since up to now the relatively small institute of Ukrainian sisters had rarely found itself in blooming financial health, certainly any large house anywhere seemed to be well beyond its economic sphere. Apparently, however, the provincialate was not a place haunted by apprehensions, since if not entirely sympathetic to taking on a costly venture, the councillors must have been basically favourable toward it. For, surprisingly enough, in September of 1940, after the matter had been taken under advisement, Sister Elizabeth began to look at properties in the eastern states. To this task she brought her usual determination and independence of mind, together with her flair for taking risks and a taste for battling every financial dragon that might appear to thwart her missionary designs.

What she was looking for she found in the small New York village of Sloatsburg. Her fancy was caught and held by the sweeping spaciousness of 'Table Rock,' the 180-acre Hamilton estate set against the background of the Catskill and Ramapo mountains, approximately thirty-five miles upstate from New York City. Its simple but splendidly built home, resting on an elevation of 840 feet, and overlooking a small lake, acres of rolling fields, and well-cleared woodland with winding bridle paths and trails, captured her imagination. Already she envisaged more than just a summer home for the sisters. Before she even held the deed to the land, she had already conceived the idea of an apostolate for the old and the young in these fascinating surroundings. And in her mind's eye she had already renamed the estate 'St Mary's' Villa of Table Rock.

Her dreams were momentarily shattered when she discovered that the attached price tag was $75,000. As had happened so often before, however, when the apostolic desires and high courage of the sisters had been thwarted by the expected – an almost empty purse – she simply called upon the entire Province of Christ the King to present the matter to the Lord in prayer. In the meantime she organized a *kvesta* to raise funds and applied her no-nonsense fiscal policies toward obtaining a loan, in the event that one day the price might become right. And it did – on June 29, 1941 – at which time she and the estate's distinguished owner, Mrs Juliet Pierpont Morgan Hamilton, signed the deed of purchase. The shrewd, personable provincial superior seemed to have an uncanny knack for coming up with precisely the kind of last-minute solutions that had kept many of the institute's missionary drives alive in the past. 'It is almost a miracle,' enthused the annalist, 'that we have bought this magnificent property, with its fifty-six-room sandstone villa and other buildings for the sum of $48,500.'[34] No one doubted that this was true, but bargain though it may have been, the purchase had drained the institute of most of its savings and had required it to accept a $35,000 loan.

On July 15, 1941, Sister Lubov Chawrona, Sister Julia Katherine

Nowicky, Sister Gertrude Lesiuk, and Sister Sylvester Stephanie Gulka occupied St Mary's Villa to prepare for the commencement of their first apostolate at the site – work with the elderly. Significantly, from the very outset, the most vocal support for the proposed St Joseph's Home for the Aged came from members of the clergy, among them Rev. V. Bilynsky, who wrote: 'Through the contributions made by our people and those of other nationalities, St Mary's Villa has come into existence as a haven for Ukrainian pioneers and their descendants ... And on July 4, 1942, the Sisters Servants will rejoice more than anyone when the Ukrainian Catholic Church in America, through His Excellency, Bishop Constantine, will bless the result of their labours, and Ukrainians will see concrete proof of their quiet but fruitful apostolate.'[35]

Father Bilynsky was absolutely right. The new joy experienced by the sisters in every Canadian and American convent on the occasion of St Mary's official dedication on July 4 went beyond their dramatic achievement. Just seven years before they had shown their readiness to help their Church in America through an obscure assignment at Stamford. Today, in the presence of Bishop Bohachevsky and Bishop Ladyka, clergymen, religious, and three thousand faithful, they were again publicly proclaiming their willingness to bear an extra burden if, by opening this fifteenth house in the United States, their people, both the old and the young, would reap the fruits of their sacrifice.[36]

Also lending her rather impressive weight to these sentiments was Mrs Hamilton. 'She is delighted,' commented the annalist, 'that the home which she loves and in which she received so many of God's blessings has passed into the hands of people who care.'[37] Indeed, from the moment of its dedication, Sister Elizabeth's imaginative apostolic package for Sloatsburg was recognized as the centre-piece of the institute's otherwise modest programme in American parishes. Within two years the Villa became a vacation and study centre for many sisters; St Joseph's grew to be a pleasant home for many pioneers, and from September 1944 St Mary's Villa Academy of Table Rock opened its doors to its first students.

The initial enrolment totalled exactly eight sophomores and one junior. Sister Cornelia Mantyka, known to be a 'model of exactitude,' who had spent most of her teaching years in the secondary school classrooms at Mundare, Yorkton, and Winnipeg, was ideally cast in the role of founder and former of the institute's latest residential high school. During the first year she was both the principal and the faculty – being the only teacher on the staff. And it was she, together with Sister Sozonta Iskiw, the superior;

Above, left, is Sister Josaphata Hordashewsky, who founded the Sisters Servants. Beside her is Sister Ambrose Lenkewich who came to Canada in 1902, guided and became first major superior of the young Canadian group.

The Sisters and faithful stand before their first home, which served as provincialate, novitiate, public chapel, and school. This picture was taken about 1908.

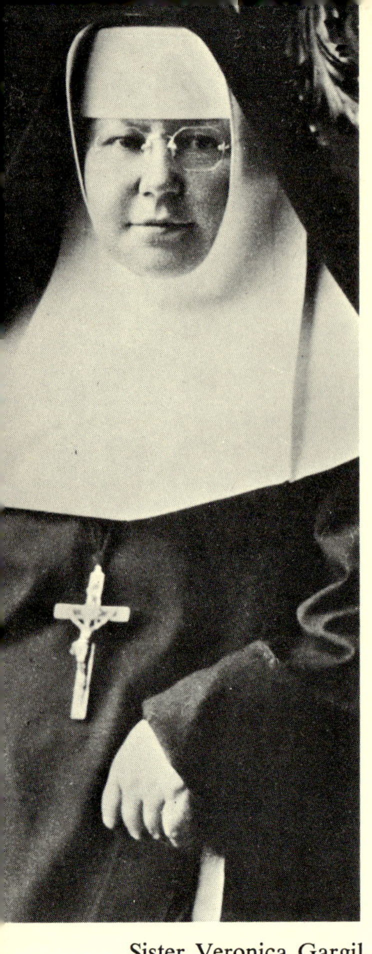 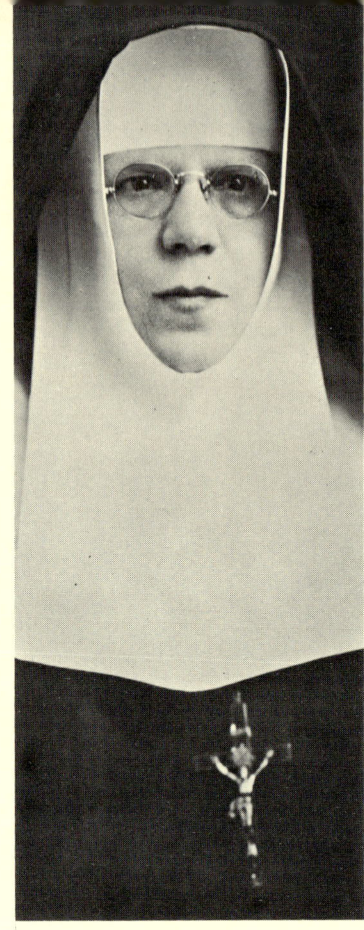 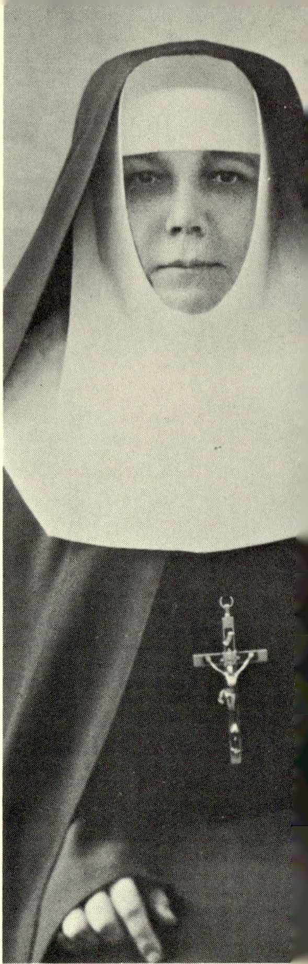

Sister Veronica Gargil, the first superior general of the institute, elected in 1934, major superior Sister Athanasia Melnyk, and Sister Elizabeth Kassian, first provincial superior.

Delegates to the first general chapter pose at the pier in Montreal, before boarding the *Ascania*.

Left to right: Sister Josaphata Tymochko, Sister Ambrose Lenkewich, Sister Athanasia Melnyk, Sister Elizabeth Kassian.

Sister Bernadette Warick succeeded Sister Elizabeth as provincial superior in 1949.
She was followed in 1959 by Sister Boniface Sloboda.
Sister Jerome Chimy took office as superior general in 1956.
In honour of a visit to the provincialate in Toronto by His Eminence, Josyf Cardinal
Slipyj, Sister Boniface presents him with a memento from the Sisters Servants.

Sister Frances Byblow held the post of provincial superior until 1970, when she was succeeded by Sister Justine Kowal. Below, Sister Frances presents a Papal Blessing, displayed by Sister Pauline Stachiw, to benefactors, especially the Knights of Columbus, at the fiftieth anniversary of St Ann's Children's Home in Ituna, Saskatchewan.

Sister Eleanor Pauline Lenyk, the prefect; and the nine students, who set the tone and spirit that has animated St Mary's ever since.

The following year, with a trebled enrolment and another teacher, Sister Joan Magriy, on the staff, the academy held its first commencement. There was one lone senior, Helen Sadasky of Bridgeport, Connecticut. She was without doubt the most clever, most popular, and most beautiful girl in her class. Every academy 'tradition' was created for her, and she had the distinction of being its first alumna.

Oddly enough, in the early years, the main lifeline of support for St Mary's was the grimy New York subway. Here, for many hours each day, in between their prayers for the passers-by and their unofficial counselling and consoling bureau for tens of passengers who stopped each day to share their troubles with these sympathetic listeners, Sister Barbara Prediliuk and later Sister Taida Letawsky, Sister Basil Starko, and Sister Andrea Anastasia Senyshyn graciously accepted alms. It is little wonder that they soon came to be known by hundreds of New Yorkers as 'our angels of the subway.'[38] Without question they were also the angels of St Mary's, for through this most humble of all assignments they sustained the academy until a capacity enrolment enabled it, in large part, to support itself. If anything the story of Sloatsburg is a chronicle of high hopes, ambitious commitments, and astonishing risks. And it does seem to give the lie to those who do not believe that the meek shall inherit the earth.

The year 1942 marked a golden milestone: a half-century of service tallied off since the institute's founding in 1892 — whole centuries of merit by another reckoning. In the kind of recollection characteristic of anniversaries, Bishop Ladyka ruminated over the life of the congregation thus far, in a pastoral letter issued on March 21 to the clergy and laity of his diocese: 'In His boundless love for our Ukrainian nation, it pleased the Lord to call into existence among us the Ukrainian Institute of Sisters Servants of Mary Immaculate. Throughout the past half-century, in fact from the moment of its inception, hundreds of generous girls have entered its ranks in order to make a total consecration of themselves to God; and through their prayer, the education and guidance of children, the care of orphans and the sick, to respond to the spiritual and temporal needs of our people. At first in Ukraine, then in Canada, Brazil, Carpatho-Ukraine, and the United States, our deeply spiritual and hard-working sisters have successfully carried out their remarkable apostolate ... For forty years they have served in our diocese in widely separated areas, even from the Peace River District to Montreal.'[39] In encouraging priests and people to participate in the anniversary, which was to be officially observed on August 15, the feast of the Assumption, he reminded them that 'the jubilee of our Sisters Servants is also the jubilee of our parishes, our dioceses, and our entire Ukrainian nation.'[40]

There was joy, extraordinary joy, in the Province of Christ the King as the sisters prepared to commemorate the event. Beneath the happiness and festiveness, however, there existed a sense of regret that the Province of Our Lady of Sorrows, whose fiftieth anniversary it rightfully was, had been plunged into the unpredictable tides of war. Aware of this sentiment their beloved apostolic visitor, Father Schrijvers, attempted to comfort them by emphasizing the marvellous scope and potential of each sister's vocation in the light of the Church's mandate to her religious institute. 'What the Divine Master had in view when He founded your congregation,' he pointed out, 'was to raise up a new generation of virgins with devoted hearts, ready to come to the aid of needy Ukrainians scattered throughout the world; prompt to care for their orphans, to instruct their children, to nurse their sick. What He willed of you, dear sisters, in calling you to such a lofty vocation, was that you should safeguard, through your prayer, your devotion, and your sacrifice, the true faith in your people and draw down upon them the pity and mercy of our divine Saviour. You responded generously to this appeal, and justly, at this moment, you rejoice at the sight of the good accomplished through your instrumentality throughout a half-century.' He concluded on a more sober note: 'Be glad at your good fortune in being able to celebrate this memorable jubilee in your flourishing province, but let your hearts also embrace your sisters all over the world; in particular, let your thoughts turn with sympathy to those in Europe, who are so sorely tried; especially to your superior general who feels in her maternal heart the anguish of all her children.'[41]

From the secretary of the Sacred Oriental Congregation, Eugene Cardinal Tisserant, came a consoling message which, in part, read: 'This Sacred Congregation confidently trusts that the sadness of the present moment will not cast its pall over the spiritual happiness of the sisters ... but that this joyous day will serve as an invitation to renewed fervour in the generosity of their dedication to personal holiness, to an ever more fruitful apostolate among our Ukrainian faithful, and for the glory of Christ's Church.'[42]

Inevitably, there were also those striking instances of eloquence and poignance that any significant event seems to summon forth. At this solemn moment Sister Veronica movingly articulated the yearnings of the members in the European province: 'We beg you, dear sisters, to observe most worthily this moment, so precious to us. In spirit we unite ourselves with you so that together we may reaffirm our lifelong commitment to the King of our hearts by renewing our religious vows, by humbly begging pardon for our faults, mistakes, and shortcomings, and by once again consecrating to Him our faithful service as a sacrifice of love.' Then, in the name of the entire family of Sisters Servants, she prayed: 'Heavenly Father, we praise You, we glorify You, and we thank You for all Your graces to us throughout the fifty years of our institute's existence, particularly for this current cross, so excruciatingly painful. Raising toward You, with all our being, our wounded hearts, our anguished souls, our sorrowful heads, and maimed hands, we praise You, O Lord. May Your name be glorified forever! For the tenderness of Your Heart, O crucified Spouse of souls, may You be praised! For the trials and sufferings which Your paternity permits, we humbly say: may You be praised! Your ways are mysterious, Your plans incomprehensible, but although we cannot fathom them, we readily accept each in a spirit of childlike simplicity.' In conclusion she reminded her sisters everywhere: 'Let us sincerely pray that through our perfect fulfilment of God's will and the generous acceptance of our crosses our institute may always be pleasing in God's eyes and ever remain a source of delight to His Sacred Heart.'[43]

At the novitiate house in Mundare, which was to be the scene of the province's official observance of the anniversary, the days preceding August 15 were hectic. 'The activity was unbelievable,' later commented the chronicler; 'the sisters seemed to be engaged in everything at once: cooking, baking, cleaning, and decorating – church, chapel, refectory, parlours, classrooms, and corridors.'[44]

It was primarily a spiritual festival. From the opening offering of the Divine Liturgy of thanksgiving in the convent chapel to the celebration of the Eucharist in the crowded church, the sisters were making promises: postulants receiving their religious habit made their initial oblation; several novices pronounced temporary vows; two sisters made their final profession; and all religious with perpetual vows reaffirmed their lifelong commitment to Christ. Through it all, the spirit was one of gratitude and joy.

Later that afternoon, at a luncheon served for their many clerical and lay friends in the quiet wood beside the novitiate house, a novice, Sister Justine Adrianne Kowal, voiced the sentiments of the institute's religious-in-training: 'Although we novices are just commencing our life as Sisters Servants, we cannot help but feel, most profoundly, the uniqueness of this day. We find ourselves delighting in the happiness which our congregation is experiencing at this moment of its golden jubilee, and we are grateful for the privilege of being able to participate in the holy joy of this great family of Servants of the Mother of Christ the King – a family that seems to have been especially chosen and blessed by the Lord.'[45]

A second celebration took place the next day, on August 16: a half-century of religious life for Sister Athanasia Melnyk. In the convent chapel, spilling over with postulants, novices, and professed religious, she participated in a Divine Liturgy of thanksgiving, and then, after a grand sermon by the esteemed Basilian missionary, Rev. A. Truch, she was honoured in their midst by being crowned with a golden wreath by her provincial superior. In that instant, through their joyful rendition of the newest community hymn, 'Glory to God in the Highest,' her fellow sisters gave expression to the emotion of the moment, and also accorded one final salute to the anniversary itself.[46]

In the jubilee's aftermath the dozens of congratulatory messages that had poured into the provincialate from ecclesiastical and civil leaders, together with those that had appeared in the press – all of which commended their life and works and made glittering forecasts for their future – failed to persuade the sisters that anything but a stern challenge lay before them if their response to the needs of their Church in North America was to remain relevant; that is, if they were to continue to be witnesses to God's love and tenderness in the midst of the world, after the example of Mary. In a word, so far as they were concerned, rhetoric was one thing and living another.[47]

The startling announcement on November 1, 1944, of the death of Metropolitan Andrew Sheptytsky, abruptly drove home to them just how fragile a thing life itself is. Needless to say, the news plunged Ukrainians everywhere into profound grief. As Bishop Ladyka put it: 'In the midst of the devastation of war in Ukraine, the Lord has permitted our nation to suffer the loss of its spiritual father.'[48]

Many sisters still remembered the stately churchman who had twice come into their midst, not to be served but to serve. They recalled how lovingly he had moved among them, and how they had warmed to this man who seemed to personify their Church and the land of their fathers. In 1970 his biographer, Marcel E. Wagner, underscored their impressions thus: 'Seldom, if ever, have the Ukrainian people had a Bishop of such great faith and talents, who was devoted wholly to their welfare. He was truly an outstanding Hierarch and religious shepherd. His outlook, knowledge, and heart, trials and efforts, embraced the entire people, wherever they lived throughout the world. It is more than likely that time will reveal that he was one of the greatest and most renowned of any Bishops, Archbishops or Metropolitans in the history of the Ukrainian nation.'[49]

Fortunately, owing to his uncanny foresight of possible communist penetration into western Ukraine and eastern Europe, his nation was not bereft of spiritual leadership at his death. For in November 1939, having sought and received from Rome a confirmation of his choice of a successor to his metropolitan see, he had secretly consecrated Rev. Josyf Slipyj, rector of the Lviv Theological Academy, as coadjutor bishop of Lviv.

The situation in Ukraine worsened, even as the pronounced success of the allied armies in western Europe from the summer of 1944 presaged a rapid winding down of the war. In January 1945 Father Schrijvers, still virtually the only link between the Sisters Servants in the old world and the new, informed Sister Elizabeth that he had not received 'any communication from Galicia since the last Russian invasion. And,' he added, 'we have no idea as to what will happen to our sisters after the war ... At the present time there is little that we can do, since even letters do not reach them now. We can help them only through prayer.'[50]

For a second time, too, unsettled conditions forced a postponement of a general chapter which under normal circumstances would have been convened in 1945. This meant, of course, that a review of the constitutions was also deferred. Admitted Father Schrijvers: 'we have no idea how long the situation will last.'[51] Almost on the heels of his latest message to them, a telegram dated March 7, 1945, from his superior general, Rev. P. Murray, C SS R, announced bleakly: 'Father Schrijvers, C SS R, Consultor General, died March 4th.'[52] Once again the sisters mourned a dear friend. 'This news has grieved our entire province; indeed, the whole institute,' confided a saddened annalist. 'Having lost a truly spiritual father, we feel orphaned; no longer do we have among us that devoted priest who sincerely loved our congregation and was always interested in its affairs.'

Father Murray, probably hoping to soften the blow, followed up his telegram with a letter to Sister Elizabeth: 'I offer my heartfelt sympathy to you, dear Mother, and to all your Community. We who lived with him know how much – how very much – he loved his dear Ukrainians, how fervently he prayed for them, how eagerly he grasped every opportunity to further their interests. And we know that among the dearest of the Ukrainians were the Sisters of the Immaculate Conception.'[53] His efforts to obtain the approval of their constitutions and the elevation of their institute to one of papal right in 1932, testified to this love. At first hand, the sisters had witnessed the compassion, courage, humility, the virtue of the simple, the wisdom of the just that had all shone in him. He had embodied the natural goodness and valour of the human race. That is why the sisters had no doubt that he would keep his promise, made in 1936, when he had written: 'I hope that one day I shall be in heaven, and from there I will continue to care for you and your dear institute.'[54]

The war in Europe mercifully ended in May 1945, but the iron curtain which had descended upon eastern Europe permitted little information to leak out. Luckily, it was not altogether foolproof, and thus on September 20, 1945, a letter from a Sister Servant in Czechoslovakia reached Sister Elizabeth, verifying her fears concerning the losses sustained by the Province of Our Lady of Sorrows: 'It would be impossible for me to describe to you what we have endured during the last few years,' wrote the sister. 'Our spiritual and material losses are incalculable. Some of our sisters have been killed by bombs and bullets; others have died from hardship, and still others have vanished without a trace ... Thank God that our Mother [Sister Veronica] is safe, except that she is ill. She longs to see all of you again.'[55]

That their superior general was alive was great news. More gratifying still was the notification received on December 1, 1945, that both she and a general councillor, Sister Christopher Kachkowsky, had reached Rome.[56] General details surrounding her escape to Italy were recounted by her travelling companion in an article written in 1957: 'In 1943, while Galicia was still under German occupation, Sister Veronica went to Stanislaviv for the purpose of extending anniversary felicitations to Bishop Khomyshyn. While there, she was stricken with blood poisoning, which compelled her to tarry longer than she had anticipated. Meanwhile, Soviet troops rapidly moved westward, cutting off her return to both Lviv and Kristinopil. Unexpectedly separated from her own, she joined the Sisters Servants in Prague where, to her dismay, she found that the feeling against foreigners, especially religious, was running high. Against that background, an anxious hierarchy agreed that it was imperative that she cross over to the West. Providence came to her assistance through the person of Rev. P. Myskiw, then provincial superior of the Basilians in the Czech Socialist Republic, who adroitly discovered a way to help her out of her perilous predicament. From the Italian consul in Prague he obtained permission for her to leave Czechoslovakia aboard a transport carrying Italian repatriates home. After a final moving farewell to her sisters in Ukrainian lands, she and her companion arrived in the Eternal City two weeks later, on September 30, 1945.'[57] The joy of the Sisters Servants at St Josaphat's Pontifical Seminary (where they had carried on a housekeeping and food services apostolate since 1932) knew no bounds. For their part, Bishop

John Buchko and the rector, Rev. J. Labay, warmly extended to these first 'refugees' of the institute the hospitality of the seminary, while at the Sacred Oriental Congregation, recorded Sister Christopher, 'she was accorded a gracious welcome by the officials, particularly Eugene Cardinal Tisserant, with whom she spoke at great length, and who, at this initial meeting, expressed the desire that the generalate now be established in Rome.'[58]

Against the backdrop of the war the notion of re-establishing the motherhouse of the institute in Ukraine faded with each passing day. For after the communist takeover of all Ukrainian lands, only a short breathing spell remained for the Ukrainian Catholic Church. Soon throughout the length and breadth of the country, the sisters witnessed its systematic destruction. The subtle weapon which the Soviets employed was aimed at gaining the allegiance of the hierarchy and clergy to the Orthodox Church, so that free of any alignment with the Holy See they would become the tools of an atheistic régime. Toward the close of 1945 Sister Veronica described this painful religious strangulation: 'All of our bishops have been deported; our priests have been arrested and hundreds are being transported to Siberia. The enemy of human souls knows well that when there are no shepherds the flock will scatter. Since the spring of this year a strong propaganda campaign for Orthodoxy has been fostered and from this movement has emerged the persecution of Catholics, especially of the diocesan clergy, and religious men and women. The moment when it will be necessary for our sisters to give their lives for their allegiance to the Catholic Church, or at least to spend the rest of their years in northern ice-covered lands, seems to be at hand.'[59]

And nothing was closer to the truth. On April 11, 1945, Metropolitan Slipyj and four other Ukrainian Catholic bishops were taken into custody. Then followed the arrest of leading members of the clergy, a draft of seminarians into the Red Army, and the confiscation of church properties. On March 8, 1946, a so-called 'Synod of the Ukrainian Catholic Church' declared its union with the Orthodox Patriarch of Moscow. Ironically, not one of the Church's bishops had been present to draw up the proclamation. When asked to recognize the apostasy, all five of the imprisoned prelates had refused. Thereupon began so intensified a persecution of the Church — now declared illegal — that those who wished to remain Catholics could do so only in secret. Numerous convents were suppressed, a small part of the building being left to the religious, on condition that they sign a declaration renouncing the religious state; this gave them the right to obtain work as civilians. The imprisoned bishops were tried and condemned to various penalties and deportation to Siberia. The Ukrainian Catholic Church was suddenly wrapped in silence, but it was not destroyed. It simply went underground, thus becoming, in the twentieth century, a Church of the catacombs.[60]

For the Sisters Servants in eastern European countries, who were an integral part of that Church, there were the imponderables now that they had never faced before. Cut off from the rest of their institute, they were experiencing a soul-wrenching isolation while, incognito, they sought to bring a ray of Christian hope into the drab lives of their oppressed country-men. Proudly, yet sadly, Sister Veronica informed Sister Elizabeth: 'Our sisters [in Ukraine] have declared themselves ready for everything, even the worst. May God grant that they come safely through this terrifying ordeal without breaking beneath the burden of indescribable suffering. Our obligation is to assist them through prayer, sacrifice, and the faithful fulfilment of our apostolate.'[61]

Without question, this was a disheartening picture. Sister Veronica, however, saw another side – in the reports from the Province of Christ the King, and in the anniversary publication, *Jubilee: 1892–1942*. Years of struggle and disappointment melted away before the vision of the fruitful-ness of the sisters' apostolate, which demonstrated the beauty and power of their consecrated dedication. 'What do I see as I gaze at this other can-vas?' she happily exclaimed in a letter to the provincial council. 'In many convents – some modern, some large, some modest and small – in schools, orphanages, hospitals, hostels, and mission centres, I see countless num-bers of boys and girls, young men and women, the elderly, and the sick, being taught, guided, and cared for by Sisters Servants imbued with a spirit of selfless love. I also see the novitiate filled with generous young women who will soon mature spiritually and will, in their turn, sow the seed of the Gospel in well-prepared soil. Strange indeed are the ways of the Lord.'[62]

Thus toward the close of 1945, when men everywhere, already feeling that the hoped-for peace had somehow eluded them, resigned themselves to mere coexistence in a world from which perfect fear seemed to have cast out love, the members of the Canadian-American province of Sisters Ser-vants refused to be dismayed. Buoyed by the unalloyed praise of their eminent superior general, they simply set their sights higher and confi-dently bowed to the future.

. . . and in time of peace

The years following the war brought changes in almost every aspect of Canadian and American life. Not least among these was the growth of population, much of which resulted from a steady stream of postwar immigration, especially from the refugee camps that had been hastily set up in western Europe for thousands of displaced persons – among them Ukrainians who had been sent into Germany as forced labour or who had fled their country at the end of the war to escape communist domination.

Hard pressed to deal with the historic misfortune that had descended upon the motherland, the Ukrainian Catholic hierarchy in Canada and the United States initially endeavoured to generate public compassion and support for their afflicted countrymen in Europe through a series of pastoral exhortations. The bishops hoped that, once aroused, Ukrainians would ignite the kind of incandescent populist fervour that can overcome the most formidable obstacles to accomplish worthwhile deeds. Given all the conflict and anxiety, therefore, the Church, as in the past, so now, encouraged its people to prayer, fasting, and almsgiving. In the spring of 1946, for instance, Bishop A. Senyshyn, as president of the Ukrainian Catholic Committee for Refugees, organized shortly before at Stamford, under the patronage of the Immaculate Virgin Mary – Mother of Ukraine – called upon Ukrainian Americans to lift the arms of their supportive prayer for the refugees on June 9, to observe a day of fast on June 10, and to supplement their prayer and sacrifice with alms – the sum saved by abstaining from one meal.[1]

Beyond this assistance the bishop hoped to marshal still another significant spiritual force to the cause – the Sisters Servants. Turning to the members of the Canadian-American province in his letter of May 23, he outlined the role he desired them to play in the bitter drama of the refugees that promised to loom large for several years. 'A great calamity has befallen our Church and nation,' he wrote, 'and it has not by-passed even our religious institutes, including your own. Many of your sisters are dead, while those who live are sorely afflicted. Since only the Lord can turn away this misfortune, we must pray fervently to Christ and His Blessed Mother for this intention. I therefore turn to you, Reverend Sisters, with a sincere request for your prayers and those of your students. As you are aware, the newly organized Ukrainian Catholic Committee for Refugees has issued an appeal to the faithful to participate in a national day of prayer and voluntary fast, and to offer alms in support of our suffering people. Since children are the finest apostles for good, especially among their parents and relatives, they should be conscious of the existing need and encouraged to contribute their own good deeds. In this undertaking your assistance is essential. I am certain that your sympathetic understanding will prompt you to use every means at your disposal to help save these hapless displaced persons.'[2]

The subsequent overwhelming response of clergy, religious, and especially the laity, old and young, irrespective of social position and organizational affiliation, dramatized a communal Christian awareness of the abiding need in every heart for love that would brace them, particularly against the kind of adversity that was currently the lot of their unfortunate brothers.

Unknown to most people, however, the Sisters Servants had already espoused the cause of war victims in the autumn of 1945. For in November of that year an emotionally charged cablegram from Sister Monica Bolysta in Poland, containing the startling message, 'Novitiate burned; our teaching sisters and nurses without employment; you are asked by all means to take us to Canada,'[3] had sparked a vigorous desire to help that had suddenly plunged them headlong into the complex procedures involved in obtaining governmental approval for the sisters' entry to Canada. And the attempt was crucial, considering the taut political climate in eastern Europe, which augmented the possibility of their being deported to Russia. Whether Canada would accept them was another question. As Bishop Ladyka saw it, the situation was less than reassuring: 'The obstacles of bringing your members here are formidable,' he told Sister Elizabeth, 'but perhaps the prayers of the sisters will overcome all.'[4]

Indeed, if difficulties persisted, it was not for lack of prayer. For as early as January 1946 a request for the sisters' spiritual support of the provincial council's efforts on behalf of the European sisters had gone out to all the convents. Then had begun such a spate of correspondence with Canadian, French, and Belgian authorities that no one could doubt that this matter had taken precedence over every other in the province. It is little wonder, therefore, that the sisters heaved their biggest sigh of relief when, just a scant month later, the Belgian government granted temporary residence visas to seventeen Sisters Servants scheduled to arrive from Poland in August and remain in that country until Canada admitted them. In the face of almost four months of persevering pursuit of their goal, it is not unlikely that harassed officials capitulated to the sisters out of sheer weariness. An additional piece of happy news was the promise of the Redemptorist Fathers in Brussels to assist in the venture by finding accommodation for the sisters in a Belgian convent.

The commitment of the Province of Christ the King to this project needs no embellishment: it was a merciful gesture through which the Sisters Servants in North America were reaching out in imagination, prayerful aspiration, and love to their counterparts half a world away, even though this meant that they would be solely responsible for all of the expenses involved, at a time when things still looked pretty dubious on their own financial front – despite the fact that, generally, the war had cured the economic hangover from the depression.

As envisaged by Sister Elizabeth, this matter constituted only a sub-heading, however significant, to the main chapter of the province's postwar assignments. Always ready to take an aggressive gamble for the Church, and emboldened by the characteristic generosity of its members, she chose this moment to reveal that she had two other irons in the fire. In a communication to her sisters on February 22, 1946, she announced: 'Our Holy Father is permitting us to transfer our novitiate and provincialate to Toronto, a more central Canadian location ... I also wish to inform you that efforts are under way to establish our generalate in Rome. As you can well appreciate, this latter undertaking can be realized only by our Province of Christ the King, since the other provinces of our institute can assist only through their prayer and sacrifice. I am convinced, therefore, that you will offer your hard-earned savings to support our three current projects: the purchase of a novitiate house in Toronto, a generalate in Rome, and the maintenance of our sisters in Belgium as well as the costs involved in bringing them to Canada.'[5]

Perhaps the most striking characteristic of her message was its confident tone, even though she must have suspected that she might ruffle some community feathers with her plan to plunge the province into substantial debt. For it was one thing for her to propose and another for the sisters to accept the risks that the proposal carried with it. If, however, there were any local superiors who wished that the whole idea would blow away, they must have constituted a silent minority since, as Sister Elizabeth informed her superior general, 'our sisters have reacted so favourably to our urgent request for financial aid that some have already forwarded their contributions.'[6]

Without doubt Sister Elizabeth was glad that the appeal had aroused the sisters in the way she had hoped it would, for she viewed their ready response as a testament to the urgency of the issues at hand. 'Until now we have benefited from the enterprises undertaken by our predecessors,' she declared in a subsequent repetition of her policies on August 30; 'but the time has come for us to meet our own current needs together with those of our members overseas. Justice and charity demand that besides procuring a new novitiate in Canada we should help to establish a suitable centre in Rome for our superior general and her council.'[7]

Her statement made it clear that the province's previous tendency to be too much attuned to the parochial concerns of domestic issues had been laid to rest. For years the temptation to concentrate on its own pressing affairs had been latent in the subsurface of its consciousness. Now, its move toward active support of outside enterprises was not only shifting the emphasis from isolation to involvement but was also hastening the emergence of the province as a leader within the institute. For, having measured wisely the extent of its responsibilities to the parent province and to itself, Sister Elizabeth was bringing her Canadian-American community into the main stream of interests – immediate and long-range – of the entire congregation. In effect, what the sisters were now saying to Sisters Servants in other parts of the world, particularly in Europe, was 'we're alive and well, and thinking of you.' This signified that something had happened that was hard to define precisely or to prove conclusively, but that was none the less important: the province had reached a crossover point from adolescence to maturity.

Understandably overshadowed by the plans to aid the refugee sisters and to purchase a generalate was the local proposal to transfer the provincialate and novitiate to Toronto. The desire for a more centralized site indicated that the sisters had concluded that it was now time for a change. The new stance, especially regarding the novitiate, was deemed vital to the healthy growth of the province, especially in the light of the steadily increasing numbers of girls entering the institute from eastern Canada and the United States. Furthermore, explained Sister Elizabeth to her superior general in her typically commonsensical way, 'despite continued efforts to provide adequate living quarters and facilities in the present novitiate house, the building simply refuses to meet the needs of the modern city girl who is entering our institute today. Moreover,' she contended, 'since we also plan to include a girls' academy on our new premises, our novices will have an excellent opportunity to meet Ontario high school requirements before proceeding to advanced studies at the prestigious University of Toronto.'[8]

A secondary, perhaps less obvious but nevertheless compelling, motive for the move was the acceleration in the current Canadian shift from an agrarian and rural to an industrial society. Sister Elizabeth and her advisers recognized that they had a responsibility at this time of a rapidly changing social structure to seek out plausible ways of deepening and sharpening the apostolate. It was becoming imperative, they felt, to apply new – and feasible – approaches to their work if they were to make a relevant contribution within the rapidly multiplying urban parishes, which their members were already being called upon to serve. And because they saw the need to train a postwar generation of Sisters Servants in a more vital spiritual and academic milieu, for the province's officials the choice was straightforward enough, however painful.

Sister Elizabeth and her council appreciated the fact that there were risks involved in a withdrawal from a well-established novitiate where, for over four decades, superiors had been able to depend upon the spiritual assistance of the Basilian Fathers for their young sisters; they were, however, convinced that they would court the greatest risk by providing a missionary formation for their active community in a centre that was rapidly becoming a ghost town. For although the plan to move east, as it had emerged thus far, seemed to some to contain an element of uncertainty, it did acknowledge that many of the hoarier truisms for remaining at Mundare were no longer valid. It did, for one thing, offer a clear-cut substitute for the outdated assumption that Mundare was still the centre of Ukrainian Catholic religious life in Canada.

Ultimately, whatever combination of motives may have been at work, the notion to transfer the novitiate seems to have been symptomatic of a distinct shift in the sisters' missionary style and emphasis. And since, up to now, the province's path toward its apostolic goals had usually been studded with risks, one more scarcely seemed to matter. For sentimentalists, a poignant question still remained unanswered: what function would the abandoned building serve? And only after it was announced that the house would be converted immediately into a children's residence, and a staff of Sisters Servants assigned to care for those Alberta youngsters who would live there until they were adopted, were they satisfied.

Having decided upon this course of action in the spring of 1945 when, because of the war, there was still no contact with the generalate on an official level, the council applied 'to the Holy See through the apostolic delegate for permission to transfer the novitiate, make the necessary loan for the purchase of a new building, and borrow from the sisters' dowries for this purpose.'[9] In the meantime, however, Sister Veronica arrived in Rome from Czechoslovakia. This meant, of course, that she would have to be brought up-to-date on all important provincial transactions. As a consequence, owing to her delay in approving the move to Toronto, a rare chance to obtain the Sifton property located in the northeast sector of the city, which consisted of 'a large parcel of land and a building appropriate for a provincialate and novitiate,'[10] was lost when it was snatched up by another buyer. 'We regret that we were unable to procure it,' lamented Sister Elizabeth in a letter to her superior general, 'for it corresponded perfectly to our requirements.'[11] Herein lay the rub. During the war when the council had sought permission for its larger projects directly through the apostolic delegate rather than through the generalate, no unnecessary delays had blocked the implementation of their plans.[12]

The loss of their opportunity to buy the Sifton Home became more significant as the search for a suitable house in Toronto continued; it seemed that any property which met their needs was far beyond their means. On May 15 of that year the sisters, according to the annalist, had been requested 'to seek the intercession of the Mother of God in the matter of finding a suitable building in the east.'[13] And still Toronto yielded nothing. As ever, the most important thing was not what Sister Elizabeth said but what she did. In this instance she simply ordered the provincial treasurer, Sister Gertrude Lesiuk, to extend the search to neighbouring cities.

On the feast of Our Lady's Assumption in August 1946 an unexpected telegram notified the staff and novices at Mundare that their prayers had been answered. 'One of the most attractive properties in southern Ontario, the former Wynnstay Estate, five miles from the city of Hamilton [at Ancaster],'[14] which had served as an RCAF convalescent home during the war, had been bought for the sum of $180,000, and would henceforth be known as 'Mount Mary Immaculate.' Thus in one stroke the Sisters Servants changed its name and its image.

Predictably enough, the announcement of the purchase sent eyebrows arching within and without the institute, and immediately provoked a run of speculation as to how the sisters would pay for the 102 acres and three buildings they had just acquired. Indeed, it was quite obvious that obtaining the site counted only as one hurdle overcome; the other consisted in what was shaping up to be the toughest fund-raising campaign in the province's history. All of a sudden, as appeals for support went out across the country, it seemed that Ukrainians everywhere were talking about Ancaster.

Besides financing the project, Sister Elizabeth and her advisers were compelled by the transfer to Ancaster, rather than to Toronto, to formulate new ideas about the apostolic works to be undertaken here. Plans for an academy had to be scrapped, since none of the buildings on the estate was suitable; instead, it was decided to open a temporary placement home for orphans.

Quite unexpectedly, in the midst of all this planning, Sister Elizabeth was summoned to Rome for her first postwar encounter with her superior general. The purpose of the visit, recorded the annalist was 'to participate in a conference that will review matters pertaining to the entire institute.'[15] Significantly, this unique invitation accented the dependence, at this moment in the congregation's history, of the general council and the entire European province upon their Canadian and American members for moral leadership and, of course, financial aid.

Prior to her departure from New York on August 26, 1946, Sister Elizabeth received the gratifying news that sixteen of the sisters from Poland had arrived in Belgium.[16] In view of this cheering development, she broadened her itinerary to include a visit with them.

While in Rome Sister Elizabeth's official meetings included several with the institute's newly appointed apostolic visitor, Rev. Gabriel A. Coussa, a member of the Basilian Order of Aleppo of the Melkite rite who in 1962 was destined to be elevated to the rank of cardinal by Pope John XXIII.[17] She found him to be a man of intelligence, dignity, and candour, who radiated a warmth that inspired confidence. It is little wonder, therefore, that she came away convinced that he was a most worthy successor to the late Father Schrijvers; one who possessed the potency to contribute mightily to the well-being of the institute at a time when it was in great need of forthright guidance in its spiritual and apostolic life.

Father Coussa, for his part, was probably happy to meet the woman who had kept a firm hand on the affairs of the Canadian-American province for twelve years. And she must have impressed not only him but other officials of the Sacred Oriental Congregation as well, for the same autumn she was asked to lead the sisters in North America for a third term which, unofficially, had commenced during the war in 1944. She would, therefore, be required to remain in office only until 1949.[18]

It was inevitable that throughout her sojourn in Europe Sister Elizabeth's thoughts should often stray to the novitiate at Mundare where preparations were under way for the historic move to the east. Here, seventeen novices and two postulants, together with their superiors, Sister Lawrence Dzumaga and Sister Josaphata Kizlyk, worked feverishly to pack everything. Then, in the cold predawn darkness of October 13, 1946, they boarded the CNR for Edmonton where, that evening, after a delightful visit with the sisters at the provincialate, they commenced their journey to Hamilton.

During the next four days – after the first burst of excitement over setting up a convent in a railway coach – their days fell into a fairly regular novitiate schedule. There was a time for common and private prayer; there was a time for work, when cooking and cleaning became much of a lark and more of a challenge in a lurching train; there was a time for recreation when gales of laughter, the classic manifestation of novices in religion, echoed in adjoining coaches; and there was a time for thoughtful silence as they watched the rolling, undulating landscape of the prairies slip away to be replaced by the rocks, forests, and lakes of northern Ontario and then by the orchards of the Niagara Peninsula. Thus for all the normal tediousness of travel, the trip was nothing if not exuberant. Eventually, at dawn on October 16, they detrained at Hamilton, and soon jammed the tiny convent at 144 Melrose Avenue, where Sister Minidore Ksenia Andrijiw, Sister Elias Agatha Popyk, and Sister Juliette Olga Chykorly happily cooked breakfast for their excited guests.

It was but a short drive up the Hamilton Mountain to Mount Mary on a day that was mellow for October. As their cars proceeded to the 'novitiate house on the hill' the sisters glimpsed a breathtaking pulsation of autumn colour in a postcard setting – lawns and hedges glistening green with drops from a morning drizzle, majestic blue pines, yellow and orange and crimson maples, and down in the valley a rippling pool bordered by the solitary silence of a nearby wood. After drinking deep of this quiet beauty, neither the piles of unpacked crates nor the dust and cobwebs that greeted them when they entered the front door of their new home could dampen their spirits. Indeed, this first group of novices at Ancaster felt like pioneers – imbued as they were with a youthful air of lofty resolve to bring Mount Mary to life.[19] Throughout the days and weeks that followed, the only thing that stood still was the grandfather clock that refused to go.

As soon as they had moved in, however, the sisters found themselves deprived of the spiritual services of a chaplain. Usually only on Sundays was the Divine Liturgy celebrated in their chapel, either by a diocesan priest from Hamilton or a Basilian from nearby Grimsby. Sadly enough, the real heart of the dilemma was a severe shortage of Ukrainian priests in the area.

Since a novitiate was involved, Bishop Ladyka, desiring to remedy the situation as soon as possible, was strongly in favour of seeking the assistance of the Latin-rite clergy. In a letter to Sister Elizabeth on February 12, 1947, he thus realistically summed up his position: 'The matter concerning a permanent chaplain is close to my heart, since I appreciate how painful it is for the sisters to be deprived of the daily celebration of the Divine Liturgy and reception of the Eucharist. I am, therefore, suggesting a means whereby the problem may be somewhat alleviated until I am able to appoint a priest, experienced enough to minister effectively to the spiritual needs of your members. As you can well appreciate, it is impossible for me to transfer a priest from any parish before Easter, for we have no substitutes. I am hopeful, however, that in the spring we shall receive several priests from Europe; hence it will be easier for me to resolve the problem of a chaplain for the novitiate. In the meantime, do you not think that it would be feasible to ask the Latin-rite bishops to assist us by assigning one of their priests until a clergyman of our own is available?'[20]

Aware of the quick tendency of some Ukrainians to label their priests and sisters *Latynnyky*,[21] the provincial council pointedly questioned whether it would be wise to accept the services of a Latin-rite priest – desirable and welcome though his spiritual ministry would be. In her letter of March 11 Sister Elizabeth discreetly replied: 'In an effort to avoid providing any reason for rash judgments, our council has concluded that it will be more prudent for us to continue to "do penance" than to experience the joy of sharing in the fountain of grace flowing from the Eucharistic sacrifice, for we do not wish to give rise to scandal among those faithful who are perhaps uninformed, and would resent our benefiting from the services of the Latin-rite clergy. Nor do we wish to enkindle the dying embers of prejudice that some of our people still harbour against them. It is our decision, therefore, to wait for a priest of our rite. We fervently pray that the Lord may mercifully release us from this painful spiritual trial soon.'[22] Thus the matter appeared to have reached yet another impasse, and the non-solution left nobody happy.

It was more than a little ironic, therefore, when, two days after the sisters had abandoned the notion of receiving aid outside the ecclesiastical structure of their rite, two Resurrectionist Fathers from nearby Dundas visited Mount Mary to meet with and inform them that 'upon the request of Bishop Ladyka, the Latin-rite bishop of Hamilton, Most Reverend J. F. Ryan, had requested the Resurrectionist Congregation to assign its own members to celebrate Mass in the convent on weekdays, until such time as Bishop Ladyka could assign a permanent chaplain of the Ukrainian rite to the novitiate.'[23] The end result of all the appointments was a satisfactory, if somewhat complicated, Mass schedule: on Fridays and Sundays the Divine Liturgy was celebrated by a Basilian from Grimsby; on all other days the Eucharistic sacrifice was offered by a Resurrectionist from Dundas. As for the novices, they now appreciated the priesthood as never before.

The sisters soon discovered that the opportunities to share Mount Mary with their people, notably children and youth, were almost limitless. During their first spring and summer at Ancaster their quest for new and meaningful forms of apostolic service led them into a host of varied programmes. In March 1947 they held two closed spiritual retreats for high school students, both boys and girls. From June 19 to August 9, in close cooperation with the diocesan clergy and members of the Basilian Order, they conducted two series of vacation schools for the children of the Niagara district. After a visit to the Mount that summer, Rev. Isidore Borecky, at that time the pastor of Ukrainian parishes at the Ontario centres of St Catharines, Grimsby, Welland, Thorold, Beamsville, and Niagara Falls, in a published article entitled 'A Children's Paradise at Mount Mary in Ancaster,' remarked: 'During this vacation one hundred children are experiencing the goodness of our sisters. It is a common sight to see a Sister Servant teaching the youngsters new games and songs, another revealing to them the fascinating mysteries of nature, and still another making them aware, in prayer, of the presence of God in and around them. From the beginning to the end of each day the sisters are with these children.'[24] Happily, almost from its inception, Mount Mary was never merely a beautiful but cold place, a community without spirit, for the sisters' spontaneous response to others seemed as fresh and fumbling as life itself.

Before the summer ended Sisters Servants joined their countrymen in a tribute to the Mother of God at the Canadian Marian Congress held at Ottawa from June 18 to 22. Through their missionary display – the only one by a women's religious institute of an Oriental rite – they were desirous of revealing the beauty and organization of the Church universal in its diversity of peoples and races, and also of fulfilling the chief aims of the Congress as outlined by Archbishop A. Vachon of Ottawa: 'to render homage to the Blessed Virgin, the fond mother of us all, to make better known our holy Church, and to encourage vocations.'[25]

Other significant events were still to follow. Early in August close to one hundred Sisters Servants assembled at Ancaster to participate in the first annual retreat ever to be held there, and to take part in the official opening of the orphanage, scheduled for August 31. Just three days after the commencement of the spiritual exercises, Rev. B. Wawryk, OSBM, the director, permitted an exceptional event to interrupt the morning programme – the arrival from Belgium of five of the sisters who had been up-rooted from their native land almost a year before. Accompanied by Sister Elizabeth, who had met them at Gander, Newfoundland, Sister Borysa Olga Horecha, Sister Leonia Maria Shott, Sister Rosalia Olga Kich, Sister Fotynia Irene Sucha, and Sister Maria Leontina Glogowsky were greeted and feted by their fellow sisters at a luncheon, after which, almost as though they had always been a part of the group, they entered into the retreat. And on the feast of the Assumption, August 15, together with fourteen Canadian and American sisters, four of them pronounced their perpetual vows.[26] Thus in so quiet and simple a way, and in a country which had been spared the scourge of war, they again picked up the thread of their religious life. Sister Elizabeth, especially, was grateful that her province had taken the initiative in obtaining the release of the sisters from Poland, particularly since the eleven who remained in Belgium were to form the nucleus of a new missionary involvement among Ukrainian refugees in Germany, France, and England. Their efforts had thus not only shored up the institute as a whole, but had also bolstered the European province in particular.

The culmination of all the activity which had commenced at Mount Mary in the spring of 1947 occurred on August 31. The village of Ancaster hadn't seen anything quite like it in years. By mid-morning hundreds of cars had converged on the estate. That evening the Toronto *Globe and Mail* reported: 'Five thousand Ukrainian Catholics from Eastern Canada and New York State attended the dedication and official opening of Mount Mary Immaculate, which commenced this morning with a solemn High Mass and concluded tonight with Benediction.'[27] The mood of the 'five thousand' on the Mount that day could, justifiably, have been self-con-gratulatory, since this new project for the Church had become a reality simply because they had cared enough to help.

Initially, the orphanage was opened to serve as a temporary residence for homeless children of the Niagara Peninsula, who were placed here by the Catholic Children's Aid Society of Toronto and of St Catharines and the Catholic Welfare Bureau of Hamilton. Nor was there any reason to believe that this arrangement would be altered in the immediate future. None the less it was soon modified considerably, not because of a local situation, but because of one which had developed in postwar Europe. At this time, the Holy See was stirred by a lively concern for thousands of orphans who were being shunted to refugee camps, notably in West Ger-many and Italy. Their cheerless fate provoked an impassioned plea to the world by the Vatican to aid these youngsters who, as they became subjected by circumstances to the demeaning indignities of the camps, had perhaps in all their short lives never felt poorer.

Echoing the papal appeal in his letter to Bishop Ladyka on December 31, 1947, James Cardinal McGuigan of Toronto dramatized the pitiful plight of these orphans. They were, he stated, 'huddled together in European camps and improper homes with inadequate care and with danger to their faith and morals. Therefore,' he emphasized, 'this is a most urgent charity now, and in the long run more effective even than sending food and clothing to Europe.'[28] In his prompt reply Bishop Ladyka revealed that 'the Sisters Servants at Ancaster, Ontario, as well as at Ituna, Saskatchewan, and Mundare, Alberta ... are already caring for many refugee children. However,' he promised, 'we shall be only too glad to cooperate in this charitable action in order to save the poor in body and spirit, especially helpless children.'[29] It was clear that the sisters had already given top priority to the call for assistance to war orphans.

On October 8, 1948, the annalist happily reported: 'We have received word from the Catholic Immigrants' Aid Society that orphans from overseas will soon arrive in Canada and will be placed at Mount Mary.'[30] Apparently Sister Elizabeth and her council pressed ahead at once with preparations to provide them with suitable accommodation, for the annals noted that 'the provincial council is now preparing to transfer its office to St Rita's Convent in Toronto. This will release part of the main building to the novitiate and free the Villa for the children. Moreover, two classrooms will be set up for them in one of the adjacent buildings.'[31]

All was in readiness when, shortly before dawn on May 17, 1949, thirty-three children ranging in ages from two to fifteen were met at Toronto's Union Station by clergy, religious, laity, and the press – men and women who, personally and collectively, experienced many shades of compassion, sympathy, hope, gladness, and love as they welcomed these 'displaced persons.' Suddenly, among them appeared Cardinal McGuigan, who was responsible for their entry into the country. For months he had patiently chipped away at official objections until all of the Department of Immigration's delaying tactics had been exhausted and Canada had opened its arms to embrace these children of Ukrainian, Italian, and German ancestry.

Having been catered to by the staff at Union Station's restaurant, hugged by the ladies, and blessed by the cardinal, they boarded their Greyhound bus along with four Sisters Servants and reached Mount Mary within an hour. No sooner had they shyly emerged from the vehicle than they were surrounded by forty-eight chattering children from the orphanage, every novice who could drop her work, and practically every professed religious on the premises. 'These children will most certainly enrich the numerous Canadian families who will share with them their hearth and their heart,'[32] wrote Sister Gertrude Lesiuk, the superior, in an article published in *Svitlo* (*The Light*) just three days later, in an attempt to hasten the day when the wistful desire of these youngsters for a family of their own might be fulfilled. Meantime, the sisters hoped that during their temporary stay at Mount Mary these new Canadians would rediscover that elusive human quality, which they probably had once known, that distinguishes a place to live from a place with life.

Without question the sisters' participation in the European orphan programme added a new dimension to their apostolic landscape; but when, eventually, the flow of displaced children to the Mount would become a mere trickle in the early 1950s, the staff would readily adapt to changed realities by replacing the orphanage with a nursery to meet a fresh call — that for extra-familial child care arising from a rapidly increasing percentage of Canadian working mothers.

In 1948 the last of the three community projects undertaken by the province after the war was realized; namely, the purchase of a general house in Rome. When, on February 4 of that year, Sister Veronica arrived in New York to begin her first postwar canonical visitation, negotiations were already in progress to obtain a suitable building. Finally selected was a small villa at Via Cassia Antica, 102, and its price, $50,000, was paid by the Province of Christ the King, which had assumed responsibility for the requisite loan.[33]

In Sister Elizabeth's opinion, this was one of the hallmarks of accomplishment for her province since, by helping to establish a centre for the institute in Rome, her members were instrumental in infusing the European sisters of the newly created vice-provinces of Poland, Czechoslovakia, Yugoslavia, and the mission in France, with a fresh optimism.[34] On the other hand, the deed served to make her sisters in North America more sensitive to the reality that they were members of a religious family scattered around the world, who although not all cut from the same cloth, were nevertheless united in clusters of supportive love and in responsibility for the well-being of all. Thus the grim atmosphere of uncertainty that had hitherto hung over the Province of Our Lady of Sorrows was being pierced somewhat by strong rays of hope for a more stable future in lands outside Ukraine, even though in that nation a crisis still existed.

Even three years after the war had ended, Sister Veronica was still invariably compelled to search for hidden meanings, and to sift truth from fiction out of the myriad rumours and sketchy reports that managed to reach her from Galicia or Siberia, despite the sheer physical isolation imposed upon the Sisters Servants in these regions. Against her rather meagre accumulation of facts about their life and work, she recognized that persecution seemed to have improved the quality and texture of the spirit of these women and helped them to become finer instruments for good than they had ever been before. Time and again she perceived that their dwindling hopes of ever being reunited with their fellow religious were illuminated by flashes of courage in desperate efforts to resist slow annihilation, and she marvelled at their painful sense of responsibility to their country's tiny but courageously persistent movement to freedom – national and religious.

Both this crisis and this hope were reflected in the superior general's Easter message of 1948 to the members of Christ the King Province. She expressed pain and joy in her words: 'Through me, beneath the golden banner of Christ the King, the entire Province of Our Lady of Sorrows unites to greet the sisters of our beloved institute with the words "Christ is risen!" Let us rejoice in the Lord, for this is the day that He has made! It may seem that these words do not apply to us, dear sisters, since we are the offspring of a nation which, in just reparation for a great spiritual debt, is still making its way to Calvary. This is indeed a reality, but still our holy Church invites us to participate joyfully in the feast commemorating Christ's victory over sin and death. And so, let us lift up our hearts, for we believe in the victory of justice and truth; we believe, even though for this faith we may be asked to lay down even life itself, as our constitutions so pointedly remind us.'[35]

Indeed, a joyous moment for the entire Ukrainian Catholic Church was at hand during Sister Veronica's visit to this country. For on March 3, 1948, Pope Pius XII divided the existing single diocese in Canada, headed by Bishop Ladyka since 1929, into three separate exarchates. Thus, Bishop Ladyka remained in Winnipeg 'as apostolic exarch of the central exarchate, his auxiliary being the newly appointed Bishop Andrew Roborecki. The western exarchate, with its see in Edmonton, Alberta, was headed by Bishop Neil Savaryn, OSBM, former auxiliary-bishop to Bishop Ladyka. The apostolic exarchate of eastern Canada, which was the largest in area and number of faithful, was assigned to another newly appointed bishop – the Most Rev. Isidore Borecky. The see of Bishop Borecky's exarchate, which embraced all the Ukrainians and other Byzantine-Slav faithful living east of the Ontario-Manitoba border, was located in Toronto, Ontario.'[36]

In taking this step the Holy See gave evidence of its recognition of the need to create new ecclesiastical jurisdictions and appoint additional bishops to facilitate the administration of the many parishes that were springing up in the wake of the third wave of Ukrainian immigration. From the beginning of 1946 to the end of 1965, the number of Ukrainians who gained entry to Canada under the auspices of the International Refugee Organization was 37,315.[37] Unlike the stalwart peasants in their sheepskin coats of Sifton's day half a century earlier, they were not voluntary emigrants but people who would likely never have left their homeland if the events of the war had not forced them to flee. These latest refugee immigrants, therefore, were deprived of the reassuring feeling that if conditions in the new country were not to their liking they could be free to return to their country of origin.[38] Inevitably, this influx of a new type of immigrant, which represented a cross section of Ukrainian life – farmers, skilled workers, professional men and women, scholars, scientists, musicians, and artists – would have a marked effect upon the structure of Ukrainian communities in the nation. For having among them skilled craftsmen and professionals they flocked, not to the frontier regions, but to the rapidly growing cities that were equally the magnets for native-born Canadians. Thus by 1961 there were nearly 54,000 Ukrainians concentrated in Winnipeg, 47,000 in Toronto, and more than 38,000 in Edmonton. Next in decreasing order were: Vancouver, Montreal, Hamilton, Fort William-Port Arthur (Thunder Bay), Saskatoon, Calgary, and Regina.[39]

In the light of this growth the Apostolic See proceeded to strengthen the Ukrainian Catholic Church in Canada at a time when communism in Ukraine was breaking a people by destroying their traditions and padlocking their temples. And so, a scant three months later, on June 25, Ukrainian Canadians again had cause to celebrate when Bishop Ladyka, who for almost twenty years had calmly, reasonably, and amiably devoted all his energies toward making his vast diocese an organism pulsating with a meaningful religious life, was elevated to the rank of archbishop. The Sacred Oriental Congregation thus completed the first phase of its plan to further the development of the Ukrainian Catholic Church in North America. It was indeed a time for Ukrainians to count their blessings.

The sentiments of the Sisters Servants, who saw the events as a great boon to the Church, were perhaps best capsuled in their congratulatory letter to the ordinary of the western exarchate, Bishop Neil Savaryn, on

April 3, 1948: 'Our Holy Father has given us men of faith and virtue at this unsettled moment in our history, so that through their prayer, work, suffering, and self-sacrifice they may build Christ's Kingdom in the hearts of the flock entrusted to their care, and contribute to a lasting peace among men.'[40]

Somewhat obscured by these significant happenings was a run of other changes, within their own religious province, that closely concerned the sisters. And coming as they did at the end of Sister Elizabeth's third term in office, they provided the members with a final glimpse of her personal involvement and apostolic assertiveness as their leader and guide.

In June 1948 she established the Home of Divine Providence for the Aged in the quiet Chestnut Hill area of Philadelphia, and phased out a similar apostolate in the two houses on Brown Street, which Bishop Bohachevsky had donated a decade earlier. Sister Elizabeth had concluded that neither repairs nor fresh paint could any longer conceal the fact that their days were numbered. By buying a gracious, spacious house on Chestnut Hill, she provided the staff with an eagerly awaited opportunity to remove their oldsters from the decrepit buildings in the airless north end of the city to a home set amid lots of grass and trees and flowers. Furthermore, from the practical side of things, she eliminated the duplication of staff and equipment, thereby permitting the sisters to serve their patients more effectively.

Another, no less extravagant venture, was the purchase of a building in Toronto to serve as the headquarters for the Canadian-American province. Having had to backtrack on her original intention of keeping the provincialate at Ancaster, owing to the need to accommodate an influx of European orphans, Sister Elizabeth and her council had transferred the central office to St Rita's Convent in Toronto, which proved to be too small to act as both a hostel for girls and a provincial house. Hence there was reason to suppose that it would not be too long before the tight arrangement was relieved. In the spring of 1949 the sisters began to seek another home, even though their memories of a futile search for a novitiate just three years before were still vivid.

As always, so now, what saved the enterprise was prayer. This time, however, because Sister Elizabeth had directed a special request to them, the novices at Mount Mary tackled the responsibility of obtaining the intercession of our Lady and St Joseph with nothing short of total enthusiasm – as is the way with novices. In April the provincial superior believed that she had found the best that was available: a fairly large structure in the heart of the city at 5 Austin Terrace, on the west side of

Toronto's famous showpiece, Casa Loma. The striking sandstone house was perched atop a small rise on three acres of landscaped property. When she announced that it had been procured for the sum of $55,000, 'miraculously,' she was hardly guilty of overstatement. Three months later on July 1, after all eleven tenants who had rented apartments in the building had moved out, and the usual bucket brigade had moved in – this time comprised of any Sister Servant who happened to be in or around the city – Sister Celeste Marjorie Diachinsky, the superior, and ten sisters, including Sister Elizabeth and her councillors, occupied the Convent of Christ the King.

Besides being the community headquarters, the convent soon began to serve other needs as well: a school of music directed by Sister Juvenalia Kaniuk; a centre for lenten weekend retreats for girls and women, organized by the sisters in conjunction with the Ukrainian Catholic Women's League; and a place from which teaching sisters moved out on weekdays to teach in several separate schools, and on Saturdays and Sundays to conduct catechetical classes in the city and suburbs for the benefit of hundreds of children attending public schools.[41]

The manner in which the province seemed to have mastered the complexities of keeping itself financially afloat while charting its apostolic course through shoals of conflicting opinions about where and how to fulfil its role in the Church, never failed to amaze Sister Veronica. At the conclusion of her visitation in October 1948 she had remarked that it was unbelievable that 'so much has been attained without any significant capital; in fact, one can almost say, without a penny – only by means of constant labour and sacrifice.'[42] The houses at Chestnut Hill and Austin Terrace amply verified the validity of her observation.

That autumn Sister Elizabeth reached the end of her tenure as provincial superior. She had, in a sense, served to the edge of the constitutional deadline – fifteen years. In the light of this fact Sister Veronica informed her on October 11, 1949, that the Sacred Oriental Congregation had granted the Canadian-American province 'the privilege of holding elections for a new provincial council.'[43] At long last she was to be rewarded with the chance to exchange the onerous responsibility of her administrative position for the joys of a direct missionary involvement.

In all, there were 115 sisters who met the electoral requirements: ten years of profession and two years' residence in the province. They were simply required to list their choice of candidates for the offices of provincial superior and councillors. And while it is true that the vote was merely consultative, with the Sacred Oriental Congregation reserving to itself the ultimate approval of candidates, the very fact that it was taken established a principle of provincial responsibility that had never before existed. The rare gesture was, perhaps, a recognition that, since the war, the province had transcended its young-province status to become one of the most active and advanced in the entire institute.

Within a month Sister Veronica notified the sisters that the assignment to govern the province for the next five years had fallen to Sister Bernadette Mary Warick and her council, consisting of Sister Lawrence Dzumaga, Sister Josaphata Kizlyk, Sister Gertrude Lesiuk, and Sister Sozonta Iskiw.[44]

Addressing herself directly to the outgoing provincial superior in a separate letter, Sister Veronica credited her with much genuine achievement. Indeed, she admitted, the most laudatory evidence for her was the distance the Canadian-American province had moved since her appointment in 1934. Within a span of fifteen years she had eased her province through the pinching poverty of the depression, the nagging anxieties of the war years, and the challenging uncertainty of the immediate postwar period. 'Neither I, nor my council, can permit this opportunity to pass without conveying to you our heartfelt gratitude for your devoted, selfless labour which, in its zealous endeavour to achieve missionary goals, overcame countless obstacles,' she stated. 'Among your many notable achievements are several that are especially significant: the educating of a long line of sisters, the establishment of numerous fruitful missions, the acquisition of many fine homes within the province, as well as that in Rome for the generalate.'[45] By all accounts it seemed that Sister Elizabeth and her councillors had justifiable grounds for pride, particularly in their province's eminence, for it currently enjoyed a high place in public esteem, and the number of girls seeking admission had risen sharply; during her term Sister Elizabeth had admitted a total of 178 candidates.[46]

There was, therefore, a good deal of substance in Sister Bernadette's remark to her at a farewell gathering in Toronto on November 25: 'You have been a good spiritual mother, teacher, and guide to all of us. Many sisters today gratefully acknowledge their membership in this institute to you. A number of them were your pupils in elementary or in high school, and it was there that they first learned the principles of selfless dedication to God's love and His work, not only through the lessons you taught but by the example you lived. Throughout your years in office you were the compass needle always pointing out to us the way to God.'[47]

Thus it seems to have been generally conceded that Sister Elizabeth had earned the right to bask in the expansive mood of esteem bestowed upon those who have constructively influenced the history of a particular organization or group. Since few leaders can climb the ramparts of meaningful achievement without provoking a certain backlash, she had often had darts sticking into her from every angle – some coming from bishops, clergy, and laity who had thought that she was doing too little too slowly; others from fellow religious who had felt that she was doing too much too fast. Moreover, possibly because it had always been her conviction that those closest to local needs and problems were usually best able to deal with them intelligently and flexibly, some seemed to think that she had exhibited too great a provincial independence, notably during the war years. What these critics tended to forget was that with the generalate's direction of the institute paralyzed by the war, she had been empowered by the Church to assume complete charge of the North American missions – which she most certainly had done.

Actually, no amount of criticism could depict her as a leader who had displayed little talent for sustained battle in the interests of her Church, her religious community, and her people, for she had initiated many things in their behalf and had completed them all. Nor was she now willing to relegate the rest of her years to comfortable retirement. Her long period of demanding leadership had drained neither her energy nor her determination for, confident, plucky, and adroit as ever, she accepted her new assignment at Windsor where, in addition to assuming the duties of local superior, she participated in a parish teaching apostolate, a work that had always appealed to the activist and assertive side of her mission-oriented nature.

For the new provincial superior, Sister Bernadette, the vote of confidence accorded her by the general council and the members of her province abruptly terminated a sixteen-year teaching career in the Edmonton separate school system. She had always responded to her lengthy assignment at this one mission with a saving sense of humour: whenever personnel transfers were posted she was sure to quip, 'Sisters come and sisters go, but I stay on forever.' Ironically, she would find herself compelled to live out of a suitcase for months at a time as she crisscrossed Canada and the United States in the interest of her sisters and the people they served.

Whether or not she would be able to reconcile current runaway apostolic demands, Sister Bernadette had the appearance of a happy choice. A native of Saskatchewan and a graduate of the University of Alberta, she came into the province's top position at the age of thirty-seven with considerably more assurance and coolness than anyone might have expected –

considering that she had never served as an official on the provincial level. By virtue of her character, training, and experience it was clear from the outset that she would guide the province in a different style from that of her predecessor, a style that could bring something vital to the office through her own way of leading, inspiring, and releasing potential energies. Her appointment was, therefore, a move that recognized the depth of her spirituality, the warmth of her womanliness, the force and sharpness of her mind, and her tenacity and seriousness of purpose. Likewise, it also acknowledged – at long last – that Canadian- and American-born sisters were as capable of guiding the institute as were their European-born counterparts, who had until now held most of the major community posts.

On November 29 Sister Veronica addressed the whole new leadership team that had moved into the public eye together with Sister Bernadette. 'Through their tireless efforts, your predecessors achieved many worthwhile goals,' she wrote. 'For this, we and future generations will gratefully remember them. No less do we place our hope in the present council, however, trusting that with the Lord's help it will also accomplish much for His praise.'[48]

Although the criterion they would use in shaping their policies would be the same as that which had always governed Sisters Servants in this country, namely, the needs of the people of God in this time and place, it is not unlikely that as they embarked on their course Sister Bernadette and her advisers experienced a moment of fleeting fear resulting from an awareness that their decisions and actions would have a direct bearing on the future relevance of their religious community in Canada and the United States.

CHAPTER 10

A time for change...

If Sister Bernadette had toyed with the idea of plunging into her province's affairs immediately, she was compelled to drop it quickly, for hardly had her trunk arrived at Austin Terrace than she was on her way to Rome, on January 27, in response to a summons from her superior general. And since the year 1950 had been proclaimed a 'Holy Year' by Pope Pius XII, she and Sister Sozonta Iskiw, who accompanied her, looked upon their journey as a pilgrimage. For not only were they to participate in meetings with the institute's central governing body but also to share in several exceptional religious events.

Chief among these was a private papal audience granted to eighteen Sisters Servants on March 3. 'It was an unforgettable thrill,' declared Sister Bernadette, 'to receive the papal blessing on behalf of each sister together with the members of her family and the people among whom she worked, as well as for all Ukrainians in Canada and the United States. In his few words with me,' she recalled, 'His Holiness expressed the hope that among Canadian and American girls of Ukrainian origin there would be found many with the courage and magnanimity of soul to respond to God's call to a life of religious commitment. His general message to us was an exhortation to pray for deep faith and great fortitude so that, as women dedicated in a special way to loving the Lord – who both transcends and is active in history – we would give relevant witness to all about us, and educate the heart and mind of our people concerning the love of Christ, which goes beyond the power of man to know.'[1]

Furthermore, in a privilege that is hard to come by – even in Rome – Sister Bernadette and Sister Sozonta joined Francis Cardinal Spellman and other members of a pilgrimage, organized by the cardinal, in a Mass celebrated by the pontiff in his private chapel. 'While we were there it seemed as if time stood still,' recalled the provincial superior.[2]

Shortly thereafter she returned home to commence her service in a new post, now, however, greatly strengthened by her spiritual experiences. And indeed, she would have great need of blessing since awaiting her immediate attention was an order from the generalate to close several of the province's missions. Against the background of a continuing influx of Ukrainians to both Canada and the United States, together with the recent establishment of new exarchates, the climate hardly seemed propitious for a move that was certain to sting both churchmen and faithful to resistance. For with each exarchate naturally jealous of its missionary prerogatives and needs, any deliberate trimming down of their works by the sisters might be misunderstood by the bishops.

This extraordinary change in policy emerged from Sister Veronica's reappraisal of the North American missions during her recent canonical visitation. In her opinion, what had looked like a series of missionary plums in the early 1940s might, in the 1950s, prove too much to swallow; in effect, the rapid expansion of the past decade appeared no longer sustainable. What had happened, she believed, was that superiors had been pressured into underestimating missionary demands and overestimating their rate of membership growth, thus creating a smallness of community spiritually detrimental to the sisters.

In her report to the Sacred Oriental Congregation, Sister Veronica found it difficult to mask her concern. 'From 1939, when contact between the province and generalate was virtually non-existent,' she explained, 'Sister Elizabeth, the provincial superior, came under considerable pressure from Bishop Bohachevsky to open missions with two-member staffs, even though this was not in conformity with the constitutions [which specified that each local community should consist of no fewer than four religious]. The missions were opened, however, on the basis of the bishop's assurance that the apostolic delegate had sanctioned this course of action. Today, the sisters' apostolate at these centres consists in teaching in the parochial school, conducting catechetical courses, caring for church sanctuaries, and performing a number of other charitable works recommended by our constitutions. Each member's monthly salary averages twenty-five dollars, which barely covers the cost of living. Since the two religious stationed at such convents are being required to do the work of four, the net effect has been a notable weakening in their spiritual life. There arises, therefore, the possibility that some will lose their religious zeal and even their vocation.'[3]

Thus according to the superior general, external activities were eroding spiritual life. In the light of this kind of imbalance, her implicit argument was strong: if the Sisters Servants were to give true witness, their missionary tasks would have to flow from a rich prayer life. This, she felt, was impossible so long as the crux of the matter remained overactivism. Her diagnosis prompted the suggestion that since the number of missions had proliferated beyond the province's capacity to staff them adequately, the time had come to lop off as many as would be needed to get back to a point of reality. Whether a change in the situation developed as a result of compromise or confrontation, some form of relief for the sisters was essential.

A record break in the province's decade-long pattern of succumbing to pressures came in the positive response of the Sacred Oriental Congregation to Sister Veronica's assessment of the situation. 'On the basis of our post-visitation statement concerning the Province of Christ the King,' reported Sister Veronica to Sister Bernadette and her council in November 1949, 'the Holy See, having graciously considered the sisters' zeal in the Church, places great hope in their future missionary endeavours. To fulfil this task, however, they must be fortified by a deep spiritual life. For this reason, the Sacred Oriental Congregation has decreed that no fewer than three sisters may be stationed at any convent. Wherever there are now only two religious, another member shall be immediately assigned to that community. Convents in parishes which cannot afford to maintain more than two sisters will have to be closed, with the approval of the local bishop. Until such time as the existing houses have the requisite number of religious, no new missions may be founded. It is hoped that these changes will enable many of our sisters, whose physical energy has also been drained by overwork, to regain their strength.'[4]

As early as 1946, however, Sister Elizabeth, fearing an unbridled growth, had been curtailing missionary expansion. 'Although there is still a great demand for sisters,' she had informed Sister Veronica in March of that year, 'we have felt it imperative to refuse all requests from the clergy for new works.'[5] That being the case, she could scarcely have been surprised to learn of the decision to terminate several missions. 'However,' explained the annalist, 'although Bishop Bohachevsky, in compliance with the directives of the Sacred Oriental Congregation, has requested our council to reach an understanding concerning the houses which could be combined in order to meet the constitutional requirements of four sisters at every mission, we have replied that the matter will be presented for consideration to the incoming provincial council.'[6]

The task of spooning out the unpleasant medicine fell, therefore, to Sister Bernadette who, although in full agreement with the decision, foresaw that a move like this could trigger much pent-up emotion, particularly among the relatively small number of Ukrainian priests – which was part frustration and part impatience at the enormity of the missionary task facing them in so many mushrooming parishes.

Since there was little likelihood that the termination of any mission would be greeted by unanimous approval, Sister Bernadette's assignment to coax cooperation from hierarchy, clergy, and laity was formidable. For even if the bishops did agree to a withdrawal of personnel, it was possible that, on the one hand, local pastors would feel that they had been by-passed, while, on the other, some sisters might view the action as an obituary of the province's further development. It seemed that the provincial superior could do little to mollify the predictable outcry that would arise; consequently, from the very outset of her tenure, the process of governing her province could be snarled rather than smoothed simply by her attempt to carry out the directives of her superiors.

Personally convinced that the institute was entering a period when it would have to learn to live with less growth resources, especially in personnel, Sister Bernadette believed that such fence mending as closing a few convents was only a stopgap measure; from now on, more lasting changes would have to come through a policy of placing priorities on which apostolic programmes would be carried on or initiated. She was aware that such a course was fraught with difficulties, notably since the bishops of the recently established exarchates were already expressing their hope of receiving more, not less, apostolic aid from the Sisters Servants. This was especially true after March 19, 1951, when the Holy See created a fourth exarchate for the province of Saskatchewan, assigning to it Bishop Andrew Roborecki, and nominating the Most Rev. Maxime Hermaniuk, CSSR, as auxiliary-bishop to the ailing Archbishop Ladyka. Such expansion meant that, henceforth, instead of receiving petitions for personnel from two dioceses – that of Bishop Ladyka in Canada and of Bishop Bohachevsky in the United States – as had her predecessor, Sister Bernadette would be required to cope with requests from seven bishops in five exarchates, beginning with the most immediate petition – that of providing housekeeping staffs of at least two sisters for each of the four episcopal residences in Canada.

It was one thing to resolve to counter the adverse effects of further fragmentation by not taking on additional works, and quite another to stand firm in the face of considerable compulsion to do so. Sister Bernadette recognized that in the immediate future the Sisters Servants would need to have a great deal of patience with themselves, perhaps more than with anyone else, as they discovered that they could not respond to all demands for schools, hospitals, well-prepared catechetical teams, leaders of parish movements, and the like. Since such an attitude would not exclude a certain emotional concern, they would no doubt feel more than a tinge of regret as they raised their eyes to the whitening harvest and looked in vain for the hands to gather it. But this, she was convinced, was better than approaching Christ with nothing but their incompetence as a gift.

Conscious of the implications involved, Sister Bernadette none the less moved promptly and firmly to implement the directives concerning the missions. On February 3, 1950, she closed the convent at Hamilton and by 1952 had withdrawn the sisters from Sydney, Nova Scotia; Hartford and Ansonia in Connecticut; and Sayre and Wilkes-Barre in Pennsylvania. Rather than constituting an excuse for the Sisters Servants to edge toward the apostolic sidelines, the abandonment of these six centres and the immediate transfer of their personnel to others strengthened and revitalized the life and work of the members in several communities. Furthermore, by 1952, this telling move permitted eighteen sisters to proceed to advanced studies – the largest group which the province had ever been able to release from the apostolate for year-round academic or professional training.[7]

Alongside Sister Bernadette's awareness of the need for her sisters to attain a formal education and to develop special skills in accordance with the general pattern of specialization becoming dominant in modern society was a measured assessment of the subtle transformation in religious attitudes emerging after the war in an already materialistic society. A sad erosion of spirit was compelling Pope Pius XII to call for pioneering in fresh spiritual countercurrents at the threshold of a decade that seemed to presage an era when Christians would no longer be able to count upon the surrounding culture to support their faith. 'Let the dangers and trials which today overwhelm the human race seem to religious as so many means of bringing back the souls of the faithful to the practice of the precepts of the Gospel,' declared the pontiff in September 1950.[8] Perhaps it was in response to such entreaties by the Church that Sister Bernadette's conferences to each local community during her annual canonical visitations stressed the cultivation of true 'mission virtues': humility, accessibility, adaptability, affability, confidence, hardiness, initiative, frankness, and loyalty.[9]

Her own verve, as much as her pronouncements or policies, persuaded the sisters that if they prayed enough, probed enough, and pushed enough there was little they could not accomplish for their people and the praise of the Lord. This euphoric sense of hope and possibility that she kindled lay in her ability to raise the sisters' confidence about their own capacities and about the institute's – the kind of confidence that is a prerequisite to any achievement. When in 1951 the members of the province were requested to assist in a revision of their constitutions, they were not only willing but ready to make their contribution toward bringing the institute up-to-date.

The problem of appropriately rewriting the rule, prior to presenting it to the Holy See for definitive approval, had remained unresolved for almost twenty years primarily because, as Sister Veronica explained, 'wartime and postwar circumstances had militated against convoking a general chapter to introduce any required modifications or changes.'[10] Now, however, their apostolic visitor, Father Coussa, felt that the time was historically ripe to proceed with this work, especially since he had observed that, however sound their aims, the constitutions of 1932 did not meet the demands of the moment. 'Father Coussa has plainly asserted that our rule is already outdated and requires changes,' confirmed Sister Veronica in her letter to Sister Bernadette in February 1951.[11] And she agreed with him. For during her visitation in the Province of Christ the King in 1948 she had shared the dismay which the Canadian sisters had been experiencing for years; that is, a feeling of helplessness in having to apply – often ill-advisedly – the constitutions conceived for eastern Europe to the sisters' life and work in North America. Members here had often reiterated their conviction that what was needed was adaptation to local areas so that the rule would reflect the interests of Sisters Servants everywhere. They had maintained that the incorporation into the constitutions of the net effects accruing from missionary experience in Western nations would enrich the institute as a whole. Now, at last, in much the same vein, their superior general took pains to point out to the Sacred Oriental Congregation the fallacy of trying to apply the European mind to the North American scene. 'Our constitutions, which were originally adapted to conditions existing in our European dioceses, fail to meet the exigencies of our life and activity in the Canadian and American exarchates,' she declared; 'hence the need for a broader, more encompassing rule is obvious.'[12]

With the institute so ready to meet the winds of change, the Holy See announced that work on the constitutional revision would begin forthwith. In communicating this news to Sister Bernadette the superior general added: 'I request that, after consultation with your advisers, several experienced local superiors, and teachers, you submit a draft to the general council consisting of your recommendations for changes in the rule.'[13] Besides seeking suggestions from the few sisters mentioned by Sister Veronica, the provincial superior invited every religious in her province to forward her personal observations regarding the relevancy of the constitutions to her daily life and work.[14] By so doing she demonstrated her conviction that consultation is the first step in the creation of shared goals and responsibilities. In this instance her bold commitment of the entire province to a careful study of the rule was instrumental in creating a community interest in a project that had remained in abeyance for so many years.

After carefully sifting through the proposals submitted by individuals and groups, the provincial council produced a draft of specific modifications and changes based on the sisters' life and activity in the Canadian and American missions. It was hoped that at least a few of their recommendations would receive positive consideration in Rome. That obviously would not be the best that could happen, but if that were the worst the council would be happy.

Father Coussa contended that the time was likewise at hand to deal with a second paramount issue: the selection of a superior general and council through a consultative vote of the sisters. For even in 1951 a general chapter of election could not be convened, owing to the large proportion of houses and members still encaged by the iron curtain. The responsibility of choosing suitable candidates was therefore allotted by the Holy See to the members of the general and provincial councils in all of the institute's provinces in the free world, to superiors of religious houses with a minimum of six sisters, and to all perpetually professed members who met the minimum age requirement of thirty-five years. The electors were instructed to mail their ballots directly to the Sacred Oriental Congregation.

Perhaps because this was the first such election in the institute's history, the apostolic visitor felt compelled to remind the electors of their grave duty. 'You are well aware that elections are an important matter in the life of a religious congregation,' he wrote in his letter of June 25, 1951, 'since on their result hinges either meritorious progress or sad retrogression, depending on whether the Holy Spirit or human manipulation influences their outcome. The Church exhorts you to avoid being guided by human considerations regarding those who are to be chosen, for a superior general and her council constitute the heart of a religious institute, and from the nature of this heart will depend future growth, both spiritual and temporal. Since this heart should be a source of animation for all members and their apostolate, each voter bears a serious responsibility before God, the Church, the institute, and souls, in her selection of candidates. Familial bonds, friendships, personal or national advantage, should not affect her choice; rather, in reaching her decision, each sister should be persuaded by noble aspirations – God's glory, the good of the Church and the congregation. Then too, since the constitutions describe the qualities expected in the institute's officials, the ultimate choice will conform to the Lord's wishes in so far as it corresponds to the guidelines laid down in the rule.'[15]

The general consensus seems to have been that Sister Veronica Gargil, who had discharged her duties as major superior since 1934, possessed the attributes and experience that projected a meaningful leadership, for on the basis of the vote the Apostolic See called upon her to remain in office for a third term. Her renomination was a personal honour for this personable woman, and proof enough that she had carried her seventeen-year burden of service with such grace, dignity, and love that her fellow sisters on both sides of the Atlantic saw her as one of the giants of their institute. It was also significant that for the first time a member of the Canadian-American province – Sister Gertrude Lesiuk – would form a part of the changed personality of the new general council, whose task it now was to weather the challenges to the institute in the first half of the 1950s.[16]

In 1951 the Province of Christ the King observed its fiftieth jubilee, and for a brief moment the Sisters Servants on this continent found themselves thrust into the limelight, as a burst of public acknowledgement in the press and from the pulpit emphasized a measure of their service to the Church. There were, however, many facets of the half-century that the sisters themselves sought to commemorate. In the end the most striking and perhaps most enduring was their tribute to the pioneer sisters for the leavening and direction they had provided through the years. 'On November 2, 1902, the first Sisters Servants, among them Sister Ambrose [Lenkewich], established our beloved institute on this continent,' noted Sister Bernadette in her letter to the sisters toward the close of 1951. 'Today, as we stand on the threshold of our Golden Jubilee, we are conscious of the countless graces and merciful goodness which Divine Providence has so munificently bestowed upon us, and which are reflected on the horizon of the past fifty years. How, then, can we express our gratitude for these gifts? To our predecessors, under whose competent leadership our province flourished, we can best manifest our appreciation through a prayerful and an exemplary life.'[17]

Thus, instead of reviling their roots, they were affirming and encouraging generation ties by reaching back to the past for perspective, solace, and meaning. And out of their awareness that the continuity between past and present is far stronger than many prophets admit, emerged a solidarity that was readily apparent among all members, young and old. Specifically, the confidence they radiated was strikingly obvious in their anniversary publication, *Jubilee Memoir*, in which they tallied the results of a fifty-year survey of their apostolic achievement. Primarily, however, it was a salute to the pioneers, for it dramatically illustrated how they had threaded their way through a maze of obstacles to stitch together a province. It was also an eloquent reminder to the present generation of Sisters Servants that what the past was seeking was a new period of introspection, self-analysis, and candour.

Gauged by the statistical yardsticks recorded in the *Memoir*, the assessment by the secretary of the Sacred Oriental Congregation, Eugene Cardinal Tisserant, of the Sisters Servants on this continent as a group of women who had been tested but had not been found wanting, would scarcely have stirred a ripple of disagreement. For his statement was not a mere triumph of rhetoric over reality. 'At the present time,' the cardinal asserted, '250 professed sisters and novices in nineteen Canadian, and sixteen American, missions continue to fulfil an admirable apostolate: they teach in a variety of schools, nurse in their hospitals, direct hostels, orphanages, and homes for the aged, care for church sanctuaries, bake altar bread, sew liturgical vestments, conduct courses in catechetics and religious music, prepare children for their first reception of the Eucharist, and foster organizations such as the Apostleship of Prayer, Marian Sodalites, and Altar Boys' Clubs. All of these works, highly esteemed by bishops, clergy, and laity, contribute much toward the strengthening of the Catholic Faith in the souls of their people who have settled in these countries.'[18]

For his part, Father Coussa probably had no intention of prejudging the future when he fondly pointed out that the province was blooming with still other indications of continuing health, and concluded: 'A review of your activity during the past fifty years permits us to expect that your tomorrow will be as bright and glorious as your today, and that the mustard seed which has now become a tree will not cease to multiply its branches and leaves so that in its shade young people, the neglected aged, the sick, the poor, and all those whose anguish calls forth your Christian compassion will continue to find sustenance, protection, and rest.'[19] Mincing no words, however, he borrowed from St Paul to sound a warning: 'Be careful that no one is deprived of the grace of God and that no root of bitterness should begin to grow and make trouble; this can poison a whole community' (Heb 12:15).[20]

Since an anniversary also calls for festivity, the milestone was commemorated at every centre in which the sisters carried on an apostolate. From May 4, 1952, when Bishop Isidore Borecky offered the Divine Liturgy of thanksgiving in St Nicholas Church, Toronto, in the presence of three thousand people, until the following November, Canadians and

Americans united with the sisters in special liturgical services and concerts to honour the occasion. Even Sister Veronica found herself swept into the stream of celebration during the course of her canonical visitation that had begun on March 27 of that year. In one city after another she witnessed in her members an unabashed pride in their heritage as Sisters Servants. And in the face of their exuberance it seemed that her approval of two new missions, one at Kitchener and another at Calgary, to be opened in August, was a special jubilee gift to them.

At this half-century mark in their history there was a need for the sisters to become double witnesses by making certain that each charitable undertaking, such as each of the two latest missions, took on a value surpassing the merit of its concrete activity through an abiding mystical and evangelical motive 'that transfigures the countenance of a poor hungry person, a sickly child, a person repulsive with leprosy, a formidable criminal, and a feeble man on his deathbed into the mysterious countenance of Christ.'[21] Such a motive would also make them truly free to set new priorities, free to meet unmet needs, free to make their own mistakes, yes, but also free to score further splendid successes with, in, and for the Mystical Body.

During that jubilee summer Sister Josaphata Kizlyk rounded out her sixteen-year stewardship as directress of the province's novitiate. As in 1936, when she had perceived the call of the Spirit in her superiors' wishes that she leave her native land to undertake the task of training Canadian novices, so now she again demonstrated an active and responsible obedience by relinquishing her duties at Ancaster to her successor, Sister Boniface Julia Sloboda, and heading for Toronto where, as a provincial councillor and an imaginative teacher in the city's Ukrainian evening schools, she would continue to place her intellectual, pedagogical, and artistic gifts at the service of others.

Right from the start of her tenure as directress she had endeavoured to instil in her novices a profound sense of commitment to their religious vocation and loyalty to their institute. Above all she had accented the concept that a Sister Servant did not offer her people goods, but goodness; not services merely, but love, stemming from a prayerful union with the Lord, that proved itself in service and sacrifice.

The interesting aspect of this transfer of office was that only after a half-century had elapsed was a Canadian-born religious appointed to this position. Sister Boniface, who had gained invaluable experience during a two-year period as Sister Josaphata's assistant, readily accepted her responsible post. She recognized, however, that certain modifications and changes would have to be implemented soon if the novices, now mostly third and fourth generation Ukrainians, as well as non-Ukrainians who were entering the institute with scarcely a smattering knowledge of the Ukrainian language, were to be adequately prepared for a meaningful apostolate among their people. None the less, in spite of any uncertainty that may have existed about how best to adapt to the new needs of a new generation of sisters in a new age, Sister Boniface and her assistant, Sister Eleanor Lenyk, took root at Mount Mary Novitiate with a will and a genuinely winning way.

While a fresh force of young girls was being prepared to step into the ranks of Sisters Servants, those who had made the way ready for them were passing from the scene. Among them was Sister Ambrose Lenkewich, one of the province's major figures, who died at Komarno, Manitoba, at the age of seventy-seven. The sisters mourned her but were comforted by her full life. For inevitably the news of her death brought back many memories of this remarkable pioneer. The sisters recalled how, after the unexpected death of Sister Taida Wrublewsky in 1903,[22] and the return to Ukraine in 1908 of Sister Isidore Shypowsky and Sister Emilia Klapowchuk, the two other original missionaries,[23] she alone had remained to fashion the Province of Christ the King. And she had built it on a rock. For although the rains of trial had come and the sea of suffering had washed over it time and again, it had grown out of an obscure farmhouse at Mundare into a flourishing Canadian missionary movement. And she had witnessed its crossing of a national boundary to take root in the United States.

Although the personal devotional life of a religious is hard to know, Sister Ambrose had not been able to hide hers. As the author of her obituary revealed, 'Sister Ambrose, though perhaps small in physical stature, proved to be a spiritual giant. This soul of prayer and sacrifice was chosen by God to become the leader of the first sisters in the institute's second province, Canada. Her love of the Church and her obedience to its teachings were outstanding, revealing themselves in her relations with all bishops and priests. An awe-inspiring humility pervaded her life, and was exemplified in her profound gratitude for even the smallest kindness. Poverty in its finest details became her love and often her suffering. In all, she manifested a strength of will and a sense of duty, punctuality, and a readiness to serve.'[24]

On May 19 she was buried at Edmonton where she had commenced her Canadian apostolate. It seemed right that she should rest beside her co-missionary, Sister Taida. 'Just as half a century earlier they had been together, so now they were together again,' remarked the annalist. 'So it is, two chosen daughters of the Immaculate Virgin, like two grains of wheat put into the ground, await the voice of the archangel's trumpet and the glorious resurrection.'[25]

On May 31, 1953, the sisters experienced a rather heady and exhilarating moment – the dedication of their first girls' high school in eastern Canada. The audience attending the opening of Mount Mary Immaculate Academy at Ancaster was a rich mixture of hierarchy, clerics, leading representatives of major religious, political, and civic groups, patrons, parents, young people, and children, all of whom, after the official ceremonies, spilled over into the spacious academy corridors from the classrooms, laboratories, dormitories, dining room, and auditorium that came under much meticulous scrutiny that day. The *Canadian Register* reporter, for one, seemed taxed for adjectives: 'Mount Mary Immaculate Academy, Ancaster, conducted by the Sisters Servants of Mary Immaculate, is one of the plushiest boarding and day schools in Ontario. It is a modern, two-storey, buff-brick, stone-trimmed structure, Georgian in design, which features all the latest in school equipment and boarding school accommodation.'[26] And, he enthusiastically added, 'with the opening of Mount Mary Academy, part of the problem of the overcrowding at Cathedral High School (girls) might be solved ... For although the sisters belong to the Greek rite [*sic*] of the Catholic Church, it is not to be considered that the school is exclusively for girls of Ukrainian origin. The teachers are all natives of Canada and the United States and have their teaching certificates from the Ontario College of Education.'[27]

For their part, however, the clergy and over a thousand of their faithful who participated in the event saw the school as a Ukrainian Catholic institution which would assert the ethnic and religious identity through a definite accent on the achievements, cultural attitudes, and ethical ideals that Ukrainians could comfortably share with their fellow Canadians. This concept was articulated among others by the president of the Ukrainian Youth Association of Canada, Mr V. Kushmelyn, who stated: 'The achievement of the Sisters Servants of Mary Immaculate is a significant accomplishment which bears witness to their total dedication to the welfare of Ukrainian youth. We believe, therefore, that through their Christian and cultural emphasis in education the girls' academy at Ancaster, Ontario, will be engraved in golden letters in the history of Ukrainian immigration in Canada.'[28]

In actual fact the sisters' commitment to build the high school had come in reply to a series of searching questions: With the European orphan refugee programme being phased out, would an apostolate in the nursery that had replaced it warrant the maintenance of the estate? In view of the fact that their geographical location had the major shortcoming of cutting them off from direct contact with youth in parishes, how could young people be served at Mount Mary?

Consideration of various enterprises were dwarfed by a long-standing belief among Sisters Servants that a well-directed academy had much to offer a girl, especially at a time when most city high schools averaged a student population of at least one thousand, and when it was difficult for a principal to be well-acquainted with the members of his staff, and for his teachers to recognize their students outside the classroom. Sister Bernadette, herself an educator, was strongly convinced that in the life of a student little could substitute for the kind of personal instruction, close teacher-student contact, spiritual and ethical guidance, emphasis on intangibles such as truth and beauty, and the special atmosphere of study and camaraderie that had distinguished the academies of the Sisters Servants for almost a quarter of a century. There was little doubt in her mind that a small well-staffed high school could equal any large collegiate as a centre of creative intellectual, spiritual, and cultural ferment.

Actually, the idea of erecting a school at Mount Mary had been conceived almost as soon as the property had been purchased, but the resultant huge debt had swiftly sapped any plans for rushing into construction. It had thus become basically a question of when and how. The first glimmer that the tide was beginning to run strong in the direction of building the school appeared on May 28, 1951, when, as the annalist reported, 'our provincial superior and her council today seriously explored the possibility of erecting a residential and day school for girls at Ancaster – a considerable undertaking in these uncertain times.'[29] Apparently some solid plans emerged from that meeting for, as the annalist indicated soon afterwards, 'various contacts are being made with architects and construction firms.'[30]

As for the other side of the coin – the financial – a problem soon loomed large: the province simply lacked the wherewithal to pay for a school that, it was estimated, would cost $550,000. Thus, as a target, an academy at Mount Mary was praiseworthy; as a projection, so expensive an undertaking was optimistic. The sober fact was that the community would have to sell a portion of its property at Austin Terrace and St Rita's Convent on King Street to raise just 10 per cent of the total sum. They were, indeed, starting from below scratch. The question that haunted Sister Bernadette and her advisers, therefore, was whether the province could funnel enough money from its communal earnings to supplement, and pay for, a $355,000 loan, in order to guarantee that the school, once begun, would be completed.

Given this rather sombre situation, it was a thin hope at best that animated the provincial superior as she saw dollar signs – 550,000 of them – pointing away from a new school. But it was at this moment that she displayed the most essential quality of any leader, one that no experience can teach: the courage that comes from strength of character. In a step that proved to be one of the high-water marks of her superiorship, she launched the project, even though it was, to date, the province's biggest gamble – not only from the financial point of view but also because there was hardly an oversupply of qualified personnel to staff another secondary school. Thus when she did assume the risk, it was simply because she believed that the apostolic case advanced by the sisters for taking it was overwhelming. Probably her chief asset at this time was one of the best business brains in the institute, a fact that revealed itself in the ensuing weeks of her negotiations with Mr J. H. Haffa, the architect, and Mr G. Hardy, the contractor. She also gave evidence that when encouraging voices were few and far between she could choose rationally and calmly among sometimes risky alternatives. The result was that on July 27, 1951, Bishop Borecky turned the sod at the site of the proposed academy.

That, it turned out, spurred the sisters' efforts in a bid to channel any extra penny saved from their personal income into the provincial building fund, since only a negligible sum had been raised from their appeal to the public for monetary assistance.[31] By October 19, 1952, when the bishop blessed the cornerstone of the almost completed edifice, it was abundantly clear how successful their attempt had been. Declared an editorial in *Nasha Meta (Our Aim)* on May 30: 'We express our sincere congratulations to the Sisters Servants on this latest admirable contribution to Christian education, an accomplishment that will greatly benefit our Ukrainian youth. May the beautiful girls' academy at Ancaster live, grow, and prosper!' Without question the feat which produced such respectful amazement in the press had been made possible only by an infusion of prayer, pluck, and luck.

Although the sisters now had a building they needed a student body to give it life. Naturally, since the school had been well publicized, particularly in the Ukrainian press, the staff waited for a ground swell of Ukrainian applicants. It never came. The enrolment for the scholastic term 1953–4 was exactly twenty-eight girls, registered in grades seven to twelve, in an academy that had been erected to accommodate two hundred students. The amazing thing about the thirteen of those who were Ukrainian was that they had come to Mount Mary from such scattered Ontario centres as Sudbury, Nipigon, Owen Sound, Trenton, Kitchener, Windsor, Toronto, Hamilton, Ancaster, and even Vernon in British Columbia. Needless to say, the small enrolment was a keen disappointment for the members of the faculty – Sister Cornelia Mantyka, principal; Sister Joan Magriy; Sister Dominic Genevieve Slawuta; and Sister Ivanna Madeleine Loya – as well as for the superior, Sister Sozonta Iskiw, and the prefect, Sister Sylvester Gulka. They were learning the hard way that while the depth or shallows of public response cannot usually be gauged until long after the response is over, even immediate effects of favourable press runs and letters from individuals and organizations are unpredictable.

Initially, therefore, the academy's future appeared murky, and its staff foresaw a long hard road. The school would have to prove itself, particularly to many new Canadians, who were unfamiliar with the work of the Sisters Servants in secondary education both in Canada and the United States. Many Ukrainians based their assessment of the academy on their knowledge that, in Europe, members of the institute had specialized predominantly in a nursery school apostolate. Not surprisingly, therefore, they questioned the competence of the teachers and automatically assumed that the scholastic standards in the school were inferior.

It was apparent that even the statement of Miss Anne Skrypka of Grimsby, Ontario, at the dedication ceremonies in May had done little to change their viewpoint. At that time, she had unhesitatingly asserted: 'As a graduate of Sacred Heart Academy at Yorkton, Saskatchewan, which is conducted by the Sisters Servants, I can vouch that every parent and every girl can have great confidence in this school. The instruction and guidance provided by our sisters will help each student to grow in an appreciation of her faith, religious rite, culture, and heritage. Here a young woman will attain the good breeding and poise that is fostered in gracious surroundings. And after four years of instruction and guidance by dedicated teachers, a graduate of Mount Mary Academy will leave her alma mater excellently prepared to meet the challenges and responsibilities awaiting her.'[32]

A growth in popular confidence was not too long in coming, however, for within three years 50 per cent of the student enrolment, which had tripled, was Ukrainian. An article in *Meta* about this time revealed the positive outlook that was beginning to prevail in some quarters, besides indicating that the work being done at the school was being observed with considerable interest: 'Students of Mount Mary Academy, Ancaster, which is conducted by the Sisters Servants of Mary Immaculate, are achieving noteworthy successes, not only in the sciences but also in the arts – music, choral work, painting, drama, and handicrafts. It is apparent that the education and training received by young women at Ancaster has not stiffened into rigid scholastic forms but has developed into the fulness of all that is intelligent, beautiful, and noble – the best that modern pedagogy can offer.'[33]

Plainly, however, such an evaluation was not shared by all, for from time to time the academy was subjected to a broadside of criticism that seemed to nettle its supporters even more than its faculty. The chief charge was that the sisters were accepting young women of other races and nationalities into the school and thus doing their own people a disservice. Parents and relatives of Mount Mary's students were quick to rise to the academy's defence. So far as they were concerned the attempt to blame the staff for the lack of Ukrainian students was to seek an excuse, not a reason. Thus, for example, in an article printed in *Meta* on July 21, 1956, Mr Peter Bihus, a grandfather of one of the girls enrolled that year, stoutly professed satisfaction with the school's performance. 'Too often some of our people undercut the good name of the academy under the guise of various pretexts, generally through the subtle accusation that the school is not Ukrainian enough,' he contended. 'The fact is that our Sisters adapt instruction to the reality of time and place. And since our children are preparing themselves for a career, not in Ukraine but in Canada, the entire programme in the school is geared toward educating them to live and work in this country ... Moreover, I am convinced, after carefully observing the attitude of my own granddaughter and that of other students, that there is no foundation to the charge that the teachers are stifling an esteem for, and love of, their Ukrainian heritage ... Furthermore, while it is true that the school has been established primarily for the benefit of our children, it is also true that when the annual deadline for new applications passes and Ukrainian students are unheard from, the sisters willingly accept girls of other nationalities. As anyone knows, the very cost of school maintenance demands adherence to such a policy.'[34]

In reality, what was occurring at Ancaster and at every other academy directed by Sisters Servants, was an attempt to make citizenship work two ways. The sisters believed that their Ukrainian students, by retaining a pride in their national origin, could effectively interpret Canadian culture to Ukrainians, and Ukrainian culture to Canadians, particularly to their fellow students of other ethnic groups. Experience had taught them that the lasting friendships formed by Ukrainian girls with students of other nationalities and cultures, such as those from Central and South American nations, almost automatically seemed to eliminate prejudice – which usually springs from an unconscious animosity toward the unknown. Their correspondence with the members of the staff after their return to their own country indicated that these daughters of diplomats, businessmen, and professionals not only affectionately remembered their teachers and schoolmates but also retained a warm regard for Ukrainians in general.

By the end of the decade, grass-roots support such as that of Mr Bihus, the dedicated commitment to their students of teachers, and chaplains – Rev. M. Pelech and his successor, Rev. B. Humeniuk – along with the achievements of its graduates and the annual academic success of its students, created a greater degree of acceptance. Thus, during the 1959–60 term 83 per cent of the one hundred resident students were Ukrainian.[35] Judging by this kind of development the sisters appeared to have staked out a sound educational apostolate at Mount Mary.

At the same time as the academy was opened in September 1953 Sister Bernadette, acting on a directive received from her superior general two years before, opened two missions in Bishop Daniel Ivancho's Byzantine-Slavonic Exarchate of Pittsburgh, which had been established in 1924 to serve the Rusins – Oriental-rite Catholics who had emigrated to the United States from the Subcarpathian region, Slovakia, and Yugoslavia.[36] Perhaps the most puzzling aspect of the instructions received from the generalate was that no sooner had the provincial council been requested in November of 1949 to close a number of small American convents, than it was being instructed in the autumn of 1951 to move into still another diocese.[37] Local imperatives have a way of modifying even the most firm decisions, notably as in this somewhat radical exception in the complexion of Sister Veronica's position. The chief factor in this surprising turnabout seems to have been a plan to eventually replace those Canadian and American sisters initially assigned to missions in the Pittsburgh exarchate with several European refugee sisters, currently in western Europe, who had previously worked with Rusins in eastern European countries. Such a substitution of staff from overseas could mean, of course, that these missions would fall under the jurisdiction of the superior general and her council.[38]

In September 1951, acting upon directives from the generalate, Sister Bernadette had sought Bishop Ivancho's permission to accede to a request by Rev. J. Tylawsky for a mission in his parish at St Clair, Pennsylvania. In his prompt reply the bishop had blessed and hailed the project as evidence of a true catholicity of spirit. 'I wish to assure you and your zealous Community of Handmaids of our Blessed Mother of our every cooperation which you will need and which we can afford,' he had promised, 'in order that this sacred enterprise may not only commence auspiciously, but that it may thrive by heavenly increment, and God willing, that this may be the beginning of a holy and most useful new religious growth in the spiritual life of our beloved Diocese.' The prelate had also expressed a glowing faith in the future growth of the institute among the Rusins: 'It is my fervent hope that we shall not, for long, have to ask nuns of Galician ancestry to forego work in their own element for our sake, but that our own young women will dedicate their lives by joining this new Sisterhood in our Diocese. Herewith I authorize any eligible young lady of our ancestry to join your Community, with your gracious consent and cooperation, to prepare herself in your Novitiate for future work in our Diocese.' Looking beyond the predictably fragile beginnings, he had concluded: 'It is my ultimate hope and prayerful desire that there should be established in our own Diocese, as soon as possible, our own Province of your Sisterhood. We should anticipate difficulties, but these should only serve to convince us of the real merits and historical significance of this holy work.'[39]

Gratefully acknowledging these warm words of welcome, Sister Berna-dette had admitted: 'Your apostolic blessing, your assurance of every cooperation and your paternal encouragement have brushed aside our hesitancy and fear of faring forth into a new diocese.'[40] In the end, how-ever, the final decision of when to send three sisters to St Clair did not have to be made, since a subsequent on-the-spot look at the situation by the provincial councillor, Sister Gertrude Lesiuk, had revealed that in the small mining community there were too few parishioners to justify the founding of a mission.

There the matter had rested for two years until it was reopened by Bishop Ivancho in the summer of 1953, when he invited Sister Bernadette to visit two possible centres for the Sisters Servants' apostolate in his exarchate – Youngstown, Ohio, and Passaic, New Jersey. She and her adviser, Sister Lawrence Dzumaga, liked what they saw in both cities. At Passaic the renovations to the public school, which young Father John Stim's parish had recently purchased, held promise of comfortable class-rooms in one part of the building and a homey convent in another. At Youngstown they foresaw a number of apostolic possibilities for the estate procured by the parish – one section of which had already been set aside as the site for a new parochial school.

In view of the general council's position in the matter, it was not for the provincial superior to decide whether to accept the project; to determine when or how to match the pastors' requests with action – that, by all accounts, was a poser Sister Bernadette was forced to ponder. Her decision came swiftly, however, for in September 1953 both missions were in operation, with Sister Cyprian Eleanor Homa, Sister Apollinaria Emily Strutynsky, and Sister Veronica Mary Demchuk stationed at St Michael's Convent, Passaic; and Sister Sebastian Mary Smaha, Sister Theodora Anne Pomirko, and Sister Germaine Olga Bohdan at Our Lady of Perpetual Help Convent, Youngstown.

No sooner was the sisters' move into the Pittsburgh exarchate announced than there was a pained indignation from some Ukrainians, including hierarchy and clergy, particularly in the United States.[41] Generally, they seemed to have been stung into the kind of protest that betrays an exposed nerve – in this case, an antagonism toward Ukrainian sisters serving Rusins, even though the people in question were closely related to them as members of Christ's Mystical Body, the Church; as members of a Slavic race; as members of an Oriental rite. The jaundiced outlook manifested at this time focused a grim spotlight on the kind of parochial passions that sometimes affect normally sensible and rational people.

Sister Bernadette, who bore the brunt of direct and indirect vocal accusations, accepted the criticism with characteristic aplomb. She and her fellow religious could only prayerfully hope for the slow convergence of attitudes that could promote greater understanding and tolerance. They knew from experience that their Ukrainian people possessed not only a great spiritual depth but also an ability to express this spirit in their relationship with other peoples. What perturbed the sisters was that for too long after the Second World War some Ukrainians, among them clergymen, had been talking too much politically and too little spiritually. And when nationalism becomes a religion, Christianity becomes, at best, a weekend obligation. The sisters were concerned that, as a consequence, their youth might grow up knowing what a Ukrainian was, but without knowing what being a Ukrainian Catholic involved except, perhaps, going to a different church.

What the sisters were trying desperately to do was to steer a course that avoided extremes on either side – of an unthinking, chauvinistic, self-righteous, nationalistic mentality on the one hand, and, on the other, of an undifferentiated involvement with everyone but their own people who, they knew, needed them. And because they understood the claims that the human family legitimately makes upon those consecrated to serve the Church, they recognized that in the best interests of the entire people of

God they were obligated to be ready to phase out certain types of work, to restyle and transform, and even to move to new places – as they had in the case of the Pittsburgh exarchate. In their estimation, this was true progress; hence they remained ready to offer whatever they possessed of patience and imaginative guidance to bring about an evolution of tolerance within their Church.

The onus of moving the Sisters Servants toward a comprehensive view of the temper and trends that would emerge in North America in the latter half of the decade was to rest with Sister Bernadette who on May 25, 1954, was confirmed in office for a second term. As she and her council – now comprised of Sister Jerome Mary Chimy, Sister Lawrence Dzumaga, Sister Julianna Pankowsky, and Sister Boniface Sloboda – felt their way through the next five years, the degree of perception and wisdom, imagination and daring which they would bring to their leadership would determine the degree to which the life and works of their members on this continent would be meaningful in an increasingly depersonalized and lonely society.

A unique opportunity for every sister to strengthen herself and those she served to withstand the anxieties already arising from the breathless pace of social and technological change, presented itself when Pope Pius XII appealed to Catholics to observe 1954 as a 'Marian Year,' and thereby commemorate the centenary of the proclamation of the dogma of the Immaculate Conception. The basic thrust of the pontiff's message was hopeful, for it was nothing less than the offering of a spiritual antidote against the fever of materialism.

Pointedly, Sister Bernadette urged her members to observe the occasion in a special way: 'May this centennial year of the Immaculate Mother of Jesus and our Mother, the patroness of our institute, be a significant one for us and men everywhere,' she wrote. 'May it be a year of purification and sanctification, of reparation, and of profound thanksgiving to God for His incomprehensible love. As Servants of Mary Immaculate, let us intensify our prayer life. In our devotion to God's Mother, let us spontaneously and creatively reveal our admiration for her, and praise the peerless richness of the sublime gifts with which God filled her from the first moment of her conception.'[42]

The spontaneous positive attitude to the papal appeal by the sisters should not have surprised anyone, since at the core of their response was a deep personal love of Mary Immaculate; therefore, to encourage others to go to Christ through her was a goal that inspired them. And so it seemed that whenever and wherever there was a Sister Servant that year she was apparently careful not to spare herself, for the 'Provincial Marian Year Reports' reveal that for twelve months, in every regular, or vacation, missionary assignment, some kind of spiritual renewal programme was in progress.[43] Perhaps it was the genuine enthusiasm of these women that warmed hundreds of men, women, and children to the notion that a real devotion to God's Mother was a blessing in anyone's life. For their part, as the Marian Year drew to a close, the sisters were grateful that they now were more vitally involved in the Church's initiative and action than ever before.

CHAPTER 11

A time to be fruitful...

If Pope John XXIII's unexpected announcement in 1959 of a plan to convoke the Twenty-First Ecumenical Council – the first since Vatican I of 1869–70 – would throw open the windows of the Church to let in the fresh air of change, so Pope Pius XII's pointed and pithy appeals for adaptation and renewal in the 1950s unlatched these windows and prepared the groundwork for Vatican Council II.

Since religious men and women have always constituted a vital part of the Church, Pius XII emphasized the need for a deepening and strengthening of the spiritual life of every member in every institute. As early as September 1950 he carefully defined for religious the nature of true renewal. 'This complete renewal of ourselves and of all that touches us is not in any sense an abdication or an unreflecting contempt of all that our forbears have laboriously established, and which should be regarded by each one as the glory and honor of his Institute,' explained the pontiff. 'Rather, it consists in not growing numb with inertia, in translating into life the great examples of the Founders, in an intense nourishing of the flame of piety, in putting everything to work so that the holy laws of each Institute will not degenerate into an assemblage of exterior regulations uselessly imposed, whose letter, in the absence of the spirit kills, but that each law may become truly a means of acquiring supernatural virtue and that those who are bound to use these means may conceive an ever greater desire of sanctity and may employ every effort, after the example of the apostle St Paul, for the salvation of their brothers.'[1]

In effect, what Pius XII was stressing was that Christian life is not a fixed, abstract concept, but a reality that is lived amid continual change. As such, it must take into account the social conditions in which it lives, and continually watch over its relationship with the environmental moment, so that it is on the alert to update itself, when necessary. Lest there be any misunderstanding about the kind of change he advocated, the pontiff specified that adaptation 'to the progress of the manners of the present does not at all mean that souls consecrated to God should lend themselves, in any way whatsoever, to the exigencies of the world, and to its foolish seductions and its appeals. Rather, it is their duty to serve as example to all men by the integrity of their lives; to use, as far as this is possible, all the progress in knowledge and techniques for the advantage of religion.'[2]

With such considerations in mind, Pius XII addressed the members of the First International Congress of Religious, which convened in Rome in 1950. He declared: 'It is our opinion that the time has come to convoke this Congress. Changing circumstances to which the Church must be prepared to adapt itself, opinions which have originated and have been propagated even within the Church, relative to the very elements and nature of moral perfection, pressing demands of the apostolic labor to which you give yourselves in a spirit of great generosity and enthusiasm, such have been the motives that have strongly led you to undertake these discussions and these studies.'[3]

In response to the wish of the pontiff that national congresses be held to implement the work of the World Congress within particular nations, the Church in the United States sponsored such a meeting for major superiors of congregations of men and women at Notre Dame University, South Bend, Indiana, within two years. Representing the Sisters Servants' American missions, Sister Bernadette and Sister Jerome Chimy were among the fourteen hundred delegates who met there in August 1952 to discuss the renewal of the spiritual and active life of their institutes. At that time, this remarkable assembly of superiors was told: 'The world yearns to see the face of God. The world wants God to explain the riddle of life. The weary weight of this unintelligible world cannot be borne by mankind alone. The world wants to see the Christ of God yoked to the same plow as it pulls. Until the world sees Him in His followers, it will continue to wallow in the slough of despond and wander in the valley of the shadow of death.'[4]

Rather than exhausting the means for furthering a deep religious life in the United States, this congress opened up vast fields for progress. Among other things, plans were made to establish special conferences and schools for the study of the religious life and the preparation of those vested with the responsibility of forming it in others.[5] The following summer, therefore, the first Institute of Spirituality for superiors and novice mistresses was held at Notre Dame from July 31 to August 7. Of the sixty-eight Canadian sisters participating in the courses, together with 859 American religious, eleven were Sisters Servants.[6]

Shortly thereafter, the Sacred Congregation of Religious declared its intention of holding a similar meeting in Canada during the summer of 1954, and indicated that this would be a National Congress open to all religious men and women of Canada without discrimination of race or language.[7] Specifically, added Rev. J. Rousseau, OMI, general secretary of the congress, 'on the authority of Cardinal Tisserant, Religious of the Oriental Rite are to be included.'[8]

From July 26 to 30 twelve Sisters Servants, headed by Sister Bernadette, took part in the congress held at Ville St-Laurent, near Montreal. Thus, from its very inception, members of the Canadian-American Province of Christ the King entered into the vibrant movement by the Church to provide religious with an opportunity to gain the theoretical principles of their vocation and also of working out their applications to the problems which were already facing them in a rapidly changing society.

Mindful that blind concentration on self-centred parochial concerns was simply a stubborn turning away from current religious trends and realities, Sister Bernadette unhesitatingly sent her members to the annual congresses and Institutes of Spirituality, thereby perceptibly shifting the Sisters Servants toward a more assertive stance within the Church universal. In fact, in several respects, her action broke new ground.

For one thing, by enabling many newly appointed local superiors to receive direction from a competent faculty at the outset of their tenure in office, she eventually provided her province with imaginative leaders who were better prepared to take bold, decisive steps to bring a breath of fresh religious thought into their convents and diverse apostolic interests among Ukrainian Catholics. For another, the numerous personal encounters and relationships of Sisters Servants with members of various religious institutes were a most visible attraction and result. At religious gatherings in the past they had often endured the exquisite humiliation of being nicely written off as Greek Orthodox nuns who must have been invited to the meeting by mistake. Such sterile encounters had produced in some sisters a self-consciousness that was manifested in a reluctance to share their insights and the fruits of their missionary experience at these conferences. Now, however, there was emerging a confident and active participation, together with a measurable strengthening of personal and communal ties with other institutes, and a healthy appreciation of their own unique role within the Church as members of an Oriental-rite congregation.

Finally their exposure to new approaches permitted Sister Bernadette to respond to Pope Pius XII's call to religious for appropriate simplification of their religious garb. In an address to superiors general of women's orders and institutes on September 15, 1952, the pontiff clarified his oft-expressed idea on the matter: 'The religious habit must always express consecration to Christ; this is what we all expect and desire. For the rest, let the habit be suitable and in keeping with the requirements of hygiene. We could not but express Our satisfaction when, in the course of the year, We saw that one or another of the Congregations had already drawn up some practical consequences on this point.'[9]

After weighing the possible repercussions among the members of her province, Sister Bernadette, who seemed to ignore non-essentials with the most breathtaking courage, made known her support of a modification in the headpiece and habit, particularly for hygienic reasons. To her delight she discovered that not only were her councillors ready to give it a try but that a goodly proportion of the sisters seemed interested. It was fortunate, too, that in the shadowland between flexible positions and changing realities Sister Bernadette's personality and opinions had considerable substance — and few substances which came into contact with her remained unaffected. Hence, although a brisk flourish of acceptance of the hitherto unthought of simplification of the traditional garb was hardly to be expected, the provincial superior soon found that most sisters were gladly cutting away unnecessary yardage from the headpiece and habit; by the beginning of 1956 most of the members were wearing a more comfortable religious dress.

Essentially, therefore, the Sisters Servants in North America came through their involvement in the initial religious movements advocated by the Holy See with a measure of pride in their religious rite, confidence in their institute, and faith in their future role within the Church.

Suddenly, however, in the spring of 1956, the entire institute found itself leaderless. For at midnight on March 22 Sister Veronica Gargil died in Rome at the age of seventy-two, having been a member of the institute for fifty-seven years and its major superior for twenty-two of them. The startling announcement of her passing left her fellow religious throughout the world saddened by the realization that they had lost a friend and that their congregation had lost a gifted and commanding champion of its religious causes. Even as she had lain on her deathbed in a Rome hospital, her work had gone quietly on; the Ukrainian translation of the new constitutions, which had been definitively approved by Pope Pius XII two months earlier on January 18, were sent to the publisher just twenty-four hours before she died. It was a fitting legacy from the woman who, asserted an editorial in *Svitlo,* had been one of the institute's most eminent members.[10]

Sister Veronica had not entered the superiorship in 1934 with any queasy thoughts that she was inadequate to the office of governing a newly reorganized institute. She had intended to prove herself, not with any sense of aggrandizement or arrogance, but because she knew that she had a job that had to be done. And she had done it. Indeed, her integrity, fairness, and independence of mind had won her an unshakable reputation for soundness, and had inspired her sisters to new heights in their life of consecration. For she had believed that courage was not a matter of parades and medals, but a virtue which helped men and women to live a selfless life with Christ in God. Thus what the sisters had lost was something as subtle as her personal presence. In a tribute to her the Edmonton weekly, *Ukrainski Visty*, said: 'Resolute and prudent, gracious and kind, she enjoyed the confidence and affection of her fellow sisters, and the respect and good will of those outside the religious institute of which she was the superior general.'[11] It is scarcely surprising, therefore, in the light of this general feeling of loss, that the most pressing question was quite specific: could anyone fill her post? And the considered answer? Perhaps.

Soon afterwards, on May 17, Sister Bernadette informed the sisters that, in accordance with the constitutions, an extraordinary general chapter would convene in Rome on September 8 of that year for the purpose of electing a successor to Sister Veronica, and a new general council. She also notified them that they would be called upon in the immediate future to elect four sisters who, together with her, would comprise the Canadian-American delegation in Rome.[12]

As might well be expected, the provincialate became the scene of a welter of comings and goings on July 3–4, as forty-two delegates, elected by the members of the province on May 26, arrived in Toronto before proceeding to Ancaster, where the chapter officially commenced on July 7. 'The sisters experienced a sense of unity and strength in the provincial gathering, as well as a finer awareness of their membership in a worldwide religious congregation,' remarked the annalist.[13] At the same time, however, there existed an undercurrent of dismay and frustration which sprang from an intense disappointment that the recently approved constitutions did not embody any of the provincial recommendations submitted to the generalate in 1951.[14] And although their reaction was tactfully muted, there was little doubt that the sisters considered the submergence of their Canadian and American community and missionary interests in the overriding European priorities as one of the major weaknesses of the latest edition of the rule.[15]

Against this backdrop Sister Bernadette's summons of the participants to steadfastness and hope at the chapter's opening session seemed designed to forestall a grave crisis of morale that could severely sap the energy and stability of the province. It may be that she hoped to harness the same emotion in framing fresh resolutions. Whatever the motivation, however, it obviously bolstered community spirit before it could noticeably begin to sag. This kind of posture, in fact, was an accurate reflection of Sister Bernadette's leadership style. On July 7 the sisters elected Sister Jerome Chimy, Sister Lawrence Dzumaga, Sister Boniface Sloboda, and Sister Joan Magriy to accompany their provincial superior to the general chapter as representatives of the Province of Christ the King.

Having dealt with this responsible task, the assembly moved to a consideration of the question of most pressing importance: how to live an authentic spiritual life in their active religious province at this time in history. In their deliberations the delegates showed little inclination to let things – which had long before proved inadequate or irrelevant – remain as they were. The proceedings of this meeting, therefore, marked a new high point in the maturing of the province, for, under Sister Bernadette's steady hand, the chapter skirted none of the topics that had been flatly overlooked by the constitutional committee at Rome in its preparation of the rule. Perhaps because its members had not been substantially attuned to changing trends in Western nations, the problems presented by the Canadian-American community may have seemed like only distant mutterings. Once again, therefore, in the hope of seeing some results that would be more than casual, the sisters endorsed twenty-four resolutions tailored to deal specifically with perplexing issues concerning their life and apostolate, which were to be presented to the general chapter. By this bold action they demonstrated that the current swell of provincial concern was not just a passing bellow.[16]

Two months later seventeen Sisters Servants from Europe, Canada, and Brazil met at St Josaphat's Pontifical Seminary in Rome, where the first general chapter to be convoked since 1934 was to be held. It was ironical that this significant event, so keenly anticipated by Sister Veronica in recent years, should ensue directly from her death.

No sooner had the chapter been declared validly convened on September 8 by Bishop John Buchko, apostolic visitor for Ukrainians in western Europe, than the delegates fulfilled their weighty obligation to their members everywhere by electing a superior general and four councillors. To the chagrin of some and delight of others – notably the sisters of the Canadian-American province – the institute that day came under the assertive management of forty-four-year-old Sister Jerome Chimy, a woman of great sensibility and sympathetic understanding, who had served on Sister Bernadette's council for the past five years. Her stunning election shattered once and for all the illusion that leadership for the congregation as a whole could be provided only by the oldest province –

that in Europe. Likewise significant was the election of Sister Gertrude Lesiuk and Sister Lawrence Dzumaga – also members of the Province of Christ the King – to the general council.[17] For their new job Sister Jerome and her advisers would need heart – and much more. For they would direct the institute at a time when a startling transformation in the political, social, and cultural life of many nations was already being wrought at the cost of an erosion of spirit beyond calculation.

Following the first two sessions of election, the delegates met an additional seven times. At these gatherings – in membership a veritable mingling of East and West – it became clear to the Canadian-American delegation that the speed of social metamorphosis on their continent, to which their sisters were endeavouring to adapt, far outstripped the glacial pace of change in several of the institute's provinces and vice-provinces, notably of those in eastern Europe and Brazil. They therefore felt that there was a lack of understanding among the chapter delegates of their problems. At the same time, however, they recognized that their own lack of firsthand knowledge of the milieu in which their fellow sisters had to live and work limited their own appreciation of their difficulties. Inevitably the meetings were marked by collisions of personalities, the shaping and thwarting of policies, the asserting or rebuffing of proposals. None the less, hidden within these seemingly ordinary assemblies was the stuff of high drama, since any directives which might ensue would directly affect the life and apostolate of every Sister Servant.[18]

Seven days after it began, the chapter ended. With the profound sense of relief that usually follows the fulfilment of a demanding duty, Sister Bernadette, Sister Joan, and Sister Boniface prepared to return home, leaving behind their two former companions – Sister Jerome and Sister Lawrence – in whose hands, together with the remaining members of the general council, the bark of the institute had been entrusted.

Upon their return to Toronto they discovered that during their short absence the Ukrainian Catholic Church in Canada had sustained a great loss in the death on September 1 of seventy-two-year-old Archbishop Ladyka. To pay their last respects to a bishop who had evidenced so much strength of character, so much tolerance, so much compassion, so much dignity that his death had visibly saddened people of his own and other nationalities and faiths across the nation, Sisters Servants from several western missions, including Edmonton, Mundare, Regina, Yorkton, and Ituna, had journeyed to Winnipeg, where they had participated in the funeral services. The sisters mourned the passing of a churchman whom they had loved and admired. They had known Archbishop Ladyka especially as a kind and gracious spiritual father, who had encouraged and admonished them; who, at times, may even have been disappointed in them, but who had always highly esteemed each sister for her gift of herself in a life of consecrated service within the Church. Perhaps more than anyone else he had maintained that in success or failure the ultimate goal of Sisters Servants in this country had been proved, time and again, to be nothing other than bringing men to God.[19] He would be sorely missed.

Later that fall, on November 18, the Holy See climaxed its organizational development of the Ukrainian Catholic Church in Canada and demonstrated a sincere interest in it by creating an ecclesiastical province and naming Bishop Maxime Hermaniuk, C SS R – who had served as apostolic administrator of the Winnipeg exarchate since April 14 – as archbishop of Winnipeg and the first metropolitan of Canada. The new ecclesiastical province was comprised of all four Canadian exarchates, which were now termed 'eparchies' and their bishops 'eparchs.' Its erection was a meaningful milestone, for it brought to an official end the mission status of the Ukrainian Catholic Church in this nation.[20]

In similar fashion Pope Pius XII exhibited a warm regard for the Ukrainian Catholic Church of the United States by establishing the apostolic exarchate of Stamford, Connecticut, on July 20, 1956, assigning to this new jurisdiction the parishes of the apostolic exarchate of Philadelphia situated in the state of New York and in all the New England states. As its first titular he appointed Bishop Ambrose Senyshyn, at that time auxiliary and vicar general to the apostolic exarch of Philadelphia. Moreover, the pontiff nominated Rev. Joseph M. Schmondiuk as auxiliary to Archbishop Bohachevsky, and Rev. Stephen J. Kocisko as auxiliary to Bishop Elko, who himself had been named apostolic exarch of the Byzantine Slavonic-rite diocese of Pittsburgh as recently as September 5, 1955.

Obviously, there was nothing niggardly and patronizing in the attitude of the Holy See toward Ukrainians and Rusins in its painstaking action to introduce structural relationships within the Church which would be truly representative of each of these ethnic groups. In fact, these developments turned out to be a prelude to a further broadening of their religious landscape. For on July 12, 1958, the Ukrainian apostolic exarchies were replaced by an ecclesiastical province, consisting of the archeparchy of Philadelphia and the eparchy of Stamford. Soon afterwards apostolic eparchs were named to these new residential sees: on August 6, Bishop Bohachevsky as metropolitan of the Philadelphia archeparchy, and, on November 1, Bishop Senyshyn as eparch of Stamford. 'The unexpected erection of two metropolitan sees beyond the boundaries of Ukraine is of great significance in the history of our Church and concretely confirms the solicitude of the Holy See for the Ukrainian Catholic Church in the free world,' commented *Meta*.[21] This same sentiment was echoed on behalf of Sisters Servants everywhere by the community annalist: 'These worthy appointments in both Canada and the United States are a concrete manifestation of the Holy Father's love and concern for our people, and a sensitive recognition of the sacrificial struggle by so many of them in eastern Europe in defence of the Church and their national identity.'[22]

At the same time as they were witnessing this vital evolution within their Church, the sisters were involved in furthering their apostolic interests in the Canadian west – their earliest missionary terrain. And so, in the period 1956–9 they saw the face of their missions at Winnipeg and Yorkton undergo significant alteration.

In 1955 a succession of events and a surge of feeling by the sisters converged to initiate this movement at Winnipeg. It all began when the religious personnel assigned to St Nicholas School became intent on improving their living conditions, in what can be regarded as a desperation move on their part. For while it was true that personal comfort and privacy for the sisters at any of their Canadian houses was still a myth, since dormitories were very much the order of the day, conditions in Winnipeg were among the worst: after a period of forty-four years, religious working at St Nick's were still quartered in the cramped, uninsulated attic. With patience and grim determination, therefore, Sister Matthew Nykoliuk, the local superior, set about to alter this deplorable arrangement. By September she had conceived a plan to purchase a piece of land adjacent to the school and construct a residence upon it. That was at least a cheerful proposal, but there was precious little cash on hand to do anything concrete about it until a *kvesta* could be carried out. Sister Matthew, for one, strongly believed that the Ukrainian public would readily support the enterprise.

In an unscheduled visit to Winnipeg on September 15 Sister Bernadette underscored her own concern in the matter. For while to many local sisters the construction of a suitable residence beside the school seemed an eminently sensible solution to their difficulties, to their provincial superior this rationale was cold comfort after her hard-eyed appraisal of the proposed $75,000 project. She perceived that the undertaking might bring as many burdens as benefits; in her mind, the question that forcefully obtruded itself was how the sisters here could maintain a separate convent when they were scarcely able to operate the school. Moreover, it seemed hardly likely that the individuals and groups who, in the face of continually spiralling costs of education freely advised the sisters about how to support the school, without themselves offering much help, would enthusiastically back a financial drive for a residence. While much of Sister Bernadette's anxiety stemmed from her realization that the sisters' meagre income could neither construct nor maintain a separate house, her misgivings were reinforced by the fear that civic authorities might at any time condemn as unsafe the school, now almost a half-century old. In such an event a residence would be superfluous.

Aware that by suggesting a reconsideration of the plan and thus stalling the project or perhaps even scotching it she ran the risk of an impasse in which the transparent need of the sisters for a convent might remain unmet, Sister Bernadette took a chance: she recommended that the sisters consider purchasing a building suitable either for a hospital or a home for the aged which, while answering a human need, would not only support itself but would also provide living quarters for its own personnel as well as that of St Nicholas School. Her highly unusual proposal raised expectations that for the first time since the sisters had come to Winnipeg to teach in 1905, some shift in their local apostolate might be imminent. Thus while, on the one hand, Sister Matthew's first hesitant steps to solve her housing problem were thrown off stride, on the other, Sister Bernadette's argument of the merits of delay obliged her to tiptoe nimbly through some misunderstandings. None the less, the provincial superior hoped that the discussions between her and the local community might eventually hammer out a plan that would do more than simply leave both parties evenly dissatisfied.[23]

Oddly enough, no sooner had the original building project begun to founder than it was replaced by another – one that initially seemed still farther out of the realm of possibility: the purchase of the former Children's Hospital of Winnipeg for a senior citizens' home. Metropolitan Hermaniuk notified Sister Matthew that the hospital, located in the central part of the city at 165 Aberdeen Avenue, was for sale, and recommended that it be obtained for a nursing home for the elderly. Moreover, besides encouraging the sisters to undertake this merciful apostolate, the prelate also enlarged their view of the advantages – medical, spiritual, and cultural – which they could offer Ukrainian pioneers in a centre such as Winnipeg.[24]

The main hospital building scarcely enticed the sisters when they first looked it over. With its boarded windows and doors it had a bombed-out, end-of-war appearance. About all lingered the stale odour of litter, dirt, and rotting wood. Yet in its essential structure, the hulk was solid and no more unattractively designed than hundreds of other older buildings that formed the bulk of Winnipeg's business stock. And so, although it was evident that renovation of this building as well as the former nurses' and interns' residences would be a costly project, the sisters felt that in the long run it might just prove a worthwhile venture.

Once convinced of its potential, Sister Matthew, who was not a woman to exert herself for nothing, spent little time wondering whether the moment was opportune for such an initiative. Exhibiting her characteristic verve and vigour, she informed her provincial superior of the hospital's availability – for the sum of $250,000 – and set about to muster support for its attainment. Fortunately for the entire enterprise, the combination of necessity and opportunity gave her the chance to stir the interest of a good friend, Mr Mark Smerchanski, whose sheer tenacity of purpose had always impressed her. The energetic mining geologist, prominent business-man, and current governor of the University of Manitoba, was a shrewd, extremely intelligent, mercurial gentleman with a remarkable package of abilities – business, administrative, catalytic. He responded with alacrity to Sister Matthew's appeal for advice and assistance, channeling his efforts first to investigate the possibility of buying the hospital and second to marshal every means at his command to facilitate its purchase. So sus-tained were his attempts that on January 4, 1956, Mr F. Ernst, who was responsible for the sale of the property, informed Sister Bernadette that Mr Smerchanski was prepared to supplement the sisters' deposit of $10,000 (half of which was donated by Metropolitan Hermaniuk and half by the St Nicholas School Committee) with a $30,000 loan, and to assume the responsibility as guarantor, as well as to act as a trustee in the sisters' behalf.[25]

As word of the transaction leaked out, few were uncertain that the Sisters Servants could bring it off. To Sister Bernadette, however, it didn't seem as if the purchase were just around the corner. Apart from the ad-vance by Mr Smerchanski – which had enabled her to make the required deposit of $40,000 – she found little cause for optimism. Indeed, for a few uncertain weeks it seemed that any hope of borrowing the entire sum of $250,000 in order to take possession of the hospital on November 1, 1956, was absurd, especially since the province had just contracted a loan to construct a new wing at Sacred Heart Academy at Yorkton.[26] Under-standably, therefore, the case for an immediate Manitoba-wide campaign for funds, as a partial solution, was overwhelming.

Taking his cue from the notable success, until now, of the sisters' apostolate among the elderly in Manitoba's rural centres of Dauphin,

Sifton, and Komarno, Metropolitan Hermaniuk offered his support by making the first monetary offering, and by lending his voice to the cause that had already gathered considerable momentum. Thus in February 1956 the hierarchy of the exarchate issued a forceful appeal for assistance to 'all the clergy, and all leaders of our Ukrainian organizations in Manitoba.' The message took an urgent line that was meant as much to foster a genuine appreciation of the enterprise by the public as to summon people to its support. In the past, it pointed out, a great number of aged Ukrainian pioneers 'had been compelled to seek health care in institutions where they could not converse in their own language, where they could not participate in liturgical services in their own rite, and where the entire atmosphere seemed foreign. Among them,' it observed, 'there are still many who cling to the hope that the Ukrainian community at large will eventually understand their trying circumstances and come to their aid.' Obviously, the bishops desired to show the public that it had a vital interest in promoting the project. In particular, they took pains to stress that the new home would welcome all elderly citizens, regardless of their religious denomination, and that their liberty of conscience would be respected.[27] That this point counted heavily in favour of the undertaking is evidenced by the fact that soon after the appeal was issued the chronicler recorded that 'forty Ukrainian organizations, including non-Catholic, and several strictly national groups, have made donations totalling $21,000.'[28] Largely because of this kind of official concern, together with persistent canvassing by the sisters, and Sister Matthew's all-consuming work of getting others interested and motivated to take some of the fund-raising responsibility upon themselves, the campaign eventually netted a sum of $100,000 – almost, but not quite, enough to cover the cost of renovation and remodelling.[29]

On December 11, 1956, Sister Matthew and Sister Fotynia Sucha moved into the nurses' residence to oversee the general facelifting that could be undertaken this early because of a second $35,000 loan advanced by Mr Smerchanski. Three days later, the dankly cheerless hospital began to be recast into something decidedly more attractive. With careful dispatch Mr Smerchanski kept an eye on the implementation of the plans for the renovation of the building, drawn up by Mr A. Nitchuk, and carried out by the contractor, Mr P. Dyrda. And so smoothly did the work proceed that on February 2, 1957, the *Winnipeg Tribune* announced that 'within the next two months the first aged and infirm will move into a building with a new name, the Holy Family Home.'

That spring, applications from would-be residents began to pour in, and on May 26, 1957, under sunny skies, Metropolitan Hermaniuk blessed and officially opened the Holy Family Nursing Home 'in the presence of distinguished members of the hierarchy, clergy, provincial and federal governments, and approximately two thousand guests.' The home, according to the Hon. D. Campbell, premier of Manitoba, was 'a cultural and humanitarian centre' which had been made possible by the courage of the Sisters Servants and the generosity of their people.[30]

Long after the official ceremonies, the home bulged with visitors. The new excitement, however, was most intoxicating for the Ukrainian oldsters themselves, particularly those who had been in other institutions; here it could not be said that they were out of sight and too often tragically out of mind. As for the sisters, the stakes in the new institution were crystal clear: their future orientation in government-controlled, health-care centres. In effect, it was to be the proving ground for them in more complex nursing organizations.

As it turned out, a goodly portion of the rapturous rhetoric of that day was later fulfilled. For if they had enjoyed good luck in obtaining the property and beginning their apostolate here, the sisters adeptly capitalized on it. The first local superiors who followed Sister Matthew – namely, Sister Melita Sophie Krawchuk and Sister Naucratia Emily Hawryliuk – with the assistance of an active Advisory Board, first headed by Mr Smerchanski, and an effective Ladies' Auxiliary presided over by his wife Patricia, introduced so many refreshing changes of style in the administration of this home, which served approximately 140 patients, that it became an institution of significant scope and validity; by 1969 it would win such general acclaim and respect from the government and the people of Manitoba that it would become imperative to construct a 124-bed addition, in order to shorten, at least by a fraction, a seemingly endless waiting list.

The spill of events associated with Holy Family Home did not eclipse a matter of concern that had emerged at their other Winnipeg institution, St Nicholas School. Ever since 1932, when grades nine and ten had been introduced, St Nick's had served as both an elementary and high school. During the 1950s, however, several factors began to militate strongly against continuing the secondary division. In the first place, updated courses, especially in the sciences, called for advanced laboratory equipment which the school could not afford. In the second, a notable lack of indoor and outdoor space and facilities, especially for the senior boys' compulsory physical education classes, began to be felt. Finally, since the average enrolment in grades nine through twelve averaged about twenty-five students each year, it seemed ludicrous to set aside several high school teachers for so small a number. After much serious consideration, Sister Bernadette decided that as of September 1956 the school would accept registrations in the elementary grades only. But no matter how logical this move seemed to her, Metropolitan Hermaniuk insisted that to let the high school go would be a serious mistake.

Against the background of all these stresses, and with both sides groping for an accommodation, it was inevitable that the provincial superior should bend her resolution to the weight of objection. She therefore suggested the establishment of a temporary high school for girls on the main floor of the newly acquired nurses' residence, adjacent to Holy Family Home – the idea being that if it flourished a permanent girls' academy or co-educational secondary school could be constructed.[31]

Although the initial reaction of press and people was overwhelmingly favourable, the announcement elicited a comparatively muted response among high school teaching sisters who appeared skeptical about opening an academy in Winnipeg when it was common knowledge that St Nicholas School had hovered perpetually on the lip of financial crisis since its opening in 1911. And although it had doggedly hung on, unlike the tradition of success stories, it still had not had its reward – the financial backing of the archdiocese – a fact which seemed to imply that many Ukrainians had not yet come to grips with the reality that it takes more than idealism to keep a school open. Under the circumstances, one of its great triumphs was that it had survived to educate children into the 1950s. In its relationship to the proposed academy, however, the controlling truth was that its steadily declining enrolment in the elementary grades indicated that it was hardly likely that it could provide the high school with any significant number of its own graduates; this, of course, would mean that almost immediately the new school would find itself in similar economic straits. Moreover, many sisters recognized that a further spreading out of teachers might bring their high school undertakings to a standstill. They therefore considered the opening of an academy in Winnipeg to be a luxury which, at the present time, the Sisters Servants could ill afford. Thus, for the moment, they remained respectful of the project but doubtful of its prospects.

Given this sentiment among the sisters, perhaps the most important plus sign was the encouragement of Metropolitan Hermaniuk. In an appeal dated June 9, 1957, on behalf of the proposed academy, he eulogized the sisters' pedagogical skill, heralded a glorious future for the academy under their direction, and petitioned parents to register their daughters for the scholastic year 1957–8. In a specific description of the project, he explained: 'Our good Sisters Servants of Mary Immaculate will open a new high school for girls in Winnipeg this coming fall. Part of the large building at 131 Aberdeen Avenue, which originally served as the nurses' residence of the Children's Hospital, will be converted into an academy which will offer grades nine through twelve. In addition to the courses prescribed by the Department of Education, students will be assured a full religious and cultural programme.'[32]

Concrete proof that the plan to open the school at the beginning of September was not a passing fancy was indicated by the amount of hectic remodelling that went on at 131 Aberdeen Avenue throughout the summer of 1957. Swiftly, walls making up the long row of former nurses' rooms on the first floor came tumbling down, and just as rapidly they were replaced by attractive classrooms, library, and auditorium. So demanding was the work of renovation and organization that it drained almost the last ounce of physical strength possessed by Sister Benedict Eva Sereda, who had assumed her duties as superior and principal of Immaculate Heart of Mary Academy on July 14. As a consequence, this able administrator and teacher was required to resign her position in favour of her assistant, Sister Bernarda Chrunik, whose previous experience in high school management proved invaluable as she temporarily took up her new duties, among them, the planning of the academy's official opening that was held on September 1.[33]

On that day, a large crowd of well-wishers joined the members of the staff, which, besides Sister Bernarda included a second teacher, Sister Angelica Patricia Hodowansky, a music instructress, Sister Gertrudine Theresa Scherba, and a prefect, Sister Anastasia Mary Pryma, to participate in the blessing and dedication conducted by Metropolitan Hermaniuk, to watch Education Minister B. K. Miller cut the ribbon and declare the academy officially opened, and to listen to the address delivered by Professor Paul Yuzyk, a member of the Department of History at the University of Manitoba.

From its inception the academy was a pursuit that went slowly: the first academic year, 1957–8, had a total registration of thirty girls in grades nine and ten. And even though the sisters' other academies had had much smaller enrolments and much shakier beginnings, unlike them, Immaculate Heart refused to grow. Prospects for a larger student body receded with each new term; by 1960, when the school was conducting grades nine through eleven, not one of its first three scholastic years had shown a registration above sixty students.[34] Indeed, if it had not been for benefactors such as the Ukrainian Business and Professional Girls' Club, the St Josaphat Council of the Knights of Columbus, Rev. M. Pelech, and Rev. A. Luhovy, who gladly offered their moral and financial support through the years, the academy would have been submerged by operating costs alone within a year after its opening. If nothing else, therefore, Immaculate Heart Academy in Winnipeg was a gesture whereby the Sisters Servants demonstrated their willingness to take a substantial risk in the interest of a Christian education for their youth.

At the same time as preparations were under way at Winnipeg during the summer of 1956 to take possession of the Children's Hospital, plans to extend Sacred Heart Academy at Yorkton, Saskatchewan, the oldest high school directed by the Sisters Servants in Canada, finally got off the drawing board. On a serene Sunday evening on June 17, Bishop Andrew Roborecki blessed and broke the ground for a new wing which, according to *Meta* had 'within the past decade become a dire necessity.'[35]

The fortunes of Sacred Heart had fluctuated since its opening in 1917 as an elementary school and orphanage. The 1920s had seen a gradual but steady growth of confidence in the sisters' work at the school by parents, as manifested by the increasing numbers of their children who enrolled, and by the Department of Education, as evinced by the favourable reports of its inspectors; on March 6, 1928, for example, inspector B. W. Wallace 'left a glowing report of the excellent work being done by the sisters at the institute.'[36] In 1932, just as the depression was tightening its grip on Saskatchewan, Sister Elizabeth registered the first grade nine students and thus brought Sacred Heart into secondary education, with herself as the first high school teacher in its history. And the incentive for this step was the sisters' contact with a group of high school girls from rural areas who had been accepted into residence in September 1927 so that they could attend the Yorkton Collegiate Institute. This initial association with girls of high school age kindled the sisters' interest in working with them more directly.

Although throughout the 1930s the school was trapped by outside circumstances – mainly the depression spiral that had ensnared most other private high schools in Saskatchewan – no psychology of uncertainty was evident. The sisters had become used to the fact that their classrooms were half-empty or overcrowded according to whether there was a good or bad crop on the prairies. During the 1926–7 academic year only five families of the forty-five day pupils attending the school paid small fees; the decade of the 1930s, which was one of almost unrelieved misfortune for Saskatchewan, trapped them still further. And no wonder. 'Drought, wind, grasshoppers, rust and unprecedented low prices for farm products brought on an economic catastrophe,' recalled the *Yorkton Enterprise* in 1965. 'From 1930 to 1939 the average income of the province of some 900,000 people was $80,000,000. At the height of the Depression one-half of the farm population had been forced to seek government assistance. A commission appointed by the Dominion government reported that Saskatchewan had suffered a steeper decline in income in a comparable time than any other part of the civilized world.'[37] Thus the prospect of seeing any immediate infusion of private or public aid was more remote than ever. Moreover, with cash or credit increasingly scarce, a simple barter economy was on the rise; fees for tuition and residence were paid for in wheat, meat, vegetables, or dairy products.

Neither time nor age, depression or war, however, seemed able to dull the sisters' creativity or blunt their initiative. In 1934, when the total registration in grades one through eleven was 109, with fourteen students in the secondary classes, Mr M. A. Trapp, inspector of schools, filed a detailed report to the Department of Education about the school, its staff, and its academic standards: 'The Sacred Heart Institute – originally, the Sacred Heart Orphanage and Convent – is an educational institution carried on under the guardianship of the Greek Catholic Church. It has no apparent means of support other than philanthropy and what fees can be collected from the parents of the pupils who attend. The building is a large brick structure, fully modern, and of the boarding school type. Although the classrooms are on the small side for the present accommodation (some rooms, only), they have a remarkable homeylike appearance with their beautiful hanging ferns and tastefully decorated walls. The teaching staff consists of a Sister Superior (at present not appointed) assisted by three sisters. The sisters are properly qualified teachers having attended normal schools in the western provinces. I was pleased to know that the Saskatchewan course is being followed and that the standing of the grades compares favourably with that found in the majority of our graded schools of the same class.'[38] The appraisal was encouraging. And when in 1937 the school held its first high school commencement exercises, bestowing graduating honours upon two Saskatchewan girls, Adele Byblow of Springside, and Anne Kwiatkowski of Hendon, Sacred Heart was well on its way toward establishing a proud record of academic, social, and cultural achievement in secondary education.

During the war years, which saw a period of abundant rain and good crops on the prairies, and a greater demand for foodstuffs with consequent higher prices, more families could afford to send their children to 'the sisters' school in Yorkton.' On October 18, 1945, when registration had reached a capacity of 118 students, the principal, Sister Mechtilde Byblow, informed the registrar of the Department of Education that the name of the school had been changed from Sacred Heart Institute to Sacred Heart Academy.[39] Simultaneously, the elementary grades had been transferred to one wing of the neighbouring St Mary's Redemptorist Monastery. Two years later, in 1947, when the academy had graduated ninety-eight grade twelve students, it was placed on the list of schools to be visited yearly by high school superintendents. Thereafter the high school developed at a brisk pace.

Neither before nor after the school had devoted itself primarily to secondary education was it without needy children. 'The sisters deserve full marks for the assistance they rendered underprivileged youngsters from Yorkton and the surrounding district,' contended Mr H. M. Jackson, who was the city clerk of Yorkton from 1932 to 1959, and who had watched the development of Sacred Heart. 'They filled a definite need in our community, providing for, and teaching, children for whose upkeep and education the city paid next to nothing. Nor was the school a closed corporation, for whenever they had extra accommodation, the sisters welcomed youngsters of other ethnic and religious groups with startling impartiality. Even Protestant children who were doing poorly in the local public schools received academic help from them.'[40]

After the war the school was cramped for space: not another desk could be squeezed into the classrooms, nor another bed into the dormitory. To alleviate this congestion, at least slightly, explained the *Yorkton Enterprise,* 'in 1948 an H-hut and a mess hall were obtained from the Yorkton airport. The H-hut served as a dormitory and the mess hall was converted into a recreation hall and auditorium. Small as this transaction may seem to the average person today, to the Sisters at that time it was a tremendous undertaking financially. They placed their trust in God and in the good will of the citizens of Yorkton and the surrounding districts. Many who understood the good intentions of the Sisters and the role they have played in forming the future citizens of this province offered assistance. The Sisters were deeply appreciative of this help. Rev. Sister Benedict [Sereda], superior at the time this project was carried out, received the full cooperation and understanding of the mayor of Yorkton in the person of C. G. Langrill.'[41]

Perhaps it was slight progress to use RCAF barracks; none the less, with their acquisition, things were a shade more comfortable than before except during the bitterly cold Saskatchewan winters when the sisters and girls, whose bedrooms were in the flimsily constructed H-hut, often felt as if they were sleeping outdoors. Amazingly, however, instead of decreasing, the enrolment steadily increased. Graduates were followed by their sisters, nieces, cousins, and other relatives – near and distant. In truth, the academy's students were its best advertisement.

In 1952 Sacred Heart pioneered with St Joseph's College in the introduction of Ukrainian as an accredited language course in Saskatchewan high schools in grades nine through twelve. This was the culmination of many years of striving to convince the Department of Education that Ukrainian as a modern language course would be of great cultural benefit to a large segment of the population in the province. But the road to this achievement had been a long and often disappointing one.

By the end of the 1930s the staffs of both the academy and college had discovered that knowledge of a second language dies young in an atmosphere of benign neglect. Whereas during the first fifteen years of the schools' existence students had had a good command of the language, the early 1940s indicated that this was no longer the case. And while previously the spoken and written word between parents and children had been Ukrainian, many parents now began to speak and write to their daughters at Sacred Heart and sons at St Joseph's in English. Teachers in both schools began to find that students complained about having to spend a lot of study time on a language for which they received no academic credit as they did for French or Latin. Despite their protests, however, few students were permitted by their parents to drop Ukrainian. But a combination of hazardous times and misguided patriotism during the Second World War convinced some parents that their children should not be compelled to study the language. 'We reached an impasse,' recalled Brother Methodius Koziak, principal of St Joseph's College at the time; 'but we did not intend to allow the Ukrainian students to drop the study of their language' even though many now had the backing of their parents to do so.[42] Continuous contact with Ukrainian youth in and outside their classrooms through the 1940s led both the Sisters Servants and the Christian Brothers to conclude that there was a growing illiteracy in Ukrainian among their people, for they found that greater numbers of students were entering their schools with little or no knowledge of the language.

Their calm and realistic view – formed by many years of teaching in schools in which the majority of their students were of Ukrainian origin – regarded the introduction of Ukrainian as the paramount order of the day for two reasons. First, a fluency in the language would make it easier for the young to appreciate their Ukrainian heritage. They believed that the crabbed and mean tendency of Anglo-Saxons to look upon ethnic people as foreigners was weakening, and that, being freer than ever before to be themselves, the time was at hand when Ukrainians would learn to appreciate Canada's ethnic diversity and their own vital place in it. Their concept of the kind of attitude that should characterize Ukrainians in this country seemed to be similar to that enunciated in October 1970 by Mr Watson Kirkonnell, former president of Acadia University, who insisted that 'every person, whatever his origin, ought to be proud of the cultural achievement of his ethnic group in world history, and thereby inspired to a contribution in his own style to the cultural life of Canada.'[43] And they were also in agreement with his view that the future of Canada is not a cultural mosaic, where ethnic traditions have each been preserved for their own sake, but a tapestry where the gifts of all have been woven into a single cultural achievement; that is, that ethnic groups weave their cultural differences into 'a proud consciousness of Canadian diversity.'[44] They did not see Canada as some vague, illusory melting-pot in which all ethnic groups were mixed like salt and pepper, but rather as a multiracial society in which ethnic communities, living as one nation, sought to weave a plurality of cultural strands into a single fabric.

A second, if not less important, reason for their desire to see Ukrainian as an accredited language course was their growing concern that young people with little or no knowledge of Ukrainian might find little meaning and authentic experience in the Ukrainian rite, which used Old Slavonic in liturgical services. The experience of the sisters in their missions throughout Canada and the United States, as well as in far-flung country parishes during their summer catechetical work, persuaded them that the Ukrainian Catholic Church in North America was beginning to feel more fully the problems of transition from a relatively serene to an explosively restless age, with all the associated cultural and generational strains. They were convinced that solving the problem of language in the liturgy could prove to be the single most critical question in the life of their Church in the latter half of the century, for already that which some Ukrainians viewed as the spectre of the use of the vernacular in their Church was beginning to emerge.

In the light of the times it is not difficult to understand why the teachers at Yorkton sought to eliminate apathy by providing an incentive for their students to study Ukrainian. As educators, however, they knew that to force something upon students was not only distasteful but also dangerous, since it could be rejected; hence they concluded that the problem would be resolved only when the Department of Education recognized the Ukrainian language as a credit subject in Saskatchewan high schools. No doubt to some this possibility seemed farfetched – an educational attempt tinged with wishful thinking.

While the sisters and brothers were certain that they could no longer consign their views on the matter to silence, they had always sensed that over-reaction could move the Department of Education into a negative stance. Thus as early as 1942 Brother Methodius, representing Sacred Heart Academy as well as St Joseph's College, had begun a cautious exploration of the possibility of altering current departmental policy regarding Ukrainian.[45] For a time it seemed that the chance of obtaining positive results was decidedly slim. No one ran out of patience, however, for as long as there was frequent communication with the department, there remained a faint glimmer of hope.

Finally, in the scholastic year 1946–7, the Department of Education pumped life into what might have begun to look like a moribund cause by endorsing a proposal permitting students of the academy and college to write the official University of Saskatchewan examinations in the Ukrainian language to obtain credit toward a degree. This move inspired the staffs of both schools with hope that education officials were at least interested in the problem; none the less they recognized that their goal of Ukrainian accreditation in high schools was still far distant, and that it would be reckless to confuse the wish with the fact.

Four years later, on May 15, 1952, the most significant move to date was made to promote an understanding and accommodation of Ukrainian interests by the Department of Education: a newly formed Ukrainian Curriculum Committee, comprised of several prominent educators, presented a brief concerning the accreditation of Ukrainian to the Hon. W. S. Lloyd, minister of education. The committee, comprised of Brother Aloysius Doiron, vice-principal of St Joseph's College; Dr G. W. Simpson, head of the Department of History at the University of Saskatchewan; Dr C. H. Andrusyshen, a member of the Department of Slavic Studies at the University of Saskatchewan; and Mr P. J. Worobets, superintendent of schools at Rosthern, Saskatchewan, based their arguments on cultural values and not on political expediency or on Ukrainian national aspirations.[46] 'St. Joseph's College and Sacred Heart Academy, Yorkton, Sask., have been giving a course in the Ukrainian language to their students ever since their foundation,' began their accompanying letter to the minister. 'Since 1946, the University of Saskatchewan has allowed our Grade XII students to write the examination in Ukrainian I, on a credit basis. This course has proved to be very successful and advantageous to the students and has been carried without detriment to their High School studies. Therefore, the teachers of these two schools feel certain that the addition of Ukrainian as a modern language option to the Programme of Studies in the Secondary Schools of Saskatchewan will also be successful and advantageous for the reasons outlined in the enclosed memorandum.'[47]

The brief explained the issue thus: 'The study of French will always occupy a central place on the High School curriculum because of the unique English-French character of the Canadian Nation. The dynamic for the study of French is thus assured. We do not wish to alter this situation. In addition to French and English, Canada also ought to avail herself of the language resources of other ethnic groups for the maintenance of language study where such groups exist in considerable numbers and where there continues to be a real desire to have such a study placed on a sound academic basis.

'In Saskatchewan, citizens of Ukrainian origin constitute the third largest ethnic group in the Province. On the basis of the population figures of 1946, the three largest ethnic groups other than English are: German (92,750), Ukrainian (71,764) and French (37,027).

'There are some districts where Canadians of Ukrainian origin constitute a majority of the population. The younger generation in these districts is not interested in perpetuating Ukrainian "nationalism." The older generation is quite naturally desirous that their children should have an understanding and respect for the cultural background of their ancestors and that some of them, at least, should have a competent knowledge of the language in which that culture is embodied and may be extended under conditions of freedom. Thus the youth of Ukrainian origin, as educated Canadians, will be able not only to be exponents of Canadianism for the younger generation, but also they will reassure the older generation that the contact with the past will not be completely broken or lost. In performing this double task, young Canadians should find considerable inspiration and satisfaction. Thus we believe that there exists in the situation a potential educational dynamic which may be utilized not on a wide scale but to a limited degree where conditions are particularly favourable.'[48]

The department's response to this overture was gratifying. 'We are interested in the proposal and impressed with the argument presented in the brief, and with the outlined courses,' asserted Mr H. Janzen, director of curricula, in a letter to Brother Methodius on May 23. 'It now becomes our responsibility to examine carefully the proposed books and courses to make certain that no unnecessary difficulties might arise once such courses are authorized for use. You are aware that we have several Superintendents of Schools of Ukrainian origin upon whom we can rely greatly in this task of examination and comment. We shall give our immediate attention to this matter.' Thus within a week after receiving the memorandum, the Department of Education had moved into the delicate realm of specifics. And, remarkably enough, as the scholastic year ended on June 30, 1952, it seemed that the improbable aspiration of the educators at Yorkton's two Catholic high schools was soon to be fulfilled, for, admitted Mr Janzen, 'I can report progress upon the consideration of including Ukrainian in our high school programme of studies. We have reached the stage where we are willing to consider it on an experimental basis for a period of two years at St. Joseph's College, Yorkton, and at Sacred Heart Academy, Yorkton.'[49] Shortly thereafter, on September 2, Mr Janzen wrote: 'Enclosed please find two copies of the outline for Ukrainian in the high schools ... We have decided to attempt this experimental outline for two years at each of these two institutions.'[50]

At a time when the need to build confidence in themselves as an important ethnic group in the nation was so transparent, a refusal from the Department of Education would have been a disappointing setback. Fortunately, the issue had a successful conclusion. On the basis of the excellent results attained by both schools in the teaching of Ukrainian during the two-year experimental period, the department extended the privilege of offering the Ukrainian language course as an optional subject to all high schools in Saskatchewan. This policy established an important guidepost for the Departments of Education in other Canadian provinces, and what remained to be seen was just how fast and how effectively similar courses would be introduced by them.

Besides being actively involved in the Ukrainian language issue, Sacred Heart Academy was grappling with the problem of overcrowding, for in the late 1940s and early 1950s a notable increase in student applications demonstrated that even the H-hut did not go nearly far enough to meet the prevailing need. Yet the situation could not be solved without money, and it would not go away. And so, year after year, the sisters waited to harvest the fruits of their patience. But the odds seemed stacked against them as, between 1942 and 1957, private high schools – with their accompanying debt and personnel requirements – had been established at Sloatsburg, Ancaster, and Winnipeg. For the moment, therefore, the staff took their academy's diminishing prospects for a building extension with philosophic calm, and conserved their psychic energy for the first opportune moment to press their demands. With each passing academic term, however, life in the H-hut – which now had two classrooms, as well as bedrooms – was becoming well night unbearable through about eight of the ten school months. In his report to the Department of Education in January 1953 the visiting superintendent delicately described the situation: 'Grades X and XII are housed in converted Air Force buildings, and a home economics department is operated in a third building. With the exception of the convent proper, the other buildings are temporary and it is intended to replace them. Rooms in the main building were warm and comfortable, but the other buildings were rather cold on the day of the visit, as it happened to be one of the very severe winter days.'[51]

Wishful thinking was beginning to wear thin for both teachers and students when in 1952 Sister Monica Mantyka and her grade ten class took a surprising initiative. Many at Sacred Heart couldn't believe it when Helen Komaryk, class president, went to the Toronto-Dominion Bank to open an SHA Building Fund account with a deposit of $1.00 – the sum netted from a class collection. And the action proved to be more substance than shadow, for before the school term ended in June the girls were involved in bake sales, candy sales, second-hand book sales, raffles – all for the 'new building.' Not only were they dreaming dreams but they were paying the price in hard work and personal sacrifice. And they could hardly have picked a more appealing bailiwick, for the cause so heartened every teacher and every student, past and present, that before long students of other grades and from other graduating classes began to make their own contribution to the fund which, in due time, would provide the $10,000 needed to pay for the building plans. It became clear that Sacred Heart was witnessing a veritable ferment of enthusiasm.

In March 1957 the visiting superintendent unwittingly pushed the drive for a new wing by supporting the staff's contention that they were desperately in need of almost everything – more space, more equipment, more teachers. 'Every member of the staff was felt to be not only competent in the work of teaching, but to have excellent relations with the student body,' he reported. 'The greatest difficulty, and the severest limitation upon the work of the school, is occasioned by a shortage of accommodation, and consequent lack of facilities.'[52] By this time, however, Sister Bernadette and her council had embarked upon the erection of a $700,000 wing that would enable the sisters to accept two hundred students, and had simply taken in stride the fact that when a new building blueprint came to the Sisters Servants a mortgage was seldom far behind.

Construction commenced in the fall of 1956 and continued through the winter. On April 25, 1957, the *Yorkton Enterprise* brought its readers up-to-date on its progress: 'With the arrival of warm, sunny spring days, work on the construction of the Sacred Heart Academy extension has taken a new impetus. The $600,000 [$700,000] structure, designed by P. Thornton of Vancouver and turned over for construction to Piggott Construction Ltd. of Saskatoon, was begun late last summer, when excavations were completed by Matheson Bros. of Yorkton. Work on the foundations began immediately and cement mixers made repeated journeys to and from Logan and Black Ltd. as men and weather competed in an effort to offset possible winter interruption. There was "concrete" proof that much progress had been made, for shortly after Haggblom's Bricklayers of Saskatoon appeared on the scene, the first brick settled comfortably into the southwest [southeast] corner of the new wing on November 14 ... With the early start this spring and the summer months ahead, the entire building should be ready for occupancy for the 1957–8 school term.'

As the school took shape, the residents of Yorkton contemplated its educational – and other – possibilities. 'Sacred Heart Academy's potentialities are reviewed in the minds of many,' reported the *Enterprise*. 'The sisters foresee the endless numbers of students from all over the province of Saskatchewan as well as Manitoba and Alberta who will avail themselves of the opportunity of a thorough scholastic and moral training, thence to take their place as good Christian women in our society. Those who were pioneers in the development of this educational institution see their hopes for a larger academy realized in the magnificent edifice. Such women of vision were the Reverend Sisters Elizabeth [Kassian], Joan [Magriy], Cornelia [Mantyka], Benedict [Sereda], Mechtilde [Byblow] and others. Yorkton will boast of one more fine building added to its recent expansion program. A new school is being built, and this city's coveted position as an educational center of Saskatchewan is thereby strengthened. Yorkton's business will undoubtedly be increased by 200 shoppers as well as their parents who will consequently be drawn to this city.'[53]

On June 2, 1957, almost twelve months after the ground-breaking ceremony, Bishop Roborecki blessed the cornerstone and placed it into position in an impressive ceremony attended by provincial and local dignitaries. Then, shortly after the new year on January 12, 1958, the students gave a loud cheer when it was announced that the classrooms and dormitory were ready for occupancy.

The official opening, set for May 25 of that year, was hailed beforehand by the *Enterprise*. 'The solemn dedication,' it announced, 'is to be held on Sunday, May 25, with His Excellency, Most Reverend Andrew Roborecki, D.D., Bishop of Saskatoon, officiating. Work on this splendid building which cost in excess of $700,000 began in the fall of 1956 and is now completed and makes a distinct contribution to Yorkton.'[54]

Scarcely anyone who came to Yorkton for the occasion would dispute the conclusion of the *Enterprise* reporter who wrote: 'Those in residence here will find a "home away from home" – comfortable bedrooms, a spacious dining hall and a restful lounge that eclipses anything else of its kind in the city. There is a fully equipped science laboratory, home economics workrooms, commercial classroom. There are, in addition, five classrooms. Music rooms for individual practice are certain to add much to the school's fine arts program. The library is truly outstanding with approximately 2000 of the best books, and an excellent reading room. The auditorium-gymnasium will facilitate an intensive physical education program including folk dancing, basketball, table tennis, volleyball and indoor sports. There is also a fine stage and dressing room. The lovely new chapel is at the extreme north end of the building. A cupola, traditional in Byzantine church architecture, rises high above the sanctuary. Slightly curved beams of laminated wood grace the ceiling. Viewing this overall picture of the new school, it can be noted that the academic, social, cultural, and spiritual training of the students is assured.'[55]

The description was succinct and accurate, for almost every feature bore the mark of a practical mind and an artistic hand, which, to a great extent, happened to be the mind and hand of Sister Bernadette. And if most of the adjectives heard that day sounded a bit hyperbolic, the tone seemed to be less a result of excitement than general approval of the results. But as the visiting sisters sauntered through the remodelled 'old building' adjoining the new wing, they could not help but think: there are years of hard work in this school; there are years of suffering.

Later on that Sunday afternoon in May, Bishop Roborecki 'took scissors from a silver tray and cut the gold, white, and blue ribbons that ran across the great doors. Peter Thornton of Gardiner, Thornton, Gathe and Associates, the architects, Vancouver, handed the keys to Reverend Mother Jerome, SSMI, Superior General. Then Reverend Mother Bernadette, SSMI, Provincial Superior, and Reverend Sister Frances, Sacred Heart Academy Superior, together opened the great door. Bishop Roborecki and clergy proceeded to the academy chapel where the blessing of the entire building began. It was an impressive ceremony, which was followed by the combined commencement exercises of Sacred Heart Academy and St Joseph's College.'[56]

Many remarks were made about the school in the official speeches that day, but it was Mayor W. S. Fichtner who pungently summed up the general consensus concerning the new edifice when he said: 'No finer event could mark Yorkton's 75th anniversary than the dedication of such a splendid school. From a meagre beginning, Sacred Heart Academy has grown until today we see the fulfilment of your most cherished ambition, in the formal opening of this new wing. I can well imagine, if Sir Winston Churchill were here today, he'd say: "some wing." '[57] But neither the mayor nor the sisters – particularly the principal, Sister Bohdana Olga Pidskalny – or their guests could have foreseen, that day, that this wing would need to be supplemented by a second extension within a decade.

The sisters' educational apostolate at Yorkton and their health-care mission at Winnipeg were typical of the kind of works with which they were associated in Canada and the United States. In the middle of the 1950s, however, with their hands already full of God's work, they moved into yet another sphere of religious activity: the organization of annual pilgrimages at their missions in Youngstown, Sloatsburg, and Ancaster.

In its improbability and sheer nerviness the undertaking was notable, particularly since the sisters had little direct experience in such an apostolate. But their sensitivity to the spiritual needs of their people prompted them to carry on a compelling crusade to try to recapture a mood of hope and faith. Moreover, they knew that there was an intangible personal goal to be gained by each pilgrim – old and young – which alone could ultimately justify all the mysteriousness and incomprehensibility of life's often cruel and callous realities.

In an open letter, published in *America*, to Sister Celeste Diachinsky, the superior at Sloatsburg, Archbishop Bohachevsky acknowledged that the sisters were tilling fertile ground. 'Our God-loving people have known how to express their religious sentiments from the earliest of times,' he stated. 'They express them individually, but also collectively, remembering the words of our Savior: "For where there are two or three gathered together in my name, there am I in the midst of them." This desire for collective worship of God produced, among us in the Old Country, the custom of making pilgrimages to so-called public sanctuaries. Hallowed shrines sprang into being in places where the Lord manifested His graces in a special manner to those who hastened to Him in their necessities. The Lord sent these bountiful celestial gifts of His upon a faithful people through the intercession of the Immaculate Virgin Mary, our Protectress and Mediatrix. Because of that, our native land was covered with many places of pilgrimage that were renowned by reason of various miracles.

'Disregarding the burden of the day's heat, our believing people used to leave their everyday labor and hasten to the shrine of Our Lady of

Hoshiw or Zarvanytsia, of Krekhiw or Sambir, in order that they might glorify God's holy name and through Mary's intercession procure for themselves necessary graces. At present these shrines have been desecrated, but a faithful nation still prays before the miraculous icons preserved underground. Therefore,' the archbishop concluded, 'it is with appreciation that one must greet the solicitude of the Sisters Servants in Sloatsburg who, desiring to renew the pilgrimage tradition of the Old Country, arrange for very beautiful pilgrimages at their convent on the mount in Sloatsburg, on the occasion of the Immaculate Virgin Mary's most solemn feast; namely, the occasion of her Assumption.'

Having sketched briefly the historical background of the pilgrimage tradition among Ukrainians, the archbiship graciously blessed this apostolate: 'May God grant that these pilgrimages bring the greatest possible glory to the Lord in the Holy Trinity, and to the Immaculate Virgin Mary, while to those who take part in them, may they bring spiritual joy and temporal as well as eternal recompense.'[58] With this kind of backing by the hierarchy, the pilgrimages seemed easily capable of success.

The first one organized by the Sisters Servants was held at their convent of Our Lady of Perpetual Help at Youngstown, Ohio, on June 27, 1954. On its outcome hung not only the question of similar undertakings there but the shape of the sisters' pilgrimage apostolate in other centres. Fortunately, no greater enthusiasm could have been registered anywhere than among the pilgrims who crowded the small chapel for the celebration of the Divine Liturgy or the recitation of the rosary or the Stations of the Cross. Those present remember it as a day when prayer was palpably in the air. And one striking indication of the way Bishop Elko together with members of the clergy and laity perceived the religious issue was the degree of recognition and support they accorded the pilgrimage. For within two years, from this modest beginning, emerged a grand pilgrimage in 1956, which was conducted through two days.

In terms of sheer numbers the Rusins staged an impressive turnout on both July 21 and 22 of that year: approximately twenty thousand pilgrims participated in the religious programme. On the first day: a pontifical Divine Liturgy celebrated by Bishop Elko, a prayerful candlelight procession, and an all-night vigil before the Blessed Sacrament; on the second: the Divine Liturgy offered every hour from 7:00 AM until noon in one of three rites and six languages – the Byzantine rite in Old Slavonic (Rusin), Old Slavonic (Ukrainian), Rumanian, and Hungarian; the Maronite rite in Syro-Aramaic; and the Latin rite in Latin. And to cap it all, thousands gathered on the spacious grounds before St Michael's Church, in the nearby suburb of Campbell, to participate in the Divine Liturgy offered in the Byzantine rite, but in the English language, by Bishop Fulton J. Sheen. 'In anticipation of the large numbers who would receive the Eucharist, the sisters prepared twelve thousand communion hosts,' recorded the annalist.[59] And perhaps to emphasize the devout spirit animating that huge assembly of faithful, the Youngstown chronicler noted that 'until then, the Lord had blessed us with a beautiful day, but during the Liturgy the azure sky turned to a menacing grey; then came the storm. It was almost unbelievable that throughout the deluge which followed scarcely anyone moved from his spot before the altar; bishops, clergy, sisters and laity prayed quietly with Bishop Sheen as he calmly continued the service.'[60]

The 'Assumption Pilgrimage' in Sloatsburg was officially inaugurated on August 14, 1955. Most of the initial reaction to the event was enthusiastic, with the press confidently predicting that 'with the cooperation of the priests and people, it may prove to be the forerunner of the greatest annual devotion in honor of Our Lady's Assumption among the Ukrainian Catholic faithful in the United States.'[61] In pursuing their ideal to foster devotion to the Mother of God, explained *America*, 'the Sisters petitioned the Holy See for an indulgence to all the faithful who would visit the Blessed Virgin Chapel of their Academy in Sloatsburg on the Sunday before the patronal feast of their province. The Holy See acceded to the Sisters' request and on January 25 of this year granted a Plenary Indulgence by rescript of the Sacred Apostolic Penitentiary, Office of Indulgences, on the conditions of Confession, Holy Communion, and prayers for the Holy Father's intention.'

The preparation of the pilgrimage could greatly affect public opinion; hence months of painstaking planning preceded the event. The spontaneous contribution in advice and assistance of St Mary's knowledgeable chaplain, Rev. B. Feddish, and members of both the diocesan and religious clergy, including the Basilian, Redemptorist, and Franciscan Orders, proved invaluable to the sisters. But despite the popular enthusiasm and their own boundless confidence, they still faced overwhelming odds. Simply to accommodate and feed the anticipated thousands of pilgrims would be no simple feat. 'At St. Mary's Villa itself,' observed the *America* reporter, 'the Sisters, shorthanded as they are because of summer and vacation schools in the parishes, are working overtime to make this Pilgrimage in honor of the Assumption of their Patroness a memorable spiritual feast for all the pilgrims.'[62]

They must have succeeded admirably, for in a newspaper account entitled 'Assumption Pilgrimage in General Glances,' one of the pilgrims presented a revealing picture of a day at the pilgrimage – a view that was typical of the Sisters Servants' pilgrimages in general: 'A beautiful, bright and sunny day. Attendance slightly over last year's. Number of pilgrims well over three thousand. Forty-four priests present, including three monsignors. Long lines of penitents. One thousand five hundred Holy Communions. Nine Masses. Assumption Chapel in St. Mary's Villa Academy crowded all day with pilgrims at prayer. Stirring sermons in Ukrainian and English. Program run smoothly and on time. Pilgrims orderly and devout. Shrines decorated artistically, and inspiring. People impressed with improvements at St. Joseph's Home for the Aged and pleased with service at new refreshment pavilion. Blessed Virgin Mary Sodality and altar boys in procession from Blessing of St. Joseph's Home to Our Lady of the Villa Shrine and Blessing of water. Ukrainian Catholic Cathedral choir of Philadelphia in fine voice sings High Mass beautifully. Everybody pleased; volunteer help tired but happy. Sisters exhausted but thankful to the Blessed Mother and good people.'[63] Thus perhaps the most remarkable single fact about this significant event was that it lived up to almost all expectations. And the most convincing proof of this was, first, the support accorded the sisters in the construction, in 1958, of Our Lady of Lourdes Grotto and Stations of the Cross, designed by the American Franciscan architect Brother Cajetan J. B. Baumann, and, second, the increasing crowds of pilgrims. In 1967 ten thousand people took part in the Assumption Pilgrimage at Sloatsburg. The issue was spiritual, and hence profound.

In July 1957 the sisters in Canada reached out to their people of the eastern eparchy in a similar endeavour. The diocesan weekly, *Meta*, informed its readers that the 'worthy and meritorious religious Congregation of Sisters Servants of Mary Immaculate, which has its novitiate and girls' academy at Mount Mary, has received from the Apostolic See the privilege of indulgence attached to certain days of the year. On the basis of this privilege, this religious centre becomes the first indulgenced site for Ukrainians of the Toronto eparchy.'[64]

For several years the sisters at Ancaster had played host to an annual gathering of faithful from nearby centres, especially from Toronto, Hamilton, Kitchener, Grimsby, and St Catharines, who, after participating in an outdoor celebration of the Divine Liturgy, had enjoyed a day on the enchanting academy grounds. It now remained to be seen whether a pilgrimage in the true sense of the word would prove any more popular than the picnic-oriented gatherings of the past. Thus even though there was no lack of pilgrimage talk in religious circles, prior to the event, the question of the hour was: how well would the laity of southern Ontario respond to a strictly spiritual programme? For the sisters were keenly aware that, no matter how sincere and admirable the goals were, they were not in control of all the factors concerning the pilgrimage. For example, their expectation of a substantial influx of pilgrims could be upset by a major disturbance stemming from such a thing as an important conference, convention, or concert being scheduled for the same day by any influential Ukrainian Catholic, or strictly national, organization.

In the planning stages one of the most encouraging features for the sisters was the eagerness of the laity to help: the diocesan branch of the Ukrainian Catholic Women's League adopted the pilgrimage as an annual project; the Knights of Columbus of Sheptytsky Council no. 5079, from the western district of Toronto, offered their personal services and financial help; several choirs, youth's and children's groups, volunteered to participate in the devotions. Needless to say, Bishop Borecky together with members of the diocesan and religious clergy helped the sisters greatly by planning the religious programme with them.

July 7 dawned bright and clear. From early morning fresh waves of pilgrims arrived at the Mount, and soon hundreds of automobiles were parked on the southwestern portion of the grounds. Throughout the day, one thousand people united themselves in prayer with their bishop, their priests, their sisters, and each other. 'These Pilgrims are the faithful children of our Church and nation, who, through a devout Christian life and an honest dedication to duty are building a promising future for Ukrainians in Canada,' contended *Meta*. 'At peaceful Mount Mary, bathed in a brilliant July sunshine, an abundance of heavenly graces and blessings must have been showered upon the faithful of the entire eparchy,' the newspaper concluded.[65]

If, at the beginning of the sisters' pilgrimages in Youngstown, Sloatsburg, and Ancaster, the press seemed to be indulging in hopeful hyperbole, their predictions were fulfilled by increasing crowds. But just how meaningful the experience was, and is, to the thousands who return each year, no one can determine exactly, for who can measure the grace which is communicated to each soul? And this, after all, is what the pilgrimages are all about.

In the spring of 1959, the final year of Sister Bernadette's second term in office, the provincial superior witnessed the completion of one other building extension, this one at Via Cassia Antica, 102, in Rome. For on April 19 of that year Eugene Cardinal Tisserant, secretary of the Sacred Oriental Congregation, assisted by the congregation's assessor, Father

Coussa, and two Ukrainian bishops, Bishop J. Buchko of Rome, and Bishop G. Bukatko of Yugoslavia, officially blessed a new four-storey wing of the generalate, which had been paid for with the sum of $80,000 borrowed by the Canadian-American province. In an article describing the event *Svitlo* acknowledged that this selfless gesture by the Sisters Servants of North America would be of paramount consequence 'not only in the history of this institute but also in that of the Ukrainian Church, since this extension, besides housing the generalate, will also provide a novitiate for European postulants, and a centre for the preparation of sisters for the challenging apostolate facing religious in modern times. The enlarged convent, therefore, will vitally link the Sisters Servants' missions throughout the world.'[66] In other words, the Province of Christ the King had once again – as it had when it purchased the original house at Rome in 1948 – invested in the future of the entire institute.

Just eight months later the generalate brought the North American community to its most momentous juncture since it was founded at the turn of the century, for on December 8, 1959, the Canadian-American missions were divided to form two completely independent provinces, one in Canada and the other in the United States.

For several years members of the Ukrainian American Catholic clergy had been loud in their contention that after almost a quarter-century the Sisters Servants' membership and houses in the United States should be incorporated into a completely autonomous religious province. And as 1960, the year in which the sisters would be observing the twenty-fifth anniversary of their apostolate in that country, drew nearer, a growing number of American-born and Canadian members, who had served in the United States for a longer period of time, began to support the notion that the American community was mature enough to govern itself. Hence by the time the superior general, Sister Jerome, arrived in New York on February 13, 1958, to conduct her first visitation of the Canadian-American province, there was little attempt to camouflage a very real desire for autonomy.

This impetus, which stemmed from an understandable yearning to play a stronger, more vigorous role in the formulation of local policy, was perhaps more sharply defined by the tremors of social change that were currently running through the United States. Moreover, the deep feelings that had begun to manifest themselves in a protest against the status quo seem to have galvanized into an internal conflict in which the American identity was palpably involved. It became Sister Jerome's delicate task, therefore, to be a sympathetic listener to conflicting views regarding the issue. For it was soon evident to her that, while some persons viewed the sudden flare-up of emotion as simply a tempest in a teapot, community passions could eventually leave resentments that might take years to heal. None the less, even though she adroitly avoided any firm commitments for or against the division of the province, even the most skilful diplomacy failed to quash rumours that a separation was imminent.

Subsequent developments confirm that Sister Jerome's visit did indeed hasten the inexorable progress of the American mission toward autonomous status. Asserts Rev. A. Welykyj, in his history of the Sisters Servants: 'From this visit was born the conviction that the American community was mature enough to become an independent entity within the institute.'[67] Sister Jerome, however, must have emerged from her experience with an informed and compelling feeling that there existed a strong disapproval of the proposal to cut deep into the current structure of the province.

The fundamental objection to such a move was that, since the institute had a total of just fifty-two American-born religious, it would be impossible for this small number to maintain the present scope of their apostolate in the nation without the assistance of Canadian personnel. Hence some members maintained that no division should be made immediately simply because there existed a driving desire for independence, but rather only when adequate resources, particularly in membership, could be tapped; otherwise, without outside assistance, the new province could find itself with a crippling personnel crisis on its hands from the very outset.

Evidently, to the superior general, the disadvantages did not appear excessive in relation to the benefits; on November 5, 1959, Sister Jerome revealed her conviction that the American members were ready to assume responsibility for their own future – to take their own risks and make their own mistakes: she informed Sister Bernadette that she was creating a new province. 'Having in view the welfare and development of our beloved congregation,' she declared, 'I have decided, together with my council, to establish an independent province of our institute in the United States of America ... The enclosed decree of erection of the American province under the patronage of the Immaculate Conception of the Blessed Virgin Mary is to be read on the day of this feast, December 8, 1959.'[68]

In reality, the news had been made public as early as August 5 by the Philadelphia diocesan newspaper, *The Way*, which had announced: 'By rescript of the Sacred Congregation [for the Oriental Churches] of February 11, 1959, exactly at the close of the centennial celebrations of the Lourdes Apparitions, a happy event has been added to the history of the

Congregation of the Byzantine Rite Sisters Servants of Mary Immaculate: the birth of a new Province.

'Up to that date, the only *de facto* Religious Province under the title of Christ the King, with its seat at Toronto, Ont., extended from Canada, where the flowering was the greatest, to the United States, embracing 42 religious homes, boarding schools, orphanages, [parochial] schools, old age homes and hospitals. The constant development of the Province and the good gains that were being realized and always more intensified have rendered advisable the division of the old immense Province and the erection of an independent Province for the United States. The seat of the new Province will be established in the very metropolis of Philadelphia, Pa.

'The new Province consists of 17 religious homes scattered throughout the United States, from Philadelphia, Pa., to Detroit, Mich.; from Sloatsburg, Buffalo and Rochester, N.Y., to Passaic, N.J.; from Ansonia, Conn., to Youngstown, Ohio. The Sisters number 86 professed, the majority with perpetual vows. A larger number of homes, 25, and of the religious, 200, remain in the Canadian Province.'[69]

Although the information was scarcely a surprise either in Canada or the United States, it triggered the faint shock waves of any transition to a new era, especially since the only sure thing about it was that the long-rumoured step had been taken. In order to assure an orderly transition, therefore, Sister Jerome delegated her councillor, Sister Lawrence Dzumaga, a Canadian by birth but now an American citizen, 'to execute the division of the Canadian-American province, and to announce the nomination of the new provincial superiors.'[70]

The extent and vigour of the generalate's plan of erection left little doubt that it was aimed as much at fostering the long-range growth of the new province as preventing any immediate adverse effects. The official decree indicated that of the total membership of fifty-two professed American-born Sisters Servants, nine were currently assigned to Canadian missions, while of the eighty-six sisters listed as comprising the membership of Immaculate Conception Province, forty-one were Canadian by birth, although seventeen of these were already naturalized American citizens. The retention of this proportion of Canadians in the United States – almost 50 per cent – indicated the general council's recognition that a sudden withdrawal of almost half of the province could have created havoc within its apostolate. In addition, the decree's statement that the novitiate at Ancaster would continue to serve both provinces for the time being demonstrated the willingness of the generalate to give the incoming American provincial council the time needed for its internal organization, and for the preparation of its personnel to fill new posts, such as those associated with formation programmes.[71]

Metropolitan Bohachevsky, who had welcomed the first Sisters Servants to the United States in 1935, noted that the seeds of the new province had been a long time germinating amid circumstances that were less than conducive to steady growth. 'It was necessary to face many trials, bear many burdens; it was necessary to be imbued with a great spirit of dedication and sacrifice in order to persevere and not retreat from your marked goal,' he stated. 'One can therefore affirm that the initial labour of the sisters of your institute was the mustard seed which has brought forth abundant fruit. Today, your eleven parochial schools, private girls' academy, three homes for the aged and infirm, and centre for the sewing of liturgical vestments, in our metropolitan see, are precisely these fruits.'[72] But even though the prelate seemed to be merely emphasizing the obvious, there was an unmistakable suggestion in his acknowledgment of past achievement that neither probable practical difficulties nor challenging problems would overwhelm the members of the new province – only a lack of the kind of drive that had characterized its pioneers.

Paradoxically, on December 8, 1959, the day selected for the official announcement of the division of the Province of Christ the King, both Canadian and American Sisters Servants discovered how inextricably they were bound together. At the provincialate in Toronto, in the presence of the assembled community, Sister Lawrence read a message from the superior general to the sisters of the Canadian province. After acknowledging their individual and collective contribution to the American mission, Sister Jerome concluded: 'I believe that the American sisters will always be grateful to their mother Province of Christ the King for carefully laying their foundations. I am also certain that they will never forget the extraordinary assistance accorded it by Sister Elizabeth Kassian, who established the first mission homes in their nation, and Sister Bernadette Warick, who furthered their development.'[73]

Then, amid an almost tangible hush of expectancy, Sister Lawrence named the sisters who would form the new Canadian and American councils: in Canada, Sister Boniface Sloboda, as provincial superior, would be assisted by Sister Modesta Anita Lukey, Sister Cornelia Mantyka, Sister Frances Byblow, and Sister Dominic Slawuta; in the United States, Sister Vincent Rosalie Yaremovich, as the first provincial superior of the newly formed province, would govern it together with her councillors: Sister

Rose Katherine Halytsky, Sister Juvenalia Kaniuk, Sister Sebastia Mary Shewchuk, and Sister Cyprian Homa.[74]

After congratulating the members of both councils, Sister Lawrence addressed a message of appreciation to Sister Bernadette who, for ten years, had directed the institute's missions in the vast territory that had comprised Christ the King Province. Dwelling not on tangible monuments, such as the educational and health-care centres that had sprung up during her administration, but instead on the intangibles which she had bequeathed to the province, Sister Lawrence said: 'During her tenure as provincial superior Sister Bernadette, by forgetting herself in a readiness to assist her sisters, has passed on to us a spirit of generosity and selflessness. More vital still, and a gift which we now gratefully acknowledge, is our deeper involvement in things spiritual, a movement she fostered throughout her two terms in office. In the days to come, therefore, may her awareness of this precious legacy be her sweetest reward.'[75]

To Sister Vincent, the incoming American provincial superior, Sister Lawrence remarked: 'The superiors of our institute have entrusted you with a grave responsibility – that of giving good leadership to your sisters, and of nourishing the growth of this first offshoot of our Canadian province as diligently as the provincial councils, since 1935, have tended the American mission. Build this young province, under the patronage of the Immaculate Conception of the Virgin Mary, on a foundation of love and gratitude toward those who founded and nourished it. In this way, you will assure its future fruitfulness.'[76]

The climactic moment for the American community came four days later at its provincialate, the Home of Divine Providence in Philadelphia, when Sister Lawrence proclaimed the Immaculate Conception Province officially erected. The prevailing mood was both jubilant and solemn, for while the sisters rejoiced in the successful culmination of a quarter-century of missionary endeavour, they could scarcely help wondering what the future held for their province as it prepared to take its first steps in the formation of its own destiny.

The Canadian Province of Christ the King, on the other hand, had so much to be proud of, so much to be grateful for, so much to look forward to. On that historic December 8, with the birth of the American province, it reached the stature of maturity. And this, of course, meant that if it were to remain true to itself and to the Church there could be no end to its new beginnings.

A time to love . . .

Historical perspective, always an elusive quality, becomes even less likely of attainment when the writer is in the midst of events concerning living personalities and fluid situations all of which will one day be evaluated by historians in a position to 'look back' on what by then will have ceased to be the current scene. Accordingly, this epilogue is little more than a statement of some of the facts and an indication of some of the developments which characterized the ten years immediately following the creation of Immaculate Conception Province for the United States at the close of 1959, an event that marked a new phase in the history of the Canadian Province of Christ the King.

*   *   *

Religious institutes in the 1960s seemed to have been caught up in a season of restlessness. For it was a time when their members were shoving each other to one side or another of a line of judgment; when some were labelled 'liberals' and others 'conservatives'; when some expressed dismay over the leisurely pace of change in the Church and in their orders and congregations, and others bemoaned the breathless dispatch with which the 'old' was being replaced by the 'new.' Without doubt, religious men and women – among them the Sisters Servants – were passing through a crisis of uncertainty, frustration, and reorganization. Many considered these to be basically healthy signs, evidencing a re-evaluation of what religious life should be. Almost all, however, agreed that the trend toward bold self-appraisal was inherent in the decrees issued by the Second Vatican Council, which called for a new understanding of the Church and its mission, and hence entailed new attitudes and procedures.

The world had greeted the formal opening of the General Ecumenical Council by Pope John XXIII on October 11, 1962, as the beginning of an exciting new era, not only for the Catholic Church but for Christians everywhere, since its aim, according to Pope John, was nothing less than 'to evoke a new Pentecost, calling for a renewal of the Church in her head and in all her members, for her reformation in the reflection of Christ in the Gospels.'[1] It was to be a demonstration of the Church always living and always young, declared Pope John in 1961 – a Church 'which feels the rhythm of the times and which in every century beautifies herself with new splendour, radiates new light, achieves new conquests, while remaining identical with herself, faithful to the divine image impressed on her countenance by her Spouse, who loves her and protects her, Christ Jesus.'[2]

Three years and sixteen promulgated documents later, on December 8, 1965, the Council was concluded ceremonially with a Mass in St Peter's Square by Pope Paul VI, who took the opportunity to stress again the significance of Vatican II: 'In this privileged point of time and space, there converge together the past, the present, and the future – the past: for here, gathered at this spot, we have the Church of Christ with her tradition, her history, her Councils, her doctors, her saints; the present: for we are taking leave of one another to go out toward the world of today with its miseries, its sufferings, its sins, but also with its prodigious accomplishments, its values, its virtues; and lastly the future is here in the urgent appeal of the peoples of the world for more justice, in their will for peace, in their conscious or unconscious thirst for a higher life, that life precisely which the Church of Christ can and wishes to give them.'[3]

On October 28, 1965, just three months before they concluded their deliberations, the Council Fathers promulgated the *Decree on the Appropriate Renewal of the Religious Life* in an endeavour to set up appropriate guidelines for adaptation and renewal within religious institutes. Some communities, in their eagerness to respond to the Church's summons to update themselves, tended to forget that pruning a living body as complex as a religious institute requires a delicate touch. There was a danger to the entire religious family when such a reforming attitude was prompted largely by deference to passing history and to contemporary fashion, that is, to values not supported by reasons compatible with divine truth and authentic human dignity. In some cases the structures of religious institutes became the object of a certain reforming intolerance, as if everyone might form at his own pleasure a new, historical, spiritual model of his order or congregation. On the other hand, there were those who, in their desire to cling to the concept that the good old days were the best ever, seemed to forget that such nostalgia can be a seductive liar, evoking bowdlerized pictures of times past with all the shadows painted out, thus obscuring or distorting the lessons to be learned.

The ills of any society or group cannot be corrected overnight, and any attempt to do so creates other ills as bad or worse than those already dealt with. Hence in any experimentation that religious institutes would undertake in their spiritual or apostolic life they would have to be willing to accept an element of failure – inherent in every experiment. And the only salve to their pride, honour, and dignity would be honesty and no pretences – to recognize the mistake as a mistake, to refrain from pretending it was a mistake, and to find tolerance in the universal human knowledge that to err is human.

The responsibility of guiding the Sisters Servants through this challenging period was assigned, first, to Sister Boniface Sloboda, provincial superior from 1960 to 1965, and then to Sister Frances Byblow, who held this position during the years 1965–70. Throughout their tenure in office both superiors were to lead a religious province which, on the one hand, was a community groping to find the best way to honour its commitment to the Church and, on the other, a community that was moving outward in an age of increasing interdependence. In the light of this trend there developed a closer association of Sisters Servants with other religious institutes and the laity, as well as a closer collaboration among themselves in Canada and in other countries.

A significant first step in the direction of establishing closer ties with members of other communities on home ground began at Yorkton in the autumn of 1961. The *Yorkton Enterprise* noted on August 17 that the Sisters Servants at Sacred Heart Academy were hosting the Canadian Religious Conference (Western). 'In attendance are more than 60 Sisters representing 14 religious orders in Alberta, Saskatchewan and Ontario,' reported the newspaper. 'Rev. J. F. Madden, csb, Superior of St. Michael's College, Toronto, is directing the three-day conference, with study groups, open forums and discussions on the heavy agenda.'[4] In recording the event the annalist pointed out that 'some sisters participated in a Mass in a rite other than the Latin rite, and received the Eucharist under two species of bread and wine for the first time in their lives. Indeed,' she concluded, 'the kind of amiability that dominated the conference should permeate all of our relationships as we anticipate the Ecumenical Council.'[5]

The ecumenical concept that all men are summoned to united effort – a mutual enrichment – took on a new dimension for the sisters during the decade as they worked together with the laity to promote the development of old missions and to establish new ones to a degree never before realized. In 1962, at Willingdon, Alberta, the combination of twenty-five years of selfless nursing by the sisters, of dedicated and efficient medical service by Dr W. G. Lazaruk, and of a district full of grateful citizens made it possible for the *Vegreville Observer* to announce on September 27 that 'in their Silver Jubilee Year [in the town], the Sisters Servants of Mary Immaculate will open the doors of the new Mary Immaculate Hospital to the residents of Willingdon and the surrounding district. The present hospital, which was built in 1937, will be renovated as a staff residence.' Thus this construction project, which Sister Boniface had inherited when she assumed office in 1960, had been brought to a successful conclusion by an interested and concerned Christian community working together.

Almost simultaneously, in the spring of 1961, the Winnipeg diocesan newspaper *Postup* (*Progress*) informed the public that 'The parents' committee of St Nicholas School has decided to begin construction of a new school building this year to replace the oldest of our educational institutions in Canada, which, during almost sixty years under the direction of our tireless Sisters Servants, has given Ukrainian society in this country nearly ten thousand citizens who are conscious of their religious and civic responsibilities. The proposed edifice, estimated to cost $200,000, will be constructed on the site of the old building at 650 Flora Avenue.'[6] The remarkable thing about this venture was that the members of the executive of a newly formed building committee under the co-chairmen, Mr W. Paschak and Mr W. Sahan, were former students of St Nick's.[7] And it was a former teacher of the school, Sister Jerome, who, on April 28, 1963, at the official opening of a new school with a new name – Immaculate Heart of Mary School – acknowledged their unique contribution to their alma mater. She said: 'The significance of this event is enhanced by the fact that the success of this great undertaking lies in the generous sacrifice, untiring effort, initiative, and determination on the part of former students. This is indeed a most gratifying service.'[8]

In a letter to the sisters in November 1967 informing them of certain building projects that were already under way, their provincial superior, Sister Frances, announced that 'the people of Calgary, at their own cost, are in the process of building a "jubilee home" for the sisters.'[9] By so doing, Calgarians were ensuring that the Sisters Servants would not leave their parish because of inadequate living quarters, which, because of a substantial debt in the province, they could not presently afford to replace. Meanwhile, to other missions which were not as fortunate she wrote: 'Cheer up – Edmonton, Regina, Vegreville – we'll get there yet. In the meantime, keep the ceiling up and the rain out.'[10]

At Holy Family Nursing Home in Winnipeg, largely through the indefatigable efforts of Mr Ron White, chairman of the home's building committee, all necessary professional and financial negotiations with various levels of government in Manitoba were nearing completion by 1965 to make way for the expansion of the institution's facilities for the aged. At that time, Mr Fred James' fund-raising committee mounted so massive an effort to secure the necessary cash that on December 17, 1970, a new extension costing $1,770,000 was officially opened. Perhaps the most distinctive reward to the sisters, the members of the advisory board, women's auxiliary, and the residents, for their collective work and prayers that had built this magnificent nursing home, was a memorable visit on July 14, 1970, of their Royal Highnesses, Prince Charles and Princess Anne.

In September of that year, the trust and confidence of the Sisters Servants in the men and women who had done so much for them at Winnipeg was manifested when Sister Frances announced the appointment of Mr Jack Kisil as administrator of the home. 'Our Community has always worked very closely with the laity,' she explained later, 'for we feel very strongly that the ideals of Christian charity can best be realized in cooperation with others of good will. In Mr Jack Kisil we found a layman to whom we could give our full trust in the chief executive position of this nursing home.'[11]

Not only parishes, towns, and cities but entire provinces came to work with the Sisters Servants. In Saskatchewan in October 1969, 'in blocks of twenty miles, Saskatchewaners walked up and down the province because the Knights of Columbus were sold on the idea that what St Ann's Children's Home at Ituna stood for was worthy of support, and they invited their fellow citizens to become involved.'[12] And so, it was a big day when Herb Ekvall, state deputy of the Saskatchewan Knights of Columbus, took the first step in the walkathon, known throughout the province as the 'Hyke for Tykes.' This immense undertaking enabled the Knights to provide a long-awaited extension, including a gymnasium, for the children at St Ann's. The seed of their accomplishment had been planted several years before, however, as Sister Frances reminded everyone, 'by a small nucleus of Knights ... that meets regularly with the Sisters and was set on its feet in 1963 by Judge Andrew Kindred with the help and continued assistance of Con Finucane and Pat Gleason.'[13] And, as is usual, the work of the Knights was of necessity supplemented by the contribution of women – in this instance by the Saskatchewan Catholic Women's Leagues of both rites, who helped to furnish the new building.

The Diamond Jubilee in 1967, when the Sisters Servants observed the seventy-fifth anniversary of their founding and the sixty-fifth year of their apostolate in Canada, provided a prime example of the understanding way in which the laity was sharing in their accomplishments. In almost every Canadian centre where the sisters were actively engaged in missionary works, their people planned to celebrate the event with them. The focal point of the observance, however, was Toronto – the seat of the community's provincialate. And so, in this city during the weekend of May 20–22, nothing was able to dilute the occasion's traditional, and quite special, commingling of private joy, public goodwill, and national esprit. Josyf Cardinal Slipyj stated in his message to the sisters: 'The seventy-fifth anniversary of your generous work among Ukrainians in Canada fills with joy not only your home ... but also our entire Church, for your labour ... is an apostolate on behalf of our entire Church and nation. May Almighty God accept our prayerful thanksgiving for your success in the past and abundantly bless your future.'[14]

On May 20, at the theatre of Central Technical Collegiate, the jubilee got off to a dramatic start when the combined talents of Toronto's Ukrainian drama, choral, orchestral, and ballet groups presented a 'Jubilee Montage' in two parts – the first depicting the cult of the Blessed Virgin in Ukraine, and the second the birth of the Institute of Sisters Servants in Zhuzhyl and their subsequent missionary endeavours on three continents. The production was realized only because people like Sister Juvenalia Kaniuk, Mr Orest Pawliw, Sister Christine Emily Opalinsky, Nadia Buchan-Pawlychenko, and Professor J. Kowaliw had selflessly contributed their musical, literary, and choreographical ability in a great cooperative effort. And for the first time the choir, composed of sisters and lay women (many, graduates of Mount Mary Academy, Ancaster), rendered the majestic *Sisters Servants Jubilee Cantata* composed by Sister Juvenalia. The crowds came away enthusing that it was the finest Ukrainian presentation Toronto had seen. Perhaps it wasn't exactly that, but it was unquestionably a popular programme which had linked the sisters with their people in a real union of heart and mind.

Sunday, the 21st, was a day of prayer and thanksgiving. It was highlighted by the Divine Liturgy of thanksgiving at St Josaphat's Cathedral concelebrated by Bishop Isidore Borecky and Bishop Michael Rusnak, at which Archbishop Sergio Pignedoli, apostolic delegate, preached the homily. The following morning in the provincialate chapel the archbishop and the sisters offered the Eucharistic sacrifice for the deceased members of the community whose memory was very much alive to those participating in this anniversary.

That evening the Religion and Culture Society of St Demetrius Parish, under the presidency of Mrs Ella Manastersky, honoured the sisters and guests at a dinner at the Skyline Hotel. The presence of representatives of Church and State and laity from many Canadian centres symbolized a common interest and a common goal: promotion of the common good.

Nor could Mrs Manastersky and her executive have selected a more meritorious guest speaker – so far as the sisters were concerned – than Dr Stephanie Potoski of Yorkton, Saskatchewan.[15] The first Ukrainian in the world to have been honoured by the papal distinction, *Pro Ecclesia et Populo*, she had been intimately associated with the apostolate of Sisters Servants for many years. Indeed, it would need a special occasion and a formidable array of speakers to capture in words all that she had done for Sacred Heart Academy in Yorkton, commented Sister Frances, 'for although she appears not to be subject to limitations of time and space, I cannot recall a single instance when she refused a service or was, in the least way, unwilling to help.'[16] Dr Potoski herself stated in the opening lines of her address: 'I consider it a great honour to be permitted to participate in this birthday, partly because, during my entire life, I have no recollection of not knowing these sisters. If one accepts the age of four or five years as that of a child's earliest recollection, then I can safely say that my association and friendship with this congregation spans almost half a century. For this great privilege, I thank God.'[17]

Her appraisal of the contribution to Canada by the sisters was augmented by the message from Prime Minister Lester B. Pearson, who stated: 'Through your pioneer work, especially in western Canada, in establishing schools, orphanages, hospitals, and other charitable institutions, you have contributed much to the betterment of many Canadians. In so doing, you have won the deep respect and gratitude of those with whom you have been associated, as attested to in the many tributes to your great work on this memorable anniversary. Canada is a better country because so many like the Sisters Servants care enough for the less fortunate among us to devote their talents and time to their service.'[18]

The most touching note was added to the evening when a letter was read from Sister Athanasia Melnyk, the only living member of the original group of nine who had formed the nucleus of the institute in 1892, and who, together with her congregation, was celebrating her Diamond Jubilee as a religious. She wrote: 'The initial task to which Almighty God called our institute – to be educators, nurses, social workers, mothers to abandoned children in the villages of western Ukraine, and advocates for our people before the Lord – we conscientiously strived to perform under the guidance of our bishops and clergy. A similar responsibility was unreservedly accepted and fulfilled with great sacrifice by our sisters upon the commencement of their missionary work in Canada, Brazil, the United States, and in the other countries to which Divine Providence sent them.

'My own role in this noble work has almost ceased, for my voice is hushed now, my mind slower, my body so enfeebled that I am confined to a wheelchair. But although I have stepped aside to permit others to take my place, my soul still burns with love for my people – the people for whom, in accordance with God's will, I have given seventy-five years of my life as a Sister Servant. This love, which constitutes my prayer for my nation, I shall place before the Lord and His Mother in eternity.'[19] Three months later she was there. For she died on August 6 in Winnipeg, the city which had welcomed her as a young missionary sixty-two years before.

The final festivities were held in Toronto on November 12 at an Anniversary Tea sponsored by the Ukrainian Catholic Women's League. The Sisters Servants had always worked closely with, and esteemed highly, the League, organized in eastern Canada by one of their former students from Sacred Heart Academy, Mrs Julius Katherine Crouse. Sister Frances voiced the sentiments of her fellow sisters when she stated: 'Today you are expressing your appreciation to the Sisters Servants of Mary Immaculate by honouring them with a Jubilee Tea. For us this cup of tea is a treasured symbol of your friendship, your goodness, your generosity. Through your diocesan president, Mrs Anne Chaiko, I sincerely thank you for what you have done and are doing for us in eastern Canada – even if just to recall your assistance in building the Ancaster Academy, or your aid to the war orphans who were cared for there for some few years; your colossal contribution to the annual Marian pilgrimage at Ancaster; an annual tea sponsored by some branch of yours in almost every one of our houses in this diocese; your support of the Mother Ambrose Scholarship Fund. I say with complete conviction that every Sister Servant knows that whatever her apostolate she can always count on the assistance and the cooperation of the Ukrainian Catholic Women's League.'[20]

In the aftermath of the celebrations, among the numerous congratulatory messages that continued to arrive at the provincialate, there was one which encouraged all members of the province. It was from the apostolic delegate, Archbishop Pignedoli, who at the jubilee banquet had named them 'the smiling sisters.' He wrote: 'I know that this is a difficult time for so many in the Church, especially the sisters. But I feel confident after my visit with you that you have the spirit and the courage that will carry you through this time of trial which is also a time of great hope. You have such a beautiful vocation, and until now your dedicated witness to God has enriched the Church. That the horizons of this dedication are broadening to take in the world, that all men are in need of the sight of your witness, will mean adjustment, but one that should not frighten or depress us.'[21]

Given the uncharted crosscurrents of novel ideas and proposals for change that were circulating among religious in the 1960s, and a need for the kind of adjustment referred to by Archbishop Pignedoli, it became clear that the Sisters Servants would have to bring into focus their own responses to the challenges posed by Vatican II. And the groundwork for this task was laid at the pre-conciliar general chapter convened in Rome on September 8, 1962 – a little over a month before the opening of the Council.

The significance of the sisters' meeting at this historical moment was stressed on September 9 in a Vatican Radio broadcast by Rev. A. Welykyj, secretary of the pre-conciliar, and conciliar, commission for the Eastern Churches,[22] who said: 'No human power can destroy those who are united in spirit. This oneness that extends across three continents – from the far-flung reaches of Siberia to San Paolo, San Francisco, and Vancouver – is concretely represented at this Second Rome Chapter, which is being held in the shadow of St Peter's on the eve of the Ecumenical Council. For this assembly is not comprised merely of twenty [eighteen] delegates; this is the entire institute meeting as one with its past, its present, and its future.'[23]

Since, in accordance with their 1956 constitutions, this was an ordinary chapter convoked for the purpose of electing a general council, the delegates fulfilled their primary role as electors on September 8, the day the chapter officially began. At that time Sister Jerome Chimy was re-elected as superior general, and two Canadians, Sister Julianna Pankowsky and Sister Cornelia Mantyka, were chosen to assist her as councillors.[24] Then, until September 19, the Canadian delegation, headed by Sister Boniface, and including Sister Bernadette Warick and Sister Cornelia Mantyka,[25] participated in a study of the recommendations which had flowed in from their sisters around the world.

Their implementations, which were approved by the Holy See on November 24, 1962, incorporated the fruit of careful consideration and discussion, and indicated that in a very real sense the delegates had examined the institute's present, reviewed its past, and planned its future.[26] Moreover, their close association in an undertaking that profoundly concerned each sister served to cement friendships and foster a greater appreciation than ever before of one another's provincial concerns, which were as diverse as the countries from which these sisters had come. The adoption of more positive attitudes and viewpoints was a sound foundation upon which to prepare for the subsequent extraordinary general chapter of affairs recommended by Paul VI in his *motu proprio* of August 6, 1966. 'The most important role in the adaptation and renewal of the Religious Life belongs to the Institutes themselves, which will accomplish it especially through general chapters,' stated the pontiff.[27]

Before another chapter was convoked, however, an opportunity for local consolidation through a fresh exchange of ideas presented itself to the Canadian Sisters Servants on April 8–9, 1964, when the First Conference of the Superiors of the Province of Christ the King was held at Winnipeg. The meeting came as an interesting innovation during Sister Jerome's canonical visitation in Canada, which had commenced in January of that year. Both she and Sister Boniface hoped that from it would ensue a closer cooperation among members of the province through an harmonious leadership. The annalist explained that together with the superior general and provincial superior, the twenty sisters present 'shall discuss problems of general concern, and shall also study our apostolate with a view toward improving it wherever possible.'[28] The Winnipeg meeting was a suitable prelude to the worldwide gathering of Sisters Servants in Rome four years later, for it provided local superiors with the opportunity to express their views on all aspects of community living.

The charge of organizing the momentous chapter of election and affairs scheduled for 1968 belonged, of course, to Sister Jerome. And perhaps her best qualification for this obligation was her surprising, and gratifying, appointment by Pope Paul VI, in 1964, as an auditor of Vatican II. 'Alberta Nun Gets Nomination in Council,' headlined Edmonton's *Western Catholic* on December 9 of that year, noting with satisfaction that it was one of Alberta's own daughters, originally from Radway, who would be present at the fourth session together with the only eight other auditors from religious congregations of women. Her proximity to the Council proceedings provided Sister Jerome with first-hand knowledge of the documents that were studied – especially that concerning religious life – and an understanding of the reasons motivating the Council Fathers to promulgate them.

In October 1966 she informed all members that preparations would commence immediately for the first session of a general chapter scheduled for September 1968. 'If it [the chapter] is to solve the difficulties we face today we must begin to make ready for it through prayer and study, in the spirit of the Council,' she declared. 'In order that every sister may have the opportunity of studying the main topics to be treated at the chapter and of contributing suggestions and proposals for the general good of the congregation and of the provinces, a questionnaire is being sent to each one. I ask you to study and complete it in a spirit of loving service to God, the Church, and the institute.'[29]

Shortly thereafter the sisters of the Canadian province were introduced to a renewal plan conceived by their provincial superior, Sister Frances, which was also designed to enable them, through personal observations and suggestions, to assist their superiors in planning for the future. On March 20, 1967, she established a Central Commission for the Revision of the Constitutions, comprised of nine sisters. Its task: to prepare a framework for a province-wide study of their religious life in the post-Vatican era, and to compile the results for presentation to the general chapter.[80]

The project devised by the commission, under the chairmanship of Sister Mechtilde Byblow, was called 'Explorations for Renewal''; the members hoped that for the community it would be a time of prayer, of quiet study and objective discussion. To assist the sisters as much as possible, Sister Dominic Slawuta, Sister Bernadette Warick, Sister Justine Kowal, Sister Cassianna Eva Slywka, and Sister Claudia Helen Popowich formulated study guides, selected appropriate readings, and prepared questionnaires for each of the following topics: Spiritual Life, Community Life, Apostolic Life, Organization and Government, and Formation. The programme began in August 1967 and terminated in December of that year. By means of regional meetings, specialized retreats, and the completed questionnaires, much information was gathered and certain trends ascertained. In addition, with the permission of the general council some experimentation was initiated in prayer and apostolic schedules, and in religious garb.

The information compiled by the commission enabled it to present a blueprint of an agenda for the provincial chapter held at Sacred Heart Academy, Yorkton, from April 17 to 22, 1968, and attended by thirty-five delegates. Soon after, in a letter to the Canadian community on June 12, Sister Frances wrote: 'The provincial chapter has come and gone with two delegates, Sister Bernadette [Warick] and Sister Justine [Kowal] ready to take along to the general chapter the recommendations that were so carefully worked out at the sessions in Yorkton. Tomorrow, Sister Mechtilde [Byblow] and Sister Monica [Mantyka] sail from New York ... to Rome where they will become members of the International Commission set up by Mother General to prepare the general chapter agenda.'[81]

In her comprehensive report to the sisters at the end of the first session, which had convened in Rome on September 8, 1968, Sister Frances advised them that the chapter had established 'a Community Commission, headed by Sister Bernadette [Warick] that will begin immediately to draft a renewed rule in keeping with Vatican II.'[82] In addition, the delegates had elected a new general council, with Sister Jerome Chimy as superior general and Sister Dominic Slawuta as the only Canadian councillor.[83]

Two years slipped by amid study and experimentation. Finally, on

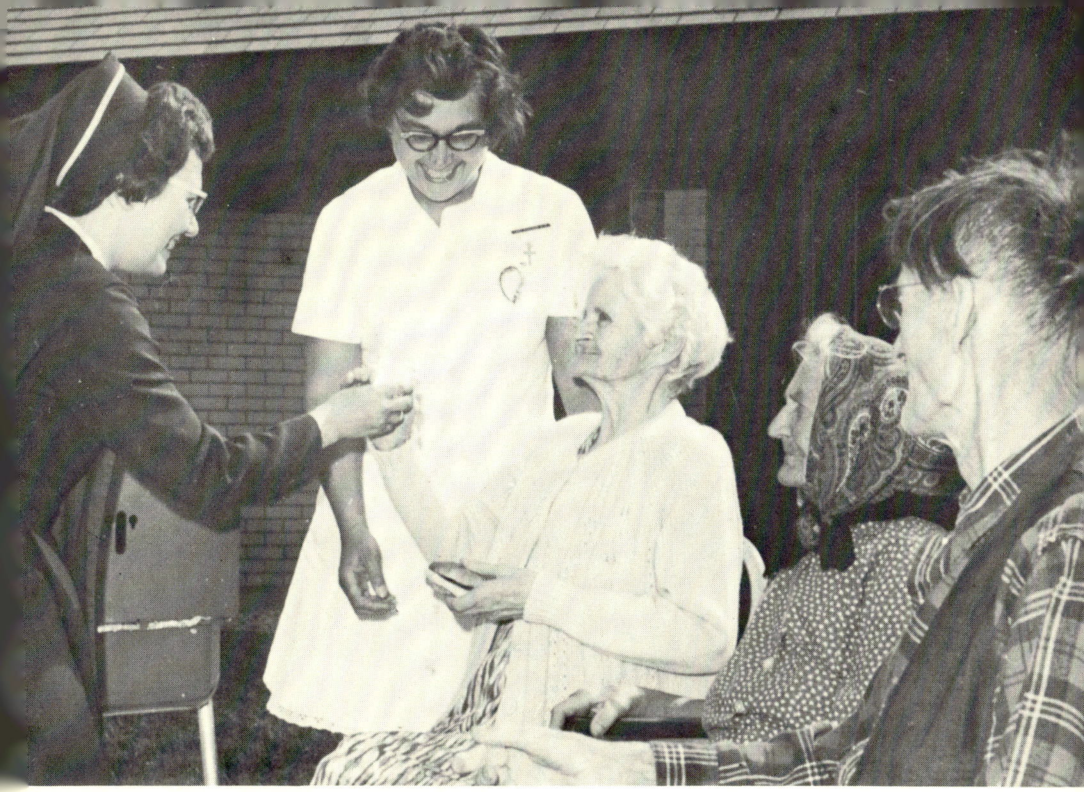

In Dauphin, older people from very different walks of life have mutual bonds at St Paul's Nursing Home. Sister Nestor Kyba helps make a good barbecue even better. Sister Eleanor Lenyk shares the satisfaction of these men in their work.

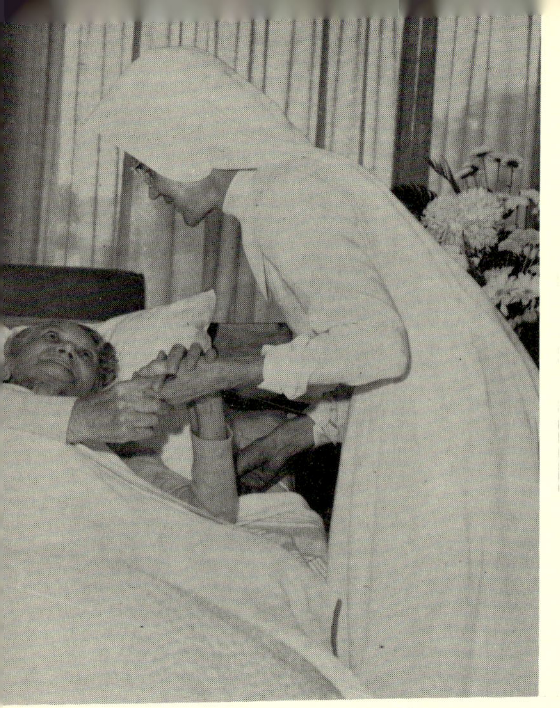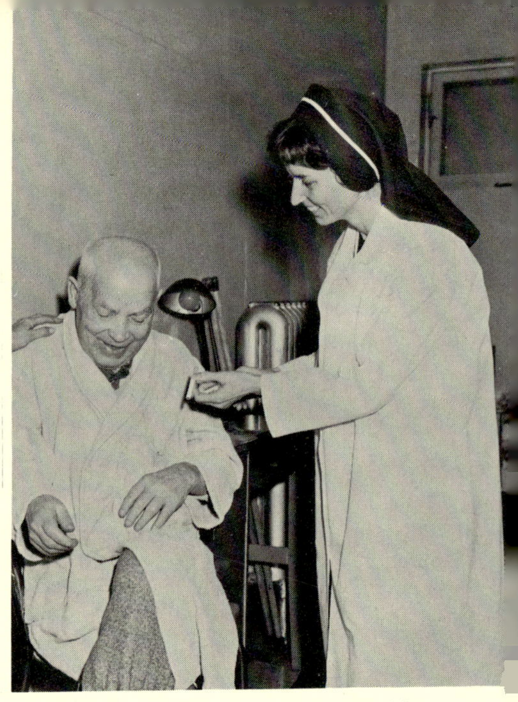

It seems as though Sister Eleanor and Sister Leontia Stadnyk manage to be 'all things to all men,' and in ways that match the occasion!

The Edmonton, Alberta, Senior Citizens' Home enjoys an unusual member – one of Sister Petronella Dybka's kindergarteners, who are celebrating Easter with a concert for the residents of the Home.

 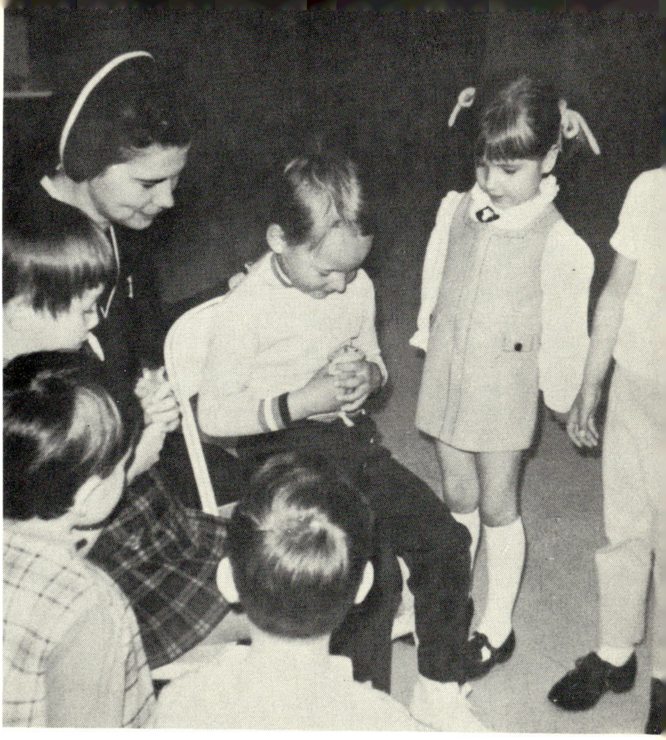

In Holy Spirit School, Hamilton, Ontario, Sister Virginia Pryslak uses both English and Ukrainian to share the gospel message. Sister Petronella might just be asking the Lord to help her keep smiling at her small mouse visitor.
Below, Sister Modesta Lukey is passing on a bit of her uncanny ability to make anything grow.

Here are our girls, full of the variety of life. Sister Juvenalia Kaniuk is advising one of her former voice students, and recent gold medallist of the University of Toronto School of Music, Oksana Bluy. There are many interests, generated by as many girls, at Sacred Heart Academy, Yorkton, Saskatchewan. Sister Ignatius Lesyk in the language lab, Sister Laura Prokop taking a moment to socialize in the dining room, and Sister Junia Kunanec teaching in the art studio, each help to create, within a diversity of people and ideas, an affectionate school unity.

In nursing, there is plenty of pathos, joy, and even fun! This premature child presents Sister Stephanie Olynyk, in Kitchener, Ontario, with an opportunity to experience the happiness found in giving of oneself. And Sister Celestine Lozinsky, an instructor at the Ottawa General Hospital School of Nursing, shows that there is more to man than meets the eye.

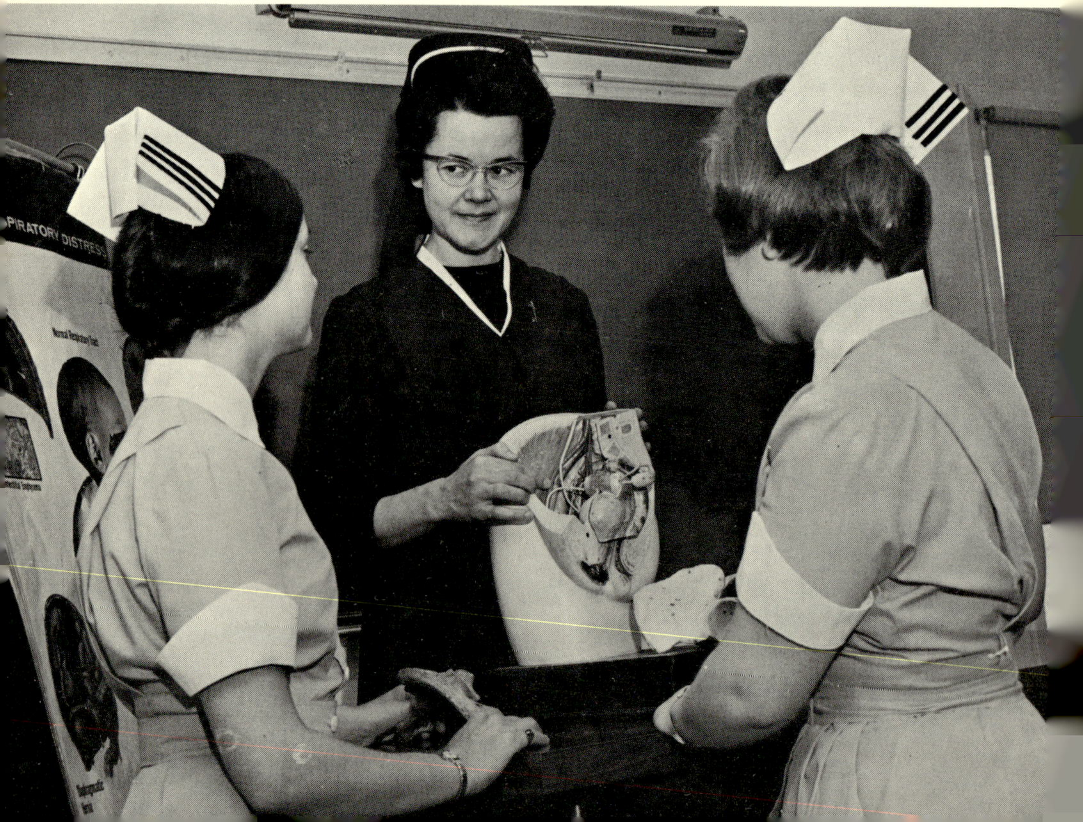

These pictures record a rare occasion at Holy Family Nursing Home in Winnipeg, when their Royal Highnesses, Prince Charles and Princess Anne, visited the patients in July 1970. Sister Innocentia Baraniuk, administrator, and Mr Fred James, chairman of the Advisory Board, welcome the royal guests.
Below, a multiple sclerosis patient shows her delight at meeting a Prince Charming.

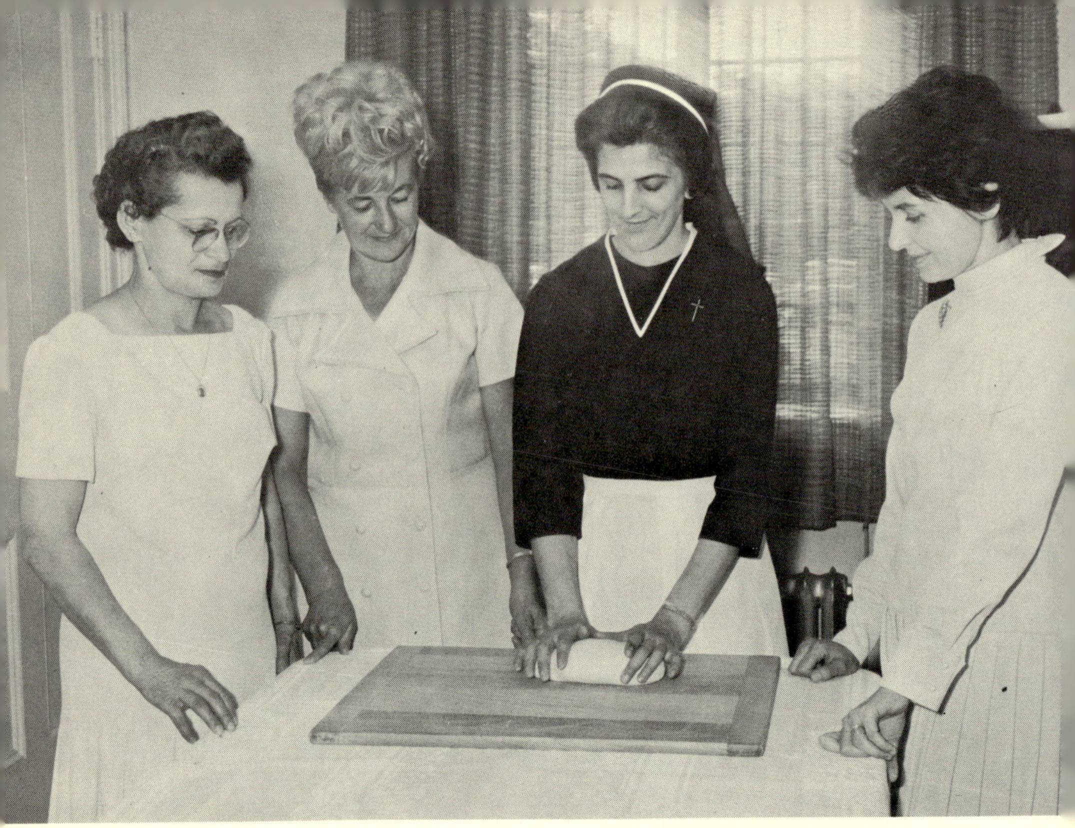

Sister Martha Zulyniak shares the experience of making altar bread with Mrs Marian Didic, Mrs Ella Manastersky, and Mrs Natalie Popowich of Toronto, thus preparing them to provide Communion Hosts for their own, and neighbouring, parishes.
Members of the Ukrainian Catholic Women's League, Miss Tatiana Diachinsky, Mrs Anne Chaiko, Mrs Katherine Crouse, and Mrs Theresa Stayshyn, discuss plans for future events with Sister Celeste Diachinsky over a cup of tea.

The annual Marian Pilgrimage is an event of deep religious significance. During the Divine Liturgy, on the grounds of Mount Mary Immaculate Academy in Ancaster, Ontario, thousands of individuals become one in their common Father. The Divine Liturgy is celebrated here by His Excellency, Bishop Isidore Borecky. In the opinion of these three children, the second Station of the Cross merits a closer look. Helping pilgrims choose a souvenir is Sister Joan Magriy, who has been a part of the Pilgrimage since its conception in 1957.

Perhaps Sister Hilary Lenyk, teaching summer catechism in Courtland, Ontario, is sharing Pope John XXIII's vision: a world ruled by love.

July 22, 1970, the second session of the provincial chapter was opened at Mount Mary Academy, Ancaster, for the threefold purpose of electing candidates for the succeeding provincial council, evaluating the fidelity of the province to the deliberations of the general chapter of 1968, and finalizing directives specifically for the province.[34] Within two months, on September 19, Sister Frances was in Rome with Sister Bernadette and Sister Justine to participate in the final session of the general chapter which examined, discussed, and voted on the new constitutions presented to it by the Post-Capitular Commission that had been set up to revise the 1956 rule. The result was a constitution valid until the next chapter, to be convoked in 1974, at which time it would again be re-examined.[35] Thus the manner in which any subsequent rule would be shaped would depend on the way in which Sisters Servants responded to, and were affected by, the future.

Perhaps as a result of closer communication with Europe through the general chapters, the Canadian sisters began to display a striking flexibility and mobility in accepting assignments to countries other than the United States. For even though they had stepped forward to assist European missions in the 1950s, by 1965 there were Canadians in four European nations – England, France, Germany, and Italy. Specifically, Sister Florence Wus and Sister Demetrius Anastasia Seniuk served at Bradford, England; Sister Irene Pauline Sawchuk at Mackwiller, France; Sister Constance Malko at Munich; and Sister Naucratia Hawryliuk, Sister Benedict Sereda, and Sister Adrianne Katherine Charandiuk at Rome. In October 1967 Sister Jerome informed the members of the entire institute that the Sacred Congregation for the Oriental Churches had accorded it the distinction of accepting a member from the Province of Christ the King, Sister Claudia Popowich, to work directly for the Holy See at the congregation in Rome as an administrative secretary for the oriental missions.[36]

It was inevitable, too, that sisters should study abroad. In 1964 Sister Frances Byblow began graduate work in theology at Regina Mundi College, Rome, and Sister Juvenalia Kaniuk studied music at Florence and Vienna; later Sister Marion Zerebesky furthered her studies in the Montessori teaching method at London.

From 1969 another form of education – travel abroad – presented itself when the sisters were requested to act as chaperons on tours sponsored by the Ukrainian Catholic Youth to both western and eastern Europe. After their trip in 1970 Sister Celestine Margaret Lozinsky and Sister Victoria Hunchak shared their reflections with the sisters of the province: 'We can say without exaggerating that this tour thrilled and inspired us. We will never be the same again. How can we, after marvelling at the breathtaking beauty of the Carpathian Mountains, the Bavarian Alps, the Pieta, St Peter's, the ancient treasures of the British Museum, the Cathedral of Cologne? But perhaps the most inspiring experiences involved not places and things but all the wonderful persons we met. Particularly, our sisters. The warmth, sincerity, hospitality, thoughtfulness shown us will always remain deeply imbedded in our hearts. The heroic life our sisters lead in Ukraine made us proud to be Sisters Servants. The example of their sincere dedication and perseverance despite hardship, isolation from the rest of the community, and fear, confirmed us in our vocation. We were amazed at how the same identical spirit animates us all.'[37]

While an occasion for travel abroad presented itself to a few sisters toward the end of the decade, both Sister Boniface and Sister Frances, during their respective terms in office, readily perceived that in a world where continuing education and preparation for a second or third career were being increasingly taken for granted, the community could do no less than train its members accordingly. Recognition of the need, of course, did not mean that the decision would be painless, since it meant pursuing a vital but seemingly contradictory policy: to provide adequate training for non-academic personnel in their convents and institutions by withdrawing them from an active apostolate. By so doing, however, both superiors were moving beyond the blueprint that had been followed in the province thus far, that is, emphasizing the academic and professional upgrading of its teaching and nursing staffs.

The new plan was initiated by Sister Boniface in the summer of 1961 when Ukrainian-language courses were offered by several experienced Sisters Servants to their own members. Later, when a programme in the Chilton/Didier method became available, the sisters took advantage of this course – oriented to the linguistic and psychological principles of the audio-visual approach to language – at Toronto, Edmonton, Winnipeg, and Yorkton.

Not dismayed or discouraged by the difficulties involved in revitalizing the province's forces, particularly in releasing sisters from their assignments, Sister Frances accelerated the trend not only to professionalize staff but above all to give the individual sister a feeling of confidence in her ability to meet the demands of the times. Her task for finding appropriate courses was eased by the organization of programmes for religious personnel of Catholic institutions. Soon, therefore, Sisters Servants were graduating in new areas. Sister Fotenia Katherine Spilchak and Sister Andronica Anne Spilchak successfully completed a four-summer Institute in Food

Service Management at the University of St Louis, Missouri; the sisters in charge of Marydale, a centre for the treatment of emotionally disturbed children that had been opened in Edmonton in 1963, were enrolled in institutes of child care at St Louis; others came to St Michael's College, University of Toronto, to participate in Institutional Food Services seminars, in institutes of sacred scripture, theology, and modern catechetics, especially the Canadian Catechism (commonly called the Come to the Father Programme), developed in the 1960s on the basis of the theology of the renewal and contemporary educational processes. To this latter programme the Sisters Servants were making a unique contribution; upon request from the National Office of Religious Education, Ottawa, in 1970, they were engaged in the revision of the entire catechism series, notably by acting as consultants on matters pertaining to the Eastern rite.

There were other areas where the sisters were moving outward to share their knowledge and experience. In January 1965, at the request of Bishop Andrew Roborecki, Sister Nestor Kyba was released from her duties in the institute's own hospital to become a temporary administrator of the diocesan St Joseph's Home for the Aged at Saskatoon. Four years later Sister Nestor, then administrator of St Paul's Nursing Home, Dauphin, Manitoba, was one of four nursing home administrators selected by the Canadian Welfare Council in Ottawa to represent Manitoba at a national seminar in Montreal.

In that same year, 1969, several significant assignments were undertaken by the sisters, and appointments accepted. In Toronto Sister Marion Zerebesky presented a paper on the philosophy and psychology of the Montessori Method to a group of supervisors, inspectors, superintendents, and university personnel at York University. At Yorkton Sister Ambrose Stachiw, chairman of the Inservice Committee for Teachers of Religion, organized an evening course for adults; Sister Mechtilde Byblow and Sister Dominic Slawuta lectured in school library services and history, respectively, at St Joseph's College University Division; moreover, in March 1970 Sister Mechtilde was appointed as one of the nine members of the English Evaluating Committee for Library Resources by the provincial supervisor of school libraries. At Ottawa Sister Cassianna Slywka was a lecturer at the Ukrainian Catholic Youth Leadership Seminar. In Saskatoon Sister Christine Opalinsky joined the staff of the Separate School Board as a supervisor in religion. Thus their apostolic works remained basically unchanged, but a fresh concept of self-giving had been introduced into their form of service.

An outline of the Sisters Servants' contribution in Canada was sketched by Sister Frances for a distinguished guest, Josyf Cardinal Slipyj, during an historic visit to the provincialate on June 15, 1968. Cardinal Slipyj, the sole survivor of all of the Ukrainian Catholic bishops who had been imprisoned in the Soviet Union, had been released from captivity in 1963, upon the intercession of Pope John XXIII, after spending eighteen years in Soviet labour camps. In December of the same year the Sacred Oriental Congregation had declared that this metropolitan of Lviv was to be regarded as Major Archbishop. Then on February 22, 1965, Pope Paul VI officially created him a cardinal – the first for Ukrainians in seventy years.

Needless to say, the cardinal's reception upon his arrival at Toronto International Airport on June 14, 1968, was tumultuous. A mood of respect, awe, and even downright adulation emerged unmistakably amidst the pressing crowds who greeted his appearance with thunderous applause. And that was only the beginning; in the receptions and gatherings that followed leaders of a multitude of Ukrainian organizations vied with each other in heaping praise upon this distinguished churchman. All in all, it was perhaps the most lavish personal tribute ever accorded a Ukrainian church leader in Canada.

Amid a hectic round of official functions, Cardinal Slipyj found time to meet with the Sisters Servants at 5 Austin Terrace, and to acknowledge Sister Frances' greeting on behalf of her fellow sisters: 'Placed by Divine Providence in twenty-four missions across Canada, the Sisters Servants today rejoice in the visit of your esteemed person to the adopted land of our fathers, the Ukrainian Canadian pioneers.' Then, in a statistical summary, she presented the cardinal with a picture of the apostolic work of sisters in this country during the year just past, 1967: '2,340 children in day schools; 1,959 in Ukrainian courses; 328 in music schools; 4,057 in catechetical classes; 1,752 prepared for their first Holy Communion; 1,447 nursed in our hospitals; 172 cared for in homes for the aged; 149 in children's homes; approximately 1,000 in youth organizations; 58 prepared for the Sacrament of the Sick; 17 prepared for baptism; 1,599 sick persons visited in their homes or in hospitals; food and clothing provided for 2,152 needy persons; responsibility for 31 church sanctuaries and sacristies.' In her closing remarks the provincial superior said: 'I do not emphasize this service to praise ourselves but to demonstrate our desire to respond to the needs of our people in this country. When you, our Major Archbishop, will celebrate the Divine Liturgy in the chapel of this provincial house, the collective apostolate of the Canadian Sisters Servants will constitute our offering at this Eucharistic sacrifice.'[38]

That the cardinal should manifest a genuine interest in their apostolate was not surprising, but, like most ecclesiastical superiors, he was also concerned that a real spirituality should animate it. For that matter, so were the institute's major superiors, since at the moment the Church was struggling through a troubled mid-passage punctuated by defections among the secular clergy and religious men and women, and a loss of faith among the laity. Moreover, religious themselves were becoming deeply apprehensive about widely publicized statements of priests and sisters concerning the ills they claimed were affecting their institutes.

Understandably, the existing confusion in religious circles was bound to affect and, in many cases, blight the religious vocation of some of their most promising young members. For, battered by doubts about the relevancy of religious life to contemporary society, worried about what their personal role as religious in the current scene should be, and unnerved by the uncertainty in which the entire Church seemed to have been trapped, sisters from orders and congregations in all parts of the country – including Sisters Servants – were reverting to the lay state. At the same time, new vocations were dropping to their lowest point yet.

Actually, the Sisters Servants had begun a programme of spiritual renewal and apostolic preparation for their temporary professed sisters in 1964. In July of that year a staff of Sisters Servants and priests had organized and directed a programme consisting of lectures, conferences, discussion groups, and workshops for thirty-two junior sisters at Mount Mary Novitiate, Ancaster. From 1966 these sisters participated in summer renewal programmes organized at Ottawa for young members of all religious congregations of women. There were few Sisters Servants in all age groups, however, who did not recognize that, perhaps more than ever before, the world had great need of the worshipful heart of a St Benedict, the infectious joy of a St Francis, the concern for the poor of a St Charles de Foucauld, the merry zeal for life of a St Philip Neri, the flaming love of a St Teresa of Avila – the kinds of religious values that are nourished by a real personal relationship with God. This was in fact the form of renewal advocated by Vatican II. And the most natural response to the Council's signals that this was indeed the way was a movement initiated by members of the Society of Jesus at the Guelph Centre of Practical Asceticism. In May 1969 these priests offered a seven-week course (which included a thirty-day spiritual retreat) specifically designed for sisters responsible for the spiritual guidance of young religious. It was their belief that modern ascetical theory and experience would enable a sister to make correct spiritual discernment in her own life and in the lives of those whom she would guide. They therefore hoped that their programme would correct the imbalance or lack of integration in individual religious between academic learning and authentic prayer experiences, which they considered to be the fundamental problem underlying the current tension-filled religious upheaval and intensifying all questions on religious life.[39]

Little did the first Sister Servant to register for the course, Sister Justine Kowal, dream that from May to September 1970 fifty-nine sisters would follow her example to devote thirty days to prayer. But it was Sister Frances who publicly gave voice to their gratitude for the unique experience of being personally guided through the Spiritual Exercises of St Ignatius when she wrote to the sisters of the province on October 14: 'Words fail me to communicate the gratitude of these sisters, contained in their "thank you's" for the opportunity to make this retreat. Nothing happens without God and in His loving providence He provided this for our Community.'[40]

One final significant event welcomed by the sisters before the decade of Vatican II ended was the official announcement of a new provincial council on December 31. Appointed to guide them for the next five years were Sister Justine Kowal, provincial superior, Sister Ambrose Stachiw, Sister Frances Byblow, Sister Ruth Yakimyshyn, and Sister Celestine Lozinsky. Thus, on New Year's Eve, together with their new leadership, they looked forward to the 1970s and beyond as a time when, hopefully, the spiritual renewal begun by the Council would become a reality in the Christian community.

*   *   *

God uses men when men are willing to be used. And He had permitted that Sisters Servants – past and present – would give of their vision, their energy, and their labour to men, women, and children on this continent. The seed of this challenge was firmly planted by Sister Ambrose and her small missionary band when they detrained at Edmonton on a crisp November night at the dawn of the century. From that moment, as Sisters Servants have continued to make common cause with the Church in this land, their love has spoken with many voices, but service has been its common tongue.

Notes

Abbreviations of the archives containing documents consulted

Archives of the Apostolic Delegation, Ottawa	**AADO**
Archives of the Archdiocese of Edmonton	**AAE**
Archives of the Archdiocese of St Boniface	**AASB**
Archives of the Ukrainian Archeparchy of Winnipeg	**AUAW**
Archives of the Basilian Fathers, Grimsby	**ABFG**
Archives of the Basilian Fathers, Mundare	**ABFM**
Archives of the Brothers of the Christian Schools, Yorkton	**ABCSY**
Archives of the Sisters Servants, Philadelphia	**ASSP**
Archives of the Sisters Servants, Rome	**ASSR**
Oblate Archives, Edmonton	**OAE**
Oblate Archives, Ottawa	**OAO**
Provincial Archives, Regina	**PAS**
Provincial Archives, Toronto	**PAO**
Public Archives of Canada, Ottawa	**PAC**

1 *A time to be born . . .*

1 'Ukraine, located in a strategic position north of the Black Sea in Europe on the cross-roads to Asia, encompasses a vast territory of some 250,000,000 acres, being larger than Germany or France. The Ukrainian population on the ethnographic territories in Europe comprises about 38,000,000, which is larger than the French or English populations in Europe. Her natural resources and production in agriculture and industry make Ukraine one of the wealthiest countries on the European continent. The Ukrainians are a distinct nation, with their own separate language and culture. They should not be regarded or classified as Russians, any more than the Scots and Irish as English.
  'In the past, Ukraine was once an empire and an independent state. Today she is designated as the Ukrainian Soviet Socialist Republic, being an integral part of the Union of Soviet Socialist Republics. The U.S.S.R., the successor of the Russian empire ruled by the tsars, conquered the Ukrainian National Republic after the First World War and has continued the Russian domination and exploitation of Ukraine by force, as well as of numerous other nations and countries ... There are some 11,000,000 Ukrainians outside the border of their homeland, being scattered throughout the world ... About 1,500,000 of Ukrainian descendants live in the United States of America. Over a half-million are a dynamic part of the population of Canada, where they have made significant contributions to the economy, political administration and the whole life of the country.' Senator Paul Yuzyk, *Ukrainian Canadians: Their Place and Role in Canadian Life* (Toronto: Ukrainian Canadian Business and Professional Federation, 1967), pp. 99–100. For a brief historical survey of Ukraine, see Appendix A, pp. 321–2.
2 See A. Welykyj, OSBM, *Istoria Sester Sluzhebnyts / History of the Sisters Servants of Mary Immaculate* (Rome, 1968), pp. 593–4.
3 See Ostrohirka (pseud.), 'Zolotyi Yuviley Z'hromadzhennia Sester Sluzhebnyts, 1892–1942,' / 'The Golden Jubilee of the Sisters Servants of Mary Immaculate, 1892–1942,' in *Kalendar Ukrainskoi rodyny na rik 1942 / Calendar of the Ukrainian Family for the Year 1942* (Mundare: Basilian Press, 1942), p. 41.
4 *Ibid.*, p. 43.
5 'Rite' means more than liturgical customs; it can be referred to as a community that has its own identity, its own practices, customs, and discipline. Cf. *Decree on the Eastern Catholic Churches.*
6 See G. Luzhnytsky, *Ukrainian Church between East and West* (Philadelphia: 'Providence' Association of Ukrainian Catholics, 1954), pp. 526–9.
7 J. Lomnitsky, *Bohoslovskyi Vistnyk / Theological Herald*, III, 3 (Lviv, 1902), pp. 285–92, quoted in D. Tkachuk, 'Hto zasnuvav Z'hromadzhennia Sester Sluzhebnyts Neprochnoho Zachatia Prech. Divy Marii?' / 'Who Founded the Congregation of Sisters Servants of Mary Immaculate?' in *Dobryi Pastyr / The Good Shepherd*, no 1 (Stanislaviv, 1933), p. 169.
8 Rev. Jeremias John Lomnitsky was born in western Ukraine on Feb. 8, 1860; he entered the Order of St Basil the Great on Sept. 28, 1882, and was ordained on Jan. 17, 1886. He was deported to Russia on Feb. 5, 1915, and died in Sambirsk on July 3, 1915.
9 Tkachuk, p. 168.
10 Luzhnytsky, pp. 526–7.
11 Tkachuk, p. 167. Father Tkachuk names the three Basilian priests who accompanied Father Lomnitsky to the Zhuzhyl mission as Rev. V. Kulyk, Rev. M. Hmilewsky, and Rev. I. Tysowsky. Rev. Cyril Siletsky was born on March 24, 1835, and died on April 28, 1918.
12 Galicia is a province of western Ukraine; although the accepted English geographical

name for this territory is 'Galicia,' its Ukrainian form in transliteration is 'Halychyna' (see Appendix A, pp. 321–2). For a description of Zhuzhyl, see S. Bachtalowsky, 'Zhuzhyl: Spomyny z misii / 'Zhuzhyl: Memoirs of a Mission,' in *Yuvileyna knyha Sester Sluzhebnyts, 1892–1942 / Jubilee Book of the Sisters Servants of Mary Immaculate, 1892–1942* (Edmonton, 1942), pp. 72–3. Regarding the Byzantine heritage, one of the most important non-Slavic components of early Ukrainian culture, see I. Ševčenko, 'Byzantine Elements,' *Ukraine: A Concise Encyclopaedia*, ed. Volodymyr Kubijovyč (Toronto: University of Toronto Press, 1963), I, 933–5: 'The first precise reference to the spread of Byzantine Christianity among the "Rus" was made by Patriarch Photius (867). Thus it dates from the greatest period of Byzantine missionary activity. The decisive step, however, was taken by Prince Volodymyr (Vladimir) only a century later (988 or 989).

'By adopting Christianity and marrying Anna, the sister of Emperor Basil II ... Prince Volodymyr became a member of the Byzantine imperial family, and his land was included in the ideal Byzantine family of states ...

'The first churches were built after Byzantine models, initially by imported architects, later by local masters carrying on the Byzantine tradition. The interior decoration of the early churches not only duplicated Byzantine religious iconography and displayed Greek explanatory inscription, but also was inspired by Byzantine imperial imagery (for example, the Hippodrome frescoes in the St. Sophia Cathedral of Kiev) ...

'The later political fate of the Ukrainian lands, which fell first under the domination of Lithuania and later under that of Poland, laid them open to western cultural influences. However, it would be an error to underestimate the survival of "Byzantium after Byzantium" in Ukraine.'

13 Tkachuk, p. 167.
14 *Ibid.*, p. 169.
15 'Provincial Chronicle SSMI: History of the Congregaton, 1902–37,' I, 11. Most of the period 1902–36 in this chronicle was written after 1936 when the original was taken to Europe by Sr Veronica Gargil during her first visitation to Canada.
16 The constitutions of any religious institute 'is a set of laws or directives, made and approved by legitimate authority, by which the life of an institute is regulated. The terms "rule" and "constitutions" are often used one for the other.' F. Geser, OSB, *The Canon Law Governing Communities of Sisters* (St Louis: B. Herder Book Co., 1947), Canon 82. For verification of the fact that it was Father Lomnitsky and not Father Siletsky who presented the constitutions for approval, see Tkachuk, p. 171.
17 Two bills introduced in the Austro-Hungarian parliament in Jan. 1874 dealt with the legal status of monasteries and the recognition of new religious societies. The Pope, on March 7, expressed his grief at the assertion in these bills that the supreme power in all matters concerning the external life of the Church belonged to the state. It was in view of these powers assumed by the government that state authorization to erect the new institute had to be obtained. See C. Wolfgruber, 'The Austro-Hungarian Monarchy,' *Catholic Encyclopedia*, vol. II.
18 Tkachuk, p. 171.
19 *Ibid.*, p. 170.
20 This situation was discussed at the Provincial Synod held in Lviv on Sept. 24, 1891. See Luzhnytsky, pp. 528–9.
21 *Jubilee Memoir 1902–1952: Sisters Servants of Mary Immaculate* (New York, 1952), p. 61.
22 Tkachuk, p. 171.
23 See E. Vytanovych, 'Galicia,' and S. Vytvytsky and S. Baran, 'Western Ukraine under Poland,' in Kubijovyč, I, 698–707, 833–47.
24 Tkachuk, p. 172.
25 One opinion in articles discussing the question of who designed the original garb is that Sr Josaphata did so in cooperation with Father Lomnitsky. See Tkachuk, p. 171, and *Jubilee Book SSMI*, p. 55.
26 See 'Customs of the Sisters Servants of the Province of Christ the King: the Habit,' pp. 38–9, a mimeographed booklet containing customs and directives which were observed in the congregation from the first general chapter held in Lviv on July 4–5, 1934, until

they were replaced by the customs adopted at the second general chapter held in Rome on Sept. 8–15, 1956.

27 'Provincial Chronicle SSMI,' I, 14.

28 *Ibid.,* p. 13.

29 Tkachuk, p. 170. The substantial cash amount was eventually raised through an appeal backed by Father Siletsky and carried out by the Basilian Fathers; fortunately, it met with a generous response that provided the partial cash payment for the house.

30 This is the date now accepted by the institute. See *Katalyog Z'hromadzhennia Sester Sluzhebnyts na 1965 rik / Catalogue of the Sisters Servants of Mary Immaculate for the Year 1965* (Rome, 1965), p. 5. Former community publications cited two differing dates: 'Finally an unforgettable day arrived: August 28, 1892 – the official birthday of the Congregation of Sisters Servants.' *Jubilee Book SSMI,* p. 56. 'The Congregation of Sisters Servants of Mary Immaculate, which had done so much for the glory of God and the religious enhancement of our people, was founded on the feast of the Assumption, August 15, 1892.' *Jubilee Memoir SSMI,* p. 61.

31 'Provincial Chronicle SSMI,' I, 15.

32 Father Lomnitsky was absent from the afternoon ceremonies because he had suddenly been called away by an urgent telegram sent by his major superior, Rev. G. Schepkowski. See Tkachuk, p. 172.

33 The following girls formed that first significant group of nine: Sr Josaphata Michaeline Hordashewsky (Lviv); Anne Kiselyk (Seblova); Maria Sendetsky (Seblova); Anne Muzyka (Zhuzhyl); Teklia Polikha (Zhuzhyl); Maria Zinko (Zhuzhyl); Pelagia Karaban (Zhuzhyl); Teklia Dudrak (Zhuzhyl); Theodosia Melnyk (Zhuzhyl). See 'Provincial Chronicle SSMI,' I, 16.

34 *Ibid.,* p. 17.

35 The full names of these sisters now were: Sr Eusebia Anne Kiselyk; Sr Melanie Maria Sendetsky; Sr Alexandra Anne Muzyka; Sr Eudoxia Teklia Polikha; Sr Paraskevia Pelagia Karaban; Sr Macrina Maria Zinko; Sr Theophilia Teklia Dudrak; Sr Anastasia Anne Melnyk; Sr Athanasia Theodosia Melnyk; Sr Arsenia Anne Hordashewsky.

36 Based on an interview with Mrs Anne Lopechuk of Toronto, a former member of the institute who worked in the nurseries of the congregation in Ukraine until 1922, and who had witnessed their development from the earliest beginnings.

37 Tkachuk, p. 173.

38 *Ibid.,* pp. 172–3.

39 *Catalogue SSMI 1965,* pp. 29–32.

40 'Provincial Chronicle SSMI,' I, 22.

41 *Ibid.,* p. 23.

42 *Ibid.,* p. 21.

43 'Moleben' is a short and popular paraliturgical service, usually in honour of Christ, the Virgin, or the saints.

44 'Provincial Chronicle SSMI,' I, 18–19.

45 *Ibid.,* p. 20.

46 Tkachuk, pp. 179–80.

47 *Jubilee Book SSMI,* p. 63.

48 *Catalogue SSMI 1965,* p. 10. In her office of major superior, Sr Josaphata was assisted by two councillors: Sr Constantine Sukhoversky and Sr Monica Komysh. In a letter from Metropolitan Andrew Sheptytsky, dated Oct. 22, 1902, from Lviv, to Sr Josaphata, the date Sept. 26 is given as that on which she was nominated; hence, the discrepancy in the date of her nomination in various printed articles seems to have arisen from the fact that this letter is dated Oct. 22. See the photostat copy which is reprinted in *Jubilee Memoir SSMI,* p. 66.

2   *A time to seek . . .*

1 'Ukrainskyi Yuviley' / 'Ukrainian Anniversary,' *Ukrainski Visty / Ukrainian News,* Edmonton, Jan. 26, 1967.

2 'Austria,' *The Times,* London, April 7, 1896.

3 V. J. Kaye, *Early Ukrainian Settlements in Canada 1895–1900* (Toronto: University of Toronto Press, 1964), pp. xxv–xxvi.

4 *Ibid.*, p. xxvi.

5 'Galicians and Ruthenians,' *Yorkton Enterprise*, March 18, 1915.

6 G. W. Simpson, 'The Names "Rus," "Russia," "Ukraine," and Their Historical Background,' *Slavistica*, no 10 (1951), pp. 17–18, quoted in Kaye, p. xxv.

7 G. W. Simpson, 'Foreword,' in Kaye, p. ix.

8 Letter of Dr Joseph Oleskow to the Department of the Interior in Ottawa, Lemberg, Austria, March 16, 1895. File no 1 Oles., PAC, also quoted in Kaye, pp. 3–4.

9 Canada, House of Commons, *Debates*, LVII, April 29, 1902, 'Immigration Act', pp. 3739–41.

10 Canada, *Sessional Papers*, XXXIV, no 10, 1900, Paper no 13, Report no 2: W. T. R. Preston, inspector of agencies in Europe, to Lord Strathcona, Dec. 23, 1899, pp. 12–13.

11 *Regina Leader-Post*, Sept. 13, 1951.

12 The three phases of Ukrainian immigration were: 1891–1914; 1922–45; and 1947–65. See V. J. Kaye, 'Three Phases of Ukrainian Immigration,' *Slavs in Canada*, Proceedings of the First National Conference on Canadian Slavs, Inter-University Committee on Canadian Slavs (Edmonton, 1966), pp. 171 ff.

13 Report to W. D. Scott, superintendent of immigration, Ottawa, Nov. 20, 1903, quoted in Kaye, *Early Ukrainian Settlements*, p. 276.

14 Report to Frank Pedley, superintendent of immigration, Ottawa, Jan. 31, 1899, quoted in Kaye, *Early Ukrainian Settlements*, pp. 298–9.

15 B. N. Bilash, 'Bilingual Public Schools in Manitoba 1897–1916,' unpublished MA thesis, Department of Education, University of Manitoba, 1960, p. 98.

16 J. S. Woodsworth, *Strangers within Our Gates* (Toronto, 1909), p. 287.

17 Kaye, 'Three Phases.' Also, in a mimeographed article dated 1966, entitled '75th Anniversary of Ukrainian Settlement in Canada,' Senator Paul Yuzyk gives the following statistics under the sub-title, 'Achievements in Canadian Politics': 'To date there have been 63 Ukrainian members of the provincial Legislative Assemblies, some having been re-elected many times, and four of whom have served as cabinet ministers ... Of the 63 provincial members, 20 were in the Alberta Legislative Assembly, 11 in Saskatchewan, 30 in Manitoba and 2 in Ontario ... Representation of Ukrainians in federal politics was not achieved until 1925, when Michael Luchkowich, American-born teacher, was elected in Alberta. Since that time 13 Ukrainians have served in the House of Commons, one of whom, Michael Starr, former mayor and businessman of Oshawa, Ontario, served as Minister of Labour from 1957 to 1963 in the Conservative Government of Prime Minister John G. Diefenbaker. There have been 3 members of the Canadian Senate appointed for life, the first being Wm. M. Wall (Wolachatiuk), a High School principal of Winnipeg (1955–1962), the next John Hnatyshyn, a barrister of Saskatoon, and myself (Paul Yuzyk, professor of history, Winnipeg).' See also Yuzyk, *Ukrainian Canadians: Their Place and Role in Canadian Life*, pp. 25–31. Note: Lieutenant Governor Stephen Worobets became the first citizen of Ukrainian origin to be named to this position in the Commonwealth.

18 J. T. M. Anderson, *The Education of the New Canadian: A Treatise on Canada's Greatest Educational Problem* (Toronto: J. M. Dent & Sons, Ltd., 1918), p. 53.

19 *Svoboda* was the first Ukrainian national newspaper in the United States. It was published weekly at Jersey City, NJ, until May 28, 1895, then in Shamokin, Pa., until Aug. 27, 1896, and since then in Mount Carmel, Pa. Since at the turn of the century Canada did not have a similar publication, many Canadians were subscribers of, and contributors to, that newspaper.

20 M. Prots, 'Correspondence: from Yorkton, Assa., Canada,' *Svoboda*, Jan. 17, 1901.

21 M. Wysochynski, 'Correspondence: from Stuartburn, Man., Canada,' *Svoboda*, Feb. 21, 1901.

22 M. Prots, 'Correspondence.'

23 Letter of Archbishop A. Langevin to Rev. Picard, superior of the Assumptionist Order, St Boniface, July 30, 1901, OAE.

24 Actually, however, the roots of the Ukrainian Catholic Church's affiliation to the Holy See ran deep, for even as early as the year 1253 Pope Innocent IV, through his papal

legate, presented the royal crown to the Ukrainian prince, Daniel Romanovych, for his coronation as King of Halych and Volodymyr. See V. Kisilewsky, 'Ukrainian National Revival in Austria 1772–1848,' unpublished PH D thesis, School of Slavonic and East European Studies, University of London, May 1936, p. 3; also A. M. Ammann, SJ, *Storia della Chiesa Russa e dei paesi limitrofi* (Torino, 1948), p. 47.

25 Cf. *Decree on Eastern Catholic Churches*, and the *Decree on Ecumenism*, Art. 15, 16, 17.

26 'The Church Slavonic language (imported to *Rus'* mainly from the Balkans) had acquired much of its specific character in the process of the translation from Greek texts. It teems with direct borrowings from Greek and with Byzantine loan translations (*calques*) in its vocabulary, phraseology, and syntax.' I. Ševčenko, 'Language,' in Kubijovyč, p. 935.

27 See P. Yuzyk, 'The History of the Ukrainian Greek Catholic (Uniate) Church in Canada,' unpublished MA thesis, Department of History, University of Saskatchewan, 1948, p. 22.

28 'This area [Galicia], once purely Ukrainian, was influenced by centuries-long Polish rule and relinquished its upper classes who, with a few exceptions, submitted to Polonization.' Kubijovyč, p. 241.

29 ' "Polonization" was the consistent policy of the Polish kings, the nobles, and the government officials to make Poles out of the Ukrainians. "Polonized" Ukrainians generally renounced their original nationality, the Ukrainian Church, the Ukrainian customs and adopted the Polish language, the Roman Catholic Church, and Polish customs. In many cases they proved to be worse oppressors of the Ukrainians than the Poles themselves.' Yuzyk, 'History,' p. 19, n 1. 'For the masses who were born in the Uniate Church, the faith became a national Ukrainian religion. The Eastern rite was maintained stubbornly as a separate hierarchy, differing from the Orthodox and the Latin forms.' *Ibid.*, p. 28.

30 The situation in Canada in regard to the schism prompted Metropolitan A. Sheptytsky to write his first pastoral letter to the Ukrainians in Canada from Lviv, dated Aug. 25, 1901, in which he set down some of the fundamental teachings of the Catholic Church, and endeavoured to assist them in recognizing those who might try to lead them into schism. In an emphatic statement he pleaded: 'Therefore, this is my first piece of advice and my foremost plea to you: hold fast to your holy faith, cherish it above life itself.' One copy of this letter is preserved in the ABFM. Of the clergymen endeavouring to make converts among the immigrants, 'the most popular were the Russian missionaries who demanded no fee for their duties. The employment of these various clergymen caused bickering, quarreling, and dissension among the Ukrainian colonists. Several factions immediately emerged: some wanted a "Ruthenian Independent Church"; some sided with the Orthodox Church; others became adherents of Roman Catholicism; still others advocated Protestantism and there also appeared an anti-clerical group with atheistic tendencies who called themselves "socialists" or "radicals." Similar situations developed in other Ukrainian settlements throughout western Canada. This break-down into hostile factions became typical of Ukrainian life in Canada for the next two decades. The religious differences were carried over into social and political affairs.' *Ibid.*, p. 51.

31 C. Genik, 'A Voice from Canada,' *Svoboda*, March 20, 1902.

32 Rev. A. Lacombe to Archbishop A. Langevin, Calgary, March 14, 1901, AASB.

33 Report of Archbishop Langevin to the Congregation of Oblates, St Boniface, July 20, 1901, AASB.

34 For a more complete account of Bishop Pascal's efforts in Vienna and Rome, see *Propamiatna knyha Otsiw Vasylian v Kanadi / Jubilee Book of the Basilian Fathers in Canada* (Toronto: Basilian Press, 1953), pp. 99–100.

35 Rev. N. Dmytriw who came to Canada from the United States in 1897 and served as an immigration agent for the Canadian Department of the Interior, performed his priestly ministry among the settlers whenever he was able to visit a colony until Aug. 1898, when he again returned to the United States. Then Rev. P. Tymkewich arrived in Edmonton on April 8, 1898, and served the people of this area for six months before he departed for the United States; in July 1900 Rev. M. Zacklinski began his ministry

in the same area. See Bishop E. Legal, *Short Sketches of the History of the Catholic Churches and Missions in Central Alberta* (Edmonton, 1914), p. 123, OAE.
36 Rev. A. Jan, OMI, to Rev. Augier, OMI, superior general, Lemberg, July 30, 1902, OAE.
37 Archbishop Langevin to Bishop V. Grandin, St Boniface, Jan. 7, 1899, OAE.
38 During Father Lacombe's trip to Austria in 1900 he was the guest of Countess Zichy (née Metternich) while in Vienna. See K. Hughes, *Father Lacombe: The Black Robe Voyageur* (New York: Moffat, Yard and Company, 1911), p. 402.
39 Rev. A. Lacombe, 'Voyage en Autriche : Mémoires du Rév. Père Lacombe, 1900,' entry for June 28, 1900, OAE.
40 See Hughes, pp. 400–1.
41 *Ibid.*, p. 401. See also letter of Father Lacombe to Archbishop Langevin, Vienna, Sept. 14, 1900, AASB.
42 Father Lacombe to Archbishop Langevin, Paris, Oct. 4, 1900, AASB.
43 Metropolitan A. Sheptytsky to Father Lacombe, Leopol, Sept. 11, 1901, OAE.
44 Archbishop Langevin to Metropolitan Sheptytsky, St Boniface, Feb. 20, 1902, AASB.
45 C. Genik, *Svoboda*, March 20, 1902.
46 Rev. B. Zholdak to Archbishop Langevin, Brandon, Man., Dec. 25, 1901, AASB.
47 Bishop Grandin had died on June 11, 1902, and Bishop Legal had just succeeded him to the see of St Albert.
48 J. Le Chevallier, 'Notice sur le R. P. Alphonse Jan, OMI, missionnaire dans la province d'Alberta-Saskatchewan,' OAE.
49 Bishop E. Legal, 'Journal 1897–1910,' entry for Jan. 30, 1901, File D-I-600, OAE.
50 *Ibid.*, entries for May 3 and July 16, 1901. Throughout the years, the bishop's paternal interest and all-inclusive charity were gratefully acknowledged by those who, having been a part of that group, retained vivid recollections of the joy occasioned by his presence at these functions. See also Le Chevallier, 'Notice.'
51 The first two members of the club to become postulants in the institute were Mary Letawsky (Sr Taida), and Pelagia Tymochko (Sr Josaphata); they entered the congregation in 1903.
52 Le Chevallier, 'Notice.'
53 Father Jan to Father Augier, Lviv, 1902, OAE.
54 Le Chevallier, 'Notice.'
55 Rev. B. Zholdak to Father Lacombe, Lviv, n.d., 1902, OAE.
56 Father Zholdak to Father Lacombe, Lviv, Sept. 14, 1902, OAE.
57 'Provincial Chronicle SSMI,' I, 44.
58 The fact that the missionaries were leaving at the specific request of Metropolitan Sheptytsky is verified in a letter of Archbishop D. Falconio, apostolic delegate to Canada, to Cardinal Gotti, prefect of the Sacred Congregation for the Propagation of the Faith, Ottawa, Oct. 28, 1902, no 1610: 'It is a pleasure for me to inform you about the arrival to this capital of four monks of the reformed Basilian Order, one diocesan priest, and four Sisters Servants of Mary Immaculate, all of the Greek-Ruthenian rite, who arrived from Galicia for missionary work in Manitoba and in the Northwest Territories, at the request of His Excellency, Very Rev. A. Sheptytsky, archbishop of Lviv.' Quoted in G. Mojoli, 'Pryizd pershykh Vasylian do Kanady v svitli documentiv' / 'The Arrival of the First Basilians to Canada in the Light of Documentation,' *Jubilee Book OSBM*, p. 69.

3   *A time to plant ...*

1 The date accepted here is that given by Rev. P. Filas in the 'Chronicle of the Basilian Fathers [1902–12],' I, ABFM.
2 Sr Ambrose Lenkewich was born on Jan. 18, 1876; and Sr Emilia Klapowchuk on July 18, 1882.
3 Taida M. Letawsky, SSMI, 'Nashi pochatky v Kanadi' / 'Our Beginnings in Canada,' personal memoirs taped in Edmonton in 1962. The information regarding Sr Taida Wrublewsky's background is also based upon an interview by the author with Sr Taida Letawsky – the institute's first Canadian postulant – at Philadelphia in July 1966.

4 See 'Chronicle of the Basilian Fathers,' I.

5 *Ibid.*

6 See Rev. S. Dydyk, OSBM, 'Memoirs,' in *Svitlo / The Light*, trans. Rev. J. Skwarok, OSBM (Toronto: Basilian Press, Jan. 1959).

7 Ambrose M. Lenkewich, SSMI, 'Z nashykh pochatkiv u Kanadi' / 'Our Beginnings in Canada,' *Kalendar Ukrainskoi rodyny na rik 1942 / Calendar of the Ukrainian Family for the Year 1942* (Mundare: Basilian Press, 1942), pp. 58–60.

8 Rev. B. Zholdak to Rev. A. Lacombe, Lviv, Sept. 14, 1902, AAE. The sisters were under the impression that the religious with whom they had resided in New York had obtained the reductions. See Lenkewich, 'Our Beginnings.'

9 Since the date of this visit varies in each of the memoirs written by the missionaries themselves, an accurate date has been difficult to establish. However, on Oct. 28 and 29, 1902, Archbishop D. Falconio, apostolic delegate, notified Cardinals Rampolla and Gotti in Rome and Bishop E. Legal at St Albert that they had arrived and had visited him in Ottawa. See 'Letter Book of Archbishop D. Falconio, 1899–1902,' entries numbered 1609, 1610, 1611, AADO.

10 Archbishop A. Langevin to Metropolitan A. Sheptytsky, Montreal, Oct. 25, 1902, AASB.

11 Archbishop Langevin to Bishop Legal, Montreal, Oct. 25, 1902, AASB.

12 Dydyk, 'Memoirs,' Jan. 1959.

13 'Chronicle of the Basilian Fathers,' I.

14 'Strathcona,' *Edmonton Journal*, Feb. 7, 1902. For the date of the missionaries' arrival in Edmonton, see *In Tribute to the Basilian Pioneers* (Mundare: Basilian Press, 1963), p. 39. However, other sources claim that the date was Sat., Oct. 31, 1902. See *Jubilee Book OSBM*, pp. 85–6.

15 See Dydyk, 'Memoirs,' Feb. 1959.

16 Father Zholdak to Bishop Legal, Lemberg, Aug. 1902, AAE.

17 Bishop Legal to Father Lacombe, St Albert, Oct. 2, 1902, OAE.

18 Legal, 'Journal 1897–1910,' entry for Nov. 1, 1902.

19 See Lenkewich, p. 58.

20 *Ibid.*

21 'Arrival of Missionaries,' *Edmonton Bulletin*, Nov. 3, 1902.

22 Bishop Legal is referring to ten Sisters of Kamaria who were sent to Canada from France at the request of Rev. A. Jan, and accompanied him to Edmonton on his return trip from Austria. They arrived in Edmonton on Oct. 21, 1902. See Le Chevallier, 'Notice sur le R. P. Jan.'

23 Legal, 'Journal,' entry for Nov. 1, 1902.

24 *Ibid.*

25 *Ibid.*, Nov. 3, 1902.

26 The initials stand for 'Christian Mutual Benefit Association.' It seems that this association had a hall which was used for various town functions.

27 *Edmonton Bulletin*, Nov. 3, 1902.

28 Legal, 'Journal,' entry for Nov. 5, 1902.

29 Rev. H. Leduc, OMI, to Father Lacombe, Edmonton, Nov. 10, 1902, OAE.

30 'Provincial Chronicle SSMI,' I, 50.

31 Bishop Legal to Father Lacombe, St Albert, Nov. 14, 1902, OAE.

32 See Lenkewich, p. 59.

33 Legal, 'Journal,' entries for Dec. 1 and 2, 1902.

34 Bishop Legal to Father Lacombe, St Albert, Dec. 22, 1902, OAE.

35 See 'Chronicle of the Basilian Fathers,' I.

36 Legal, 'Journal,' entry for May 23, 1903.

37 Rev. H. Leduc to Father Lacombe, May 25, 1903, OAE.

38 Legal, 'Journal,' entry for May 25, 1903.

39 See M. H. Marunchak, *V Zustrichi z ukrainskymy pioneramy Alberty / Among Ukrainian Pioneers of Alberta* (2nd ed., Winnipeg, 1965), p. 23.

40 See 'Provincial Chronicle SSMI,' I, 53.

41 Rev. P. Filas to Bishop Legal, Beaver Lake, July 15, 1903, AAE.

42 Dydyk, 'Memoirs,' Feb. 1959.

43 See letter of Father Filas to Bishop Legal, Beaver Lake, Aug. 10, 1903, AAE.

44 Interview with Sr Taida Letawsky; see also Lenkewich, p. 59.
45 'Provincial Chronicle SSMI,' I, 53.
46 Interview with Sr Taida Letawsky.
47 Interview with Sr Augustina Hawryliuk, who entered the congregation in 1906, in Vegreville, Alta., Oct. 1966.
48 Lenkewich, p. 60.
49 *Ibid.*
50 *Ibid.*
51 Letawsky, 'Our Beginnings in Canada.'
52 *Ibid.*
53 *Ibid.*
54 Legal, 'Journal,' entry for Aug. 30, 1903.
55 Interview with Sr Taida Letawsky.
56 Legal, 'Journal,' entry for Aug. 31, 1903.
57 Letawsky, 'Our Beginnings in Canada.'
58 'Provincial Chronicle SSMI,' I, 53.
59 See Archbishop Langevin to Cardinal Gotti, prefect of the Sacred Congregation for the Propagation of the Faith, St Boniface, Dec. 8, 1903, AASB.
60 Based on interviews with Sr Taida Letawsky, Sr Augustina Hawryliuk, and Sr Suzanne Starko.
61 *Ibid.*

4   *A time to grow ...*

1 See B. Meyers, *Sisters for the 21st Century* (New York: Sheed and Ward Inc., 1965), chap. 2.
2 'Education: Teacher Training,' *Encyclopedia of Canada*, vol. II.
3 M. R. Lupul, 'Relations in Education between the State and the Roman Catholic Church in the Canadian Northwest with Special Reference to the Provisional District of Alberta from 1880–1905,' unpublished PHD thesis, Faculty of Education, Harvard University, Cambridge, Mass., June 1963, pp. 875–6. Note: 'Territories' here specifies a region having a certain degree of self-government, but not having the status of a province.
4 Archbishop A. Langevin to the Congregation of Oblates of Mary Immaculate, St Boniface, July 20, 1901, AASB.
5 Archbishop Langevin to Metropolitan A. Sheptytsky, St Boniface, Feb. 20, 1902, AASB.
6 *Ibid.*, June 20, 1902, AASB.
7 See above, chap. 3, p. 43.
8 Rev. P. Filas to Bishop E. Legal, Lemberg, April 23, 1905, OAE. The first qualified teacher, whose education through high school and the provincial Normal school was sponsored by the Sisters Servants, was Natalie Melnyk (Sr Theresa) who completed her teacher training in Calgary in 1912 and began her novitiate on Jan. 15, 1913.
9 'Edmonton Chronicle SSMI, 1902–26,' I, 8; see also pp. 7–20 for a detailed description of the sisters' varied apostolic works.
10 Legal, 'Journal 1897–1910,' entry for Jan. 11, 1904.
11 J. G. MacGregor, *Vilni Zemli (Free Lands): The Ukrainian Settlement of Alberta* (Toronto: McClelland and Stewart Ltd., 1969), pp. 211–12.
12 *Ibid.*, p. 212.
13 'Provincial Chronicle SSMI' I, 56. A discrepancy exists as to the year of this first building transaction. The provincial chronicle indicates that the school was purchased in 1905; the *Jubilee Book SSMI*, p. 84, states that it was bought in 1908.
14 Father Filas to Archbishop Langevin, Lemberg, April 17, 1905, AASB.
15 'Provincial Chronicle SSMI,' I, 70.
16 See 'Edmonton Chronicle SSMI,' I, 23–105.
17 'Provincial Chronicle SSMI,' I, 56.
18 Archbishop A. Langevin, 'Mémoire sur la situation des sujets ruthènes de la Majesté

Apostolique, l'Empereur d'Autriche, dans l'Ouest Canadien,' St Boniface, July 2, 1904, OAE.

19 Father Filas to Archbishop Langevin, Lemberg, April 17, 1905, AASB.

20 Sr Athanasia Melnyk was one of the original nine girls who entered the institute at the time of its founding in 1892. She died in Winnipeg on Aug. 6, 1967 – the year in which the congregation was observing its seventy-fifth anniversary.

21 In 1907 the sisters moved to a house on Stella Avenue; see 'Provincial Chronicle SSMI,' I, 69.

22 'Winnipeg Chronicle SSMI, 1905–39,' I, 9.

23 *Ibid.*

24 'Provincial Chronicle SSMI,' I, 62.

25 *Ibid.*, p. 63.

26 *Ibid.*

27 *Ibid.*, p. 66; see also 'Winnipeg Chronicle SSMI,' I, 10–22.

28 'Provincial Chronicle SSMI,' I, 69.

29 See 'Winnipeg Chronicle SSMI,' I, 23 ff.

30 See 'Edmonton Chronicle SSMI,' I, 23; also Legal, 'Journal,' entry for March 5, 1904. It has not been possible to determine whether this land was actually purchased by the Basilian Fathers. Some sources state that it was donated by the diocese of St Albert to the Ukrainian Catholic Mission in Edmonton; see *Jubilee Book OSBM*, p. 29.

31 Bishop Legal to Father Filas, Edmonton, Dec. 5, 1910, AAE. For details regarding this loan, refer to Bishop Legal's letter to Very Rev. A. E. Burke of the Catholic Church Extension Society in Toronto, St Albert, April 15, 1911; also Bishop Legal's letter to Bishop N. Budka, St Albert, Nov. 18, 1916, OAE.

32 Sr Josaphata Tymochko's salary was the first received by a Sister Servant from a provincial Board of Education.

33 'Winnipeg Chronicle SSMI,' I, 15.

34 *Ibid.*, p. 24.

35 See A. Sheptytsky, 'Address on the Ruthenian Question to their Lordships the Archbishops and Bishops of Canada,' Lviv, March 18, 1911, p. 5, AUAW. According to 'Report no 2: St Nicholas School,' AASB, the total cost of St Nicholas School amounted to $25,942. The fact that four lots, which were purchased for the site, together with the school building, were both paid for with money drawn from the episcopal fund has not, to this author's knowledge, been previously known. All other sources consulted claim that the entire cost was borne solely by the archdiocese of St Boniface.

36 His Excellency, Bishop Andrew Roborecki, completed his elementary school education at St Nicholas School in 1925. He was ordained a priest in 1934. He received episcopal consecration on May 27, 1948, and became auxiliary to Archbishop Basil Ladyka. On March 19, 1951, a fourth exarchate was created for the province of Saskatchewan and assigned to Bishop Roborecki.

37 A. Sheptytsky, 'Address,' pp. 5–6.

38 'Provincial Chronicle SSMI,' I, 83.

39 *Ibid.*

40 See *Constitutions SSMI, 1892*, ASSR. Part IV, Rule no 11: 'In his diocese the ordinary is the natural guardian of all the houses which are situated in it.' Part IV, Rule no 12: 'The local pastor, within the limits of his authority, is the guardian of the sisters who dwell in his parish.'

41 See Welykyj, *History of the SSMI*, pp. 149–67.

42 During a provincial chapter held by the institute in Lviv, April 20–22, 1907, new constitutions were approved to replace the original rule accepted at the time of the congregation's founding in 1892. In Canada, each mission adapted schedules of prayer and work to its own circumstances; in the area of the religious garb, a black scapular was worn instead of a blue one as in Europe; in addition, a Canadian sister received a gold ring and black cape at the time of her final profession.

43 'Winnipeg Chronicle SSMI,' I, 16–17. The first letter, signed by Sr Vladimira, secretary, announced the election of Sr Vitalia Mykush, and was received in Winnipeg on Feb. 7, 1909. The second letter, signed by Sr Vitalia, announced the appointment of Sr Ambrose Lenkewich, and was received in Winnipeg on June 8, 1909.

44 Both Sr Isidore and Sr Emilia later volunteered to work in the Brazilian mission. Here they lived and worked until their death in the same year, 1937.
45 This character sketch is based on interviews with Rev. S. Bachtalowsky, CSSR, Sr Taida Letawsky, and Sr Suzanne Starko.
46 'Rapport de la réunion de quelques prêtres du rite ruthène, a l'Archevêque de St-Boniface,' Jan. 4, 1910, p. 5, AASB.
47 *Ibid.*
48 See 'Provincial Chronicle SSMI,' I, 82–4.
49 Sheptytsky, 'Address.' This and the following quotations are from pp. 16–17.
50 *Ibid.*, p. 25.
51 *Dushpastyr / Pastor of Souls* (Lviv), Dec. 1, 1912, ABFG.
52 See A. Luhovy, *Golden Jubilee of the Ukrainian Catholic Hierarchy of Canada, 1912–1962* (Winnipeg: Progress Printing & Publishing Co. Ltd., 1962), pp. 10–12.
53 'Provincial Chronicle SSMI,' I, 94.

5   *A time to build ...*

1 A. Luhovy, *Golden Jubilee*, p. 8: 'Father A. Delaere, CSSR, of Belgian origin arrived in Canada, Sept. 28, 1899. He adopted the Ukrainian rite March 9, 1906, and dedicated himself to the spiritual needs of the Ukrainian Catholic immigrants.'
2 A. Delaere, C SS R, *Memorandum on the Attempts of Schism and Heresy Among the Ruthenians (commonly called 'Galicians') in the Canadian Northwest* (Winnipeg: West Canada Publishing Co. Ltd., 1909), pp. 37–8, AASB.
3 For the names of the sisters in the institute by 1912, see 'SSMI Provincial Entry Register' for the years 1903–12.
4 See above, chap. 4, p. 62.
5 This account is based on interviews conducted with pioneer sisters: Sr Taida Letawsky, Sr Augustina Hawryliuk, Sr Josepha Mary Bilan, and Sr Suzanne Starko; local chronicles were also used.
6 Sr Ambrose Lenkewich to Bishop N. Budka, Mundare, May 31, 1913, AUAW.
7 *Ibid.*, Oct. 17, 1913, AUAW.
8 See Lubov K. Chawrona, SSMI, 'Spomyny pro nashu pratsyu v Kanadi' / 'Memoirs of Our Missionary Work in Canada,' an article written for the SSMI provincial archives, pp. 1–3.
9 Sr Ambrose Lenkewich to Bishop Budka, Mundare, Nov. 27, 1916, AUAW.
10 Letter signed 'The Children of St Joseph's School' to Bishop Budka, Mundare, Nov. 21, 1917, AUAW.
11 Based on interviews with Sr Taida Letawsky and Sr Augustina Hawryliuk.
12 See 'Chronicle of the Basilian Fathers,' II, 11–12.
13 See M. R. Davie, *World Immigration* (New York: The MacMillan Company, 1949), p. 461.
14 *Ibid.*, pp. 490–6; also, Kaye, 'Three Phases.'
15 *Yorkton, the Commercial Centre of Eastern Saskatchewan*, comp. Board of Trade (Yorkton, 1910), p. 10.
16 See Z. M. Hamilton, 'Old Yorkton,' *Yorkton Enterprise*, July 8, 1943. From the Archives of the Saskatchewan Historical Society, File #352; also J. I. Tesla, *Ukrainske Naselennia Kanady: Poselennia i Demografichna Kharakterystyka / Ukrainian Population of Canada: Settlement and Demographic Characteristics* (Toronto: The Shevchenko Scientific Society in Canada, 1968), pp. 26–7.
17 See 'Chronicle of the Monastery of Our Lady of Perpetual Help, Yorkton, Sask., 1913,' vol. I; also 'Pioneer Days of Our Community,' written and compiled by the High School Students of Sacred Heart Academy, Yorkton, 1955, Film no 261, Local Histories, PAS.
18 See 'Yorkton Chronicle SSMI, 1915–34,' I, 3–4. This important discussion between Bishop Budka and Father Delaere might have taken place while the bishop was in Yorkton for the blessing of St Mary's Church on Aug. 23, 1914, or for the Synod held on Nov. 27–29, 1914.

19 In 1920 the sisters purchased fifteen additional lots from Mr Dunlop, part of which served as playground and the rest as a vegetable garden. This is the present site of Sacred Heart Academy.
20 Bishop Budka to the Sulpician Order of Montreal, Montreal, May 16, 1916, p. 9, AUAW.
21 See 'Yorkton Chronicle SSMI,' I, 4.
22 'Girls' Academy Will Be Erected,' *Yorkton Enterprise*, July 29, 1915. The article also stated that the building was to be '80' x 45' in size, two storeys high, with basement, and will cost between $30,000 and $40,000.' The statistics were later modified.
23 Viscount is a village in Saskatchewan on the Canadian Pacific Railway, fifty-eight miles east of Saskatoon. It is in a grain growing and dairying district.
24 Sr Nicholas Petrushkewich to Bishop Budka, Yorkton, Jan. 12, 1916, AUAW.
25 See Mechtilde M. Byblow, SSMI, 'History of Sacred Heart Academy,' an unpublished article written on the occasion of the academy's fiftieth anniversary in 1966, p. 3.
26 *Ibid.*, p. 1. The 'Provincial Chronicle SSMI,' I, 98, states that the total amount of the loan was $25,000 at 5 per cent. It has not been possible to determine from existing records whether this was the original sum borrowed, or whether a second loan of $10,000 was made at a later date.
27 Bishop Budka to Sr Ambrose Lenkewich, Winnipeg, May 25, 1916, AUAW.
28 'Sacred Heart Convent to Be Erected in Yorkton,' *Yorkton Press*, July 25, 1916.
29 Rev. N. M. Decamps to Bishop Budka, Yorkton, Sept. 19, 1916, AUAW.
30 Sr Ambrose to Bishop Budka, Yorkton, Jan. 13, 1917, AUAW.
31 'Patron Feast of Ruthenian Church,' *Yorkton Enterprise*, July 5, 1917.
32 *Ibid.*
33 See Pope Pius XI, 'Christian Education,' *Christian Education of Youth* (New York: The American Press, 1936), pp. 32–3.
34 Quoted in 'Yorkton Chronicle SSMI,' I, 14.
35 *Ibid.*, p. 15.
36 Ambrose M. Lenkewich, SSMI, 'Sestry Sluzhebnytsi' / 'Sisters Servants,' *Kalendar Ukrainskoho Rusyna na rik 1917 / Calendar of the Ukrainian Ruthenian for the Year 1917* (Winnipeg, 1916), p. 139.
37 See 'Influenza,' *Encyclopedia Canadiana*, vol. V.
38 'Winnipeg Chronicle SSMI,' I, 41–2.
39 See 'Sifton Chronicle SSMI, 1910–43,' I, 48.
40 See Byblow, p. 5.
41 See 'Yorkton Chronicle SSMI,' I, 44–5.
42 'Edmonton Chronicle SSMI,' I, 83–4.
43 *Ibid.*, p. 84.
44 Chawrona, 'Memoirs,' pp. 3–5.
45 *Ibid.*
46 Luhovy, *Golden Jubilee*, p. 15.
47 'Bishop Budka Lays New School Corner Stone,' *Yorkton Enterprise*, Sept. 11, 1919.
48 Brother Stanislaus James, FSC, *The History of St. Joseph's College (1919–1955)* (Yorkton, 1955), p. 2.
49 *Ibid.*, p. 23. See Appendix I of this booklet for the complete text of Brother Stanislaus' magnificent offering.
50 *Ibid.*, p. 2.
51 'Yorkton Chronicle SSMI,' I, 121.
52 Sr Ambrose to Bishop Budka, Mundare, n.d., 1916, AUAW.
53 'Provincial Chronicle SSMI,' I, 103.
54 *Ibid.*, p. 106.
55 *Ibid.*
56 *Ibid.*, p. 107.
57 The cost of the Edmonton extension was $16,000; that of Sifton was $30,000.
58 'Provincial Chronicle SSMI,' I, 111–12.
59 'Winnipeg Chronicle SSMI,' I, 50.
60 See Kaye, 'Three Phases.'
61 *Ibid.*, p. 41.

62 *Ibid.*
63 See 'Winnipeg Chronicle SSMI,' I, 58–9.
64 See 'Edmonton Chronicle SSMI,' I, 125.
65 One of these sisters was Sr Magdalene Euphrasia Hupalo, according to one of her students, Sr Julianna Pankowsky.
66 Rev. Josaphat Jean, OSBM, to the author, Grimsby, Ont., Feb. 9, 1967.
67 'Ruska Missionerska Shkola i Bursa v Siftoni, Man.' / 'The Ruthenian Missionary School and Bursa in Sifton, Man.,' *Kalendar Ukrainskoho Rusyna na rik 1916 / Calendar of the Ukrainian Ruthenian for the Year 1916* (Winnipeg, 1916), pp. 110–11.
68 *Ibid.*
69 Langevin, 'Rapport de la réunion de quelques prêtres du rite ruthène,' p. 6.
70 'Sifton Chronicle SSMI,' I, 2.
71 *Ibid.*, p. 4.
72 See letter of Father Jean to the author, n 66 above.
73 'Sifton Chronicle SSMI,' I, 16–17.
74 *Ibid.*, p. 33.
75 *Ibid.*
76 *Ibid.*, p. 35.
77 *Ibid.*, p. 36.
78 *Ibid.*, p. 38.
79 Sr Ambrose to Bishop Budka, Yorkton, Aug. 18, 1916, AUAW.
80 See 'Sifton Chronicle SSMI,' I, 39.
81 *Ibid.*, p. 40.
82 The author has been unable to establish the reasons why the Missionary School was dissolved at that time.
83 'Provincial Chronicle SSMI, I, 111.
84 *Ibid.*, p. 110.
85 *Ibid.*, p. 120. Archbishop A. Sinnott of Winnipeg eventually assumed a remaining debt of $12,000, and thus acquired the building and land.
86 'Ukrainians in Ontario, for instance, numbered 24,426 in 1931, and by 1941, the number had doubled.' Kaye, 'Three Phases.'
87 Based upon interviews with former pupils of these schools in Montreal, their parents, and Sisters Servants who later taught there, particularly Sr Julianna Pankowsky.
88 See 'Provincial Chronicle SSMI,' I, 121.
89 Sr Ambrose, after her appointment as Canadian assistant to the European major superior in 1909, designated the Mundare convent as the institute's motherhouse in Canada.
90 For example, in the ten-year period, 1909–19, a total of fifty-two girls were admitted to the novitiate – an average of approximately five each year.
91 See letter of Sr Ambrose to Bishop Budka, Mundare, Oct. 19, 1916.
92 Langevin, 'Rapport,' pp. 6–7.
93 It is possible that, if the ecclesiastical structure in which the Sisters Servants were working had remained unchanged (two Latin-rite dioceses), a second novitiate might have become the nucleus of two autonomous diocesan branches of the institute, since the formation of novices in two separate novitiates might have fostered a narrow parochial outlook, which is usually conducive to fragmentation. The establishment of an ordinariate for Ukrainian Catholics in Canada in 1912, under Bishop Budka, effectively removed this possibility.
94 For Sr Ambrose's letter to the sisters regarding this matter, see the 'Edmonton Chronicle SSMI,' I, 75–6.
95 Sr Ambrose to Rev. N. Kryzanowsky, Winnipeg, Dec. 12, 1924, ABFM.
96 Because the question of a dowry was involved, this transaction proved to be a complicated and time-consuming affair before it was finally straightened out. See 'Provincial Chronicle SSMI,' I, 128–9.
97 Father Kryzanowsky to Bishop Budka, Mundare, March 30, 1926, ABFM.
98 See 'Provincial Chronicle SSMI,' I, 123.
99 The building actually cost $30,000 to construct. See *Jubilee Book SSMI*, p. 82.

100 'Corner Stone of New Convent Laid,' *Edmonton Journal*, July 13, 1926.
101 Bishop Budka to the Sisters Servants of Mary Immaculate in Canada, Winnipeg, Feb. 10, 1917, AUAW.
102 *Ibid.*
103 'Every five years the local ordinary, either in person or through a delegate, must make a visitation of every convent of a diocesan institute. He may make such visitations oftener, since the religious life is subject to him. The visitator has the right and duty to question any of the religious who he thinks should be questioned to obtain information about things which are within the scope of visitation.' F. Geser, *The Canon Law Governing Communities of Sisters*, Canon 165.
104 Bishop Budka's letter to the Sisters Servants, dated Feb. 10, 1917, see n 101 above. For notification of Father Decamps' visitation, see letter of Bishop Budka to Sr Ambrose, Winnipeg, Oct. 27, 1916, AUAW.
105 See Rev. N. M. Decamps' 'Visitation Report of the Institute of Sisters Servants of Mary Immaculate,' Yorkton, Dec. 1, 1916, p. 7, AUAW.
106 Bishop Budka to 'All Convents of the Sisters Servants of Mary Immaculate in Canada,' Winnipeg, Jan. 31, 1917, AUAW.
107 Sr Ambrose to Bishop Budka, Yorkton, Feb. 15, 1917, AUAW.
108 See Welykyj, *History of the SSMI*, pp. 214–24.
109 Bishop Budka to Sr Ambrose, Winnipeg, Feb. 11, 1917, quoted in the 'Edmonton Chronicle SSMI,' I, 72–3.
110 Sr Ambrose to Bishop Budka, Yorkton, Feb. 15, 1917, AUAW.
111 Father Decamps to the Sisters Servants of Mary Immaculate in Canada, Yorkton, Feb. 27, 1917, quoted in the 'Yorkton Chronicle SSMI,' I, 24.
112 The relevant document is filed with Bishop Budka's papers, AUAW.
113 That such a dangerous division of loyalties did arise to threaten unity has been verified in private interviews with the following pioneer sisters: Sr Taida Letawsky, Sr Suzanne Starko, Sr Augustina Hawryliuk, and Sr Josepha Bilan.
114 Bishop Budka to Metropolitan A. Sheptytsky, Winnipeg, Nov. 22, 1918, AUAW.
115 See 'Edmonton Chronicle SSMI,' I, 131.
116 Bishop Budka to the Sisters Servants, Winnipeg, Feb. 10, 1917, AUAW.
117 Among Bishop Budka's papers (AUAW) there exists a document containing a number of revisions of the constitutions; however, no existing chronicles of the institute record that even these completed sections were ever received and put into practice by the sisters.
118 'The chapter of a religious institute is a legitimate assembly of those members of the community to whom the constitutions give the right to vote when matters concerning the community are to be discussed and decided.' Geser, Canon 181. This chapter in Winnipeg was held from Sept. 19–21, 1921.
119 'Yorkton Chronicle SSMI,' I, 66.
120 The new form of community prayer was officially approved by the ordinary on Oct. 23, 1921.
121 Although they bore similar surnames, these last two members were not blood sisters. Since for unspecified reasons Sr Euletheria Furtak resigned late in 1923, an election for councillors called by Sr Ambrose for Nov. 5, 1924, resulted in the election of Sr Josepha Bilan, Sr Augustina Hawryliuk, and Sr Josaphata Tymochko. See 'Provincial Chronicle SSMI,' I, 117–20.
122 In this council, Sr Ignatia Butryn was the treasurer and Sr Magdalene Hupalo the secretary.
123 See 'Yorkton Chronicle SSMI,' I, 111–12.
124 Archbishop Langevin had died on Jan. 15, 1915, and Archbishop Legal on March 10, 1920.
125 'Winnipeg Chronicle SSMI,' I, 91.
126 Luhovy, *Golden Jubilee*, p. 16.
127 *Ibid.*
128 See 'SSMI Entry Register,' for the period 1903–27.
129 Bishop Budka to the Sisters Servants, Winnipeg, Feb. 10, 1917, AUAW.

6 *A time to heal ...*

1 'Edmonton Chronicle SSMI, 1926–34,' II, 58–9.
2 'Winnipeg Chronicle SSMI,' I, 110.
3 See letters of Sr Ambrose Lenkewich to Rev. N. Kryzanowsky. The first relevant communication, written from St Ann's Convent, Ituna, Sask., is dated Nov. 8, 1924; the second, from Yorkton, bears the date Dec. 2, 1924, ABFM.
4 See *Canada One Hundred 1867–1967*, prepared in the Canada Year Book Handbook and Library Division, Dominion Bureau of Statistics (Ottawa, 1967), p. 341.
5 Hospital Committee, '20,000 Campaign for the Mundare Hospital: An Appeal to the Citizens of Mundare and District,' Mundare, n.d., 1928.
6 'Provincial Chronicle SSMI,' I, 137.
7 *Ibid.*, p. 140.
8 Nestor H. Kyba, SSMI, 'A Short History of the Medical Missionary Work of the Sisters Servants of Mary Immaculate,' written for the SSMI provincial archives, p. 2.
9 *Ibid.*
10 See Catholic Hospital Association, 'A Philosophy for Catholic Hospitals,' n.d.
11 See Rev. A. Luhovy, 'Vazhnist Zakonnych Z'hromadzhen' / 'The Importance of Religious Institutes,' *Jubilee Book SSMI*, p. 166.
12 Bishop B. Ladyka to Sr Athanasia Melnyk, Winnipeg, Aug. 14, 1929.
13 'Yorkton Chronicle SSMI,' I, 197.
14 Brother Stanislaus James, *History of St. Joseph's College*, p. 5.
15 The hostel was officially opened on May 16, 1928. Later, the hostel was also made available to working girls.
16 'Provincial Chronicle SSMI,' I, 130.
17 *Ibid.*
18 Brother André was a humble lay brother of the Congregation of the Holy Cross; he died in the Hospital of Notre Dame de l'Espérance at Saint Laurent in the ragged northern outskirts of Montreal on the night of Jan. 5, 1937, at the age of ninety-one. In every state of the United States and in every province of Canada there are thousands of people who firmly believe that they have been cured of grave illnesses through the holy work of this humble Canadian, Brother André, and the intercession of St Joseph. And through their faith in that simple man and his devotion to St Joseph, there has been built one of America's – and the world's – greatest shrines, the Oratory of St Joseph on Mount Royal, in Montreal. See Aldin Hatch, *The Miracle of the Mountain* (New York: Hawthorn Books, Inc., 1959).
19 'Provincial Chronicle SSMI, I, 131.
20 *Ibid.*, p. 143.
21 *Ibid.*, p. 131.
22 Lubov K. Chawrona, SSMI, 'Spomyny saznuvannia ukrainskoi shkoly u Davfyni' / 'Memoirs of the Founding of a Ukrainian School in Dauphin,' written for the SSMI provincial archives, p. 3.
23 This sum was over and above the cost of food and lodging which, during the first year, were provided by the parish.
24 Chawrona, 'Memoirs of Dauphin,' p. 4.
25 *Ibid.*, p. 5.
26 'Provincial Chronicle SSMI,' I, 142.
27 *Ibid.*, pp. 164–5.
28 *Ibid.*
29 See Davie, *World Immigration*, pp. 552–3.
30 'Provincial Chronicle SSMI,' I, 142.
31 'Ituna Chronicle SSMI, 1920–37,' I, 155.
32 Interview with Sr Taida Letawsky.
33 'Ituna Chronicle SSMI,' I, 155.
34 See the SSMI Entry Register,' for the period 1927–34.
35 Langevin, 'Rapport,' pp. 6–7.

36 Report of Rev. H. Workman, OFM, to Archbishop H. O'Leary, Edmonton, Nov. 26, 1927, AAE.
37 Bishop N. Budka to the teaching Sisters Servants, Winnipeg, March 4, 1925.
38 *Ibid.*
39 See above, chap. 5, p. 114.
40 Workman, see above, n 36.
41 'Provincial Chronicle SSMI, I, 132.
42 Interview with Sr Monica Mantyka at Ancaster, Ont., May 1970.
43 'Provincial Chronicle SSMI,' I, 182.
44 See *ibid.*, II, 125–6.
45 See letter of the Sacred Congregation for the Oriental Churches to Rev. J. Schrijvers, Rome, Oct. 6, 1928, AUAW.
46 Father Schrijvers to the Sisters Servants in Canada, Lviv, Oct. 29, 1928.
47 See above, chap. 5, p. 113.
48 'Yorkton Chronicle SSMI,' I, 236–43.
49 See 'Provincial Chronicle SSMI,' I, 139.
50 Father Schrijvers to Sr Athanasia Melnyk, Jan. 31, 1929, quoted in the 'Provincial Chronicle SSMI,' I, 141.
51 Sr Veronica Gargil to the Sisters Servants in Canada, Lviv, May 15, 1929, quoted in *ibid.*, I, 144.
52 Bishop B. Ladyka to Sr Athanasia, Winnipeg, Jan. 28, 1930.
53 Bishop Ladyka to Luigi Cardinal Sincero, Winnipeg, Sept. 30, 1930, p. 2, AUAW.
54 Sacred Oriental Congregation to Bishop Ladyka, Rome, May 8, 1930, AUAW.
55 Bishop Ladyka to Luigi Cardinal Sincero, Winnipeg, Sept. 30, 1930, pp. 2–3, AUAW.
56 'Provincial Chronicle SSMI,' I, 159–60.
57 *Ibid.*, p. 160.
58 Sacred Oriental Congregation to Bishop Ladyka, Rome, March 6, 1931, AUAW.
59 *Ibid.*
60 See letter of Archbishop H. O'Leary to Archbishop A. Cassulo, apostolic delegate to Canada, Edmonton, April 20, 1931, AAE.
61 See 'Yorkton Chronicle SSMI,' I, 236–8.
62 Archbishop O'Leary to Archbishop Cassulo, Edmonton, April 18, 1931, AAE.
63 It is clear from the directives of the Sacred Oriental Congregation (see n 58 above) that this last proposition could not be implemented.
64 See letter of Sr Athanasia to Archbishop O'Leary, Edmonton, April 15, 1931, AAE.
65 'Yorkton Chronicle SSMI,' I, 238.
66 'Aprobata Z'hromadzennia Sester Sluzhebnyts' / 'Definitive Approbation for the Congregation of Sisters Servants,' *Nova Zoria / New Star* (Lviv), Aug. 11, 1932, quoted in the 'Provincial Chronicle SSMI,' I, 170.
67 'Provincial Chronicle SSMI,' I, 171.
68 'A religious institute becomes a papal institute by approval of the Holy See. This approval is not given unless the institute has already been approved by its local ordinary and has given proof that it answers the purpose for which it has been established. The Roman pontiff, can, of course, erect a papal institute directly, without further formality. As a rule, however, papal approval is given through the Sacred Congregation and is given gradually.' Geser, *The Canon Law Governing Communities of Sisters,* Canon 113.
69 Father Schrijvers to Sr Athanasia and all Sisters Servants in Canada, Aug. 13, 1932, quoted in the 'Provincial Chronicle SSMI,' I, 172–3.
70 Bishop Ladyka to Luigi Cardinal Sincero, Winnipeg, Sept. 2, 1932, AUAW.
71 See 'Provincial Chronicle SSMI,' I, 179.
72 Father Schrijvers to the Sisters Servants in Canada, Brussels, Aug. 15, 1933, quoted in the 'Provincial Chronicle SSMI,' I, 184–5.
73 Father Schrijvers to the Sisters Servants in Canada, Brussels, Nov. 10, 1933.
74 Ex officio delegates are those who attend a chapter by virtue of their office; that is, the major superior and the members of her council.
75 The delegates arrived in Lviv on June 21, 1934.

76 The councillors were: Sr Vitalia Mykush, Sr Christopher Kachkowsky, Sr Tekla Rudyk, Sr Monica Bolysta, Sr Valerie Dubyk, and Sr Augustine Syra.
77 Father Schrijvers to the Sisters Servants in Canada, n.d., 1934, quoted in the 'Provincial Chronicle SSMI,' I, 207–9.
78 'Provincial Chronicle SSMI,' I, 207.
79 The provincial treasurer and secretary, Sr Ignatia Butryn and Sr Marcella Wynnyk, respectively, were appointed later.
80 Sr Veronica Gargil to Sr Elizabeth Kassian, Lviv, Oct. 28, 1934.
81 Brother Methodius (Koziak), FSC, 'Nasha Spivpratsia' / 'Our Cooperation,' *Jubilee Book SSMI*, p. 157.

7 *A time to blossom ...*

1 See letter of Sr Elizabeth Kassian to the Canadian Sisters Servants, Edmonton, Dec. 1, 1934.
2 This fact has been verified by the teaching sisters involved, including Sr Ignatia Butryn, Sr Monica Mantyka, Sr Joan Magriy, and Sr Emmanuel Dzubinsky.
3 'Provincial Chronicle SSMI,' I, 224. Regarding the periodical's title, the sisters selected it from among six possible ones: 'Sluzhbnytsia Marii' / 'A Servant of Mary'; 'Vistnyk Marii' / 'The Marian Herald'; 'Mariyskyi Vistnyk' / 'The Marian Herald'; 'Zoria Marii' / 'Star of Mary'; 'Zhurnal Sester Sluzhebnyts' / 'Journal of the Sisters Servants'; 'Vistnyk Z'hromadzhennia Sester Sluzhebnyts' / 'The Herald of the Institute of Sisters Servants.' See 'Winnipeg Chronicle SSMI,' I, 183.
4 *Zoria Marii / Star of Mary*, Edmonton, Jan.–Feb. 1935, p. 3.
5 Sr Veronica Gargil to the editor of the *Star of Mary*, Lviv, April 21, 1935, quoted in the 'Provincial Chronicle SSMI,' I, 224–5.
6 The final issue of the *Star of Mary* is dated April–Sept. 1967. After a period of thirty-two years the periodical was replaced by a provincial newsletter, the first of which is dated Nov. 5, 1967, and signed by Sr Frances Byblow, provincial superior. The newsletters deal with the current highlights in the province, concerning both individual houses and sisters. Besides to Canadian convents, these are also sent to the members of the Province of Christ the King serving in other parts of the world, to the provincialate in the United States, and to the generalate in Rome.
7 See above, chap. 5, p. 97.
8 See 'Provincial Chronicle SSMI,' I, 233.
9 Archbishop A. Sinnott to Bishop B. Ladyka, Tampa, Fla., April 3, 1935, AUAW.
10 See letter of Sr Elizabeth Kassian to Bishop Ladyka, Yorkton, April 17, 1935.
11 'Provincial Chronicle SSMI,' I, 237.
12 'Archbishop Sinnott was later willing to resell the property to the sisters for $15,000 cash; however, no agreement was ever reached. Finally, in 1941, a group of benefactors purchased a building that had previously served as an orphanage and hospital. It had been operated by a Protestant group, but had been closed because of negligible results. The new convent was blessed on Sept. 21, 1941, in the presence of a large number of Ukrainians.' *Jubilee Book SSMI*, p. 91.
13 Bishop Ladyka to Archbishop A. Cassulo, Winnipeg, Jan. 30, 1935, AUAW.
14 Interview with Sr Augustina Hawryliuk.
15 See 'Provincial Chronicle SSMI,' I, 233–4.
16 Interview with Sr Elizabeth, in which she noted that the institute had even set aside a part of its land in Willingdon for a chaplain's residence. The Basilian Fathers, however, never did assign a priest to reside there permanently, and thus one of the greatest hardships from the moment the hospital came into existence has been the lack of a resident chaplain.
17 Lubov K. Chawrona, SSMI, 'Shpytal u Velingdoni' / 'The Hospital at Willingdon,' written for the SSMI provincial archives, p. 1.
18 See *Jubilee Book SSMI*, p. 139.
19 Chawrona, 'The Hospital at Willingdon,' p. 2.
20 Social Credit was a doctrine which held that the basic flaw in the economic system lay

in the inadequate distribution of purchasing power and that the remedy lay in the distribution of periodic 'social dividends' to bring supply and demand into a more even balance. William Aberhart, who headed the party, proved unable to translate his theories into practice. Banking and currency were federal matters beyond the control of the province. See 'Social Credit,' *Encyclopedia of Canada*, vol. VI.

21 Mr R. A. McLeod, investment manager, the Mutual Life Assurance Company of Canada, to Sr Sofronia Sianchuk, provincial secretary, Waterloo, Ont., Aug. 27, 1936.
22 Chawrona, 'The Hospital at Willingdon,' p. 2.
23 *Ibid.*
24 See *Jubilee Book SSMI*, p. 140.
25 Chawrona, 'The Hospital at Willingdon,' p. 2.
26 *Ibid.*
27 *Ibid.*, p. 3.
28 'Provincial Chronicle SSMI,' I, 285.
29 Kyba, 'A Short History of the Medical Work of the SSMI,' p. 3.
30 Interview with W. G. Lazaruk, MD, at Willingdon, Dec. 1966.
31 See Kyba, p. 3.
32 Chawrona, 'The Hospital at Willingdon,' p. 2.
33 'Provincial Chronicle SSMI,' I, 234.
34 Bishop Ortynsky did not receive full ordinary jurisdiction and independence from the local Latin-rite ordinaries until Aug. 17, 1914, when his legal position was defined by the Holy See in the Decree *Cum Episcopato*. See *The Directory: Ukrainian Catholic Archeparchy of Philadelphia Byzantine Rite 1962–1963*, comp. Rev. M. Charyna (Philadelphia: America Press, 1962), p. 7.
35 See the letter of Mother Jerome Chimy to Mother Vincent Yaremovich, in *The Silver Crown*, comp. the Sisters Servants of the Immaculate Conception Province (Philadelphia, 1961), p. 33. Bishop Ortynsky forwarded a similar request to the Sisters Servants in Galicia, but because the sisters were just in the process of dispatching the first missionaries to Brazil his request was refused.
36 This figure for the Ukrainian Catholic population in the United States is quoted from Charyna, n 34 above.
37 'Chronicle of the Basilian Fathers,' I, 171.
38 See Charyna, n 34 above.
39 Interview with Sr Elizabeth.
40 'Provincial Chronicle SSMI,' I, 234.
41 The scope of the sisters' work at the seminary was broadened in 1938 when Sr Theresa Melnyk was placed in charge of the school library and museum.
42 Interview with Sr Elizabeth.
43 See 'Hartford Chronicle SSMI, 1948–54,' for the year 1948. The works outlined here are typical of those recorded in the chronicles of almost every one of these early American convents, ASSP.
44 'Minneapolis Chronicle SSMI, 1937–45,' I, 6.
45 'Provincial Chronicle SSMI,' I, 345–6.
46 Open letter of Rev. B. Turylo to the Provincial Superior SSMI, Rochester, June 11, 1942, quoted in *Jubilee Book SSMI*, p. 167.
47 This number includes postulants and novices. See 'SSMI Entry Register,' for the period 1902–35.
48 At this time the only temporary mission was that at Portage la Prairie, opened in 1936.
49 'General Chronicle SSMI,' II, 355, ASSR; also in Welykyj, *History of the SSMI*, p. 323.
50 'Mundare Chronicle SSMI,' II, 188.
51 Sr Veronica Gargil to the Sisters Servants in Canada, Edmonton, Aug. 1936.
52 Neither the provincial annals nor any of the existing local chronicles record any negative reaction to this appointment.
53 See 'Winnipeg Chronicle SSMI,' I, 158.
54 'Provincial Chronicle SSMI,' I, 304.
55 Interview with Sr Jerome Chimy, who became the institute's superior general in 1956.
56 'Winnipeg Chronicle SSMI,' I, 117.
57 Luhovy, *Jubilee Book SSMI*, p. 166.

58 'Provincial Chronicle SSMI,' I, 307.
59 Interviews with the first superior, Sr Augustina Hawryliuk, and Sr Alexandra Doiron. In 1970, at the age of seventy-eight, Sr Alexandra was still active on the staff of St Paul's Nursing Home at Dauphin, Man.
60 Metropolitan M. Hermaniuk, 'Appeal of the Ukrainian Catholic Exarchate of Manitoba for the New Ukrainian Home for the Aged in Winnipeg,' Nov. 1956.
61 Interview with Sr Augustina Hawryliuk.
62 See 'Provincial Chronicle SSMI,' I, 342. Bishop Bohachevsky made the donation in March 1937. See also p. 322. Two subsequent donations of houses in Philadelphia included one at 818 North Franklin Avenue and another at 721 Brown Street. The first of these became a sewing centre for liturgical vestments, and the second a hostel for girls working in the city's factories. See *Jubilee Book SSMI*, pp. 110–11. Both of these properties were subsequently returned to the diocese; see letter of Bishop C. Bohachevsky to Sr Bernadette Warick, Philadelphia, Jan. 27, 1951.
63 Bishop Bohachevsky to Sr Elizabeth, Philadelphia, March 1937.
64 See letter of Sr Ambrose to Sr Elizabeth, Ituna, Sask., July 1, 1935, in which this problem is thoroughly discussed and the possibility of constructing a new building is considered.
65 'Provincial Chronicle SSMI,' II, 18.
66 Interview with Sr Alexandra Doiron.
67 'Ituna Chronicle SSMI,' I, 161.
68 The loan was in the amount of $12,000 at 5 per cent.
69 'Provincial Chronicle SSMI, 1938–43,' II, 42.
70 Father Pelech's loan was in the amount of $5,000.
71 Rev. Stephen Semchuk, 'Miy poklin Sestram Sluzhebnytsiam z nahody 50-littia' / 'My Felicitations to the Sisters Servants on the Occasion of their 50th Anniversary,' *Jubilee Book SSMI*, p. 154.
72 See above, chap. 5, p. 93.
73 See 'Ituna Chronicle SSMI,' I, 161–75; also 'Provincial Chronicle SSMI,' II, 38–42.
74 The first catechetical school was held for the parishioners of Toronto's east end. See *Holy Eucharist Ukrainian Catholic Chronicle, Toronto, 1927–1969*, comp. J. Denischuk, CSSR (Toronto: Basilian Press, 1969), p. 2.
75 See Kaye, 'Three Phases'; also *Canada: A Sociological Profile*, comp. W. E. Mann (Toronto: The Copp Clark Publishing Co., 1968), p. 182.
76 'Toronto Chronicle SSMI, 1937–50,' I, 3–4.
77 See Denischuk, n 74 above, pp. 8–10.
78 'Toronto Chronicle SSMI,' I, 5.
79 *Ibid.*, p. 7.
80 Sr Veronica to Sr Elizabeth, Lviv, July 12, 1939.

8 *In time of war . . .*

1 See W. C. Langsam, *The World since 1914* (5th ed., New York: The Macmillan Company, 1943), pp. 735–9; also Welykyj, *History of the SSMI*, p. 386.
2 Pastoral letter of Bishop B. Ladyka to Ukrainian Catholics in Canada, Winnipeg, Sept. 21, 1939.
3 *Ibid.*, Sept. 4, 1939.
4 See Welykyj, p. 340.
5 *Ibid.*, p. 387.
6 *Ibid.*, p. 406.
7 Sr Veronica Gargil to Sr Elizabeth Kassian, Kristinopil, Oct. 28, 1939.
8 *Ibid.*
9 See Welykyj, pp. 388–9.
10 Sr Veronica to Sr Elizabeth, Oct. 28, 1939; see n 7 above.
11 'Provincial Chronicle SSMI,' II, 145.
12 Sr Veronica to Sr Elizabeth, Oct. 28, 1939; see n 7 above.
13 Rev. J. Schrijvers to Sr Elizabeth, Rome, Jan. 6, 1940.

14 See 'Provincial Chronicle SSMI,' II, 137.
15 *Ibid.*, pp. 158, 180. These statistics were copied from the annual statistical reports of the 'Greek' Catholic dioceses in Canada and the United States as of Dec. 1939.
16 *Ibid.*, p. 205.
17 *Ibid.*
18 Archbishop W. M. Duke of Vancouver to Bishop Ladyka, Vancouver, Dec. 15, 1943, AUAW.
19 See 'Provincial Chronicle SSMI, 1943–7,' III, 56–8.
20 See Davie, *World Immigration*, pp. 551–3.
21 Rev. J. Kutsky of Wilkes-Barre to Bishop Bohachevsky, and quoted by the bishop in his letter to Sr Elizabeth, Philadelphia, n.d., Prot. N. 1599.
22 Rev. B. Baranyk, OSBM, to Sr Elizabeth, Mundare, June 15, 1945, quoted in the 'Provincial Chronicle SSMI,' III, 186.
23 See 'Provincial Chronicle SSMI,' III, 72. Also the 'Annual Catechetical Report, Province of Christ the King, 1944.' These new missions included: Vegreville, Alta.; Winnipeg (St Mary's Girls' Institute); Fort William and Hamilton in Ontario; Sydney, NS; Phoenixville, Chester, Sayre, and Minersville in Pennsylvania; Buffalo, Rochester, and Sloatsburg (St Joseph's Home for the Aged, St Mary's Villa Academy) in New York; and Washington, DC.
24 Sr Elizabeth to Father Baranyk, Edmonton, July 19, 1945, quoted in the 'Provincial Chronicle SSMI,' III, 187–94.
25 See the 'Annual Catechetical Report, Province of Christ the King, 1935.'
26 Rev. N. Savaryn, OSBM, 'Vykhovna Diyalnist Sester Sluzhebnyts'/'The Educational Service of the Sisters Servants,' *Jubilee Book SSMI*, p. 176.
27 Rev. M. Pelech, 'Nam treba Metsenativ'/'We Need Patrons of the Arts and Sciences,' *Jubilee Book SSMI*, p. 172.
28 Semchuk, *Jubilee Book SSMI*, p. 154.
29 *Ibid.*, p. 154.
30 See the 'Annual Catechetical Report, Province of Christ the King, 1945.'
31 Luhovy, *Jubilee Book SSMI*, p. 166.
32 Semchuk, *Jubilee Book SSMI*, pp. 154–5.
33 See 'Provincial Chronicle SSMI,' II, 204.
34 *Ibid.*, p. 234.
35 Rev. V. Bilynsky, 'Dlya ukrainskoho narodu'/'For the Ukrainian Nation,' *Jubilee Book SSMI*, pp. 132–3.
36 See 'Provincial Chronicle SSMI,' II, 315–16.
37 *Ibid.*, p. 239.
38 Interviews with Sr Taida Letawsky and Sr Cornelia Mantyka.
39 Pastoral letter of Bishop Ladyka to the Ukrainian Catholic Clergy and Laity in Canada, Winnipeg, March 21, 1942.
40 *Ibid.*
41 Father Schrijvers to the Sisters Servants in Canada, Rome, Dec. 7, 1941.
42 Eugene Cardinal Tisserant to Sr Elizabeth and the Sisters of the Province of Christ the King, on the occasion of the institute's fiftieth anniversary; no place or date given.
43 Sr Veronica to Sr Elizabeth and the Sisters of the Province of Christ the King, on the occasion of the institute's fiftieth anniversary; no place or date given.
44 'Mundare Chronicle SSMI' II, 390.
45 Justine A. Kowal, SSMI, 'Address on the Occasion of the Fiftieth Anniversary of the Sisters Servants of Mary Immaculate,' Mundare, Aug. 15, 1942.
46 The hymn, *Slava, slava, na vysoti Bohu*, was composed for the jubilee by Rev. A. Truch.
47 See Elizabeth S. Kassian, SSMI, 'V urochystu khvylyu' / 'At a Solemn Moment,' *Jubilee Book SSMI*, pp. 36–7.
48 Pastoral letter of Bishop Ladyka to the Ukrainian Canadian Clergy and Faithful, n.d., quoted in the 'Provincial Chronicle SSMI,' III, 93.
49 Marcel E. Wagner, 'Metropolitan Andrij – Priest and Patriot,' *The Way*, English section, Nov. 15, 1970.
50 Father Schrijvers to Sr Elizabeth, Rome, Jan. 7, 1945.
51 *Ibid.*

52 Rev. Patrick Murray, CSSR, March 7, 1945, quoted in the 'Provincial Chronicle SSMI,' III, 124.
53 Father Murray to Sr Elizabeth, Rome, April 29, 1945.
54 Father Schrijvers to the Sisters Servants in Canada, Edmonton, Feb. 13, 1936, quoted in the 'Provincial Chronicle SSMI,' I, 224–5.
55 Letter from a Sister Servant to the Sisters Servants in Canada, Czechoslovakia, Sept. 5, 1945, quoted in the 'Provincial Chronicle SSMI,' III, 213–14.
56 See letter of Sr Veronica to Sr Elizabeth, Rome, Oct. 9, 1945.
57 Christopher T. Kachkowsky, SSMI, 'Z zhyttia Maty Vyroniky Gargil'/'From the life of Mother Veronica Gargil,' Rome, Oct. 17, 1957.
58 *Ibid.*
59 Sr Veronica to the Sisters Servants in Philadelphia, Rome, n.d., 1945, quoted in the 'Provincial Chronicle SSMI,' III, 267–8.
60 See Msgr S. Majoli, 'The Persecution of the Church in Ukraine,' *First Victims of Communism: White Book on the Religious Persecution in Ukraine*, trans. from the Italian (Rome, 1953), pp. 99–113.
61 Sr Veronica to the Sisters Servants of Christ the King Province, Rome, Jan. 1946, quoted in the 'Provincial Chronicle SSMI,' III, 268–70.
62 Sr Veronica to Sr Elizabeth, Rome, Jan. 8, 1946.

9   *... and in time of peace*

1 Bishop A. Senyshyn to the Ukrainian Catholic Faithful in the United States, Stamford, Conn., May 9, 1946.
2 Bishop Senyshyn to the Sisters Servants of Mary Immaculate, Stamford, May 23, 1946.
3 Sr Monica Bolysta to Sr Elizabeth Kassian, Chelm Lubelski, Poland, Nov. 1945; see 'Provincial Chronicle SSMI,' III, 241–2.
4 Bishop B. Ladyka to Sr Elizabeth, Winnipeg, March 7, 1946.
5 Sr Elizabeth to the Sisters Servants of the Province of Christ the King, Edmonton, Feb. 22, 1946.
6 Sr Elizabeth to Sr Veronica Gargil, Edmonton, March 1, 1946.
7 Sr Elizabeth to the Sisters Servants of the Province of Christ the King, Edmonton, Aug. 30, 1946.
8 Sr Elizabeth to Sr Veronica, Edmonton, Nov. 25, 1945.
9 'Provincial Chronicle SSMI,' III, 225.
10 Sr Elizabeth to Sr Veronica, Edmonton, Nov. 8, 1945.
11 *Ibid.*
12 Interview with Sr Elizabeth.
13 'Provincial Chronicle SSMI,' III, 300.
14 'Ancaster School Located on Magnificent Estate,' *Canadian Register*, Hamilton edition, June 13, 1953.
15 'Provincial Chronicle SSMI,' III, 309.
16 One group of ten sisters was accommodated by the Sisters of St Anthony at Leeuw St Pierre, and six other sisters by the Sisters of St Joseph at Eyseringen.
17 Father Coussa was appointed apostolic visitor for the Sisters Servants by the Holy See on May 25, 1946.
18 For letters regarding Sr Elizabeth's confirmation in office for a third term, see letter of Sr Veronica to Sr Elizabeth, Rome, Aug. 4, 1946; also, letter of the Sacred Oriental Congregation to Bishop Ladyka, Rome, Aug. 19, 1946, AUAW.
19 The group included four professed sisters – Sr Ignatia Butryn, Sr Lawrence Dzumaga, Sr Josaphata Kizlyk, and Sr Olympiada Mary Puhach; and the novices – Georgina Victoria Yakimyshyn, Judith Rose Pacholko, Pelagia Anne Sap, Albina Josephine Gregoriw, Fotenia Katherine Spilchak, Dosithea Rose Luby, Veronica Mary Demchuk, Claudia Helen Popowich, Marianne Olga Telenko, Clement Anne Basaraba, Demetriada Justine Rychkun, Christine Emily Opalinsky, Nestor Helen Kyba, Sabina Sophie

Kotowich, Dominic Genevieve Slawuta, Bohdana Olga Pidskalny, Flavian Irene Dmyterko; the postulants included (Oksana) Mary Iwaschyshyn, and (Florentine) Sophie Smysniuk.

20 Bishop Ladyka to Sr Elizabeth, Winnipeg, Feb. 12, 1947.
21 See above, chap. 2, p. 25.
22 Sr Elizabeth to Bishop Ladyka, Ancaster, March 11, 1947.
23 'Provincial Chronicle SSMI,' III, 425. The first chaplain at Mount Mary was Rev. B. Kuzma.
24 Rev. Isidore Borecky, 'Ditochyi ray na hori Prechystoyi Divy v Ankastyr'/'A Children's Paradise at Mount Mary in Ancaster,' quoted in the 'Provincial Chronicle SSMI,' III, 490.
25 Archbishop A. Vachon to the Provincial Superior of the Sisters Servants of Mary Immaculate, Ottawa, Sept. 8, 1946.
26 Sr Rosalia Kich was already perpetually professed.
27 *Globe and Mail*, Toronto, Aug. 31, 1947.
28 James Cardinal McGuigan to Bishop Ladyka, Toronto, Dec. 31, 1947, AUAW.
29 Bishop Ladyka to Cardinal McGuigan, Winnipeg, Jan. 9, 1948, AUAW.
30 'Provincial Chronicle SSMI, 1947–53,' IV, 168.
31 *Ibid*.
32 Gertrude N. Lesiuk, SSMI, 'Pryizd syritok do syrotyntsia v Ankastyr, Ontario' / 'The Arrival of Orphans at Ancaster, Ontario,' *Svitlo*, May 20, 1949.
33 See Kachkowsky, 'From the Life of Mother Veronica Gargil.'
34 These vice-provinces were created in July 1947. See Welykyj, *History of the SSMI*, pp. 443, 450, 457.
35 Sr Veronica to the Sisters Servants of the Canadian-American province, Easter 1948.
36 *Yearbook of the Eparchy of Toronto – In the Vineyard of Christ*, ed. Julian Beskyd (Toronto, 1964), p. 51.
37 See 'Ukrainians,' *The Canadian Family Tree*, Canadian Citizenship Branch, Department of the Secretary of State (Ottawa, 1967), p. 323.
38 See Kaye, 'Three Phases.'
39 See *Canadian Family Tree*, p. 323.
40 Sisters Servants of Mary Immaculate, of the Province of Christ the King, to Bishop N. Savaryn, Ancaster, April 5, 1948.
41 During the scholastic year 1969–70, for example, the sisters stationed at 5 Austin Terrace served nine city and suburban parishes, which included: St Josaphat, St Nicholas, St Basil, St Mary (Leeds Avenue), Holy Eucharist, St Mary (Shaw Street), St Peter and Paul (Scarborough), St Mary (Cooksville).
42 Sr Veronica to the Sisters Servants of the Province of Christ the King, Rome, Sept. 30, 1948.
43 Sr Veronica to the provincial council of the Province of Christ the King, Rome, Oct. 11, 1949.
44 The secretary, selected by the council, was Sr Juvenalia Kaniuk; the treasurer, Sr Boniface Sloboda.
45 Sr Veronica to Sr Elizabeth, Rome, Nov. 14, 1949.
46 See 'Summary of Postulants Admitted to the Novitiate 1902–52,' in the 'Provincial Chronicle SSMI,' IV, 421.
47 See 'Address of Sr Bernadette Warick to Sr Elizabeth Kassian, Toronto, Nov. 25, 1949,' quoted in the 'Provincial Chronicle SSMI,' IV, 227.
48 Post-visitation message of Sr Veronica to the provincial council of the Sisters Servants of the Province of Christ the King in Toronto, Rome, Nov. 29, 1949.

10 *A time for change . . .*

1 Interview with Sr Bernadette Warick; see also 'Provincial Chronicle SSMI, IV, 245–6.
2 *Ibid*.
3 Excerpt from Sr Veronica Gargil's letter to the Sacred Oriental Congregation, quoted

in a letter from the congregation to Archbishop A. G. Cicognani, apostolic delegate to the United States, Rome, Oct. 13, 1949.

4 Post-visitation message of Sr Veronica to the provincial council of the Province of Christ the King in Toronto, Rome, Nov. 29, 1949.

5 Sr Elizabeth Kassian to Sr Veronica, Edmonton, March 1, 1946.

6 'Provincial Chronicle SSMI,' IV, 221.

7 See 'Apostolic Report, 1952,' p. 36.

8 Pope Pius XII, 'True Renewal,' Sept. 23, 1950, AAS, 42, 657, quoted in *Religious Life in the Light of Vatican II*, comp. the Daughters of St Paul (Boston, 1967), p. 347.

9 See 'Canonical Visitations 1950–1957.'

10 Welykyj, *History of the SSMI*, p. 463.

11 Sr Veronica to Sr Bernadette, Rome, Feb. 10, 1951.

12 Quoted in Welykyj, p. 463.

13 Sr Veronica to Sr Bernadette, Rome, Feb. 10, 1951.

14 Sr Bernadette to the Sisters Servants of the Province of Christ the King, Toronto, May 30, 1951.

15 Rev. G. A. Coussa to the Sisters Servants in the Province of Christ the King, Rome, June 25, 1951.

16 The term of the council was to expire in 1956. Members included: Sr Christopher Kachkowsky, Sr Monica Bolysta, Sr Eudocima Woloshyn. Sr Jerome Chimy was appointed to replace Sr Gertrude Lesiuk on the provincial council.

17 Sr Bernadette to the Sisters Servants of the Province of Christ the King, Toronto, Nov. 24, 1951.

18 Eugene Cardinal Tisserant to Sr Bernadette, Rome, n.d., 1951.

19 Father Coussa to the Sisters Servants of the Province of Christ the King, Rome, March 19, 1951.

20 *Ibid.*

21 Pope Paul VI, awarding the first Pope John XXIII Peace Prize to Mother Teresa of India.

22 See above, chap. 3, p. 42.

23 See above, chap. 4, p. 69.

24 'Provincial Chronicle SSMI,' IV, 441.

25 *Ibid.*, p. 442.

26 'Ukrainian Sisters Open New Academy,' *Canadian Register*, Toronto, June 13, 1953.

27 *Ibid.*

28 Mr V. Kushmelyn to the Provincial Council of the Sisters Servants, Toronto, Oct. 14, 1952.

29 'Provincial Chronicle SSMI,' IV, 317.

30 *Ibid.*, p. 318.

31 Interview with Sr Bernadette.

32 Anne Skrypka, 'Address on the Occasion of the Dedication of Mount Mary Immaculate Academy, Ancaster, Ont., May 31, 1953,' see 'Provincial Chronicle SSMI,' IV, 453.

33 *Nasha Meta*, April 20, 1957.

34 Peter Bihus, 'Persha graduatsiya akademii'/'The Academy's First Graduation,' *ibid.*, July 21, 1956.

35 Statistics quoted regarding student enrolment are from the 'Student Record File,' Mount Mary Immaculate Academy, Ancaster.

36 See above, chap. 7, p. 156.

37 See accounts of the foundations of the missions at Youngstown, Ohio, and Passaic, NJ, in the 'Provincial Mission Register SSMI,' pp. 237, 239.

38 *Ibid.*

39 Bishop Daniel Ivancho to Sr Bernadette, Homestead, Pa., Sept. 14, 1951.

40 Sr Bernadette to Bishop D. Ivancho, Toronto, Sept. 25, 1951.

41 Interview with Sr Bernadette.

42 Sr Bernadette to the Sisters Servants of the Province of Christ the King, Toronto, Nov. 30, 1953.

43 For the religious programmes introduced by the sisters across Canada and the United States, see the 'Provincial Chronicle SSMI, 1954–60,' V, 14–29.

11   *A time to be fruitful . . .*

1 Pope Pius XII, 'True Renewal.'
2 *Ibid.*
3 Pope Pius XII, Address to the First International Congress of Religious, Dec. 8, 1950, quoted in *Proceedings of the 1953 Sisters Institute of Spirituality*, ed. Joseph E. Haley, CSC, (South Bend, Ind.: University of Notre Dame Press, 1954), p. 1.
4 *Ibid.*, p. 13.
5 *Ibid.*, p. 1.
6 *Ibid.*, p. 5.
7 See *Proceedings of the First Canadian Religious Congress*, Sections II and IV, English-Speaking Religious Men and Women, Canadian Religious Conference, General Secretariate (Ottawa, 1954), pp. 3, 9.
8 *Ibid.*, p. 9.
9 Pope Pius XII, 'Address to Superiors General of Women's Orders and Institutes,' Sept. 15, 1952, quoted in Daughters of St Paul, comp., *Religious Life in the Light of Vatican* II, p. 366.
10 See *Svitlo*, April 1956.
11 *Ukrainski Visty*, April 16, 1956.
12 See the 'Provincial Chronicle SSMI,' v, 172.
13 *Ibid.*, p. 181.
14 See above, chap. 10, p. 223.
15 Interview with Sr Bernadette Warick.
16 For a summary of the chapter proceedings and a list of the resolutions, see the 'Provincial Chronicle SSMI,' v, 188–94. This general chapter introduced the title 'Mother' for the superior general and provincial superiors, while the chapter held in 1962 extended its use to general councillors and directresses of novices. At the first session of the fourth general chapter convened in 1968, it was decided that the title need not be strictly adhered to; rather, its use would depend upon current usage in each country. In this book, the title has been used only when it appears in quoted material.
17 The remaining two councillors were Sr Olga Dykun and Sr Josaphata Woytowich. Sr Helen Dykun was re-elected to the post of secretary. To replace Sr Jerome and Sr Lawrence on the provincial council, the general council appointed Sr Joan Magriy and Sr Cornelia Mantyka.
18 Based on interviews with the members of the Canadian-American delegation.
19 See Bishop Ladyka's jubilee messages of 1942 and 1952, in *Jubilee Book SSMI*, pp. 18–20, and *Jubilee Memoir*, p. 22.
20 See Beskyd, *Yearbook of the Eparchy of Toronto*, p. 51. An archeparchy corresponds to an archdiocese; an eparchy is a diocese in a definitely established form.
21 'Ukrainska Katolytska Mytropoliya u Amerytsi'/'The Ukrainian Catholic Metropolitan See in the United States,' *Nasha Meta*, Aug. 1958.
22 'Provincial Chronicle SSMI,' v, 212.
23 Interviews with Sr Bernadette Warick and Sr Matthew Nykoliuk.
24 See 'Mission Register SSMI,' p. 22.
25 See letter of Mr Frank Ernst to Sr Bernadette, Winnipeg, Jan. 4, 1956.
26 See letter of Sr Bernadette to Mr R. R. McInnes, assistant director of finance, Manitoba Hospital Services Plan, Toronto, Oct. 2, 1959.
27 'Appeal of the Ukrainian Catholic Exarchate of Manitoba for the New Ukrainian Home for the Aged in Winnipeg,' Winnipeg, Feb. 6, 1956, [signed] B. Ladyka, OSBM, archbishop; M. Hermaniuk, CSSR, bishop-coadjutor.
28 'Chronicle of Holy Family Nursing Home, Winnipeg, Man.,' I, 15.
29 Donations totalled $100,500.95; cost of remodelling amounted to $101,630.47. See letter of Mr M. Smerchanski to Sr Bernadette, Winnipeg, June 10, 1957.
30 D. Mykytiuk, 'Otvorennia domu presvyatoyi rodyny u Vinnipegu,'/'The Opening of Holy Family Nursing Home in Winnipeg.' *Nasha Meta*, June 8, 1957.
31 Interview with Sr Bernadette.

32 Metropolitan M. Hermaniuk, 'Appeal of the Winnipeg Archdiocese on Behalf of the First Ukrainian Academy for Ukrainian Girls in Manitoba,' Winnipeg, June 9, 1957.
33 Sr Benedict was officially replaced in Sept. 1958 by Sr Claudia Popowich.
34 See the daily registers for Immaculate Heart of Mary Academy for the years 1957 to 1960.
35 *Nasha Meta*, June 1956.
36 Byblow, 'History of Sacred Heart Academy,' p. 8.
37 'The Hungry Thirties,' *Yorkton Enterprise*, Oct. 6, 1965.
38 See 'Sacred Heart Academy,' Department of Education Files, Regina.
39 Sr Mechtilde Byblow to the Registrar, Department of Education, Yorkton, Oct. 18, 1945. Department of Education Files.
40 Interview with Mr H. W. Jackson, Yorkton, Sept. 26, 1966. The sisters also assumed sole responsibility for the upkeep, high school education, and professional training of many orphans from St Ann's Children's Home at Ituna. Among these were Anne and Olga Bohdan; Anne, Olga, and Helen Komaryk; Angela and Mary Verklan; and Olga Lysay. Also educated by the sisters from the first grade were Pauline and Elizabeth Matwiy.
41 'Yorkton Business Section to Be Canvassed for Funds This Week,' *Yorkton Enterprise*, April 25, 1957.
42 Brother Methodius, 'The Ukrainian Language in Saskatchewan High Schools: The Story of Its Beginnings,' *Life Beacon* (Toronto: Basilian Press, June 15, 1957).
43 'Rejects Cultural Mosaic,' *Progress*, English section (Winnipeg), Oct. 25, 1970. Note: Acadia University is at Wolfville, NS.
44 *Ibid.*
45 See Brother Methodius, *Life Beacon*, Sept. 15, 1967.
46 *Ibid.*
47 Letter accompanying the brief from the Ukrainian Curriculum Committee (signed by the convener, Brother Methodius) to the Hon. W. Lloyd, minister of education, Yorkton, May 15, 1952, ABCSY.
48 'Memorandum to the Minister of Education Regarding the Addition of Ukrainian to the Programme of Language Studies in the Secondary Schools,' from the Ukrainian Curriculum Committee, Yorkton, May 15, 1952, ABCSY.
49 Mr H. Janzen to Brother Methodius, Regina, May 23, 1952, ABCSY.
50 Mr Janzen to Brother Methodius, Regina, Sept. 2, 1952, ABCSY.
51 'Superintendent's Report of Sacred Heart Academy, Yorkton, Sask., Jan. 16, 1953,' Department of Education Files, Regina.
52 'Superintendent's Report re Sacred Heart Academy, Yorkton, Sask., March 18, 19, 1957,' Department of Education Files, Regina.
53 'Sacred Heart Academy Extension Program Progressing,' *Yorkton Enterprise*, April 25, 1957.
54 'An Important Yorkton Milestone,' *ibid.*, May 22, 1958.
55 *Ibid.*
56 *Ibid.*
57 'Hundreds Attend Sacred Heart Dedication,' *ibid.*, May 29, 1958.
58 'Archbishop Sends His Blessings to the Pilgrims in Sloatsburg, N.Y.,' *America*, English section, June 23, 1956.
59 'Provincial Chronicle SSMI,' V, 196.
60 'Chronicle of Youngstown, Ohio, SSMI,' I, 103.
61 'St. Mary's Villa Academy Scene of Assumption Pilgrimage August 14,' *America*, English section, July 27, 1955.
62 *Ibid.*
63 'Assumption Pilgrimage in General Glances,' *ibid.*, Aug. 1956.
64 *Nasha Meta*, July 1957.
65 *Ibid.*
66 *Svitlo*, June 1959.
67 Welykyj, p. 487.
68 Sr Jerome Chimy to Sr Bernadette, Rome, Nov. 5, 1959.

69 'American Province Created for Sisters Servants of Mary Immaculate, Agency Says,' *The Way*, English section, Aug. 5, 1959.
70 Sr Jerome to Sr Lawrence Dzumaga, Rome, Nov. 5, 1959.
71 See 'Provincial Chronicle SSMI,' v, 446–9. Note: The Immaculate Conception Province did not open its own novitiate at Lansdale, Pa., until Aug. 1968 – almost ten years after its erection.
72 Metropolitan C. Bohachevsky to Sr Vincent Yaremovich, Philadelphia, Aug. 15, 1960.
73 Sr Jerome to the sisters of the Canadian Province of Christ the King, Rome, Dec. 8, 1959.
74 The members of both councils were appointed by the generalate after a consultative vote by the sisters in Canada and the United States in Nov. 1959. Later the provincial councils appointed their own secretary and treasurer. The Canadians chose Sr Valerie Sophie Krochenski as secretary and Sr Helena Kwasnicky as treasurer; the Americans selected Sr Juvenalia Kaniuk and Sr Rose Halytsky, as secretary and treasurer respectively.
75 'Provincial Chronicle SSMI,' v, 451.
76 *Ibid.*

Epilogue: A time to love . . .

1 See John J. McEleney, SJ, 'Religious Life,' in *The Documents of Vatican II*, p. 462.
2 Pope John XXIII, *Humanae Salutis*, Dec. 25, 1961, in *ibid*.
3 Pope Paul VI, 'Closing Message to the Council Fathers,' Dec. 8, 1965, in *ibid*., p. 728.
4 'Canadian Religious Conference On at Sacred Heart Academy,' *Yorkton Enterprise*, Aug. 17, 1961.
5 'Provincial Chronicle SSMI,' VI, 45.
6 *Postup*, March 19, 1961.
7 Other members of the executive included Mr S. Kruk and Mr M. Pasichny. They were constantly assisted by Mrs Olga Paschak and Mrs Jean Sahan.
8 Address by Sr Jerome Chimy on the occasion of the opening of Immaculate Heart of Mary School, Winnipeg, April 28, 1963. Note: In the 1964–5 scholastic year the school had a total enrolment of 228 students in grades one through twelve. Due to congestion, the secondary school grades were discontinued in June 1965. By Dec. 1970 the building debt, which had been assumed entirely by the sisters, amounted to $262,000 at 5¾ per cent; besides this, the sisters were still responsible for all operation and maintenance costs.
9 Sr Frances Byblow to the Canadian Sisters Servants, Toronto, Nov. 5, 1967.
10 *Ibid.*, Feb. 15, 1968.
11 Address by Sr Frances on the occasion of the opening of the new facilities at Holy Family Nursing Home, Winnipeg, Dec. 17, 1970.
12 Address by Sr Frances on the occasion of the opening of the new facilities at St Ann's Children's Home, Ituna, May 2, 1971.
13 *Ibid.*
14 Josyf Cardinal Slipyj to the Sisters Servants of Mary Immaculate at Edmonton, Vatican City, Nov. 8, 1968.
15 Other members of the Religion and Culture Society executive were Mr Wm. Popowich, Mrs Natalie Popowich, and Mrs Marion Didic. To commemorate the occasion the Society established the Mother Ambrose Scholarship Fund for furthering the education of Canadian Sisters Servants.
16 Address by Sr Frances on the occasion of the official opening of the extension to Sacred Heart Academy, Yorkton, June 1, 1969.
17 Address by Stephanie Potoski, MD, on the occasion of the seventy-fifth anniversary of the founding of the Institute of Sisters Servants of Mary Immaculate, Toronto, May 22, 1967.
18 Message of Lester B. Pearson, prime minister, Ottawa, May 1967.

19 Sr Athanasia Melnyk to the members of the hierarchy, clergy, and laity at the jubilee banquet in Toronto on May 22, Winnipeg, May 18, 1967.
20 Address by Sr Frances on the occasion of the seventy-fifth Anniversary Tea sponsored by the Ukrainian Catholic Women's League, Toronto, Nov. 12, 1967.
21 Archbishop S. Pignedoli to Sr Frances, Ottawa, June 6, 1967.
22 Father Welykyj was appointed to this position on July 9, 1960.
23 Rev. A. Welykyj, OSBM, 'Na sluzhbi Bohovi i liudyni' / 'In The Service of God and Man,' Vatican Radio broadcast, Sept. 9, 1962, quoted in the *Star of Mary*, Sept.–Oct. 1962, pp. 4–5.
24 Sr Zenovia Kmeta and Sr Christopher Kachkowsky were the other councillors elected; Sr Helen Dykun was again chosen to hold the post of general secretary.
25 Sr Bernadette and Sr Cornelia were elected to represent Canada at the general chapter by thirty-one delegates to the provincial chapter held at Ancaster from April 27 to 29, 1962.
26 For a detailed list of these implementations, see Welykyj, *History of the SSMI*, pp. 543–7.
27 *Norms for the Implementation of the Decree* Perfectae Caritatis, art. 1.
28 'Provincial Chronicle SSMI,' VI, 284.
29 Circular letter of Sr Jerome Chimy to the Sisters Servants, Rome, Oct. 1966. The questionnaire entitled 'Renewal of Religious Life in Our Congregation in the Light of Vatican Council II,' was developed under the following headings: Renewal of Interior Life and Modifications in Our Liturgical Life; Vocation; Vows; Common Life; Religious Discipline; Religious Habit; Recruitment; Formation; Apostolate; Government.
30 See letter of Sr Frances to the Canadian Sisters Servants, Toronto, March 20, 1967. Note: Members of the Commission were: Sr Dominic Slawuta, Sr Bernadette Warick, Sr Innocentia Baraniuk, Sr Mechtilde Byblow, Sr Sylvia Nakoneshny, Sr Justine Kowal, Sr Cassianna Slywka, Sr Claudia Popowich, and Sr Ambrose Pauline Stachiw.
31 Sr Frances to the Canadian Sisters Servants, Toronto, June 12, 1968.
32 *Ibid.*, Oct. 22, 1968. Note: Two other Canadians on the Commission were Sr Cornelia Mantyka and Sr Justine Kowal.
33 The remaining councillors were Sr Anisia Pastuch, Sr Basil Chykalo, and Sr Thomas Hrynewich; Sr Helen Dykun was re-elected as secretary.
34 See letter of Sr Frances to the Canadian Sisters Servants, Toronto, July 15, 1970.
35 See *ibid.*, Oct. 14, 1970.
36 Sr Jerome to the Sisters Servants of Mary Immaculate, Rome, Oct. 10, 1967.
37 Quoted in the *Newsletter*, Toronto, Oct. 14, 1970.
38 Address by Sr Frances on the occasion of Josyf Cardinal Slipyj's visit to the Provincial House, Toronto, June 15, 1968.
39 See letter of Sr Frances to the Canadian Sisters Servants, Toronto, Jan. 9, 1970.
40 *Ibid.*, Oct. 14, 1970.

Appendices

Appendix A

Facts about Ukraine and the Ukrainians

[Excerpts from Senator Paul Yuzyk, *Ukrainian Canadians: Their Place and Role in Canadian Life* (Toronto, 1967), Appendix D, pp. 100–2.]

'The Ukrainian state was established in 862 A.D., when a Viking chieftain from Scandinavia, Ruryk, consolidated several tribes with Kiev as the capital. This Kievan state, known as Rus (not Russia or Ruthenia) expanded into an empire extending over most of Eastern Europe under the rule of the Grand Princes of Kiev. The greatest rulers were Volodimir (Vladimir) the Great (980–1015), who made Christianity the state religion in 988, under the jurisdiction of the Patriarch of Constantinople; Yaroslav the Wise (1019–1054), who codified the laws, systematized the administration and fostered cultural development; and Volodimir Monomachus (1113–1125), last of the strong rulers of Ukraine. During the 10th, 11th and 12th centuries, next to the Byzantine Empire, Kievan Rus was the most powerful and flourishing state in Europe. The Mongolian-Tatar invasions commenced by the invincible and ferocious Genghis Khan in 1240 finally destroyed the ancient Ukrainian state, but the heroic resistance of the Ukrainian armies helped to save Europe from a similar catastrophe.

*   *   *

'The "Tatar yoke" was cast off over a hundred years later with the aid of the Lithuanians, who became the invited rulers of the liberated Ukrainian lands. When Lithuania united with Poland, dynastically in 1385 and organically in 1569, Ukraine fell under the rule of rapacious Polish landlords. So severe was the oppression that the Ukrainian Cossacks rose up in revolt several times. In 1648, the Cossack leader, Hetman Bohdan Khmelnytsky, swept the Polish landlords out of Ukraine and re-established an independent state, receiving recognition from several European powers. His unfortunate alliance in 1654 with the Muscovite Russian tsar later gave Russia the opportunity to force her rule upon Ukraine. Hetman Mazeppa's valiant attempt, in alliance with King Charles XII of Sweden, in 1709, was abortive, failing to overthrow the Russian domination. By this time the Russian and Polish rulers had divided up Ukraine between themselves with the Dnieper River as the dividing line.

*   *   *

'When the Polish state was partitioned out of existence by the Russian, Prussian and Austrian emperors in the late 18th century, the western Ukrainian territories of Galicia and Bukovina, from where most of Canada's Ukrainians originate, fell under Austrian rule. The largest part of Ukraine was under the despotic Russian tsars, who pursued a ruthless policy of suppressing freedom and the Ukrainian culture; the name "Little Russia" was now applied to the subjugated country. Ukrainian publications and the Ukrainian language were forbidden by decree in the 19th century. Ukraine appeared doomed to perish. It was only the Habsburg-ruled Galicia and Bukovina which showed that the flame of Ukrainian freedom and culture still flickered.

*   *   *

'The spirit of the Ukrainian people, however, could not be completely destroyed. When the Russian tsardom and the Habsburg monarchy crumbled at the end of the First World War, the Ukrainians immediately re-established an independent democratic state. By the Act of January 22, 1918, the parliament of the Ukrainian National Republic proclaimed Ukraine's independence. The new state was not strong enough to maintain itself very long; by 1921 it was overrun by Russian Bolshevik armies and partitioned by Soviet Russia, Poland, Rumania and Czechoslovakia. The Second World War (1939–1945) forcibly brought almost all of Ukraine under Soviet Russian domination behind the Iron Curtain. The Ukrainian Soviet Socialist Republic, although having representation at the United Nations, is a republic in form only; it possesses no freedom and independence and as a puppet of the Russian government in Moscow is subjected to Russification, as formerly under the tsars. The Ukrainians, together with the other non-Russian captive nations, are struggling in various ways to regain their freedom, and seek the aid of the free world.'

Appendix B

The Ukrainian Catholic Church
by Rev. R. Danylak, JUD

HISTORICAL BACKGROUND

The history of the Ukrainian Catholic Church is intimately connected with the social and political history and destiny of the Ukrainian people. Its origins must be traced back to the dim beginnings of Christianity in Ukraine. Legendary tradition has it that the first-called of the apostles, Andrew, was the first to erect the cross of Christ on the hills of Kiev. Be that as it may, there is no doubt that Christian communities flourished around the shores of the Black Sea in the first centuries of the Christian era. The veneration of Pope St Clement I, martyred at the end of the first century, was well established in this area.

Not until the eighth century is it possible to determine more accurately the penetration of Christianity into these lands. When Olga, widow of Prince Ihor Rurik and regent for her son Sviatoslav, willed to be baptized in 955, the Christian faith must have been showing healthy signs of life in the capital of the Rus empire. The 'baptism of Ukraine' under St Volodymyr in 988(9) was the sanctioning and the culmination of the progressive evangelization that had thoroughly penetrated to the roots of Rus-Ukrainian culture.

With his conversion and baptism the Grand Prince Volodymyr gave official impetus to this movement, establishing hundreds of churches, monasteries, and religious institutions. Before his death in 1015 Kiev was in its glory as the city of churches. Religious life continued to develop and flourish in the Kievan capital and to expand its missionary influence throughout the entire realm of the Grand Principate of Kiev – to the north into the duchies of Novhorod, Suzdal, and Moscow; westward, to Halych, Lviv, Peremyshl.

With the reception of Christianity Volodymyr provided an established hierarchy for this new Church, united under the jurisdiction of the metropolitan of Kiev. Jaroslav the Wise, son and successor of Volodymyr, provided for the election of the first indigenous metropolitan, Hilarion, in 1050, establishing by this act the autonomy of the Ruthenian or Ukrainian Church in the Kievan metropolitanate from the political and ecclesiastical influence of Byzantium.

At this time Byzantium had not yet ruptured ties with the Apostolic See of Rome; hence Kiev had received the Christian faith as a member of the Catholic Church. And even following the unfortunate schism of 1054, the grand princes and metropolitans of Kiev continued in communion with Rome for almost a century. The devotion of Yaropolk to the See of Peter, and the introduction of the feast of the Translation of the Relics of St Nicholas to Bari in Italy in 1087, are incontrovertible evidence of continuing ties between Kiev and Rome. With the Tartar incursions and civil strife among the contending princes of Rus, the subsequent religious picture of Ukraine remains obscure to historians. The ensuing turmoil forced Metropolitan Maxim to flee to Volodymyr on the Kliazma in 1299. In 1325 his successor, Peter, confirmed as metropolitan of Kiev and all Rus by the patriarch of Constantinople, permanently transferred his residence to Moscow – which was to prove a sorry decision for subsequent Ukrainian ecclesiastical and political history. It was in this period that the metropolitan see of Halych was established (1141–1371). This see would be restored centuries later for the Ukrainian Catholics of western Ukraine.

It is only in the middle of the fitfeenth century, with the aborted union of the Council of Florence in 1439 and the proclamation of this union in the metropolia of Kiev and all Rus by Cardinal Isidore, that the historical picture is clarified. In 1457 Kiev was confirmed as the metropolitan see by Patriarch Gregory of Constantinople with the appointment of Gregory, a disciple of Cardinal Isidore, as metropolitan of Kiev. Subsequent political intrigue induced Pope Pius II to divide the ancient Kievan metropolia in 1458 into the two metropolia of Kiev and of Moscow, confirming Gregory as metropolitan of Kiev. But it was not until the Union of Brest-Litovsk in 1596 that Metropolitan Rahoza of Kiev and his suffragan bishops gathered in synod could clearly express the muted desire of the Ukrainian people to cement their communion with the See of Peter. Unfortunately, inner dissension, the political ambitions of the Ukrainian nobility, and the relentless political scheming of Moscow and Warsaw did not promise lasting success to the heroic efforts of these saintly bishops, especially since the dissenting opposition had convoked an anti-synod. The Greek Patriarch Teofan consecrated Job Boretsky as Orthodox metropolitan of Kiev in 1620. But the idea of unity did not die even within the reconstituted Orthodox Church – viz. the efforts of Metropolitan Petro Mohyla. In 1685 the dissident bishop of Lutsk, Gedeon Chetvertynsky, submitted himself to the patriarchate of Moscow and was designated metropolitan of Kiev. Once more Kiev was a prisoner of Moscow. The Catholic metropolitan see in the Russian empire was ultimately suppressed in 1805 with the death of the last Kievan metropolitan, Theodosius Rostotsky. Nothwithstanding the few feeble attempts of the remaining bishops of the Ukrainian Catholic Church under tsarist domination to maintain themselves in existence, and the good will of Tsar Paul I (1796–1801), the Church was unable to withstand much longer the continued harassment from the tsars. Finally, through a succession of 'ukazes,' Nicholas I saw the culmination of the struggle in the eventual surrender in 1838 of three bishops who had betrayed their Church. The idea of Union in eastern Ukraine was finally destroyed.

But Divine Providence had already provided for the continuation of the idea of the Ukrainian Catholic Church. Although the bishops of Lviv and Peremyshl had refused to accept the Union of 1596, Innocent Wynnytsky, bishop of Peremyshl, declared himself a Catholic in 1692; and Joseph Shumlansky, bishop of Lviv, did the same in 1700. Bishop Dionysius Zhabrotsky of Lutsk adhered to Union in 1702.

With the suppression of the Catholic metropolia of Kiev in 1805, Pope Pius VII re-established the metropolia of Halych in 1807 in the Austrian domains, conferring upon its titulars all the rights, dignity, and prerogatives of the metropolitans of Kiev, and recognizing the metropolitan of Lviv-Halych as head not only of the ecclesiastical province of Halych but of the entire Ukrainian Catholic Church. This quasipatriarchal authority was confirmed in the recognition by the Holy See of Metropolitan Josyf Slipyj as Major Archbishop in 1963.

It was this ecclesiastical province of western Ukraine and the dioceses of Mukachev, Uzhorod, and Priasiv that provided the bulk of emigrants to Canada in the years 1890–1914, 1920–39, and, finally, after the Second World War. In 1912 the Holy See appointed the first Ukrainian bishop, Nicetas Budka, to answer to the spiritual needs of this flock. This new ecclesiastical formation was ultimately crowned with the creation of a distinct metropolia of Winnipeg in 1956.

JURIDICAL STRUCTURE

The Church as People of God exists and functions at two primary levels: that of the universal Church and that of the diocese, the particular or local church. 'The Roman Pontiff, as the successor of Peter, is the perpetual and visible source and foundation of the unity of bishops and of the multitude of the faithful. The individual bishop is the visible principle and foundation of unity in his particular church, fashioned after the model of the universal Church. In and from such individual Churches there comes into being the one and only Catholic Church' (*Constitution on the Church*, I, 23).

The Second Vatican Council clearly indicated the immediate divine origin of the authority and pastoral responsibility of bishops in virtue of their episcopal consecration as pastors of their flock – the diocese – and of their collegial responsibility under the leadership of the Pope for the welfare of the entire Church (cf. *Decree on the Bishops' Pastoral Office in the Church*, art. 8). These are the two divinely ordained pivots of the structural and hierarchical Church. And although the authority of the local bishop, even in the affairs of his own particular church, is by its very nature subordinated to the universal vigilance of the supreme pontiff, in its exercise a bishop does not become a mere executor of the Pope's sovereign authority. The bishop is truly pastor of his diocese, which constitutes a miniature image of the universal Church. The local or particular church adapts itself to the spiritual and historical conditions of its human members to serve their needs. This human configuration of the Church further expresses itself in the national or ritual agglomerations of individual dioceses in the so-called particular churches whose circumscription blends with the territorial or ethnic boundaries of single nations or rites. Such are the churches of Canada, Italy, the United States, etc. Such is the Ukrainian Catholic Church, whose members have established new homelands outside the motherland of their ancestors, retaining none the less a spiritual and cultural affinity and identity with the original people and Church. This is a further application of the conciliar principle of collegiality to the individual Churches. The bishops can act as a unity not only as members of the entire episcopal college but also in the smaller affiliations which life itself creates.

In exercising his supreme authority over the universal Church the Roman pontiff makes use of the departments of the Roman curia, who act in the name and with the authority of the Pope for the good of the churches and in the service of the sacred pastors (cf. *Decree on the Bishops' Pastoral Office*, art. 9). This function can be likened to the ministries or secretariates of civil governments. The Roman congregations, secretariates, tribunals, and offices are executive instruments of the Pope. Their relation to the college of bishops has not yet been established (cf. K. Morsdorf, 'Commentary on the Decree on the Bishops' Pastoral Office in the Church' in *Commentary on the Documents of Vatican II*, II, 174). Although theirs is a pastoral charge, the congregations do not supplant or replace the native authority of the bishops as pastors of their people. In their present structure the congregations date from the reform of the Roman curia of Pope Sixtus V. Pope Gregory XIII established a distinct congregation for the affairs of the Greeks in 1573. This eventually was fused with the Congregation for the Propagation of the Faith in 1622; and in 1627 a distinct commission for oriental affairs was established within this missionary congregation. A separate Oriental Congregation for the affairs of the Eastern Churches was established in 1917 by Pope Benedict XV. 'To it are reserved all matters which regard either the faithful or the discipline or the rites of the East. It possesses for the Churches of Eastern rites – save for the changes that subsequent papal legislation has established – those faculties which the other congregations enjoy for the churches of the Latin rite' (cf. *M. P. Cleri Sanctitati*, can. 195).

RELIGIOUS INSTITUTES

Christian life from its very beginnings found the most adequate expression in the lives of men and women who strove to follow Christ more freely and to imitate Him more nearly in the practice of the evangelical counsels. Eventually this expression of Christian conviction found its structural counterpart in the formation of religious orders and congregations. Their growth and expansion, and the rising complex needs of the Church, led to the exemption of many of these bodies from the ordinary vigilance and jurisdiction of the diocesan bishops and placed them under the immediate and exclusive jurisdiction of the Pope. As institutes of pontifical right they thus enjoy, in matters which pertain to the interior life of the community and the government of its members, a certain autonomy in an immediate relation to the universal Church. In this area the Pope exercises his supreme jurisdiction through the Congregation for Religious, in the Latin rite, and through the Oriental Congregation, for religious of the Eastern rites (*M. P. Cleri Sanctitati*, can. 195, I, 1).

None the less, in what pertains to the external apostolate, all religious, exempt and non-exempt, are subject to the authority of the local ordinaries in those things which relate to divine worship, the care of souls, sacred preaching intended for the people, the religious and moral education of the Christian faithful, as well as to the various works of the exercise of the sacred apostolate. Catholic schools conducted by religious are also subject to the authority of the local ordinaries as regards general policy and supervision. The privilege of exemption applies chiefly to the internal order of their communities, so that in them all things may be more aptly coordinated, the growth and depth of religious life better secured, and their services be more readily available for the good of the entire Church.

Appendix C

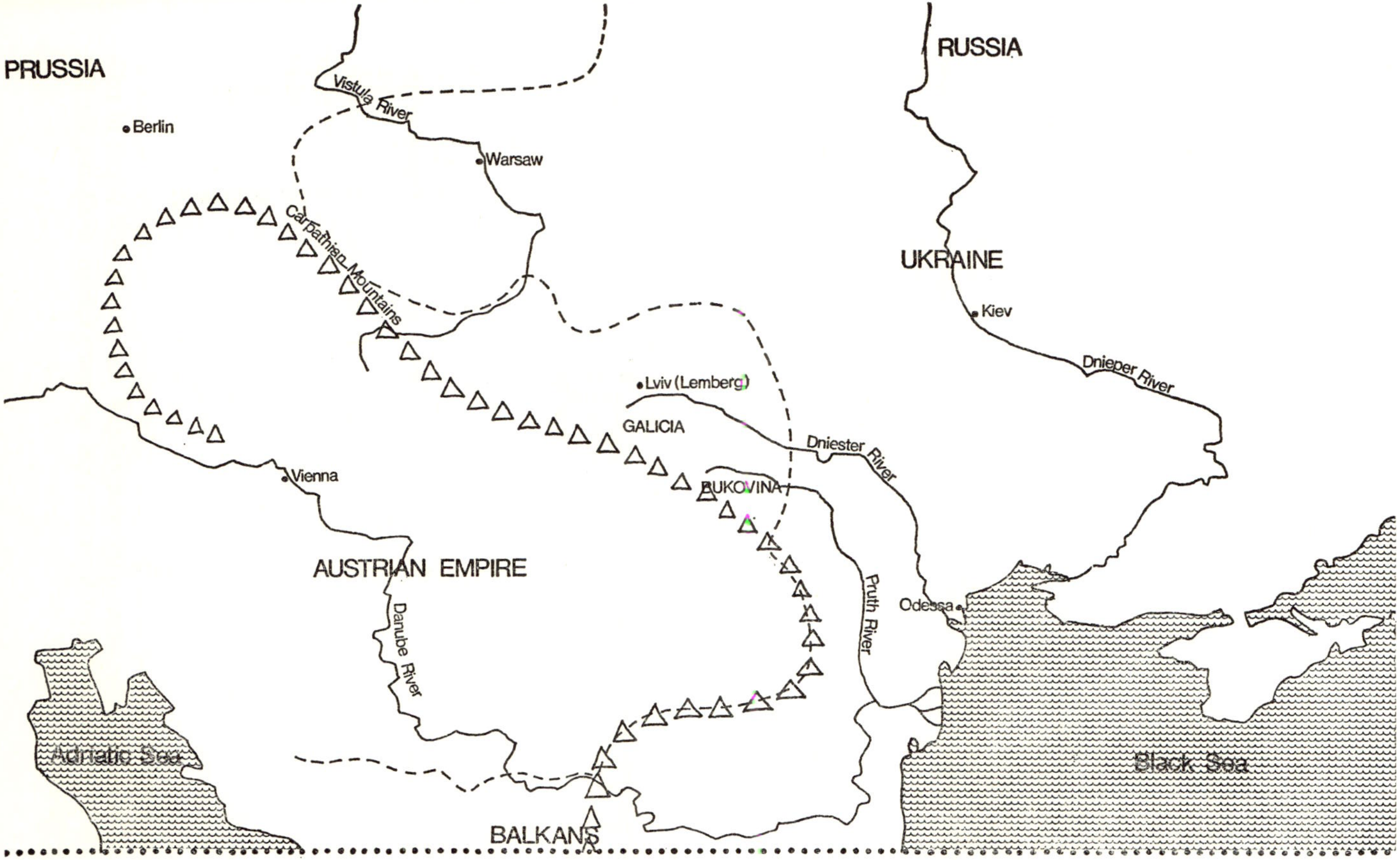

Ukraine: showing the Austrian-controlled provinces of Galicia and Bukovina, from which the majority of Ukrainians emigrated to Canada in the period 1891-1914.

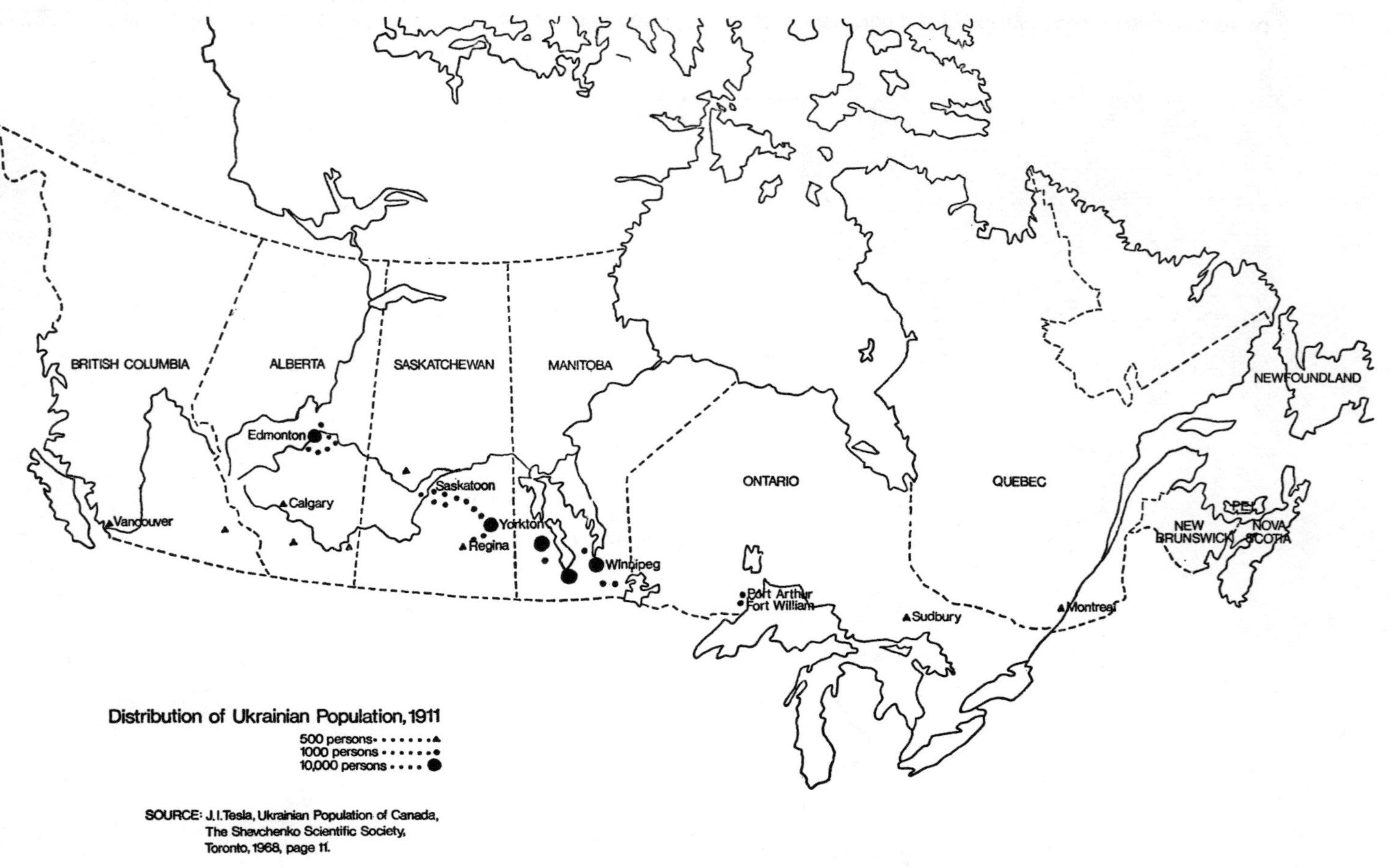

Distribution of Ukrainian Population, 1911

SOURCE: J. I. Tesla, Ukrainian Population of Canada,
The Shevchenko Scientific Society,
Toronto, 1968, page 11.

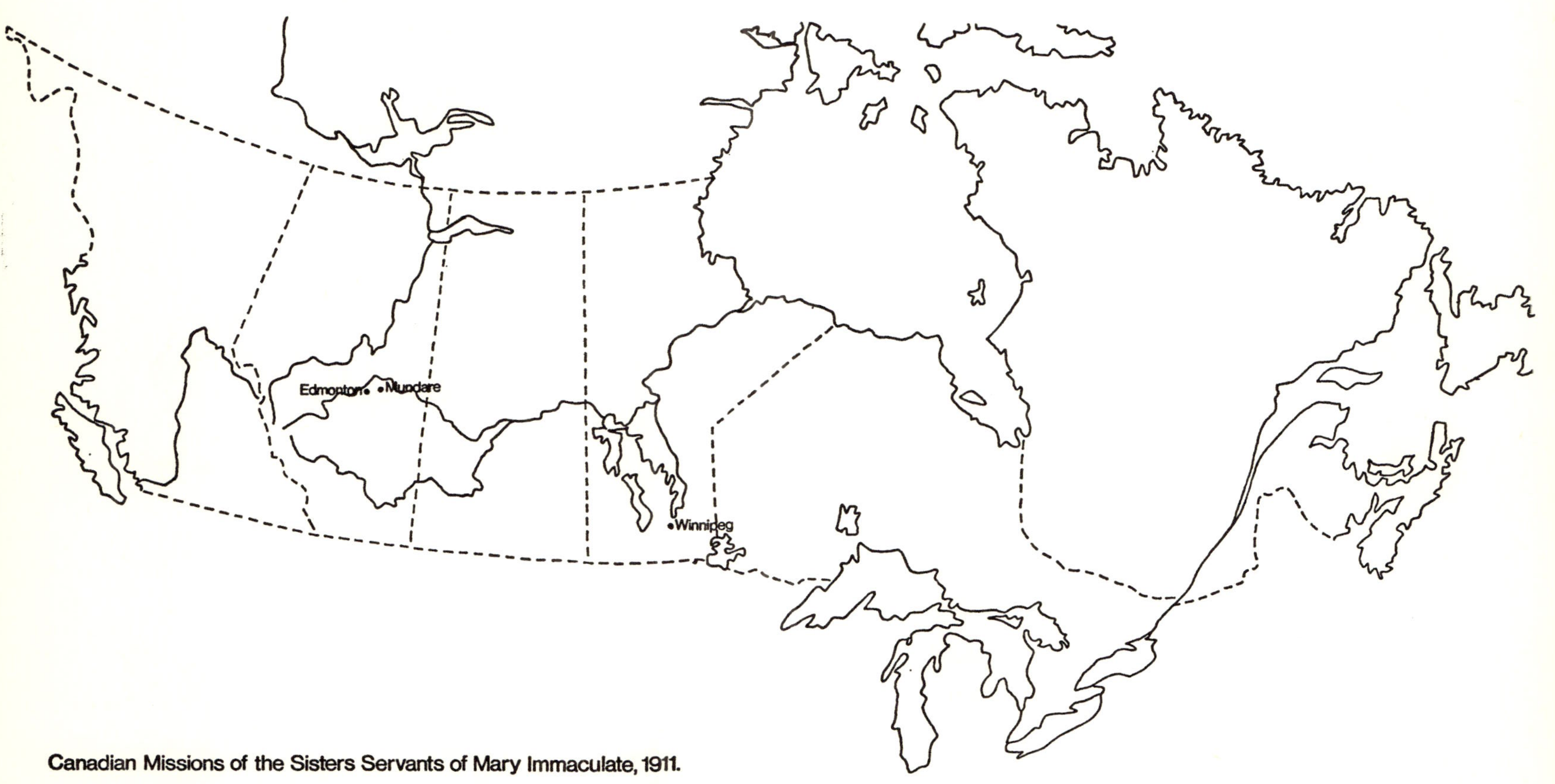

Canadian Missions of the Sisters Servants of Mary Immaculate, 1911.

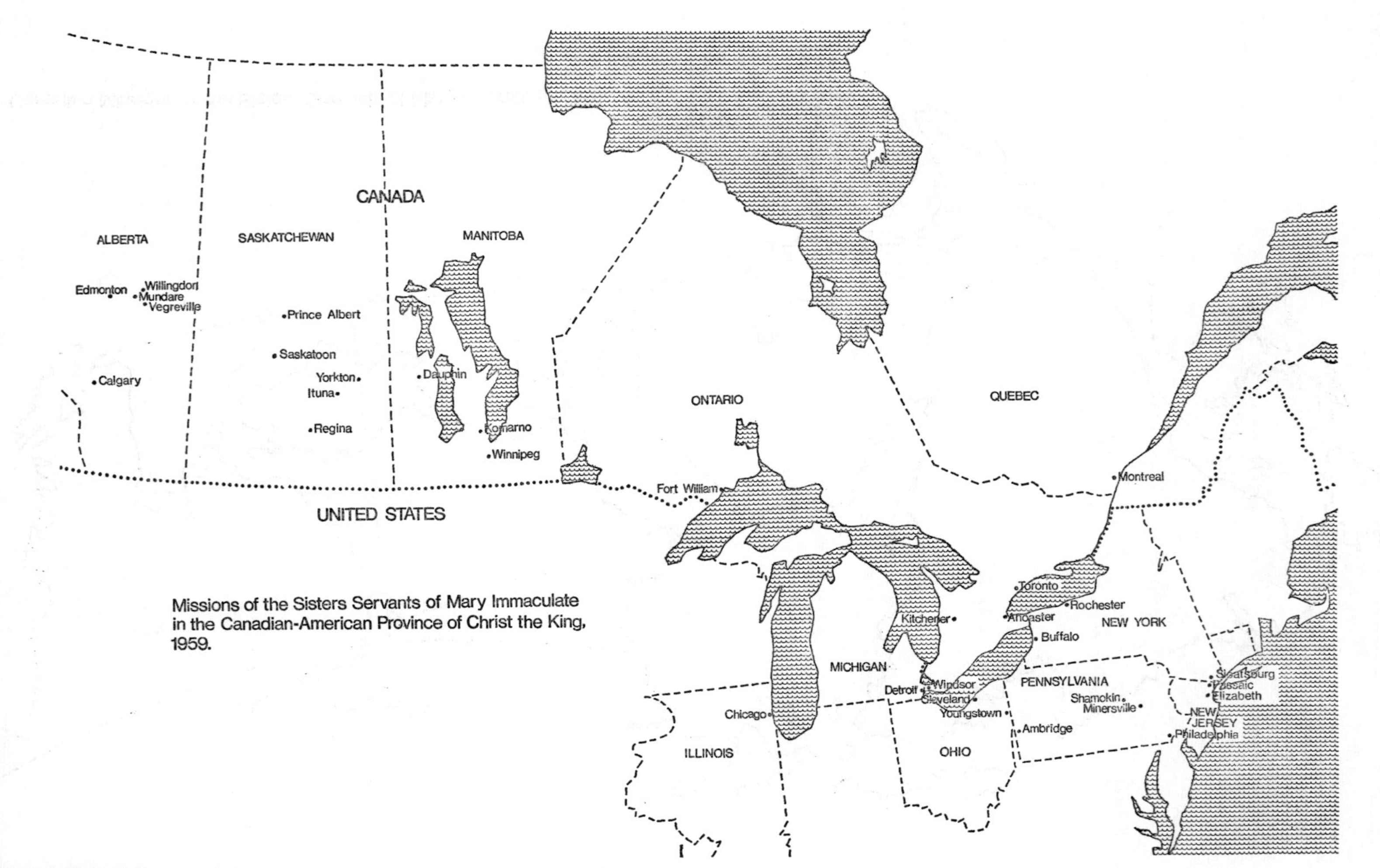

Missions of the Sisters Servants of Mary Immaculate in the Canadian-American Province of Christ the King, 1959.

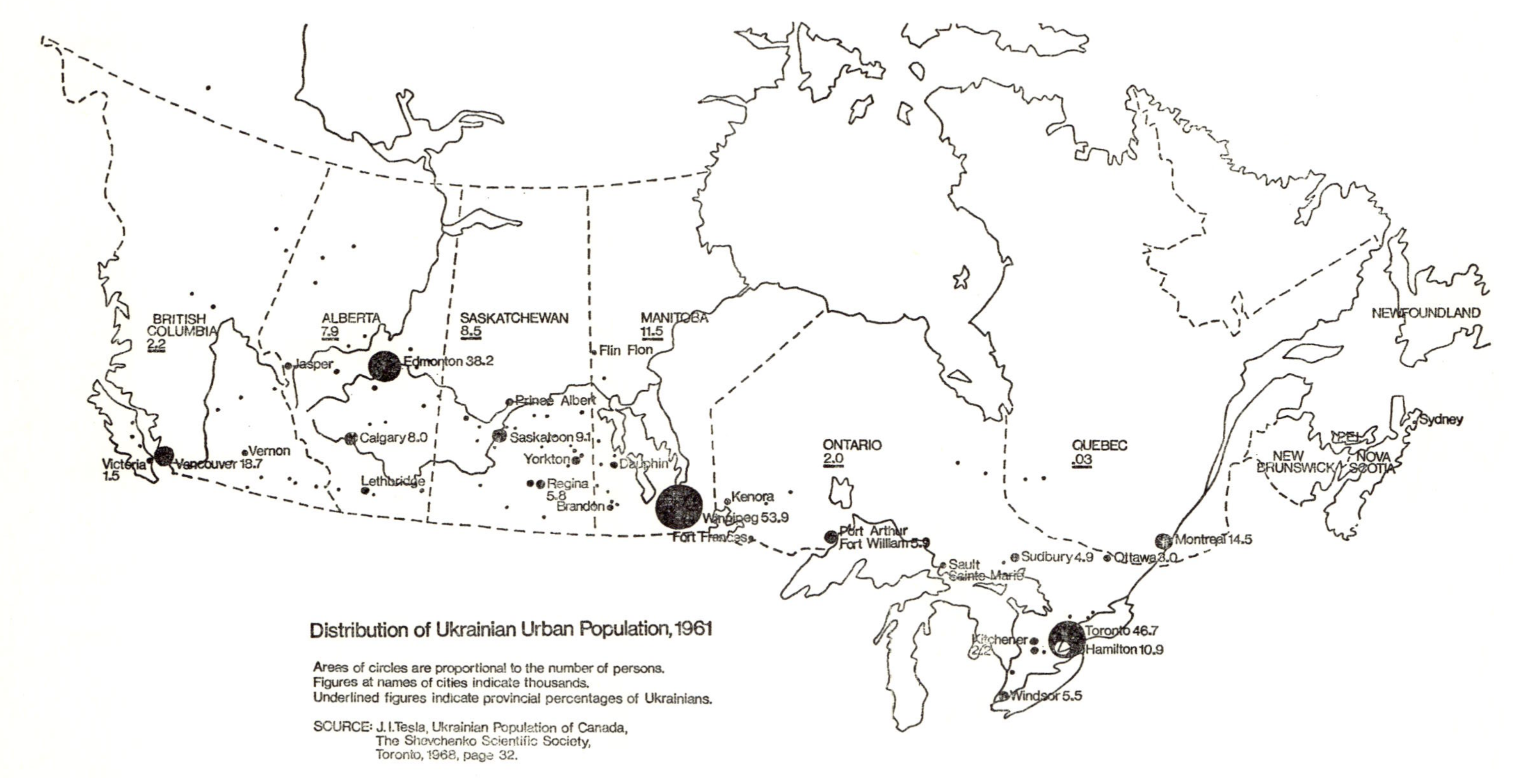

Distribution of Ukrainian Urban Population, 1961

Areas of circles are proportional to the number of persons.
Figures at names of cities indicate thousands.
Underlined figures indicate provincial percentages of Ukrainians.

SOURCE: J.I.Tesla, Ukrainian Population of Canada,
The Shevchenko Scientific Society,
Toronto, 1968, page 32.

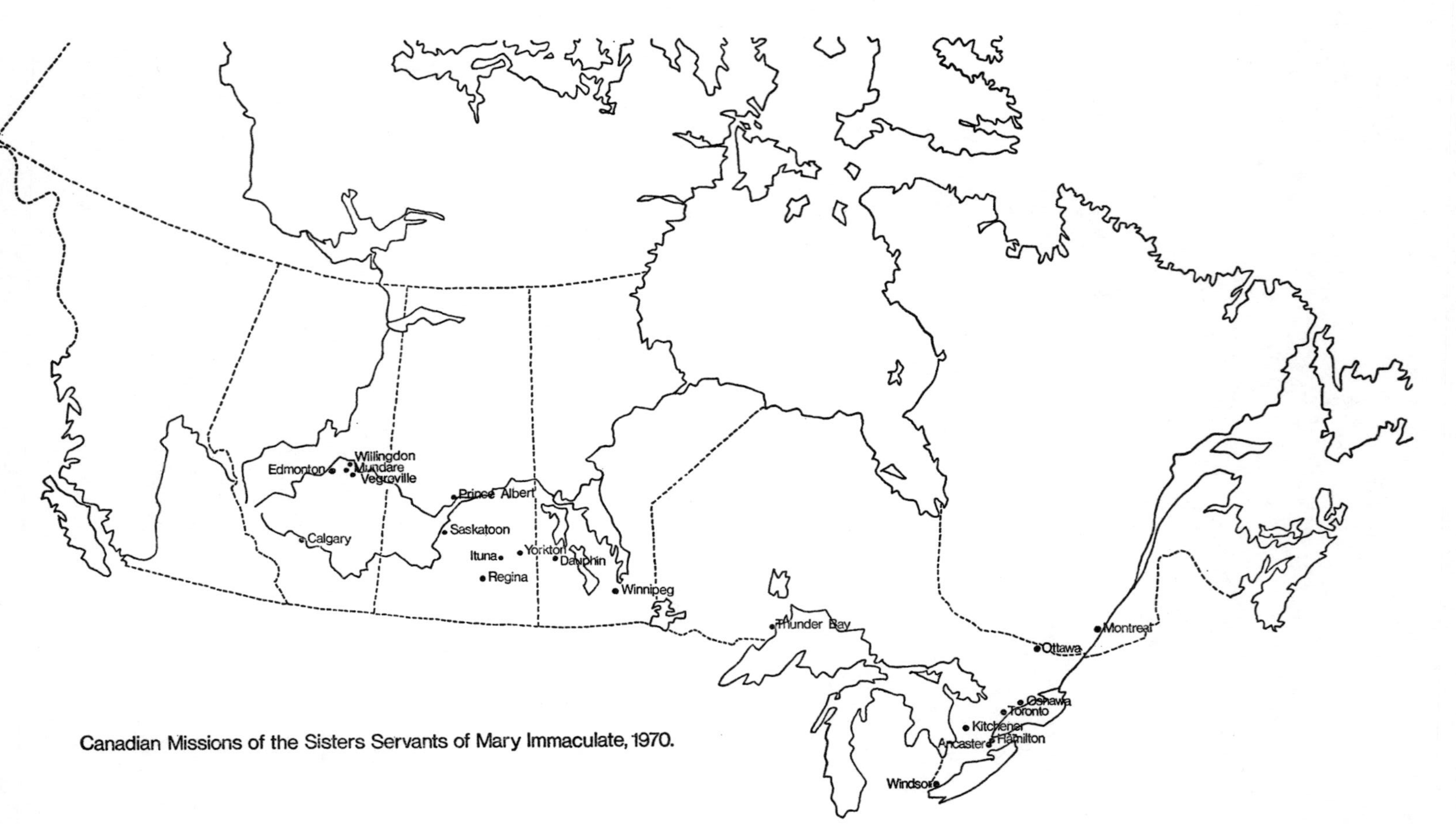

Canadian Missions of the Sisters Servants of Mary Immaculate, 1970.

Appendix D

Missions in Canada, 1902–70

ALBERTA	Founded

Edmonton
Sacristy of St Joachim's Church — 1902
   (closed in 1903)
St Josaphat's Convent — 1905
Marydale — 1965
   (closed in 1968)
Convent, 10744-70 Avenue — 1968

Mundare
Homestead Convent — 1903
St Joseph's Convent — 1926
General Hospital — 1928

Willingdon
General Hospital — 1935

Vegreville
Our Lady of Perpetual Help Convent — 1943

Calgary
St Bernadette's Convent — 1952

MANITOBA

Winnipeg
Convent — 1905
St Nicholas School — 1911
Holy Family Nursing Home — 1956
Immaculate Heart of Mary Academy — 1958
   (closed in 1963)
Immaculate Heart of Mary School — 1963

Sifton
St Mary's Convent — 1910
   (closed in 1924; reopened in 1935; closed in 1955)

Dauphin
St Paul's Convent — 1928
   (St Paul's Nursing Home)

	Founded
Komarno	
St Basil's Convent	1935
(St Basil's Home for the Aged)	
(closed in 1961)	
Portage la Prairie	
St Anthony's Convent	1936
(closed in 1943)	

SASKATCHEWAN

Yorkton	
Sacred Heart Institute	1915
(Sacred Heart Academy)	
Ituna	
St Ann's Orphanage	1920
(St Ann's Children's Home)	
Saskatoon	
Immaculate Conception Convent	1928
Regina	
Holy Family Convent	1931
Prince Albert	
Our Lady of Lourdes Convent	1956

QUEBEC

Montreal	
St Theresa's Convent	1925
(St Anne's Convent)	

ONTARIO

Toronto	
St Rita's Convent	1937
(closed in 1951)	
Christ the King Convent	1949
Windsor	
Immaculate Conception Convent	1939
(Infant Jesus Convent)	
Thunder Bay (Fort William)	
Convent	1942
Hamilton	
Convent	1945
(closed in 1950; reopened in 1965)	

	Founded
Ottawa	
Convent	1946
(closed in 1949; reopened as House of Studies in 1965)	
Ancaster	
Mount Mary Immaculate Novitiate	1946
Mount Mary Immaculate Academy	1953
Kitchener	
St Bernadette's Convent	1952
Oshawa	
Convent	1964
NOVA SCOTIA	
Sydney	
Convent	1942
(closed in 1952)	

Appendix E

Missions in the United States, 1935–59

	Founded

Stamford
  Seminary (housekeeping) — 1935
    (closed in 1940; reopened in 1943; closed in 1948)

Hartford
  Convent — 1948
    (closed in 1954)

Ansonia
  Convent — 1949
    (closed in 1955)

MICHIGAN

Detroit
  Convent — 1937

MINNESOTA

Minneapolis
  Convent — 1937
    (closed in 1945)

PENNSYLVANIA

Philadelphia
  St Mary's Home — 1937
  Home of Divine Providence — 1948

St Clair
  Convent — 1937
    (closed in 1949)

Minersville
  Convent — 1937
    (closed in 1942; reopened in 1943)

Shamokin
  Convent — 1938

Keiser
  Convent — 1939

	Founded
Wilkes-Barre	
Convent	1939
(closed in 1952)	
Ambridge	
Convent	1939
Chester	
Convent	1940
(closed in 1943)	
Sayre	
Convent	1941
(closed in 1952)	
Phoenixville	
Convent	1943
(closed in 1949)	
NEW YORK	
Syracuse	
Convent	1938
(closed in 1941)	
Buffalo	
Two convents	1941
Sloatsburg	
St Mary's Villa	1941
St Joseph's Home for the Aged	1942
St Mary's Villa Academy	1944
Rochester	
Convent	1941
MISSOURI	
St Louis	
Convent	1938
(closed in 1943)	
NEW JERSEY	
Passaic	
St Nicholas Convent	1939
St Michael's Convent	1953
Elizabeth	
Convent	1949

	Founded
NORTH DAKOTA	
Ukraina	
Convent	1940
(closed in 1944)	
DISTRICT OF COLUMBIA	
Washington	
Seminary (housekeeping)	1941
(closed in 1948)	
OHIO	
Youngstown	
Convent	1953
Cleveland	
St Mary's Convent	1956
St Joseph's Convent	1957
ILLINOIS	
Chicago	
Convent	1957

Appendix F

Provincial superiors and councils, 1902–70

1902–12   Sister Ambrose M. Lenkewich

1912–21   Sister Ambrose M. Lenkewich

Sister Nicholas A. Petrushkewich	1st councillor from 1912
Sister Taida M. Letawsky	2nd councillor from 1912
Sister Josepha M. Bilan	1st councillor from 1914
Sister Euletheria A. Furtak	2nd councillor from 1914
Sister Athanasia T. Melnyk	3rd councillor from 1914
Sister Melanie M. Sochatsky	2nd councillor from 1917

1921–6   Sister Ambrose M. Lenkewich*

Sister Euletheria A. Furtak	1st councillor
Sister Nicholas A. Petrushkewich	2nd councillor
Sister Elizabeth S. Kassian	3rd councillor
Sister Athanasia T. Melnyk	secretary-treasurer

1926–34   Sister Athanasia T. Melnyk*

Sister Josaphata P. Tymochko	1st councillor
Sister Ambrose M. Lenkewich	2nd councillor
Sister Suzanna M. Starko	3rd councillor
Sister Ignatia A. Butryn	treasurer

1934–9   Sister Elizabeth S. Kassian

Sister Ambrose M. Lenkewich	1st councillor
Sister Fevronia A. Prystupa	2nd councillor
Sister Natalia L. Klos	3rd councillor
Sister Lubov K. Chawrona	4th councillor
Sister Ignatia A. Butryn	secretary
Sister Gertrude N. Lesiuk	treasurer

1939–44   Sister Elizabeth S. Kassian

Sister Ignatia A. Butryn	1st councillor
Sister Fevronia A. Prystupa	2nd councillor
Sister Natalia L. Klos	3rd councillor
Sister Monica M. Mantyka	4th councillor

* Sister Ambrose was elected for her 1921–6 term and Sister Athanasia was elected in 1926; at all other dates provincial superiors were appointed.

	Sister Sofronia P. Sianchuk	secretary
	Sister Gertrude N. Lesiuk	treasurer
1944–9	Sister Elizabeth S. Kassian	
	Sister Ignatia A. Butryn	1st councillor
	Sister Fevronia A. Prystupa	2nd councillor
	Sister Natalia L. Klos	3rd councillor
	Sister Eleanor P. Lenyk	councillor
	Sister Monica M. Mantyka	4th councillor to 1946
	Sister Lawrence J. Dzumaga	4th councillor from 1946
	Sister Gertrude N. Lesiuk	treasurer
1949–54	Sister Bernadette M. Warick	
	Sister Lawrence J. Dzumaga	1st councillor
	Sister Josaphata S. Kizlyk	2nd councillor
	Sister Gertrude N. Lesiuk	3rd councillor to 1951
	Sister Jerome M. Chimy	3rd councillor from 1951
	Sister Sozonta T. Iskiw	4th councillor
	Sister Juvenalia M. Kaniuk	secretary
	Sister Boniface J. Sloboda	treasurer
1954–9	Sister Bernadette M. Warick	
	Sister Jerome M. Chimy	1st councillor to 1956
	Sister Lawrence J. Dzumaga	2nd councillor to 1956
	Sister Joan M. Magriy	councillor from 1956
	Sister Cornelia K. Mantyka	councillor from 1956
	Sister Julianna R. Pankowsky	3rd councillor
	Sister Boniface J. Sloboda	4th councillor
	Sister Juvenalia M. Kaniuk	secretary
	Sister Helena M. Kwasnicky	treasurer
1959–65	Sister Boniface J. Sloboda	
	Sister Modesta A. Lukey	1st councillor
	Sister Cornelia K. Mantyka	2nd councillor to 1962
	Sister Innocentia J. Baraniuk	councillor from 1962
	Sister Frances E. Byblow	3rd councillor
	Sister Dominic G. Slawuta	4th councillor
	Sister Valerie S. Krochenski	secretary
	Sister Helena M. Kwasnicky	treasurer
1965–70	Sister Frances E. Byblow	
	Sister Boniface J. Sloboda	1st councillor
	Sister Modesta A. Lukey	2nd councillor
	Sister Dominic G. Slawuta	3rd councillor to 1969

	Sister Ambrose P. Stachiw	councillor from 1969
	Sister Oresta K. Sereda	4th councillor
	Sister Ruth O. Yakimyshyn	secretary
	Sister Bernadette M. Warick	treasurer
1971–	Sister Justine A. Kowal	
	Sister Ambrose P. Stachiw	1st councillor
	Sister Frances E. Byblow	2nd councillor
	Sister Ruth O. Yakimyshyn	3rd councillor
	Sister Celestine M. Lozinski	4th councillor
	Sister Doloretta F. Shalagan	secretary
	Sister Bohdana O. Pidskalny	treasurer

Appendix G

Directresses of novices, 1903–70

1903–9	Sister Ambrose M. Lenkewich
1909–13	Sister Taida M. Letawsky
1913–17	Sister Suzanne M. Starko
1917–18	Sister Athanasia T. Melnyk
1918–21	Sister Suzanne M. Starko
1921–2	Sister Nicholas A. Petrushkewich
1922–4	Sister Josaphata P. Tymochko
1924–5	Sister Taida M. Letawsky
1925–8	Sister Suzanne M. Starko
1928–9	Sister Lawrence J. Dzumaga
1929–35	Sister Josepha M. Bilan
1935–6	Sister Natalia L. Klos
1936–52	Sister Josaphata S. Kizlyk
1952–9	Sister Boniface J. Sloboda
1959–60	Sister Bernadette M. Warick
1960–4	Sister Frances E. Byblow
1964–5	Sister Joan M. Magriy
1965–9	Sister Boniface J. Sloboda
1969–70	Sister Justine A. Kowal

Appendix H

Deceased sisters, 1903–70

	Born	Entered institute	Died
Taida Helen Wrublewsky		14. 5.1898	23. 5.1903
Josepha Mary Zaozirny	1889	31.10.1905	17. 5.1906
Paraskevia Euphrasia Gnus	28.11.1884	5.11.1911	9. 2.1918
Macrina Pelagia Faryna	1890	20. 5.1909	7. 6.1921
Theodosia Katherine Senchuk	2. 7.1885	20.12.1909	22.11.1921
Anastasia Katherine Kuzymkiw	21. 3.1882	14. 5.1912	24. 5.1924
Seraphina Michaela Pelchar	4.12.1896	13. 8.1915	5.12.1924
Antonia Anne Guz	30. 6.1902	2. 8.1918	17. 9.1925
Sylvester Mary Werbicky	27.11.1905	17. 8.1923	12. 6.1928
Stephanie Katherine Kinach	22.12.1895	8. 6.1916	23. 5.1929
Naucratia Stephanie Mizun	20.12.1909	9. 7.1925	12. 6.1930
Irene Emelia Guz	22. 7.1908	17. 8.1924	22. 7.1930
Naucratia Helen Olynyk	1912	12. 8.1930	2.10.1931
Clementia Anastasia Sheremeta	2. 2.1915	30. 8.1930	12. 6.1932
Olga Julia Turczyn	14. 6.1904	18. 2.1920	23. 8.1935
Stephanie Ksenia Diakovich	3. 7.1900	12. 5.1928	18.10.1940
Genevieve Mary Zakaluzny	9.11.1912	12. 8.1930	28. 6.1942
Veronica Maria Melnyk	3.12.1887	28. 2.1905	4. 6.1945
Magdalene Euphrasia Hupalo	24. 3.1882	1. 4.1914	23. 5.1948
Stanislaus Mary Koziak	17. 5.1908	2. 9.1932	11.11.1949
Eupraxia Maria Savry	1. 8.1901	6. 6.1917	19. 1.1950
Margaret Anna Sereda	14.10.1905	1. 7.1932	13. 2.1951
Anisia Anna Pasowisty	23. 3.1901	28. 8.1915	13. 6.1951
Ambrose Marcella Lenkewich	18. 1.1876	6. 6.1895	13. 5.1953

	Born	Entered institute	Died
Eugenia Barbara Rolack	27.12.1890	8. 7.1910	3. 9.1956
Martha Olga Bohaychuk	6. 7.1915	9. 4.1935	1.11.1957
Cecile Maria Bilinsky	6. 9.1890	1. 9.1910	13.11.1957
Josaphata Pelagia Tymochko	20.10.1882	21. 9.1903	7. 7.1958
Damian Natalie Shmokaluk	10. 1.1924	20. 7.1941	1. 8.1959
Leontia Barbara Lavriw	30.12.1888	15. 4.1911	12.11.1961
Nadia Anastasia Klymochko	6. 5.1892	20. 6.1913	17. 6.1963
Leona Mary Shewciw	14. 5.1939	30. 6.1957	30.11.1963
Minidore Ksenia Andrijiw	12. 2.1914	18. 8.1929	7. 8.1965
Maria Joanne Melnyk	1. 5.1891	11. 5.1909	14. 8.1965
Anthonine Anastasia Romano	15. 7.1918	10. 9.1942	15.10.1965
Constantine Irene Nawrocky	24. 1.1943	30. 6.1960	10.12.1966
Lawrence Josepha Dzumaga	20.12.1903	13.10.1918	19. 6.1967
Athanasia Theodosia Melnyk	10. 9.1875	27. 8.1892	6. 8.1967
Theresa Natalie Melnyk	8. 9.1895	14. 1.1913	16. 5.1968
Agnes Euphrasia Stetz	14. 5.1893	16. 1.1914	26. 2.1969
Tatianna Mary Baraniuk	20. 2.1902	18.10.1916	15.12.1969
Sophie Mary Cherwonka	20. 9.1891	12. 8.1911	10. 4.1970
Daria Paraskevia Ushkowsky	1. 8.1892	20. 9.1912	14. 4.1970
Partenia Anna Syrylo	19. 9.1916	25. 7.1940	5.12.1970

Index of surnames

Index of place names